The Poser 3 Handbook

The Poser 3 Handbook

Shamms Mortier

CHARLES RIVER MEDIA, INC.
Rockland, Massachusetts

Executive Editor: Jenifer Niles
Production: Publishers' Design and Production Services, Inc.
Cover Design: Sherry Stinson
Cover Image: Shamms Mortier
Printer: InterCity Press

CHARLES RIVER MEDIA, Inc.
P.O. Box 417
403 VFW Drive
Rockland, Massachusetts 02370
781-871-4184
781-871-4376(FAX)
chrivmedia@aol.com
http://www.charlesriver.com

This book is printed on acid-free paper

The Poser 3 Handbook
by Shamms Mortier
ISBN 1-886801-90-8
Printed in the United States of America

99 00 01 02 03 7 6 5 4 3 2 1

DEDICATION

FOR JAKE ORVIS,
THANKS

Contents

Foreword

Why Poser?

Sometime in the late 1980s I had notions of finding out how much of a cartoonist I could be. I quickly found that the process of visualizing the human form in pose and in perspective—without reference—was quite difficult. I knew what I wanted to portray, but I couldn't "see" the pose. It wasn't the details of drawing that scared me—it was the overall form.

So I went out and bought one of those wooden mannequins and quickly discovered that it was good for about six poses. Why are they built the way they are? They don't have anywhere near the range of motion of a human being—and forget about pushing beyond. So I set out to design and build a better mannequin. My research led to some very interesting materials that produced a number of odd-looking creatures. The closest I got to a usable mannequin involved using some modular tubing parts I discovered at a machine shop in Ohio. I think I eventually designed a better Bunsen burner, but the human form kept eluding me.

Then one day it struck me. I had been animating and programming professionally for several years in Hollywood (mostly with Rhythm & Hues Studios). I had all this built up 3D math knowledge and firsthand experience with the difficulties and complexities of creating computer-generated artwork as well as traditional artwork. So . . . why not combine my knowledge with my needs and make a simple-but-better "digital" mannequin?

My initial goals were very modest. I just wanted something representational of the size and proportions of a human body. And I wanted it to be extremely easy to use and pose. Direct 3D manipulation of the figure was essential. If I could simply represent directional lighting that would be great. That was all I wanted to do. I wasn't planning to write a 3D renderer or to have detailed human models that could bend. I wasn't planning to allow for animation or props or clothed models or textures or lighting or bump maps. But Poser had a mind of its own—and sometimes things just can't be stopped.

Now years have passed, Fractal Design took an interest, added some talented programmers and artists and writers and managers, merged with Ray Dream and MetaTools, added more programmers and designers—and the end result is the third release of Poser as a design tool for digitally equipped artists. Poser maintains its roots as a tool for traditional artists and sculptors, but has grown significantly to become a very useful addition to the toolbox of 3D artists and animators.

I am continually amazed at the varied users and surprising uses people find for Poser—from home hobbyists to fashion designers to architects to scientists to sculptors to professional animators to fine artists. For me, it has been especially exciting to help foster the creativity of developing artists. Art is a very healthy expression of humanity. I am still hoping that one of these days I can take a break from programming and put Poser to use on my own cartoons as I had originally planned!

Larry Weinberg
Poser 3 Master Programmer

Introduction

Welcome to the awesome animated world of MetaCreations' Poser 3. Poser 3 is a organic modeling and animation system, a place where you can design and move human, animal, and alien 3D models. With a little study and exploration, this book will allow you to master all of Poser 3's capabilities.

Preparations

To be able to use this book effectively, you must be working familiar with Poser 3. That means that, at the very least, you will have worked through the tutorials and references in the Poser 3 documentation, so you have an understanding of the basic parameters of the Poser 3 tools and processes. Chapters 1 and 2 of this book reference Poser 3 tool usage and can be used to reinforce your learning, but not to supplant information in the documentation. Most references to Poser 3 tools and their associated icons or menu listings in this book are meant to stretch your working knowledge of Poser 3 beyond the basic information presented in the documentation and to build upon the basics. So read the documentation at least once and work through all of the associated tutorials. You will find that in making these preparations, your appreciation of what is contained here, and this book's value, will be many times more useful.

The following items are essential if you are to get as much value out of this book as possible:

- **MetaCreations Poser 3.** Obviously, without the software, your appreciation of the contents of this book will be either nonexistent or severely limited. You should purchase a copy of Poser 3 or upgrade your existing Poser 1 or 2 version (piracy is illegal and hurts everyone).
- **An appropriate computer platform to run the Poser 3 software.** You

will need a PowerMac or Pentium system to make creative use of Poser 3. The systems used in the creation of the book were two PowerMacs (a 100 MHz PowerComputing 100 and an Apple 233 MHz G3) and a Pentium Pro 300 MHz system. These were adequate for both creating the illustrations in the book and rendering the animations on the CD-ROM. Faster is always better when it comes to generating computer art and animation, and Poser 3 is a very demanding application when it comes to memory and speed. If you can afford an acceleration card, that's better yet. If your computer runs at less than 100 MHz (with at least a 200 MHz system recommended), your Poser 3 renderings are going to be pretty slow.

- **RAM.** The more RAM (Random Access Memory) your computer can access with Poser 3, the better. More RAM allows for larger scenes, which in turn render faster. The systems used in the creation of this book contained 172 MB and 128 MB (PowerMacs) and 256 MB (PentiumPro) of RAM respectively. Running Poser 3 with less than 48 Megs of RAM is not advisable.
- **CD-ROM drive.** CD-ROM drives are so commonplace today that one is probably already installed on your system. A 4X speed CD-ROM is the lowest speed drive you should be using, with 24X CD-ROM drives now becoming commonplace. Since all of the animations referenced in the book are included on the accompanying CD-ROM, you have to have a CD-ROM drive to utilize the book's CD contents.

System Requirements

Macintosh PPC Processor

System 8+ (the software will run under System 7.5.5 and 7.6, but this is not recommended), Color Display, 24-bit recommended, hard disk, CD-ROM drive, 12 MB of available memory, 16 recommended (RAM), 80 MB hard disk space.

Windows

IBM PC Compatible, 486 DX or faster recommended, Microsoft Windows 95 or Windows NT v4 or later, color display, true-color recommended, hard disk, CD-ROM Drive, 16 MB of system memory (RAM), 80 MB hard disk space.

The Book's Structure

This book has been carefully laid out into three comprehensive sections: Covering the Basics, Animation, and Advanced Topics. Depending upon your skill level as an experienced Poser user and/or as a digital animator, you may desire to skip one section or another. Please do not do so. The reason for working through this whole book, no matter your experience level with Bryce or computer animation techniques, is that each section contains new and useful material for maximizing your Poser 3 encounter.

SECTION I: COVERING THE BASICS

This section includes the following chapters:

- **Chapter 1: New Features.** This chapter details the new features contained in Poser 3 and what they mean to your creative options.
- **Chapter 2: Navigating the Interface.** The Poser 3 interface is completely new, and learning to optimize its use will enhance your Poser 3 work.
- **Chapter 3: Posing and Customizing the Human Body.** Learn to shape the body in believable and humorous ways.
- **Chapter 4: Posing and Customizing Hands.** Poser 3's hands are exquisitely modeled and every joint can be moved into position.
- **Chapter 5: Creating Expressive Faces.** Combining emotions and phonemes produces faces that can express all of the human emotions and then some.
- **Chapter 6: Posing and Customizing Animal Models.** From the Dolphin to the Velociraptor in the Poser 3 libraries, and from the Chimp to the Bear on the Zygote extras CD collections, animal models are one of the most alluring aspects of Poser 3.
- **Chapter 7: Composited Figures.** Poser 3 allows you to mix and blend figures of various types, so creatures that are based in mythology and fantasy can be easily brought to life.
- **Chapter 8: Backgrounds, Props and Rendering.** Working with Backgrounds and Props allows you to create complete worlds that act as environments for your characters.

SECTION II: ANIMATION

This section includes the following chapters:

- **Chapter 9: Animation Controls.** You have to master Poser 3's Animation switches and buttons in order to shape your figure at selected keyframes on the timeline, and using Inverse Kinematics can be a big help.
- **Chapter 10: Animating Articulated Hands.** Because of their articulated complexity, Hands have to be treated with care to evoke believable movement.
- **Chapter 11: Facial, Mouth, and Eye Movements.** This chapter covers how, when, and why to animate faces, especially the use and development of phoneme and other facial morphing cycles.
- **Chapter 12: Animal Animation.** In this chapter reference is made to the *Muybridge Animation Books* and other techniques used to create animals in motion.
- **Chapter 13: Composite Character Animation.** Fantasy and mythological character choreography is covered in this chapter.
- **Chapter 14: The Walk Designer.** This chapter provides a detailed look at one of the most spectacular features in Poser 3.
- **Chapter 15: Morphing Madness.** One of the oldest myths in the world concerns the ability of magicians and special animals to shapeshift, to change from one form to another. Poser 3 gives you access to this capability for your characters.

SECTION III: ADVANCED TOPICS

This section includes the following chapters:

- **Chapter 16: Creating Hierarchies.** This chapter details the use and procedures for creating text-based animation scripts in Poser 3, new to this version.
- **Chapter 17: Handshaking.** This chapter covers how to Import/Export Poser 3D object and animation files and why and when to do it—an important chapter for RayDream, 3DS, and other 3D application users. Also covered are Bryce 3D uses and mapping Poser animations to a plane in any 3D application, as well as Painter 3D and Poser.
- **Chapter 18: Customizing Templates.** This chapter describes preparing content in bitmap painting applications, including Painter, Photoshop, and other applications, including how to map photographic faces onto Poser models.

- **Chapter 19: Cameras, Lights, and Rendering.** This chapter contains BioVision Motion Capture files, Sound Clips, Cameras, and Lights.
- **Chapter 20: Hints and Tips from Master Users.** This chapter contains hints and tips from three exemplary Poser 3 masters. Larry Weinberg is the parent and creator of Poser; Steve Cooper is the Poser 3 product manager at MetaCreations, Cecilia Ziemer is a Poser master user whose work has been published in *3D Artist Magazine,* in *Ray Dream 5 f/x* (Coriolis), and in the *Bryce 3D Handbook* (Charles River Media).
- **Chapter 21: The Zygote Media Group.** This exclusive chapter was written by the master modelers at Zygote Media Group. The Zygote Media Group was responsible for crafting all of the new high-quality animatable models in Poser 3. A tour and overview of their operations is included, as well as a modeling process walkthrough and other Poser 3 specific material.
- **Chapter 22: Poser Projects.** This chapter contains the development of six original Poser 3 projects (with all the necessary components included on the CD-ROM).
- **Appendix**

On the Book's CD-ROM

The enclosed CD-ROM contains movies, extra props and backgrounds, new templates, poses, and more unique material from Zygote. The CD-ROM that accompanies this book is loaded to the top and adds hundreds of dollars worth of Poser 3 extras.

How to Use This Book

The way that you use this book, and the priority of the information contained in it, will necessarily depend upon how much experience you have had with both Poser and computer art and animation in general. Some general categories follow that describe classes of users. If one of these categories seems to closely resemble how you might define yourself, you might find it helpful to use the underlying text as a guide for exploring this book's contents.

The Experienced Poser User and Computer Animator

If you are an experienced Poser 1 or 2 user and also have invested a good amount of time mastering your computer animation skills in other applications, you will find Poser 3 easy to understand. Because Poser 3 has tools and options not contained in other 3D applications however, you will find useful ideas throughout the whole book. If you have studied the documentation, you can spend less time on Section I of this book and most of Section II will be an easy read. Section III will probably be your main focus, since it explores details more suited to professional approaches. You should look at all of the animations and project files on this book's CD-ROM and customize them to your liking.

The Poser User with Little or No Animation Experience

If you are an experienced Poser 1 or 2 user, but have little or no animation experience, then here is how you might benefit best from this book. Skim Section I, except where the new Poser 3 tools and options are covered. Spend most of your initial time reading through and working from Section II (after you have, of course, worked through the Poser 3 animation documentation thoroughly). Since you are new to computer animation, save your study of Section III until later, after you feel comfortable creating basic animations in Poser 3. After you have reached that comfort level, you can study and customize the animations and associated Poser 3 projects contained on the book's CD-ROM.

The Experienced Computer Animator with No Previous Poser Experience

If you feel that this user category describes you best, then you can use this book to your best advantage by doing the following. Spend time learning Poser 3 first, both from its documentation and from Section I of this book. When you have a good feel for how the general tools and options work, move on to Poser 3's animation capabilities, in the documentation and as detailed in Section II of this book. Remember that although your previous experience as a computer animator may have given you a good understanding of the necessary vocabulary of the trade, Poser 3 does some things differently than other

3D applications. Compare Poser 3's animation and configuration options and methods with those you are already familiar with, and, if necessary, jot down the differences and similarities for continued exploration and study.

THE EXPERIENCED COMPUTER 2D ARTIST WITH NO POSER OR 3D ANIMATION BACKGROUND

The great thing about Poser 3 for 2D artists ready to move into 3D is that you can use the Poser 3 presets to create astounding 3D graphics and animations with ease. For the 2D artist, creating (and printing out) Poser 3 pictures is the best way to familiarize yourself with the interface design and the tools. This is suggested before you move on to various 3D and animation options. In terms of your best way to work with this book, spend a lot of time with Section I. Reread it several times, and with the Poser 3 documentation at your side, create a series of single images. When you feel ready to move into 3D and animation, do so slowly, so you can appreciate the options and power of each succeeding step along the way. You should also study as much animation as possible, on TV, in the movies, and on the Web. Also notice and pay attention to your own movements as you go about the day. At that point, you will be ready to work through and customize the projects listed in Section III of this book and to gain more advanced knowledge.

THE NOVICE USER, WITH NO PREVIOUS EXPERIENCE IN COMPUTER ART OR ANIMATION

If you were attracted to the purchase of this book without knowing why, you have made a good choice. Before you can make good use of it, however, you will have to get accustomed to computer basics. This includes a familiarity with your system and its components. You may be an artist or animator whose experience includes art and/or animation with noncomputer media. Poser 3 is a great choice when moving from "traditional" to electronic media, since you can create amazing graphics and animations with a minimum of study. More advanced projects will take deeper study and concentration, but that comes in time. When you are ready, purchase Poser 3 for your computer, and certainly after you have worked through the Poser 3 documentations, work at a steady and comfortable pace through the examples presented in this book. You will be amazed at how quickly your efforts will result in professional images and animations.

Poser 3 Conquers the Moving World

MetaCreations' Poser 3 is one of the most innovative and exciting pieces of software to ever be developed for desktop systems, rivaling in many cases the capabilities and output of systems and software costing hundreds of thousands of dollars. You can choreograph human and animal figures of every type and opulate your electronic worlds with animated beings. When completed, the results can be printed on paper for gallery presentations, sent to videotape or CD-ROMs for animated productions, or output to removable disk media for presentation to friends and associates.

Welcome to Poser 3, where characters bring the computer screen to life.

SECTION I

Covering the Basics

CHAPTER 1

New Features

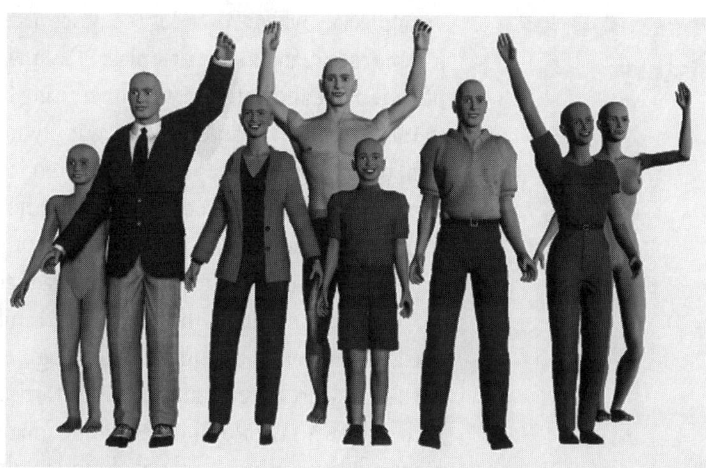

A Whole New Ballgame

Poser 3 has so many new features that at first glance you might not even notice that it carries over a number of tools and attributes from previous versions. This is due to the complete makeover of the interface, something that may initially throw experienced Poser users for a loop. This chapter focuses upon a general overview of the new Poser 3 features and explains how they are different and expanded from those in previous versions. In Chapter 2, we'll take a detailed tour of the new interface, its tools, how it influences your work, and how you can best interact with it.

Poser: A Brief History

To appreciate where Poser 3 is today, it's necessary to understand how and why it came into being in the first place. Poser was originally conceived as a way to provide a fast and accurate way for creating human figure images for 2D artists to trace over. It was developed as a utility for MetaCreations' Painter application, based on the concept of having a model or mannequin pose in the studio. Almost immediately after Poser's release however, users started to clamor for more 3D animation features. This constant pressure from Poser's user base has driven its development toward a professional 3D art and animation tool.

Poser 3 is the result of this pressure and embodies both the 2D and 3D artists' needs. The creation of posable human figure images for the 2D artist has never been so easy, accurate, or affordable. 3D artists and animators now are presented with a huge array of options and functionality in Poser 3. Just two years ago, many of these features were only found in ultra-professional workstation-based 3D applications, and many have never been seen on any platform.

New to Poser 3

OK, with some observance and respect for history, it's time to list the features that are propelling Poser 3 into the forefront of human and animal model art and animation applications with the listing of each feature, a note about why it may be important to you, and how it will influence the way you think and work is included.

NEW CONTENT

As you read through this list of new Poser 3 content, be sure to pay special attention to the features that are most attractive to you. That way, you'll know which chapters will enhance your Poser 3 learning curve.

New Models

The models in previous editions of Poser were good enough for tracing purposes in a 2D environment, but the models in Poser 3 have been redesigned from the ground up by the Zygote Media Group, a high-end professional modeling facility. Here's a list of the human models that ship with Poser 3:

- Business-attired human male/female models, lo-res/hi-res variants
- Casually attired human male/female models, lo-res/hi-res variants
- Nude human male/female models, lo-res/hi-res variants
- Child clothed/nude mode, lo-res/hi-res variants

NOTE

The model that first loads into Poser 3 is a Poser 2 model. To work on a human model that allows the extended features of Poser 3, you need to load one of the models from the Poser 3 People library.

These new models are sculpted and texture mapped, whether with muscles or attire, so that each feature is anatomically correct.

As in Poser 2, any of these models can also be a temporary proxy for other Figure types, simply by selecting that Figure from the Figure height item on the Figure menu. Alternate Figure height types include: Baby, Toddler, Child, Juvenile, Adolescent, Ideal Adult, Fashion Model, Heroic Model. The proportions of the figures' anatomical geometry are adjusted and all costuming remains intact. For instance, selecting a male Business figure and then selecting the baby Figure Height will result in a baby that is attired in a business suit (see Figure 1.1).

FIGURE 1.1 *The Businessman model looks very different when alternate Figure heights are chosen. From left to right: Baby, Toddler, Child, Juvenile, Adolescent, Ideal Adult, Fashion Model, and Heroic Model.*

TIP

If you use the Baby to Juvenile Figure heights and globally resize the figure to that of an adult, you will have a very unique adult with different proportions than the standard adult figure (see Figure 1.2).

You'll read more in Chapter 3 about ways to customize standard characters, so that each model leads to infinite variations. But a quick example would be to take a baby Figure height and use it as an adult character.

All in all, the new People models included with Poser 3 contribute to an interesting family portrait (see Figures 1.3 and 1.4).

The importance of the new Poser 3 models to your graphics and animation cannot be overestimated. If you intend to fold the renders into a 2D composition, the quality and variety of the models will address any high-end need you are faced with. If you intend to use Poser 3 animations (see Section II on animation), the quality and mutability of these new models will make your audience gasp with delight.

Articulated Human Hands

Poser 2 had over twenty articulated hand models that could be used to replace the left or right hand of a model. But, Poser 3 has traded off the limited number of hands for a hand model that you can shape into infinite poses. The

FIGURE 1.2 *The Baby Figure height globally resized to adult proportions with a wig on creates a unique adult character. See Chapter 3 for more figure modifications.*

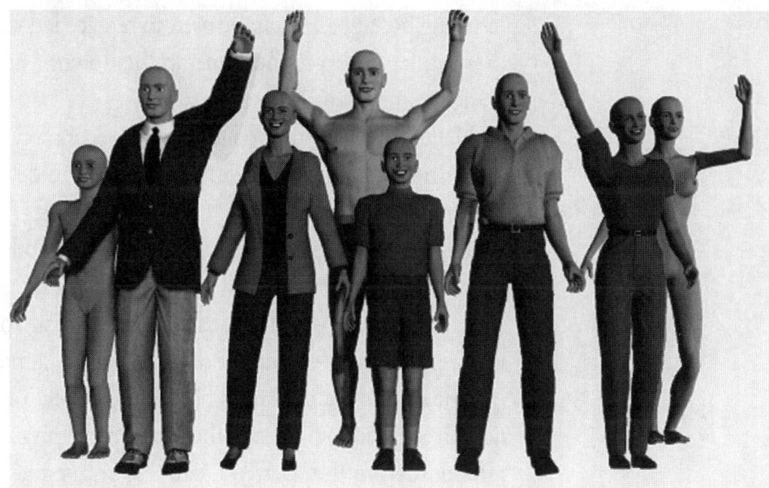

FIGURE 1.3 *A composite portrait of the new models included in the Poser 3 People library.*

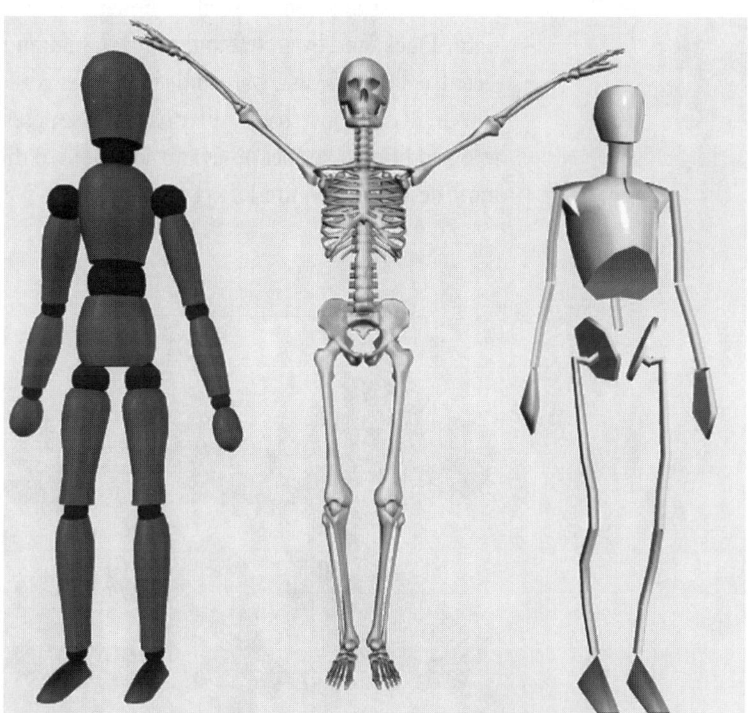

FIGURE 1.4 *In addition to the new people models, you may also select new Mannequin, Skeleton, and Stick figures.*

resulting posed hands can be used to replace left or right hands on a model, or they can be loaded to the scene on their own. The flexibility of this single upgrade is almost worth the price alone.

Hands in Poser 3 now consist of two separate categories. The first are left and right hand models in the Additional Figures folder in the Figures library. These are stand-alone models of a left and a right hand. They can be posed by rotating or resizing any of the digits that make up the model—three for the thumb and three for each finger—as well as the resizing or rotation of the base. You can create eerie animations with hands floating in the air, or, after posing a hand, apply it as a replacement for the left or right hand of a model in the scene.

The second are the Hand libraries or collections of saved poses that can be quickly applied to figures in the scene, providing a quicker way to shape a definite pose from the start. You can also resave these saved poses if you choose. The Hand library contains five separate categories of Hands: Basic (26 poses), Counting (0 to 5), Hand Puppets (seven poses), the entire Poser 2 Hand Poses library, and Sign Language (A to Z plus "and").

The "Hand Puppets" category deserves a detailed mention. These hand poses consist of seven "animal" silhouettes (Bird left and right, Dog left and right, Duck, and Swan left and right). Children love to see these shapes projected as shadows on a wall, and since Poser 3 allows objects to cast shadows, you could develop a shadow play using these poses as a start. You could also develop additional Puppet poses and add them to this library. See Chapter 10 for more details. See Figure 1.5.

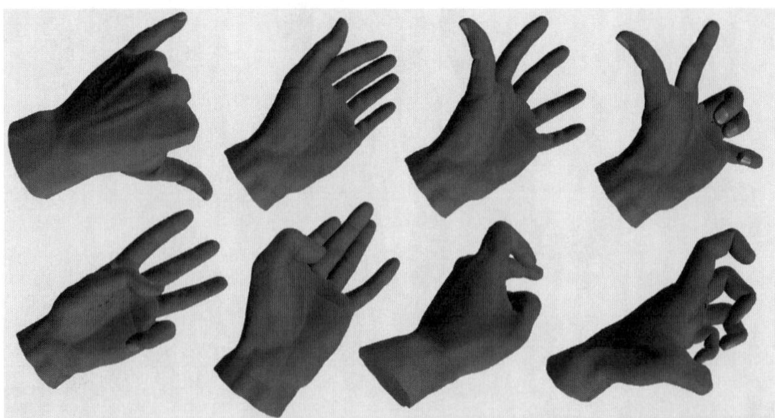

FIGURE 1.5 *The new Hands in Poser 3 are exquisitely modeled and can be posed and animated in an infinite variety of ways.*

Animal Models

Poser 1 and 2 treated the world as if it were only populated by human beings, a depressing thought, but Poser 3 ships with five animal models: Dog, Cat, Horse, Dolphin, and Velociraptor. Each of these animals has its own personality and individual controls for causing various parts of its body to morph into new shapes—mouths open displaying teeth, fins or legs bent as if in a gallop, eyes rolling and looking in targeted directions, and more. See Chapters 6 and 12 for a more detailed look at how you can modify and animate the new Animal models in Poser 3. See Figure 1.6.

Facial Expression and Phoneme Library

All of the new Animal model heads, as well as the heads of models in the new People library, have controls for adjusting various elements on the head. Most have mouth opening capabilities, and the People heads have controls for adding features that give a character a true human quality—emotion. Not that animals are devoid of emotion, it's just that the human face is unique in its capacity to twist and contort with so many different kinds of displayable emotions. Zooming in for a close-up of the new People faces in Poser 3 allows you to get a better idea of the power that emotions play in our ability to "read" each other. No narrative is needed when the face can display exactly what's going on inside your character's mind.

Just as Hands can be altered by assigning a different posed Hand from the Hand libraries, facial expressions can be altered instantly by assigning them an-

FIGURE 1.6 *The inhabitants of Poser 3's nonhuman model library.*

other pose. And just as Hands have a stand-alone pair (left and right) that can be posed individually, or placed on the screen as a singular floating object, so Heads too have their own Male and Female pair. You can place heads as nonconnected floating objects into a scene. These capabilities add a wealth of functionality to Poser 3's uses, as you'll see in Chapter 5, 7, and 11. See Figure 1.7

Custom Textures for All Models and User Templates

The textures designed for the new People models and the Animal models are realistic and proper, but that would never be enough for the artist or animator needing to personalize his or her work. Realizing this, MetaCreations decided to include the texture Templates as well. These templates can be modified in any bitmap painting application. The ability to modify the textures of any model pushes Poser 3 even farther into the creative realm. The standard Template size is 9.7 × 9.7 inches at 72 DPI and takes up about 1.4 MB of drive space. See Chapter 18 for details on customizing Templates. See Figures 1.8 and 1.9

BioVision Motion Capture Files

If you are one of the 100 million or so individuals who saw the film "Titanic," then you have already seen Motion Capture files in use. As the camera flew over

FIGURE 1.7 *Altering the expression of a face is one of Poser 3's most magical attributes, allowing for an almost infinite range of expressions. This also includes shaping the mouth into phoneme-like contortions so you can lip-sync sound files.*

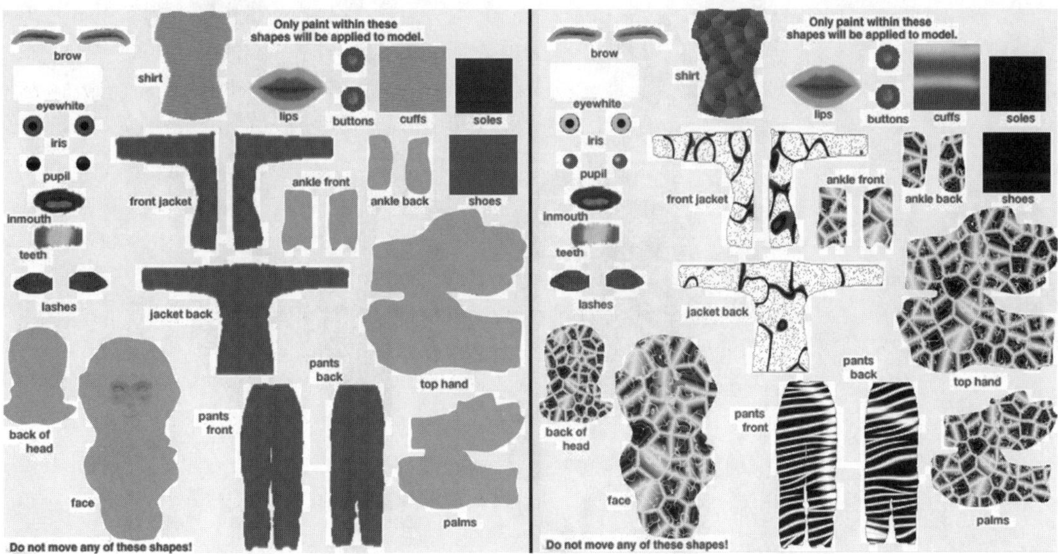

FIGURE 1.8 *On the left is the Business Woman texture Template, and on the right, as it looks after being modified.*

the deck from stem to stern, hundreds of people going about their holiday and travel tasks were visible. Attention! These were not human actors, but digital proxies. The reason they looked so real was that their motion was captured from real human models, and mapped to the digital models. This capability is present in Poser 3, so you can begin scripting your own "Titanic" movie (though perhaps with a somewhat smaller budget). The new capabilities of Poser 3 for accessing and saving Motion Capture files push it into the realm of a moviemaker's application and a professional user's dream. A number of Motion Capture files are included on the Poser 3 CD-ROM, and more are on the way from third party developers.

BVH motion capture data is an industry standard motion format. Motion capture hardware is used everyday by scientists and moviemakers alike to record complex human motion and to create ultra-realistic, highly kinetic animations. Dance, sports, and medical data motions are just some examples of typical usage. Poser 3 imports BVH motion data files and allows you to apply them to a Poser figure. The final animation generated is remarkably lifelike and would be virtually impossible to achieve in any other way. You can also save out BVH motion files, so that your Poser 3 animated moves can be read by any other application able to import this animation format.

FIGURE 1.9 *When the modified texture is mapped to the Business Woman model, a whole different character emerges, as shown in the right-hand model.*

3D Prop Library

The new Props library that ships with Poser 3 is just the start. Beyond the basic group contained here, you are expected to add your own props. Props add interest and variety to an animated scene. For more ways to use Props, be sure to read Chapters 8 and 13.

Hair Library

With all due respect to readers who may have witnessed, like I have, that it's "hair today, gone tomorrow" (sorry), Poser 3 contains a new library of Hair objects so that all of your models don't need to look like Yul Brynner anymore (unless you want them to). These hairpieces are not just blocky models, but sport such niceties as stray strands of hair. Hair, like any object, can be rotated, resized, and even retextured. Hair objects come already attached to the heads of the People models, though it usually has to be moved into place. The textures already mapped to them, however, are truly spectacular and add even more personality traits to your models. See Chapters 5 and 7 for more on Hair options and uses. Figure 1.10 illustrates some of the Hair objects.

FIGURE 1.10 *Here are just a few examples from the new Poser 3 Hair library.*

Walk Collection

The new Poser 3 Walk Collection consists of a series of animated poses that can be applied to a selected People library figure. The Walk Collection files were designed and saved out from the new Poser 3 Walk Designer (see Chapter 14). Walks can always be modified and altered after they have been assigned to a model, and then saved out again as a new file.

The Walk Designer

Using the Walk Designer control panel, you can manipulate a set of sliders that will build and blend a custom walk automatically. Then just attach the figure geometry to a curved path for very fast and realistic development of walking and running Poser people. Building a realistic walk cycle by hand was always a tedious and frustrating chore, but not any more. Now, by simply dragging a set of dials to control stride length and speed, along with a variety of body part position changes, walks can be constructed in minutes if not seconds. Be sure to read Chapter 14.

Poses, Cameras, and Lights

All three of these elements have their own Poser 3 libraries. New Poses, Cameras, and Lights can be added to their respective libraries at any time. Once retrieved and applied, they can be modified and saved again. Like everything else in Poser 3, the libraries contain elements that you are always free to put your own creative stamp on. See Chapters 3 and 19.

Morph Target Channels

What if you're making the next great science fantasy movie, and you have to show Dr. Heckle being transformed into Mr. Slide? Wouldn't it be great to develop both characters separately, pick the source and target models, and then have Poser 3 grind away to create the intermediate stages of the transformation? This process is called 3D Morphing, and you can do it easily with the new Morphing features in Poser 3. See Chapter 15 on Morphing Madness.

The RDS5 Modeling Connection

Poser 3D adds a Plugin for Ray Dream Studio 5 users that offers direct access to the Vertex Modeler. RDS5 OBJ import/export is fostered, so you can build shapes, create morph target groups, and perform other handshaking magic. See Chapter 17.

The RDS5 Animation Connection

There are times when Poser 3's animation environment, sweet as it is, just won't be extensive enough to allow you to develop the animation that's calling you. But, Poser 3 adds a plugin for animation and figure export/import into RDS5, retaining all figure geometry and key frame data. So if you are using RDS5, you'll have additional options. See Chapter 17 for details.

New Animation Options

In addition to the Animation Palette ported over from Poser 2, Poser 3 adds additional animation options. Chief among these is the Control Graph, which allows you to perform "eases" using splined curves between selected frames. There's also a new basic animation Controller at the bottom of the Poser 3 interface that allows you instant access to keyframe addition and deletion. See Chapter 9.

Sound File Support and Sound Clip Files

New to Poser 3 is the capability to import and attach sound clips to your animations. You can use a sound clip for a background music element, an effect, or even a voice-over for lip-synching.

Support for Poser 2 Figures

If you are upgrading from Poser 2, and you have a ton of Poser 2 figures that you developed over time, you will appreciate the respect given to you in Poser 3. All of your Poser 2 figures can be imported and animated. Poser 2 figures, especially the low-res type, are good to use as background elements, such as a crowd.

Rendering Modes

Recognizing that there is more to an artist's life than ray tracing, MetaCreations has added a series of new rendering options to Poser 3 output. Rendering options include Silhouette (great for creating Alpha masks as detailed in Chapter 17), Outline, Wireframe, Hidden Line, Lit Wireframe, Flat Shaded, Sketch, Smooth Shaded, and Texture Shaded. Cartoon artists and animators will absolutely flip over the Sketch option that creates an instant flat cartoon look from the scene content. See Chapter 8.

Extensibility

Extensibility means openness. Software that is extensible is software that allows other developers to write extended plugins, so the application becomes more than the sum of one developer's creative energy. Software that offers no extensibility is usually limited to smaller possibilities because the more diverse the developers that write the code, the more options the application can address. Extensibility is one of the first attributes a professional user looks for when purchasing software, because it means that the application will have a longer life span, and that its future development will be augmented by more tools and options.

Poser 3 is highly extensible, so you can expect more content for all of its libraries. Zygote Media Group, the same developers responsible for creating all of the new Poser 3 models, have also created the first five CD-ROM collections of Poser 3 plugins. Starting with a sampler CD that contains a number of high-quality models and other added files, they also offer more human and animal models, textures, and BVH motion files. Be sure to read Chapter 21, which presents the complete Zygote story and details the Zygote modeling process. In addition, we incorporate a number of the added Zygote models and other files throughout this book, in tutorial text, figures, and animations on the book's CD-ROM (see Figure 1.11).

FIGURE 1.11 *This group picture displays just some of the models offered by Zygote from its CD-ROM collection. Of high interest are Asian, Afro-American, and elderly people models.*

A MetaCreations Exclusive

Poser 3 now incorporates MetaCreations' exclusive SREE-D acceleration technology. This built-in high-speed 3D renderer allows unprecedented real-time performance, eliminating the need for platform or OS specific 3D software. Faster redraw of 3D models on screen allows for more realistic, shadowed previews, easier positioning of models, faster playback of key framed animation and higher resolution models with greater physical detail. In computer graphics and animation, speed means a more natural creative approach.

Moving Along

In this chapter, we've looked at Poser 3's new feature list. Each item was explored as to its importance and use. In the next chapter, we'll take a detailed journey through the Poser 3 interface and itemize ways you can optimize your work in Poser 3.

CHAPTER 2

Navigating the Interface

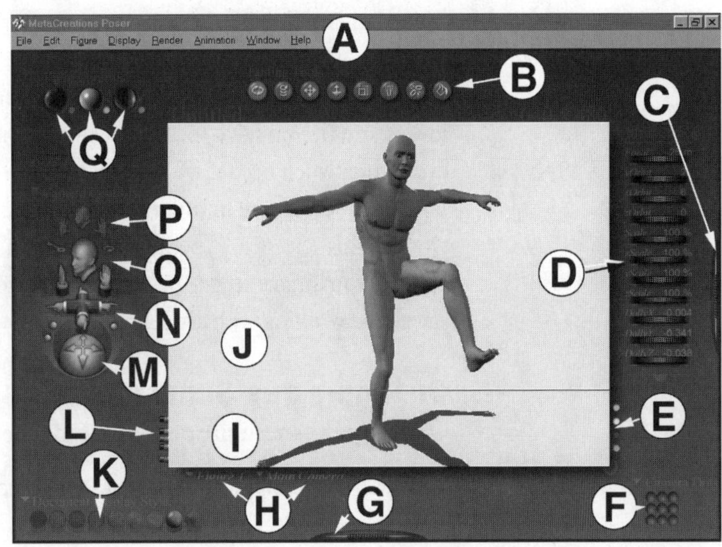

First Things First

In this chapter, we will explore all of the tools and concepts in Poser 3 and where the controls are located. Even if you are an advanced Poser user with experience in Poser 1 and 2, everything is so new in Poser 3 that this chapter will be important to read.

The first action you should take before starting your Poser 3 work sessions is to make sure that you're working in a screen size that allows Poser 3 enough elbow room. Poser 3 will work on a screen set to 640 × 480, but it will present you with some space problems at this size. The reason for this is that the actual working area in Poser 3 is differentiated from the surrounding tools and utilities. A 640 × 480 screen size means that your actual workspace can't be set much larger than 320 × 240. This is fine for multimedia work, but little else.

Thus, if you have the capacity to do so, it is strongly suggested that you change your monitor size to 1024 × 768, with the option of 800 × 600 as the lowest size (if you have to). This will allow a working area of 640 × 480 and even larger when needed. A 17-inch monitor or larger is necessary when working at this screen size in order to read text. If your system doesn't allow you to work at this screen size (because you don't have a suitable monitor or enough RAM), you'll have to get by at a screen size of 640 × 480. In all cases, you should be working with sixteen million colors.

Changing the Screen Size on the Mac

To change the screen size on the Mac, do the following:

1. Go to the Apple menu at the top left of your screen and move down to Control Panels. Once the Control Panels list opens up, double click on Monitor.
2. Once in the Monitor dialog, click on the Options button. This will display a list of monitor size options. Select 1024 × 480 if it's listed, or 800 × 600 if that's the largest setting displayed (see Figure 2.1).
3. After selecting the enlarged monitor size, your screen will be replaced by that option.

Poser 3 loves RAM. On the Mac, be sure to increase Poser 3's memory allocation as much as possible, given the amount of RAM you're working with. Do this in the standard fashion by selecting Poser 3 and bringing up its INFO window, then increase the Preferred memory as much as possible.

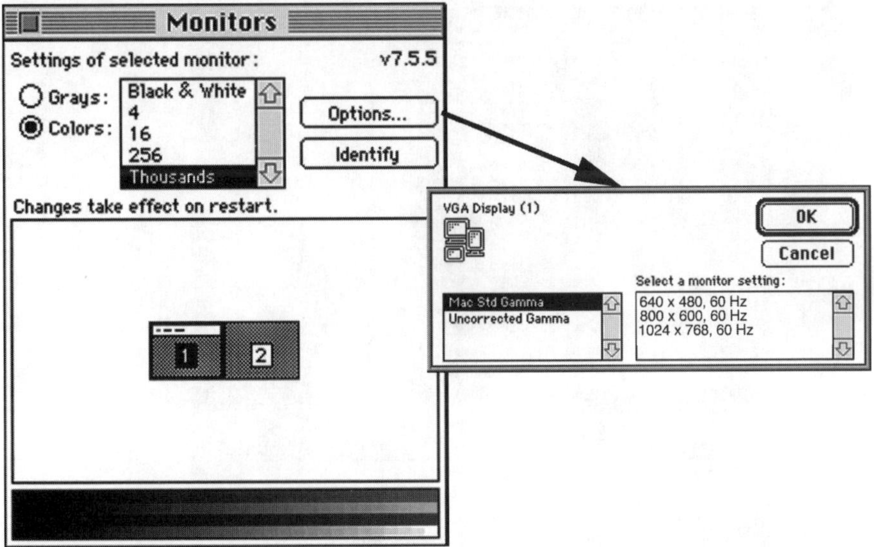

FIGURE 2.1 *The Mac Monitor dialog on the left and the Options dialog on the right with the screen sizes displayed.*

CHANGING THE SCREEN SIZE IN WINDOWS 95/98/NT

To change the screen size in Windows 95/98/NT, do the following:

1. Open My Computer and double-click on the Control Panel directory. Once it opens, double click on Display. When the Display dialog opens, click on the Settings tab.
2. Move the slider until 1024 × 768 is displayed. Select Large Fonts from the Fonts list unless you are working with a 19-inch monitor or larger. You may be asked to insert your original Windows 95/98/NT CD so the new fonts can be loaded. Hit the TEST button to see the new size, and then click OK. The screen will change to the new size (see Figure 2.2).

   Note that the computer usually restarts after this change. Instead of using the Control Panel you could also just right-click on the desktop and select Properties to adjust the screen attributes.

Poser 3

OK, now that you have enlarged your monitor settings, it's time to explore the Poser 3 interface. Open Poser 3. You will see the Poser 3 interface once the splash screens have disappeared (see Figure 2.3).

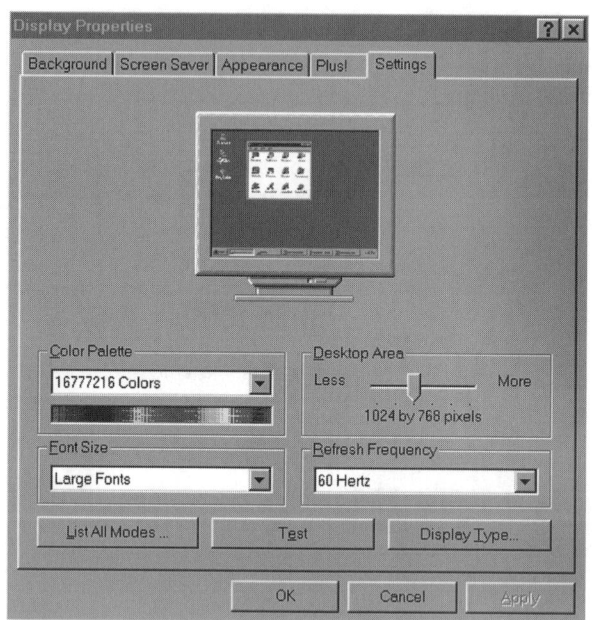

FIGURE 2.2 *Change the screen size in the Display dialog in the Control Panel directory to the new size for Windows 95/98/NT.*

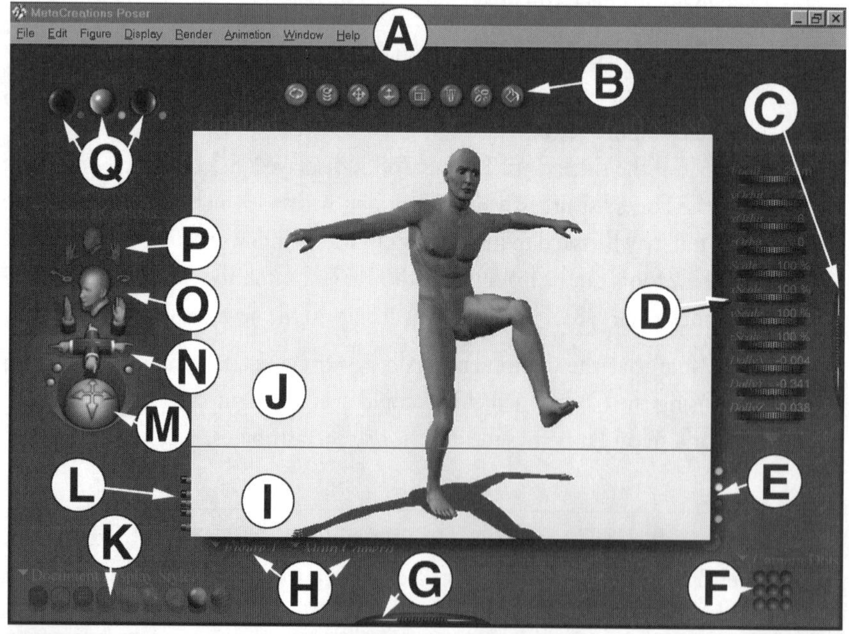

FIGURE 2.3 *This is the Poser 3 interface. All of the key letters point to various elements on the interface that we will detail in the following text. Refer to this interface schematic for locating the placement of the options pointed out in the text that follows.*

This chapter is devoted to exploring and detailing the new Poser 3 interface, but it assumes that you understand the Poser 3 documentation. Please be sure to read the Poser 3 documentation in its entirety and work through all of the tutorials. Then you can use this chapter, and indeed this whole book, as a tool for expanding your knowledge and filling in missing details.

Referring to Figure 2.3 on the opposite page, the key letters point to the following Poser 3 tools and options.

A. Menu Bar

This area is Poser 3's Menu bar where the File, Edit, Figure, Display, Render, Animation, Window, and Help menus are accessed. In this section, salient features in each menu list that you should pay particular attention to will be discussed.

File Menu

Besides the standard load/save selections, there are two very important listings in the File Menu you should pay attention to at the start: Import and Export.

Import lists a number of different types of file format data that can be read into Poser 3. This can be separated in background data (movie files or graphics used as a backdrop for your Poser 3 choreography), 3D Object Data (Poser 1 and 2 documents and libraries, and 3D props in the following formats: 3DMF, 3DS, DXF, OBJ, and Detailer/Painter 3D Texture files), and BVH motion capture files. The Import option is where to go when it's time to enhance your Poser 3 world with more items.

Export is important because it allows Poser 3 to handshake with other applications. Poser 3 allows you to export three types of data: Picture files (PICT for Mac users and BMP or TIFF for Windows users), 3D Object data (3DMF, 3DS, DXF, OBJ, and Detailer/Painter 3D Texture files), and BVH motion files. Picture file exports allow you to read the Poser graphic into a bitmap paint application (like MetaCreations Painter), where it can be customized and composited with other images. For example, the cover of this book was created by compositing Poser 3 images in Adobe Photoshop and MetaCreations Painter. Exporting objects is important because other 3D applications may have a larger set of 3D tools necessary for putting the final touches on a Poser 3 project. Motion file export is important because other 3D applications can read motion files.

At a number of places in this book, discussions illustrating the ways Poser 3 output can be redirected to alternate 3D applications are included. For example, when it comes to the sheer beauty of applying a texture or material to a Poser 3 object, Bryce 3D is an optimum choice. Poser 3 does not export animation files to Bryce 3D, but Bryce 3D can be used to place origin points on Poser 3 elements for keyframe animating. You will be astounded at the quality of Poser 3 objects exported to any of your favorite 3D applications. Applications that allow "boning" are especially suitable for Poser 3 imports, since boning allows you to animate a figure's parts without visible seams or breaks in the model. This is especially useful to 3D Studio and Studio Max users.

Edit Menu

The two most important items in the Edit Menu at the start of your Poser 3 experience are the Preferences and Properties listings.

Preferences Why is the Preferences dialog so important? Because you can configure Preferences to the way you work best in Poser 3. First, set your screen size and menu placement the way you like them. Place the Poser figure on the screen where you want it to appear when you first start Poser 3. Then, simply go to the Preferences dialog and click on Set Preferred State and wait while all of your settings are read. Make sure Launch to Preferred State and Use Previous State are on, and quit the dialog by hitting OK. Now quit Poser 3 and start it up again. You will find that all of the settings you adjusted are still there. See Figure 2.4.

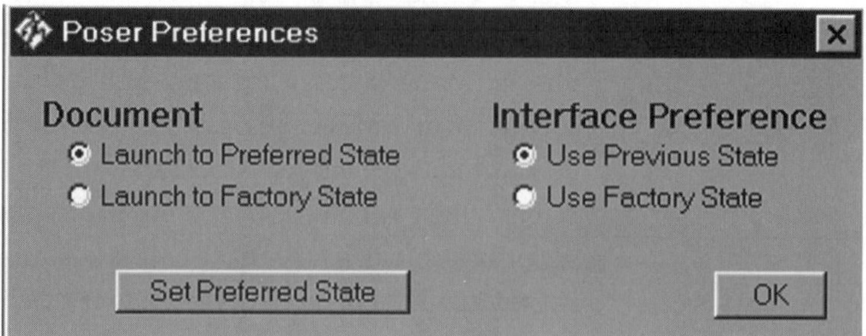

FIGURE 2.4 *The Preferences dialog allows you to configure and save the Poser 3 workspace to your liking, which becomes the new default when Poser 3 starts up the next time.*

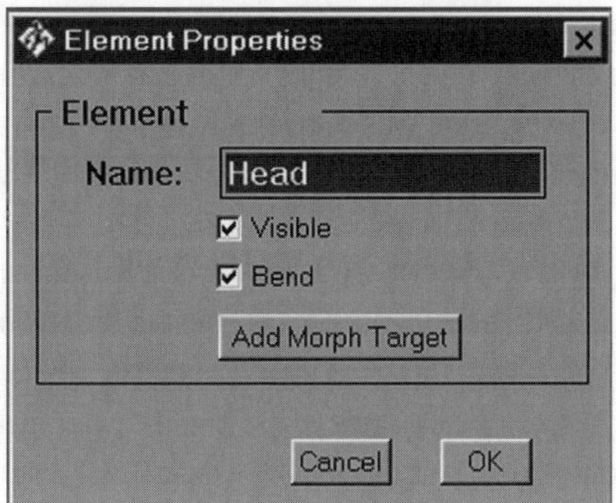

FIGURE 2.5 *The Properties dialog lists specific attributes for each part of a Poser 3 figure and also for selected Props.*

Properties The Properties dialog is important because it tells you at a glance the parameters of any selected object. In Chapters 3 to 7, various types of figure creation are covered, so knowing how and when to bring up a selected element's Properties dialog is important. The three central attributes that can be accessed from the Properties dialog are selecting a morph target for it, determining whether a selected element on a figure is visible, and whether it can bend. More information is provided on Morph Targets in Chapter 15. See Figure 2.5.

Figure Menu

A number of the items in this menu are carry-overs from Poser 2, so experienced users will take comfort in the familiarity of these listings.

Figure Height Just as in Poser 2, the same global Figure Height options are available. Simply select an option and watch your figure assume that physique. The options are: Baby, Toddler, Child, Juvenile, Ideal Adult, Fashion Model, Heroic Model. Although the option reads "Figure Height," that doesn't mean you can't use any one of these selections and resize it. A Toddler, for instance, can be resized to adult proportions in order to create a strange-looking Adult. Likewise, a Heroic Model can be resized to emulate a bizarre baby model.

Replace Body Part with Prop As we will explore in Chapters 7, 8, 13, and 22, there are powerful consequences when you replace a Poser 3 element with a Prop that open up all kinds of creative alternatives.

Set Figure Parent Any element in the scene may become the Parent of another element. Parent Actions set the actions of the Child. This is handy when you've developed a Walk Cycle and assigned it to one figure, and then need the exact same choreography to be duplicated by another figure(s).

Use Inverse Kinematics IK (Inverse Kinematics) is a carry over from Poser 2. In IK, you have to move the element at the end of a connected chain, like the foot or the hand, to move those elements farther up the chain. I would advise that you turn IK off until you've had a lot of experience animating body parts without it, then you can explore its uses. See Chapter 9.

Everyone works differently and sets defaults to accommodate personal comfort levels. For me, that means leaving IK off in most circumstances. The first thing I do in Poser 3 after importing a figure is to switch its IK settings off for all parts. By doing this, I can pose figures faster and more accurately. You can experiment both ways to discover whether using IK is suitable for your approach.

Use Limits Any figure model element can have its movements limited, allowing it to bend only so many degrees. For more realism in your figures movements, it's advisable to leave this checked. For maximum control however, leave it off.

Genitalia Male genitalia in Poser 3 has been completely remodeled and is now very realistic. Since there may be situations where this might be considered inappropriate (perhaps for small children in some classrooms), you may select to leave it unchecked.

Auto Balance Auto balance is an advanced posing feature. It's important because when it's checked on, it attempts to realign the figure according to the calculated weight of each of the body parts. The results are very subtle, but if you're looking for maximum realism, leave it checked on. See Chapter 3.

Lock Hand Parts Poser 3 hands have articulated fingers and finger/thumb joints. When a figure is being posed, it's sometimes difficult to select a hand without selecting one of the finger/thumb joints. This option can be used to prevent the problem.

Drop to Floor Dropping a figure to the "floor" is especially useful when shadows are on, because it makes the shadows that are cast appear more realistic. For maximum effect, make sure the Ground Plane is also visible.

Symmetry Poser 3 allows both left and right symmetry. Just pose half of the body, select Symmetry for that posed half, and the same pose is applied authentically to the other half of the body. See Chapter 3.

Delete Figure Any Figure in a Poser 3 scene can be eliminated, even if it's the only one present. For example, props are deleted by selecting "Delete Prop" in the Edit menu.

Hide Figure/Show All Figures When you have so many figures in a scene that it becomes hard to pose the one you want to, hide the rest. Selecting the Show All Figures command brings them all into view again.

Display Menu

The Display menu lists items that control what you see on your screen. We'll touch on just a few of the important options in this menu.

Cameras See Chapters 9 and 19 for a detailed look at Poser 3 camera use. In general, the cameras you'll be using most in Poser 3 animations are the Main, Posing, and especially the Dolly Camera. Other Cameras are more useful in the design phases of your productions.

Styles Poser 3 features a new list of Style options. A Style indicates the way Poser 3 renders to the preview display screen. The Styles you may select from include: Silhouette, Outline, Wireframe, Hidden Line, Lit Wireframe, Flat Shaded, Sketch, Smooth Shaded, and Texture Shaded. A Style can address the whole document and all of its elements, just the selected figure, or only separate elements. On the last point, this means that you could have a hand where every finger renders in a different display style.

The most important thing to remember about Styles is that although they are geared primarily towards the display screen, they can also be rendered in a final animation by selecting to render from Display Settings in the output options.

See Chapters 8 and 19 for more details on Display Styles.

Bend Body Parts Always leave this attribute checked on in Poser 3. If left off, the figure will show ugly separations between its elements.

Paper Textures Here's another new item. Paper textures add a little personality to your rendered output, but they can also serve as posing guides. The Grid option is especially useful when it comes to aligning and measuring on-screen elements in your Poser 3 compositions.

Paste into Background This is not a new Poser 3 attribute, but it is extremely valuable. Every time you activate this command, every item in the scene is copied as a snapshot that is pasted onto the background. This is not a keyframe option, so the background holds for the entire sequence. Using this feature makes it very easy to create a nonmoving background group of figures, a crowd, or even a more abstracted background design. Once the background is created, you can erase the elements that created it, and use the background for whatever new foreground material you like.

Display Guides Using the optional Display Guides as posing aids is covered in detail in Chapter 3.

Render Menu

Rendering can mean any of several possibilities in Poser 3. You can render to the Display for previewing purposes, to a file, or you can select to render a movie. As far as movies go, Mac users render QuickTime animations, while Windows users can select either AVI or QuickTime formats (as long as QuickTime for Windows is installed). You can also render single frame sequences on either platform.

Display Rendering Here you gave two main options, the same as allowed in previous editions of the application. Select either Preset Render (Fast or Clean) or Smooth Render (Fast or Clean) for previews. Preset Rendering gives you a better idea of how the materials look.

Render Options Dialog This is the most important item in the Render menu, since it's where you select and determine all of the rendering parameters for Preset rendering. To prevent being confined to your display setting size, check the New Window button and set the size and DPI of the finished rendering. Rendered output for publishing normally requires a DPI of 300 or more. You can also select the Surface material dialog from here or choose it separately from the Render menu. The Surface material dialog is where all of the elements in your scene get their color, texture, and other material assignments (see Figures 2.6 and 2.7). See Chapters 8, 9, 17, and 19 for more rendering details.

Animation Menu

The listings in this menu allow you to set your preferences for making movies, and to accomplish several complex interactions for customizing your settings. The details are covered in Chapter 9. As far as rendered output, this is also the location of the Make Movie dialog. See Figure 2.8.

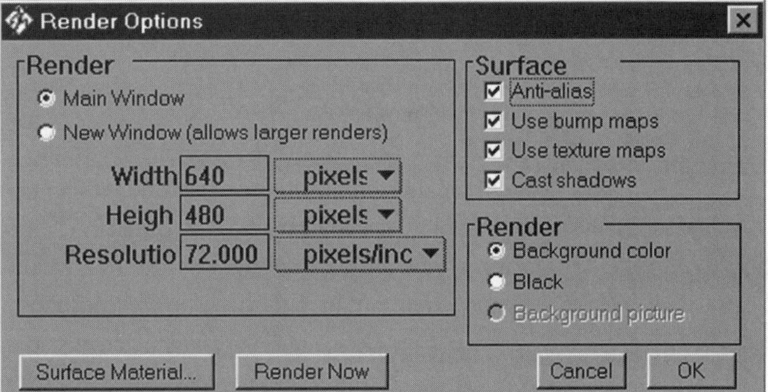

FIGURE 2.6 *The Render Options dialog.*

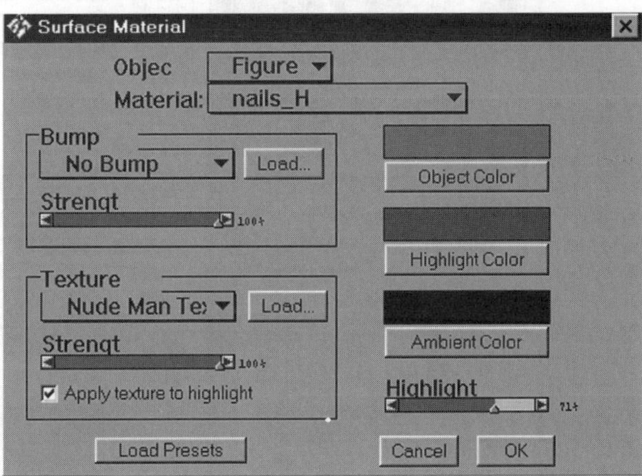

FIGURE 2.7 *The Surface Material dialog.*

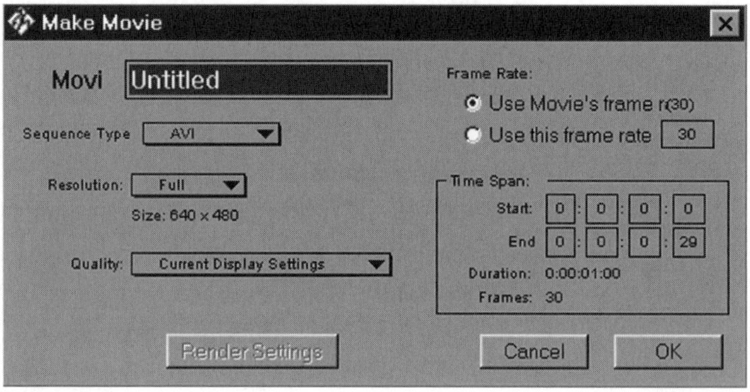

FIGURE 2.8 *The Make Movie dialog.*

Window Menu

Think of this menu as an extension of the Display menu. Checking or unchecking the items here either brings them up or hides them on the display. Most of these items can also be accessed by clicking their respective icon or button on the Display screen, or by selecting various hot-key combinations. The most important item in this listing whose location you will want to memorize is the Walk Designer dialog, which allows you to create diverse walks for the figure (see Figure 2.9). The Walk Designer itself is detailed in Chapter 14.

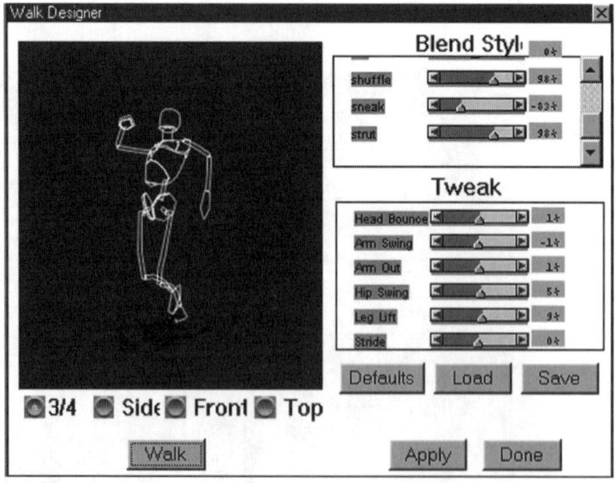

FIGURE 2.9 *The Walk Designer, one of the most startling features of Poser 3.*

B. EDITING TOOLS (SEE FIGURE 2.3 FOR KEYLETTER LOCATION)

You'll find that every chapter in this book makes some reference to one or more editing tools, so knowing where they are and how to use them is vital. Remember that they are dual-use controls. If you click and drag the cursor over them, they act on a figure globally. If you select a tool so that it lights up, and then click and drag on an element in the Document Window, only that element will be affected by the tool.

C. LIBRARY PALETTES TOGGLE (SEE FIGURE 2.3 FOR KEYLETTER LOCATION)

Click on this toggle and the Library Palettes pop to the screen. Once activated, you can access any of the Libraries to add elements to the Document, or add/delete items from a library. Only delete items that will no longer be needed. There are libraries for every element in Poser 3, including figures, props, poses, lights, and cameras (see Figures 2.11 and 2.12).

FIGURE 2.10 *The Editing Tools Group (left to right): Rotate, Twist, Translate/Pull, Translate/In-Out, Scale, Taper, Chain Break, and Color.*

FIGURE 2.11 *The Library Palettes toggle on the right side of the screen.*

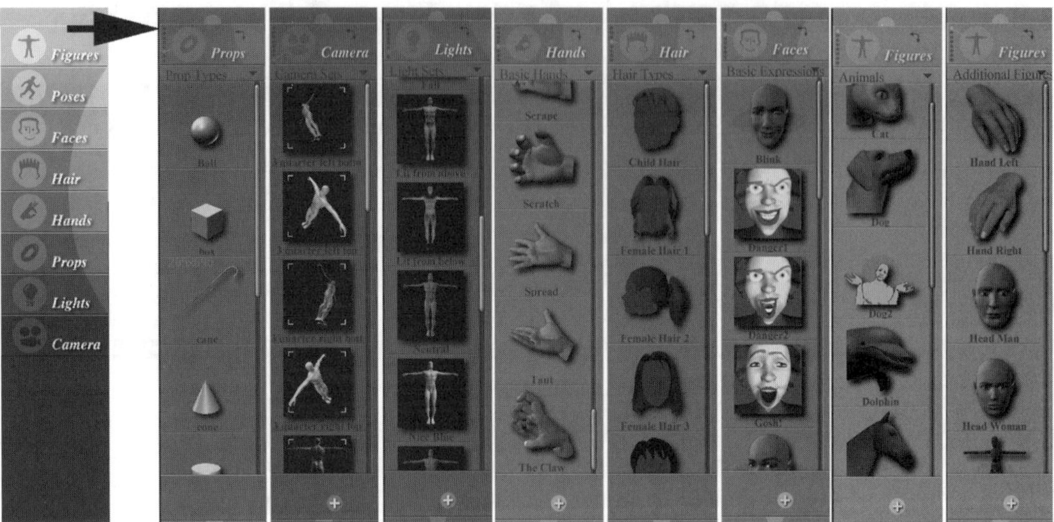

FIGURE 2.12 *From the Main Library List, all of Poser 3's Libraries become available.*

D. Parameter Dials (See Figure 2.3 for keyletter location)

Parameter settings are different for different items. A human, for instance, has different parameters than a quadruped, so the settings that need to be adjusted are different as well. See Chapters 3 to 8. See Figure 2.13.

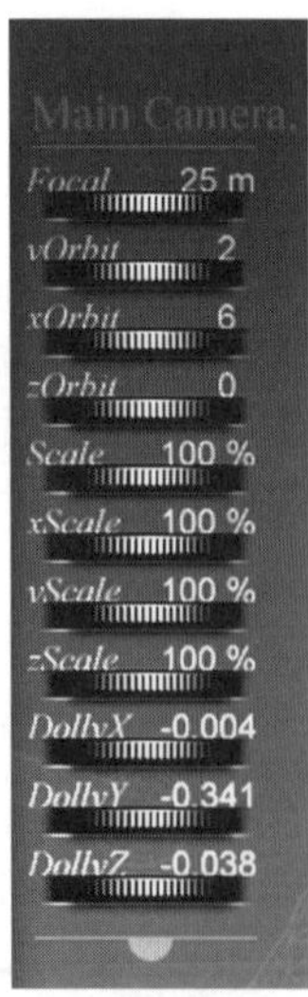

FIGURE 2.13 *Parameter Dials are used to configure any selected item's adjustable dimensions.*

FIGURE 2.14 *These controls allow you to alter the Background, Foreground, Shadow, and Ground colors.*

E. Color Controls (See Figure 2.3 for Keyletter Location)

The Color Controls give you instant access to global color settings for the Background, Foreground, Shadows, and Ground Plane. See Figure 2.14.

F. Memory Dots (See Figure 2.3 for Keyletter Location)

Memory dots can be a real time saver when it comes to recalling previous settings and views. Bryce 3D users will recognize this new Poser 3 feature. See Figure 2.15

G. Animation Controls Toggle (See Figure 2.3 for Keyletter Location)

The Animation Controls allow you to set keyframes, as well as to determine the length and frame rate of the animation. See Chapters 9 to 15 for a detailed look at Poser 3 animation options and techniques. This toggle brings up the Animation Controls. See Figure 2.16.

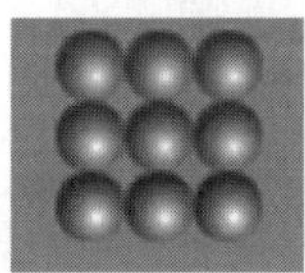

FIGURE 2.15 *Memory dots are used to return you to previously saved settings and views.*

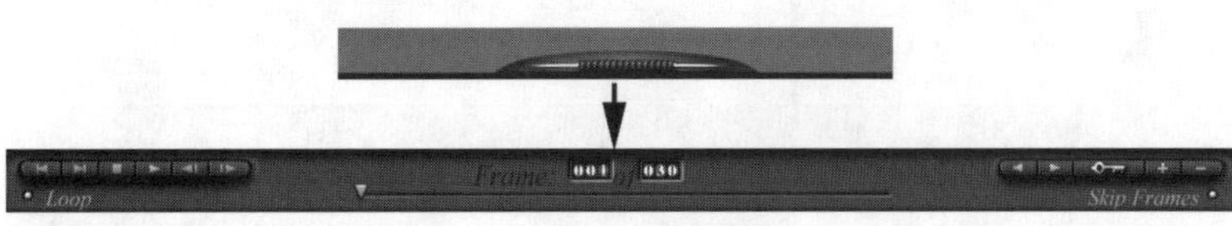

FIGURE 2.16 *Clicking on the toggle brings up Poser 3's Animation Controls.*

FIGURE 2.17 *The left control brings up the global selection, and the right control accesses the itemized list.*

H. SELECTION LISTS (SEE FIGURE 2.3 FOR KEYLETTER LOCATION)

Knowing how to use the selection lists is vital for finding the exact Document item you need to alter. See Figure 2.17.

I & J. DOCUMENT WINDOW (SEE FIGURE 2.3 FOR KEYLETTER LOCATION)

The Document Window is where you see the results of your alterations and modifications. See Figure 2.18.

K. STYLE BUTTONS (SEE FIGURE 2.3 FOR KEYLETTER LOCATION)

Clicking on one of the Style buttons changes the entire Document, the Figure, or the selected element to that Style, depending which is selected in the attached list. The buttons are quicker than using the respective menu commands. See Figure 2.19.

L. DEPTH CUEING, TRACKING, DISPLAY SHADOWS (SEE FIGURE 2.3 FOR KEYLETTER LOCATION)

These buttons activate or deactivate Depth Cueing, Tracking, and Shadows. In general, leave Depth Cueing off until you need it (though it's also a nice ani-

FIGURE 2.18 *The bottom part of the Document Window shows the Ground Plane (I), if it's switched on. The rest of the area behind your figures and props shows either a background color or the image/movie file loaded in.*

FIGURE 2.19 *Clicking on a Style Button changes the rendered Style in the display.*

mation effect). Tracking indicates the rendered quality of your Document when previewed and animated. As a default, leave Tracking set to fast Tracking (the center button) and leave Shadows on. See Figure 2.20.

M. CAMERA CONTROLS 1 (SEE FIGURE 2.3 FOR KEYLETTER LOCATION)

The Rotation Trackball allows you to rotate the camera left/right and up/down. It has no effect when you're in an orthogonal camera view. The button to the upper left controls the camera zoom. Below that is a button that controls the camera's focal length setting. To the upper right is a button that allows the camera to bank left and right. See Figure 2.21.

FIGURE 2.20 *The buttons toggle Depth Cueing, Tracking options, and Display Shadows on or off.*

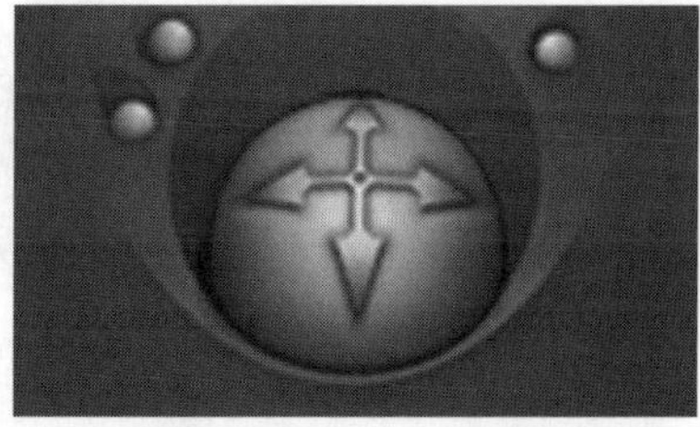

FIGURE 2.21 *The Rotation Trackball will be the Camera Control you use the most.*

N. CAMERA CONTROLS 2 (SEE FIGURE 2.3 FOR KEYLETTER LOCATION)

The crossed arms control camera movements left/right and in/out of the screen. See Figure 2.22.

O. CAMERA CONTROLS 3 (SEE FIGURE 2.3 FOR KEYLETTER LOCATION)

Instantly alter the Camera View by clicking and dragging left or right over the central icon in this group. The hand icons allow you to move the camera on either the ZY or the XY planes. The key icon is a switch that turns animation on or off, and the looping arrow icon switches on the Fly Around feature, so you can preview a scene from all sides.

P. CAMERA CONTROLS 4 (SEE FIGURE 2.3 FOR KEYLETTER LOCATION)

In this set of Camera Controls, the icons couldn't be more clear as to what they do. Clicking activates either the left or right Hand camera views, or the Head camera. Always use the Head camera when posing a face. See Figures 2.23 and 2.24.

FIGURE 2.22 *Camera movement is controlled left/right and in/out of the screen by these crossed arms.*

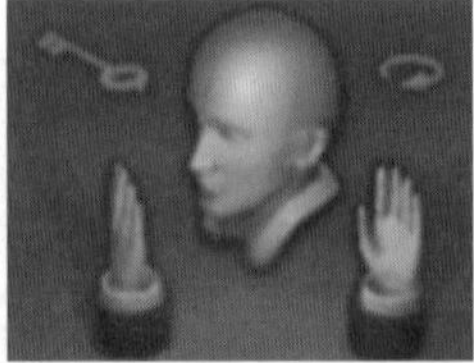

FIGURE 2.23 *The hand icons allow you to adjust movement up and down, while the key icon turns animation on or off. The looping arrow icon switches on the Fly Around feature. The central icon shows you what camera view you're in.*

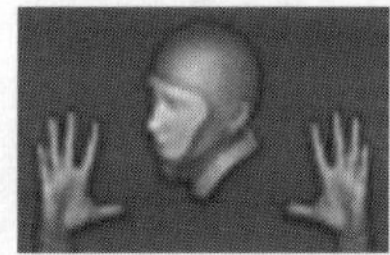

FIGURE 2.24 *The icons tell the story. Click to use either the left- or right-hand camera views, or the Head Close-up camera.*

FIGURE 2.25 *The Light Controls.*

Q. Lighting Controls (See Figure 2.3 for keyletter location)

Here's where you control the color (small beads) and direction (large radial controls) of the three Poser 3 light sources. Always consider adjusting the color to influence the mood of a scene. See Chapter 18. See Figure 2.25.

Very Important Poser 3 Data Sites

For additions and upgrades, it's vital to stay in close contact with MetaCreations and all of the other developers whose work supports Poser 3. Here are three important Web sites to visit. The first is the address of the MetaCreations page where you can download the Poser 3 Advanced Animation Guide (in PDF format). Following that are the sites for the Zygote Media Group, BioVision, and the House of Moves.

http://www.metacreations.com/products/poser3/resources2.html
Advanced Animation Guide- PDF

http://www.zygote.com/
Data on all Zygote Models

http://www.biovision.com/
BioVision Motion capture Site and Freebies

http://www.moves.com/
House of Moves data Site and Freebies

Moving Along

In the next chapter, we'll explore the posing and customization of human figure models.

CHAPTER 3

Posing and Customizing the Human Body

Paying Attention

In Aldous Huxley's famous book *Island,* he speaks about the large birds that inhabit the surrounding jungle. Every once in a while, when a character in the plot gets too far off track, the birds start yelling "Karuna, Karuna!", or "Attention, Attention!" You might think of Poser 3 as a Karuna bird, because it too calls for your attention. Attention to what? Attention to observing the body, with specific attention to how it bends and twists, and as we'll see later in Section II of the book, how it moves.

Artists and animators actually have a long history of paying attention to the human body, and when necessary or called for, the bodies of other creatures as well. It has always been thought that emulating the body in sculpture, painting, and dance was to bear special witness to a realm of the sacred. To be able to shape a piece of art in a way that reminds the viewer of the body is to remind them of the great mystery of life itself.

All visual art is the art of storytelling, of relating an unspoken narrative, a secret message. We can intuit more in a few seconds from a body pose or an expression on the face than we can from hundreds of descriptive words. I can remember my early years as an art student in Chicago. I rode the elevated trains about two hours a day, back and forth from the Loop, Chicago's downtown. I used to carry a sketchpad and make quick impressionistic drawings of the people that I saw. Sometimes, I'd spend weeks just observing a single feature, like noses. Other times, I'd try to capture the tableau of an entire group, and how their body statements unconsciously related one member to another. Karuna!

The first demand this book makes on you is to pay attention to all the life forms that surround you, human and nonhuman, day and night. If you purchased Poser with the intention of having an easy no-thought time in generating instant animations with no real care about the deeper implications potentially involved, then you are missing out on an opportunity to reinvigorate your appreciation of the world around you. Creating fast and easy populated scenes and movies in Poser 3 is certainly possible, but so is paying attention to the nuances and the finer points for an enhanced learning experience.

Karuna! Karuna! Whether in your pocket or in your head, begin carrying a sketchbook. Notice how life forms dance through your day and take that same information back to your work and play sessions in Poser 3. Karuna!

Basic Posing

Make sure that you understand how the Edit tools and Parameter Dials work before proceeding with these exercises.

OUR FIRST POSING EXERCISE

Get ready to take some mental notes, though you may write down what I'm going to ask you to do afterwards. At the end of reading this paragraph, put the book down. Either in the chair you're sitting in or another favorite chair, relax. Find a comfortable position. Take note of how each part of your body is either bent or twisted. Where are your feet? Where are your hands? Are there noticeable angles between your torso and the rest of your body? Take a mental picture of every part and how it relates to every other part. Do it, and then come back to the book when you're ready.

Hopefully, you really did have a few moments of relaxation and were able to take note of all of the things I asked you to. If you have to, while the memory of your body pose is still fresh, jot down whatever you can concerning the relationship of your body parts while you were relaxing. After that, when you're finished noting everything you can recall, open Poser 3.

Use whatever figure is on your screen for this initial exercise. Do the following:

1. Import a basic Box prop from the Props library. Place it somewhere in the center of the scene. This will be a stand-in for the chair you were just sitting in.
2. Resize the Box with the Resizing tool in the Edit tools above the Document window. Hold the Shift key down while resizing so that the Box has relative proportions to substitute for a chair, as compared to the figure's size.

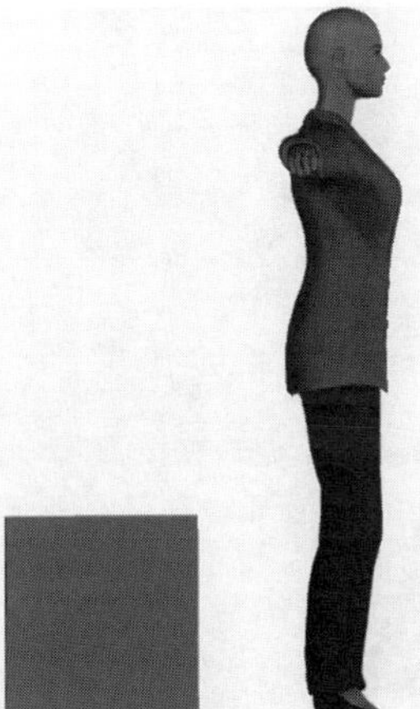

FIGURE 3.1 *The figure is moved so that it is in proximity to the resized box-chair, as seen from a side view.*

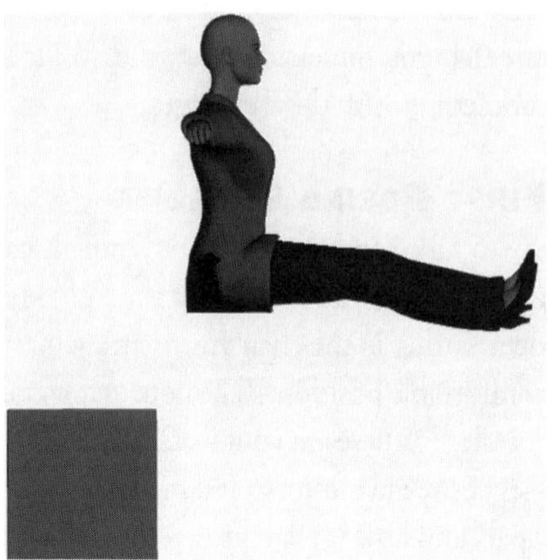

FIGURE 3.2 *The model with its thighs angled after the Bend operation.*

3. Turn off any Inverse Kinematics for your figure. Move your figure somewhere in proximity to the box-chair. Use the orthogonal side camera view and the front view. Click on Drop To Floor for both the box-chair and the figure (see Figure 3.1).
4. Select and Bend both thighs at a value of -86, using each thigh's Parameter Dials. You should now have a model as depicted in Figure 3.2.
5. Bend each of the Shins at an angle of 72. Move the model so that it sits on the box (use the Translate/Pull tool in the Edit toolbar, while keeping the mouse over the tool, and not in the Document window). See Figure 3.3.
6. This step is optional. I have added another box to act as the chair back, because that is more fitting for the chair I was sitting in (see Figure 3.4).

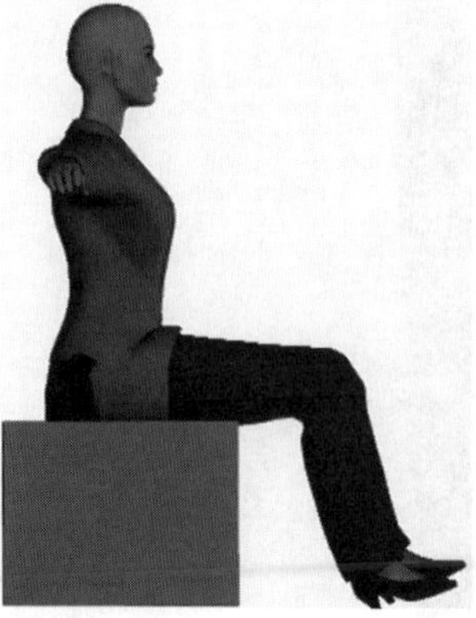

FIGURE 3.3 *The model's shins are Bent, and she is placed on the box-chair.*

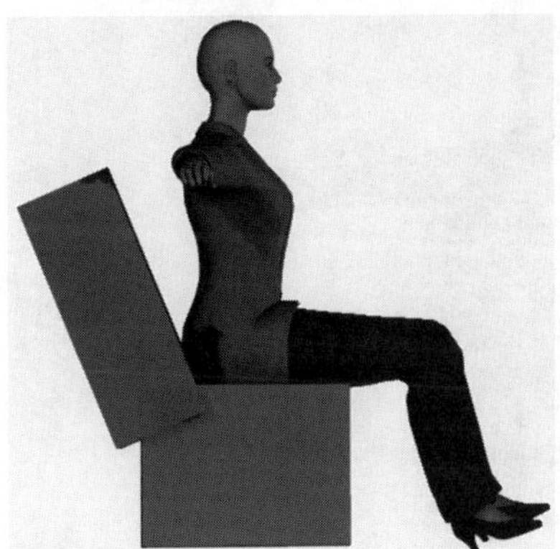

FIGURE 3.4 *A back is added to the chair.*

7. From here on, I will adjust the figure according to the pose I was sitting in. Your pose may be quite different, but you'll get a good idea of how to make your own customized adjustments by following along. The next thing I did was to angle the Abdomen by using a Bend of -30, so that the model is leaning against the back of the chair. She looks a little stiff, but I'll make the final adjustments later (see Figure 3.5).
8. Now my relaxation pose turned out rather complex, since I placed both of my hands behind my head in a locked position, to rest my head. My next step was to get the Right Arm/Hand in place. If I was using Inverse Kinematics, I could just move the hand into place and the arm parts would follow, but I'm not. Therefore, I moved the Right Shoulder, followed by the Right Forearm, followed by the Right Hand (see Figure 3.6).

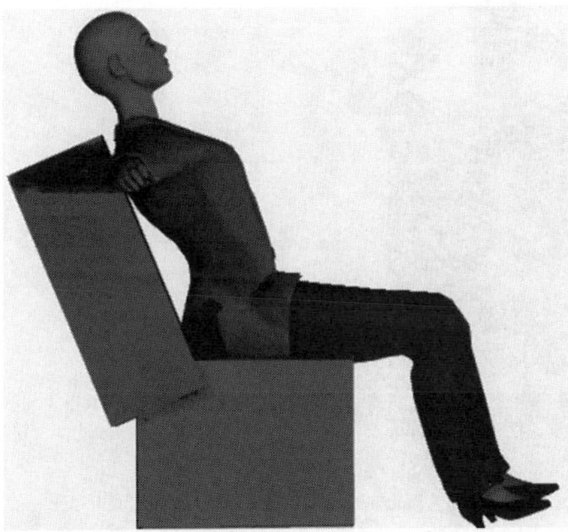

FIGURE 3.5 *The model leans back in the chair.*

FIGURE 3.6 *The Right Arm and hand are placed into position.*

When you are posing a model, switch views as necessary to get the best view for the task at hand. The orthogonal views are especially valuable in this regard.

When making global changes to a hand, always select Lock Hand Parts from the Figure menu. This allows you to select and rotate the hand without accidentally selecting the thumb or a finger joint.

9. Now for some Poser 3 magic. I used Figure/Symmetry/Right to left to instantly snap the Left Arm/Hand into place, instead of arduously modifying it separately (see Figure 3.7).

FIGURE 3.7 *The Left Arm/Hand is placed by using the Right to Left Symmetry command.*

10. At this stage, when you have the basic pose done, it's time to make small adjustments for reality's sake. First of all, destroy symmetry a little. Life forms are not completely symmetrical, not left to right or any other way. As you can see in Figure 3.8, I have adjusted my model's legs so they are not exactly at the same angle. It doesn't take a lot of movement to interrupt symmetry, just a little here and there. I also adjusted the model to fit the confines of the chair more accurately. I placed hair on her head for two reasons: to enhance reality and to hide her hands a little. I wanted to hide her hands so that a close-up wouldn't reveal that I didn't spend the necessary time locking her hands exactly together. I could have done that, but for this pose, it wasn't necessary (see Figures 3.8 and 3.9).

FIGURE 3.8 *The final pose has been accomplished.*

FIGURE 3.9 *A more interesting camera view.*

FIGURE 3.10 *Here, we've applied the same Pose to all of these Zygote models (available on the Zygote Extras CD).*

Now that you have the pose you want, the first thing to do is to save it to the Poses Library. Just go to the Poses Library and hit the Plus Sign, name your Pose, and hit OK. Since you have the Pose, you can apply it to any selected figure (see Figure 3.10).

It is seldom wise to apply a Pose across species lines. This Zygote bear model, for instance, dislikes having its forelegs placed behind its head (see Figure 3.11).

CAUTION

Karuna! A Bear has sharp teeth and claws. Do not force the Bear, or any being, into poses it doesn't appreciate.

ANOTHER BASIC POSE

This time, we'll investigate another pose, one that displays emotion. It's true that you can use Poser 3's excellent facial controls to display a wide range of emotions, but there are times when your camera is not pointed at the face of a figure. It's also possible that the face of a figure is not large enough in certain shots to allow the face to tell the story. At those times, you have to figure out a

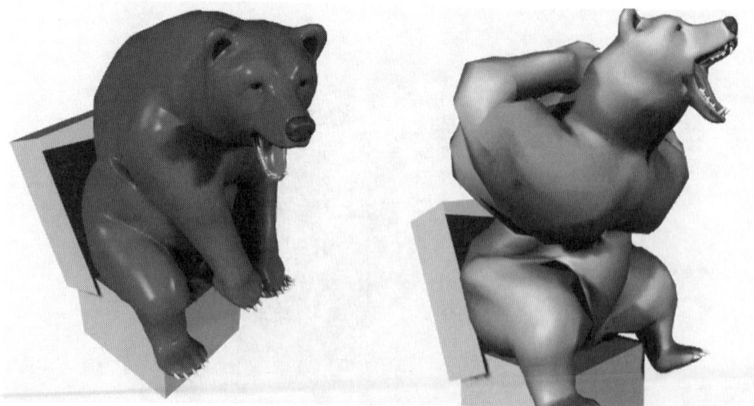

FIGURE 3.11 *When the Pose was applied to the Zygote Bear, it complained loudly. We can see this by the way the Bear's polygonal mesh warps.*

FIGURE 3.12 *Here is the figure before any customized posing.*

way to allow the body pose to work as the narrator, so that the emotion is clearly understood by the body pose alone.

Karuna! One of the best ways to study body pose emotions is to watch silent films. The poses of the characters are often exaggerated, in order to make up for the lack of audio, so the poses are easier to see. Body poses in a silent film often tell the story quite effectively.

For this exercise, instead of actually placing your body in a suitable pose, I would ask you to close your eyes and imagine the emotion of despair. Several pictures should appear before you. Perhaps some will be related to this emotion as you have witnessed it being played out on film, or perhaps even from moments in your memory. No need to linger too long on this feeling. What you're looking for is the ability to transfer your imagined sense of how a body might evidence despair to the Poser 3 figure. When you're ready, allow me to lead you through an appropriate pose as I might shape it. You can always add your own personal touches afterwards.

Note that the figure illustrated is from the Zygote Extras CD collection: the Old Man. See Figure 3.12.

1. Despair is a crushing weight, felt by the soul and the body. Imagine the figure besieged by a weight above it, and shape the figure accordingly by bending its knees slightly. Rotate the neck so that the shoulders hunch (see Figure 3.13).

FIGURE 3.13 *The weight of despair has affected the model. The knees are bent and the shoulders hunched. The figure is also Bent (20) at the abdomen slightly.*

FIGURE 3.14 *The Right Shoulder hangs limp from the emotional weight.*

2. Use a bend of 90 to drop the right shoulder (see Figure 3.14).
3. Now we'll use an old painter's trick (though nobody knows exactly who the old painter was) to emphasize the weight of the situation. When despair hits, we feel as if our extremities have suddenly grown larger. To relate this feeling ever so slightly, select the Left Hand and use the Scale dial to resize it to 125%. Then do the same with the Right Hand (see Figure 3.15).
4. The next part's a little tricky. You have to maneuver the figure's right arm and hand so it hides part of his face. Use the Head Camera for close-ups.

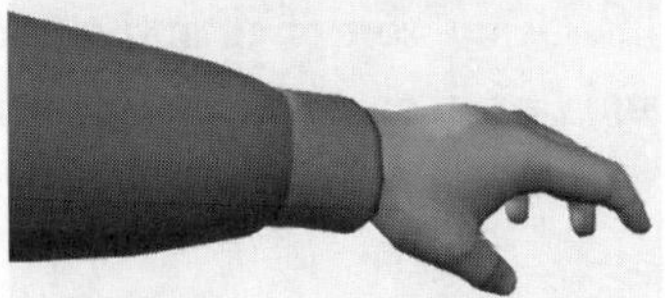

FIGURE 3.15 *The hands are enlarged 125%.*

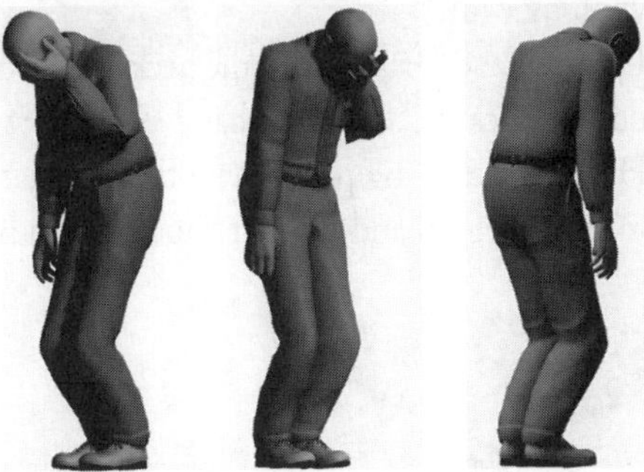

FIGURE 3.16 *The right arm and hand are rotated into position so the figure's face is partially hidden.*

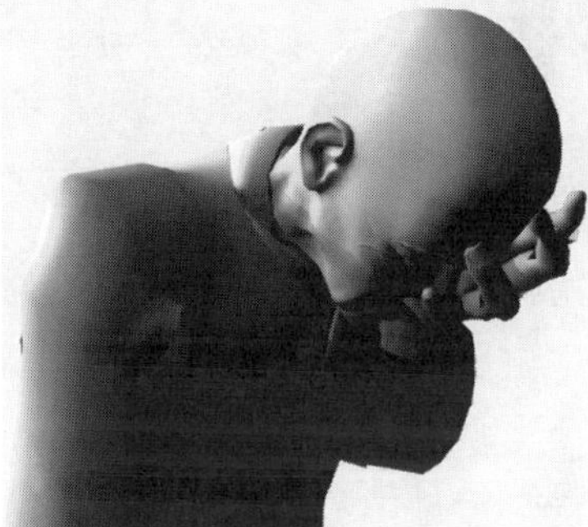

FIGURE 3.17 *A close-up of the pose.*

The idea is to get the hand close, but not to poke any fingers into the head (see Figures 3.16 and 3.17).

ONE FINAL POSE

Let's do one more pose before moving on to the customizing section. This time, just in case the despair exercise left you down in the dumps, we'll opt for pure joy. If despair is a weight that drives us down, then joy can be described as an emotion that lifts us up, sort of an anti-gravity response. Where despair makes us fold up and cave in on ourselves, joy opens us to the world and literally lifts our spirits. With all of that in mind, load a figure and follow along.

NOTE

The figures illustrate the Zygote Old Woman model, but you can use any figure you like for this posing example.

1. Load in your figure from the Library. It can be any figure you will enjoy working with.
2. Use the Bend Dial to bend the neck at -25. Go to the Hands Library and double-click on the Reach hand. When the dialog appears, select Right Hand. Repeat this operation for the Left Hand. Raise the Right Shoulder to a bend of -20 and the Left Shoulder to a Bend of 20 (see Figure 3.18).

FIGURE 3.18 *The model beams joy.*

FIGURE 3.19 *The model bends in the middle.*

3. We could stop right here, but we want a more ridiculous joy. Use a Side-to-Side parameter of -16 on the Abdomen. Then turn the Chest Parameter dial to 15. The model bends at the middle (see Figure 3.19).
4. Use a Twist of 77 and a Side-to-Side of 61 on the Right Thigh. Then use a Bend of 108 on the Left Shin (see Figure 3.20).
5. We want our model to literally "click her heels," so the Left Leg has to be brought into position. Use a Twist of -53 and a Side-to-Side of -5 on the Right Thigh. Then use a Bend of 90 on the Right Shin to complete the pose (see Figure 3.21).

FIGURE 3.20 *The Right Leg is posed.*

FIGURE 3.21 *The pose is completed, and the model skips into the sunset.*

Customizing the Human Form

Take one look at Figure 3.22, and you'll realize that Poser 3 figures can be sculpted to take on looks not quite familiar to everyday observation. If you're an admirer of Bosch or Dali, you will want to explore ways to add a touch of surrealism to your Poser 3 creations. The techniques we'll describe will require your familiarity with both the Editing Tools and the Parameter Dials.

BY GLOBAL RESIZING

Global Resizing refers to scaling a selected element of a figure (model) while holding the Shift key down with the Resize Tool positioned over the selected element, or by using the Scale Parameter Dial. Either of these operations resizes the selected element in all XYZ directions at the same time. It sounds like a pretty basic function, and it is. The results, however, can be quite interesting. In these exercises we'll move from some simple customizing alterations to more radical examples.

FIGURE 3.22 *A bizarre humanoid parades in ecstasy.*

FIGURE 3.23 *The Business Man model at the start.*

The Heads Have It

Let's apply a simple resize to the head of a selected figure. Do the following:

1. Load the Business Man figure from the People library. Resizing a head looks really bizarre on the business suited figures (see Figure 3.23).
2. Click on the Resize Tool in the Edit toolbar. Place the cursor over the head of the model, hold down the Shift key, and click-drag the cursor upward to the right (see Figure 3.24).
3. Now do the opposite. With the same Resize Tool highlighted, place it over the head, and click-drag down and to the left, with the Shift key held down (see Figure 3.25).

FIGURE 3.24 *The head of the model becomes enlarged, almost like a strange human balloon.*

FIGURE 3.25 *Now the figure has a pinhead, and the suspicion is that its intelligence has suffered a blow.*

Bomber Man

Using the same model as depicted in Figure 3.25, with its head shrunk, click on the Abdomen Element. Using the Scale Parameter Dial, select a Scale of 40 (see Figure 3.26).

Now we'll globally resize more of the model's elements. Resize the Left/Right Shins, Shoulders, and Forearms to 50. Resize the Left/Right Thighs to 125. I call this fella Bomber Man, since it looks like all he needs is a WWII flying cap and a scarf blowing in the wind (see Figure 3.27).

FIGURE 3.26 *Scaling the Abdomen down gives the model the appearance of a wasp.*

FIGURE 3.27 *Bomber Man to the rescue!*

AXIAL RESIZING

You can also use either the Resize Tool or the Parameter Dials to resize a model's elements on any selected axis. It's a lot easier with the Parameter Dials, because you have more control over each dimension. In standard computer graphics terms, this operation is called a *stretch*.

The Ostrich Lady

Import the Casual Woman from the People Library. Select her Neck, and use the Parameter Dial for a Y-Scale value of 950 (see Figure 3.28).

Now it's time to apply a more radical series of Axial Stretches. Set the Parameter Dials to the following values: Y-Scale for Left/Right Thigh, Abdomen, and Chest = 50; X-Scale for Left/Right Shoulder = 182; Y-Scale Neck = 1200; Head globally resized to about 300% with the Resize tool. Your finished biogenetic engineering experiment should look similar to Figure 3.29.

TAPERING

The Taper operation in Poser 3, whether initiated through the use of the Taper Tool in the Edit toolbar or by the Taper Dial in the Parameters Module, is the single most powerful way you can add radical customized elements to your models inside Poser. Heads are a special case for tapering, since there is no Taper Dial in the Parameters Module. To taper a head, you have to use the Taper Tool in the Edit toolbar.

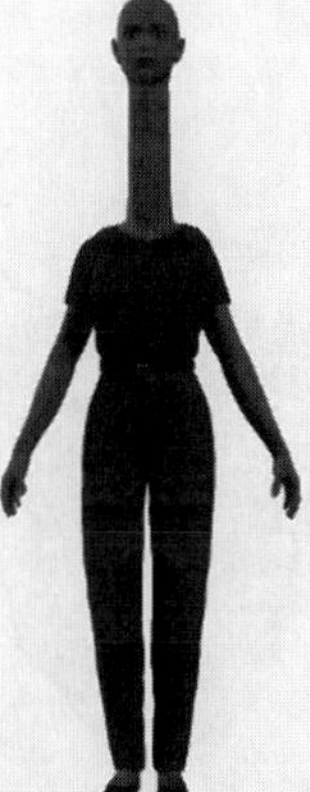

FIGURE 3.28 *They say she can see over any obstacle.*

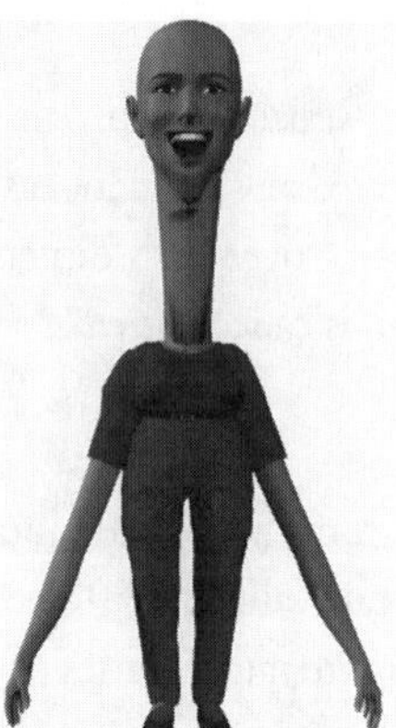

FIGURE 3.29 *The famous Ostrich Lady.*

Taperhead

The head of a model can be tapered small to large or large to small. The axis of tapering is always vertical for a head.

Pushing the Taper to extra large, so that the head is wider at the top than at the bottom and the width of the head is as wide as the outstretched arms, creates a very bizarre situation. The head flattens out into a circular plane that can be rotated against the body. All of the head parts are still fully articulated and "animatable!" (see Figures 3.30 and 3.31).

Karuna! Use the flattened head for a Sun face. Just make all of the other parts of the body invisible.

FIGURE 3.30 *Left to Right: normal head, head with large taper at bottom, and head with large taper at top.*

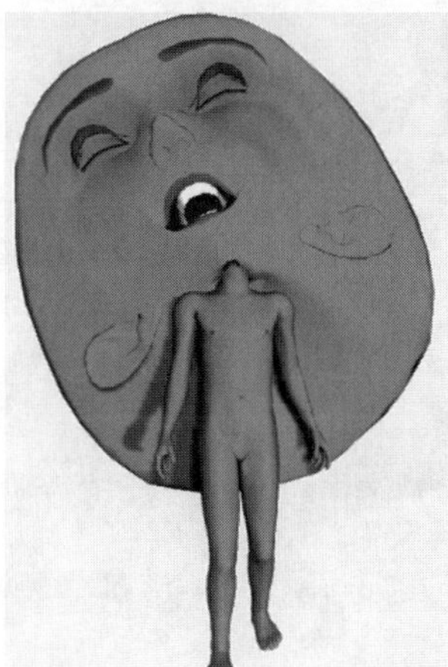

FIGURE 3.31 *When pushed to the limits, the Tapered head can become a flat plane. All the parts still move.*

Taper, Taper Everywhere

Except for the Head, all other figure elements have a special Parameter Dial devoted to customizing the Taper. You should explore the look of Tapers on all body elements. When used on body parts, Tapers can create a very cartoonish character (see Figure 3.32).

FIGURE 3.32 *Tapers were used on all of these model's body parts.*

FIGURE 3.33 *A pair of Northern Sqonks wishes you happy learning.*

Moving Along

In this chapter, we've explored methods of posing a figure and also discovered ways for customizing. In the next chapter, we'll look at hands in the same way.

CHAPTER

4 Posing and Customizing Hands

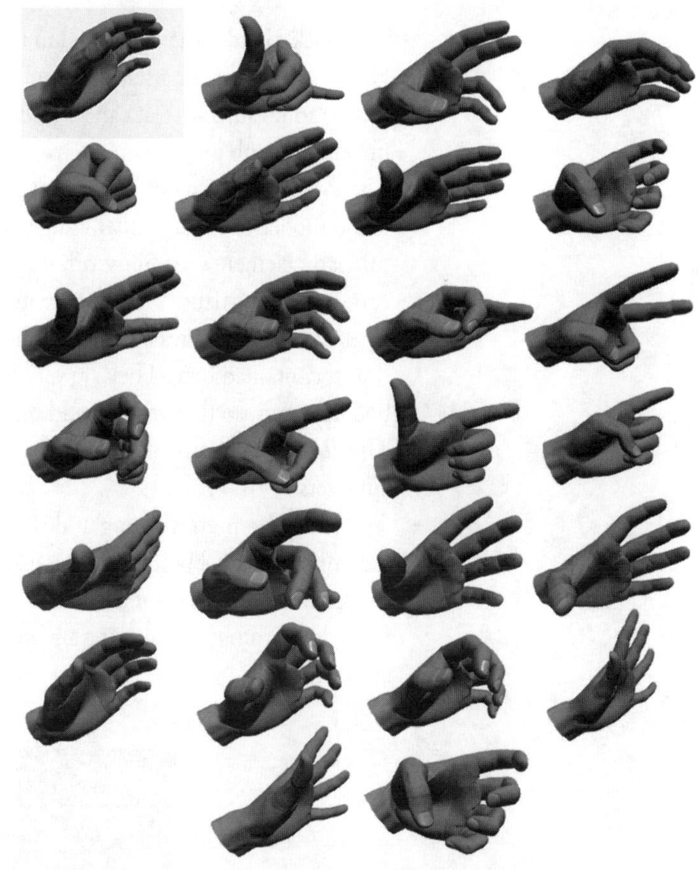

A Show of Hands

One of the most exhaustive revisions in Poser 3 versus its predecessors is the resculpting of the hand models. No longer do you have to shy away from close-up camera views of a model's hands, afraid that your audience will be presented with a gnarled and misshapen appendage. Instead, you can zoom in as close as need be, with a super-realistic hand model as your reward. To emphasize this fact, there are two camera icons in the Camera Controls at the left of the Document window that display a left and a right hand. Click on either, and the camera zooms in on the model's appropriate hand (see Figure 4.1).

Important Hand-associated items are contained in a number of places in Poser 3:

- The Lock Hand Parts command in the Figure menu. When selecting a Hand on a model, or a stand-alone Hand model. It's important to have this option. Otherwise, it can be difficult selecting the hand instead of a finger or thumb joint.
- The Properties dialog in the Edit menu. Properties are as important for Hand models as for any other model. Remember that you can selectively turn any element's visibility off, which we'll see is important when it comes to customizing Hands (later in this chapter).
- The Additional Figures library list. There are two Hand models, Left and Right, contained here. They are very important because they are disembodied hands, so that you can add them to a scene as stand-alone items. This leads to all sorts of possibilities, as we will see in this chapter and Chapters 7, 10, 17, and 22.
- The Joint Parameters dialog and the associated Use Limits command are important for Hand poses because they lock in the standard values for resizing and other modifications. They may, however, prevent you from doing things like altering a Hand to achieve an alien or monstrous appendage.

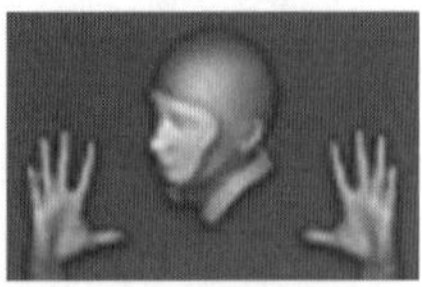

FIGURE 4.1 *The Left and Right Hand icons in the Camera Controls module zoom to a view of either hand.*

- The Pose Hands libraries. Hand Poses are listed under five separate collections in the Hands library: Basic Hands, Counting, Hand Puppets, Poser 2 Figure Hands, and Sign Language (see Figures 4.2 to 4.5).

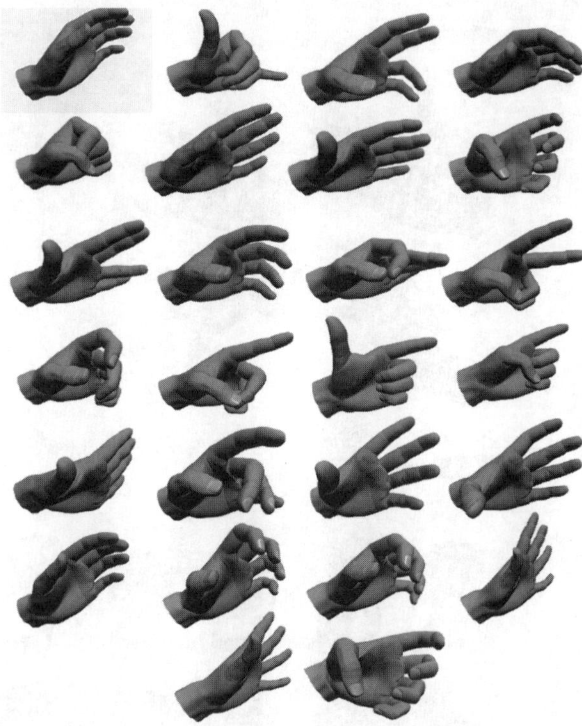

FIGURE 4.2 *Basic Hand Poses: Basic, Call Me, Coupled, Cupped, Fist, Flat Out, Fully Extended, Gnarly, Greetings, Limp, OK, Peace, Pick, Point, Pointer, Pointer 2, Pusher, Quirky Relaxed, Reach, Reaching, Relaxed Basic, Scrape, Scratch, Spread, Taut, and The Claw. Though there are some minor differences in the Poser 2 library of Hand poses, you can use this figure as an example of the Poser 2 poses as well.*

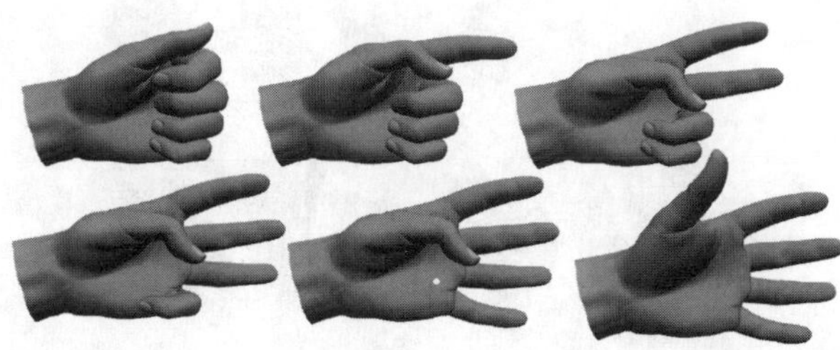

FIGURE 4.3 *Counting Hand Poses: 0 to 5.*

NOTE

A project you might want to try is to access the Hand Puppets library and to render a Hand casting a shadow of one of the animals represented.

Note that the Poser 2 poses are slightly different than those included in the Poser 3 Basics library.

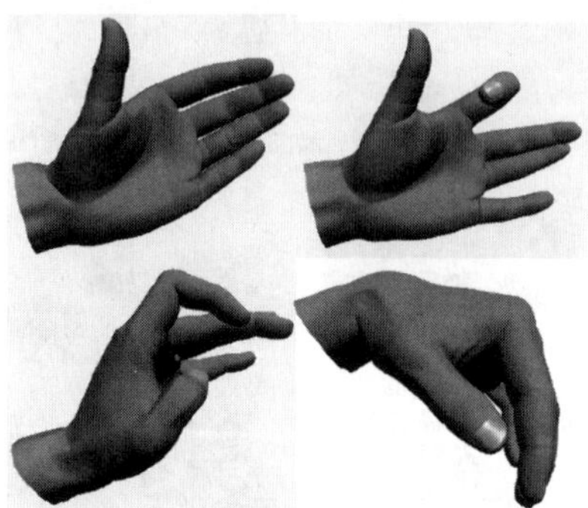

FIGURE 4.4 *Hand Puppets Poses: Bird, Dog, Duck, and Swan.*

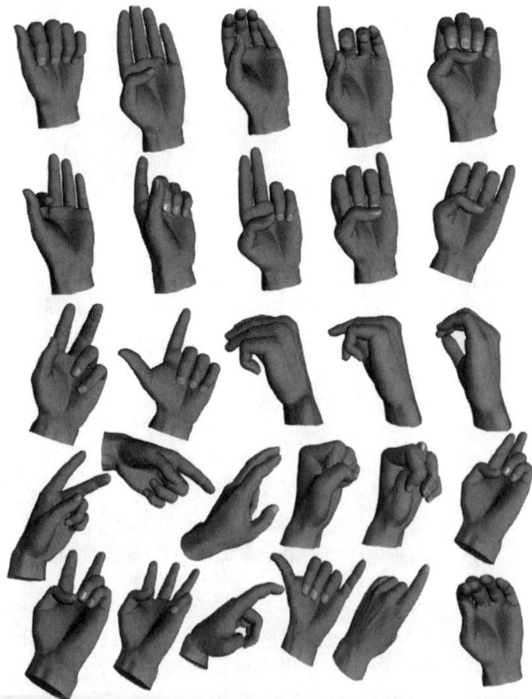

FIGURE 4.5 *Sign language hand poses: A to Z, &.*

GENERAL RULES FOR POSING THE HAND

The articulated hands in Poser 3 can be positioned into any needed pose in two ways. The first is to simply target a hand for a pose from the Hands library. You can either accept the library pose completely, or use it as a basis for making further modifications. This is the easiest way to get a hand posed. The second method, though a little more time consuming, serves best when the pose you desire is nowhere to be found (or anything even close to it) in the Hands library. In that case, you'll need to go in and pose each digit yourself. When that becomes necessary, follow these rules:

- Always use the Hand Camera view (either left or right) to zoom in close to the Hand so you can see exactly what you're doing.
- Instead of trying to click on the appropriate digit with the mouse, use the elements list under the Document window to select the exact part of the hand you want to move into position.
- For a more natural and realistic pose, make sure Use Limits is checked on in the Figure menu. This sets a boundary on possible movements and prevents you from doing things that might cause deformations in the Hand's geometry.

Karuna! If your Hand has to be holding an object, like a spear or a hammer handle, or some other prop, you can use a fist pose as the easiest way to get the Hand into a general position, then tweak the pose with the Parameter Dials.

PARAMETER DIAL ALTERATIONS FOR THE HAND

The three most important hand controls that can be manipulated by the Parameter Dials are Grasp, Thumb Grasp, and Spread. These three operators offer you global control over a selected hand. The Parameter Dials associated with selected finger and thumb joints are specific to those elements, and not to the overall hand. Grasp, Thumb Grasp, and Spread are important when you want to show some hand movement from frame to frame in an animation, but aren't interested in the fancier poses offered by specific items in the Hand Poses library (see Figure 4.6).

Customizing Hands

The general process for working through a Hand customizing process is as follows:

1. Apply the modifications.
2. Save the new Model to the Additional Figures library.

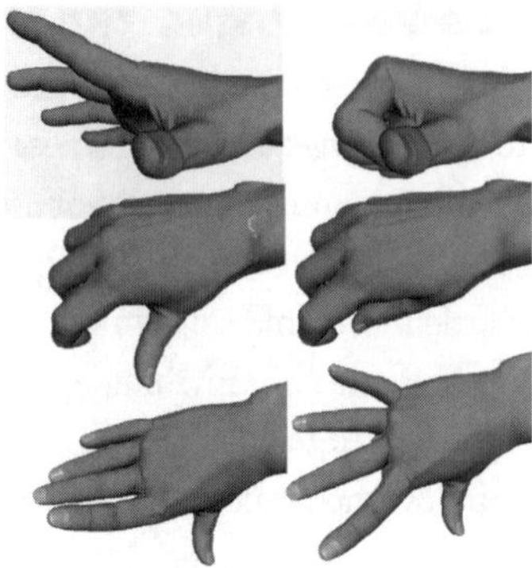

FIGURE 4.6 *Grasp closes the fingers, Thumb Grasp closes the thumb, and Spread splays open the fingers. Top: Grasp open and closed; Middle: Thumb Grasp open and closed; Bottom: Spread closed and open.*

3. Save the new Pose (if there is one) to the Hands library, preferably in a new folder named for your collection (such as MyHands or another appropriate name).

TYPES OF HAND CUSTOMIZING OPTIONS

There are some modifications that can be applied easily to a Hand in Poser 3, and some that require more planning and work. In general, the two simplest modifications you can apply to a Hand or to any of its parts are resizing and tapering. Each of these has its limits, beyond which the targeted Hand will start to warp and deform uncontrollably.

NOTE

It's always a good idea to rotate the Hand after applying any modifications, since this allows you to see if any anomalies were caused by your efforts. If deformations are caused, then you have to decide to either retrace your steps and to correct them, or to accept them as part of the new model.

When you customize Hands, there are two ways to engage in the process. The first is to load one of the stand-alone Hands from the Additional Figures library folder. This is a good option when you want to apply the hand either as a singular floating object, or to have it replace a Hand (or any other body part) on a figure already in your scene.

If you need to replace both hands of a model already in your scene, however, you may wish to take another route. In that case, use one of the Hand Camera views to zoom in on a Hand that you would like to customize. Apply the necessary modifications. When you're through, you can simply elect to use the Symmetry command to apply the same modifications to the other hand. If that completes the model, then save the model out with a new name, or save it out when all modifications are completed.

THE MOST DIFFICULT MODIFICATION

It's enticing to think that because Poser 3 contains a Visible/Invisible option in the Properties Dialog, you could easily just make some selected fingers invisible to create a two-, three-, or four-digit hand. You can do this, as long as you also address some attendant issues. When you make an element of a model invisible, you expose a hole where it once was. In the case of a Hand, the hole is most visible in the Front and Top views of the Hand. The hole will render, unless you do something to mask it. Unless you need this to happen for your own creative reasons, holes in figure parts are not desirable.

You can take place and size an elongated sphere (from a Ball Prop) to mask the hole, or use another imported object to do the same thing. But that's only part of it. From that point, the Hand (or the whole body of the model) will have to be glued to the patching object by making that object the Parent (Set Figure Parent in the Figure menu). This can present big problems when animating, because only the patching object can be set to animate. Solution? Do not make any elements of the hand invisible to achieve an alien or cartoon hand. It isn't worth it. Besides, if you really need an alien hand, you can model it in Ray Dream 5 or another 3D application (see Chapter 17), and import it for placement in Poser 3.

ALIEN HANDS

If you want to stay in Poser 3 and still need to create alien looking Hands, you have some options. Raising the Scale Value on the tip of the fingers can create bulbous or padded-looking finger tips. Decreasing the Scale of the fingertips to 10, and then lengthening the X Scale to 300 creates sharp knife-like finger tips. Playing with the Taper Values for the Hand and all of its elements can also lead to some interesting looks.

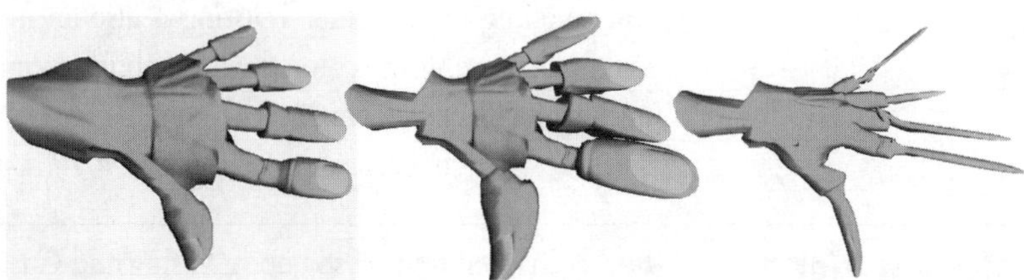

FIGURE 4.7 *A series of Alien hands, customized by using different Scale and Taper values from the Hand's Parameter Dials.*

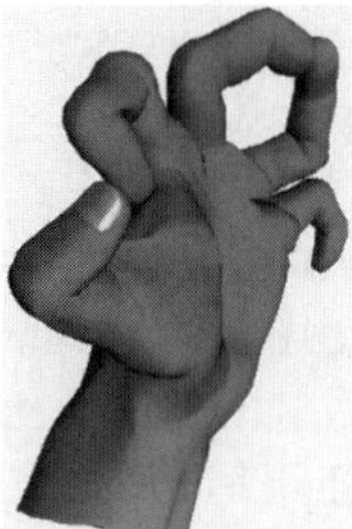

FIGURE 4.8 *By switching Limits off, you can shape the finger parts into unreal contortions.*

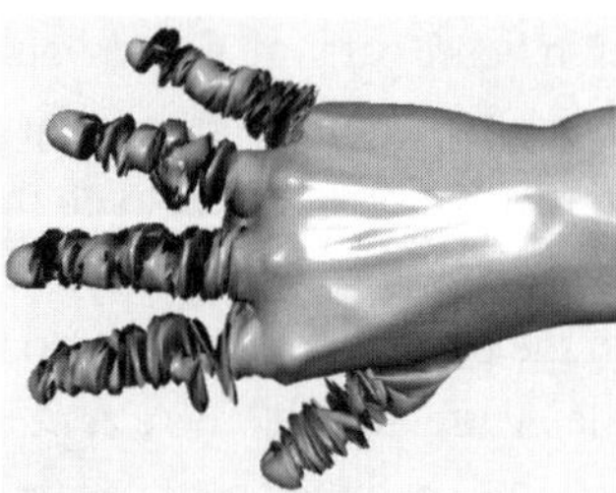

FIGURE 4.9 *Twisted fingers reshape the very nature of the Hand.*

WRITHING SNAKES

One neat effect you can perform on a Hand is to use the Side-to-Side and Bend Operations on the finger and thumb parts with Limits Off. This allows you to Bend the joints in relation to each other by angles of 90 degrees or more. When animated, this has the appearance of writhing snakes.

TWISTED REALITY

If you apply a Twist of 1000 or more to a Hand element, it will display a contorted twist that looks like the element is being wound up like a rubber band. Apply this same twist to the base of all of the fingers, and the rest of the fingers will go along for the ride. Twisting is also an interesting way to create alien looking hands. When colored with a bluish green, the fingers look like coiled steel bands (See Figure 4.9).

Moving Along

In this chapter, we focused upon Posing and Customizing Hands. In the next chapter, we'll explore the fascinating topic of Posing and Customizing Heads.

Color Plate 1. Cecilia Ziemer's exquisite planted Poser painting.

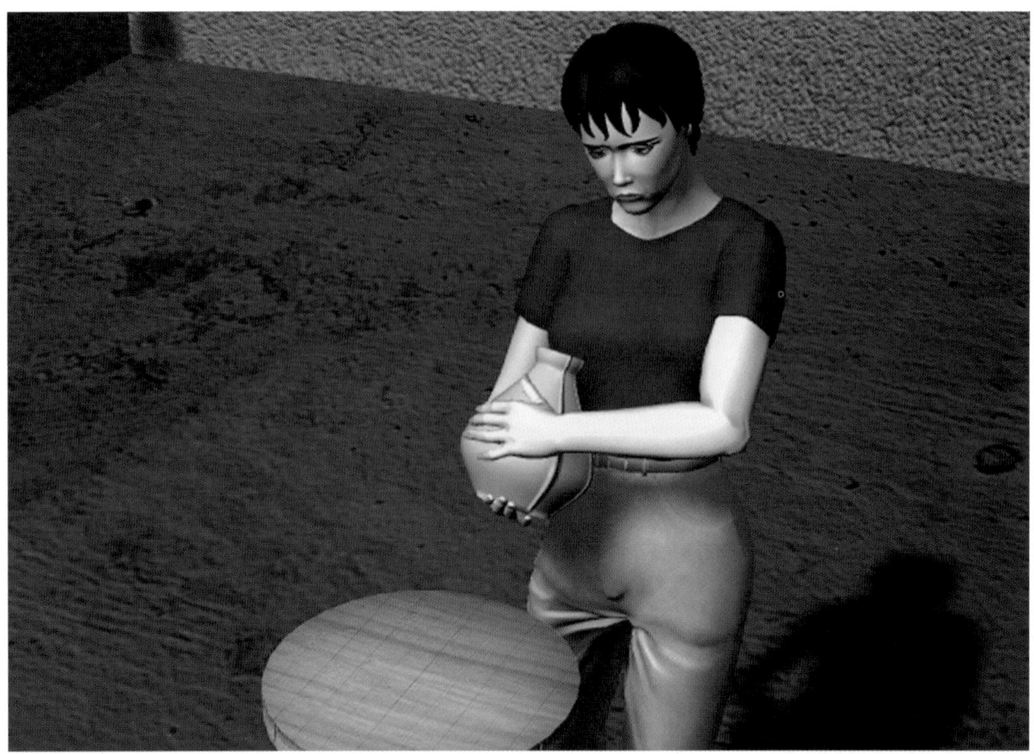

Color Plate 2. Chris Derochie's Poser renderings display how intent alters how a figure is posed, from grief at the top to "on fire" at the bottom.

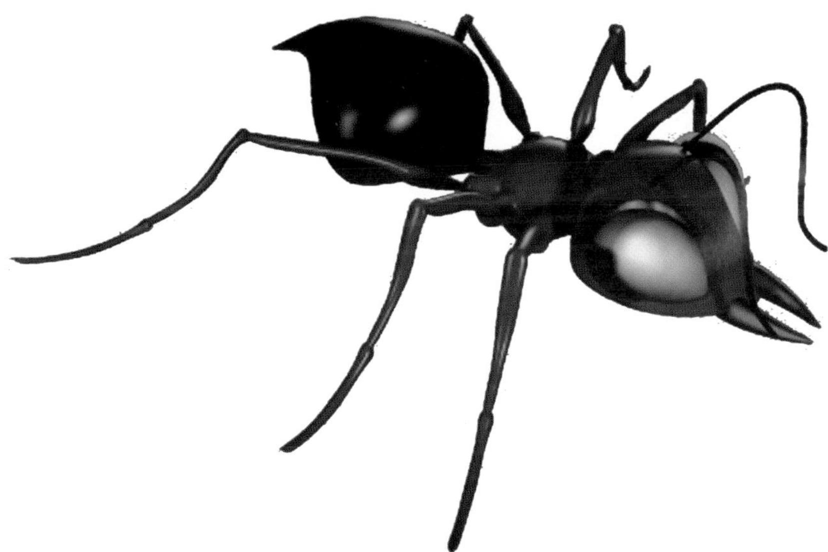

Color Plate 3. Top: The Zygote Media Group at work. Bottom: Ian W. Grey's Red Ant is included on the book's CD-ROM.

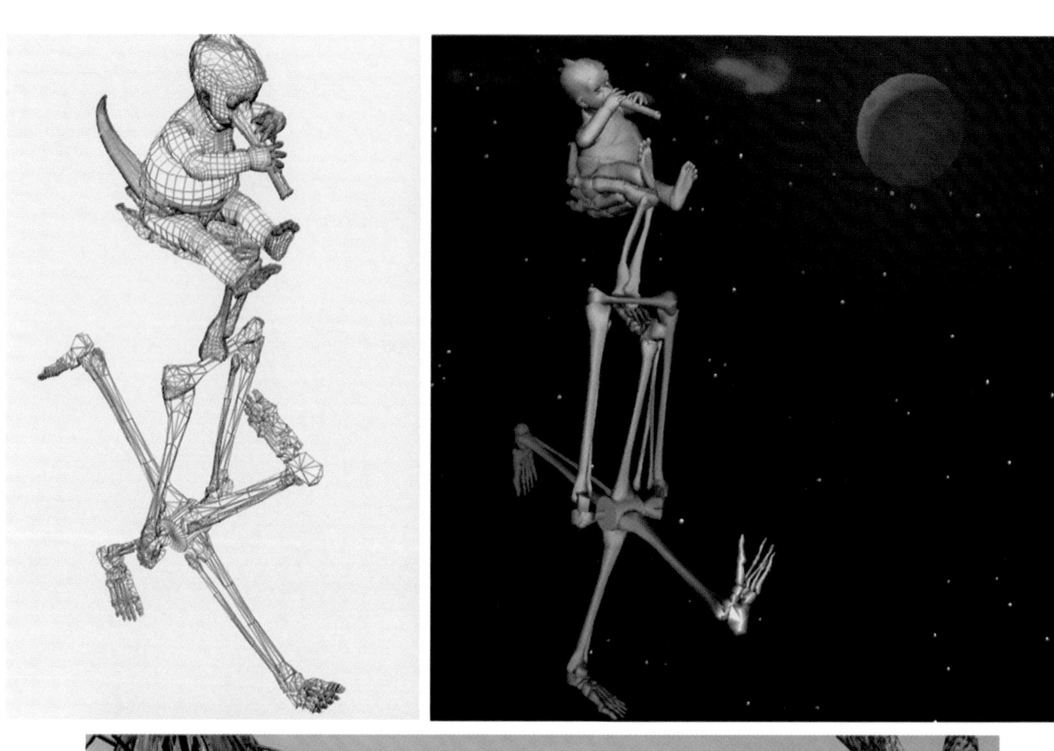

Color Plate 4. Cecilia Ziemer pushes Poser figures to the edge. Top: Bones. Bottom: Junkyard Fairies.

Color Plate 5. Top: The Carousel project from Chapter 22. Bottom: The Centaur project from Chapter 22.

Color Plate 6. Top: Two Zygote Poser Chimps in Bryceland. Bottom: The Jail Cell Poser project included on the CD-ROM, created by SB Technologies.

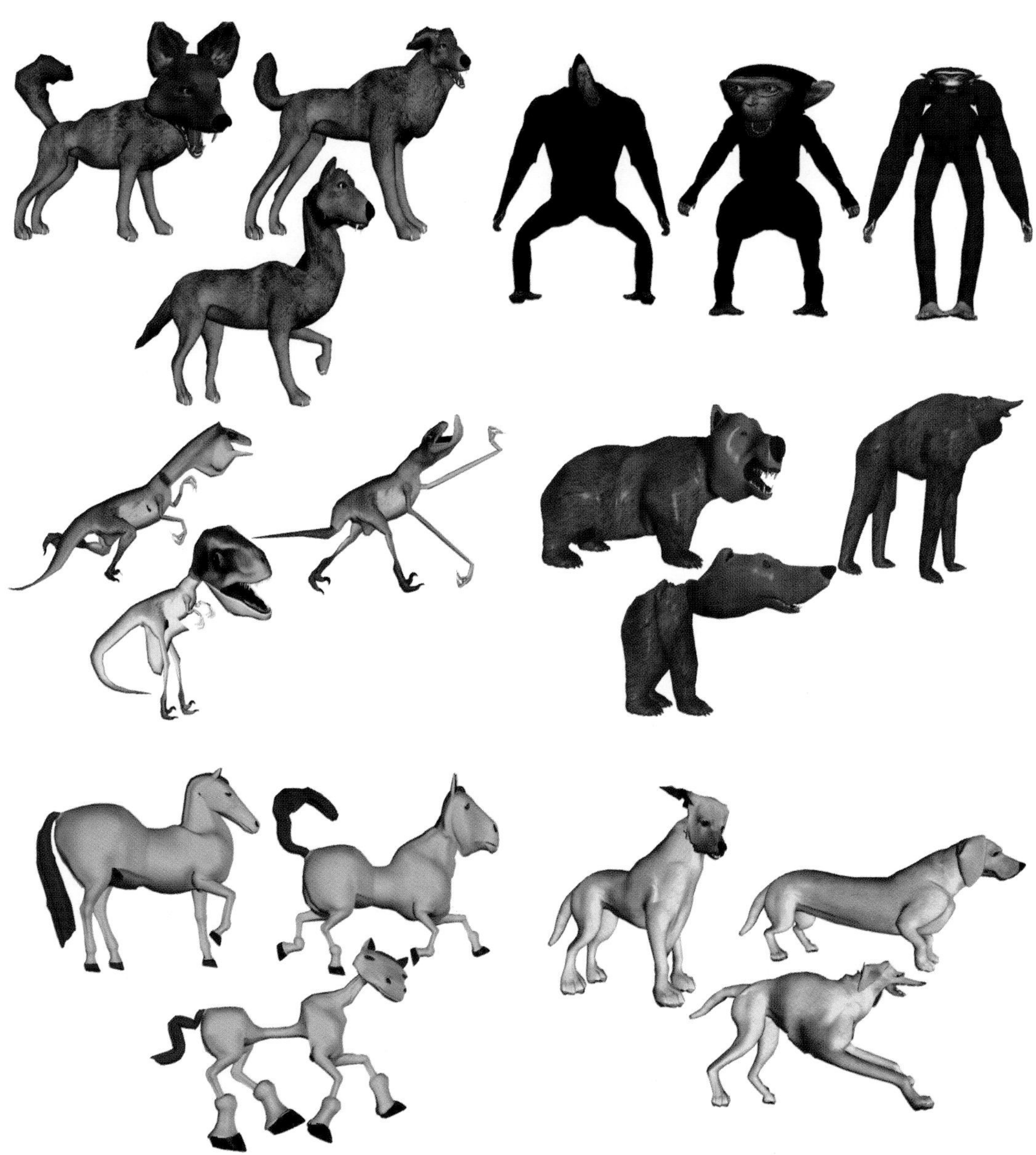

Color Plate 7. Using the Parameter Dials on Poser animals, you can create different characters. Top to bottom: Wolf, Chimp, Raptor, Bear, Horse, and Dog.

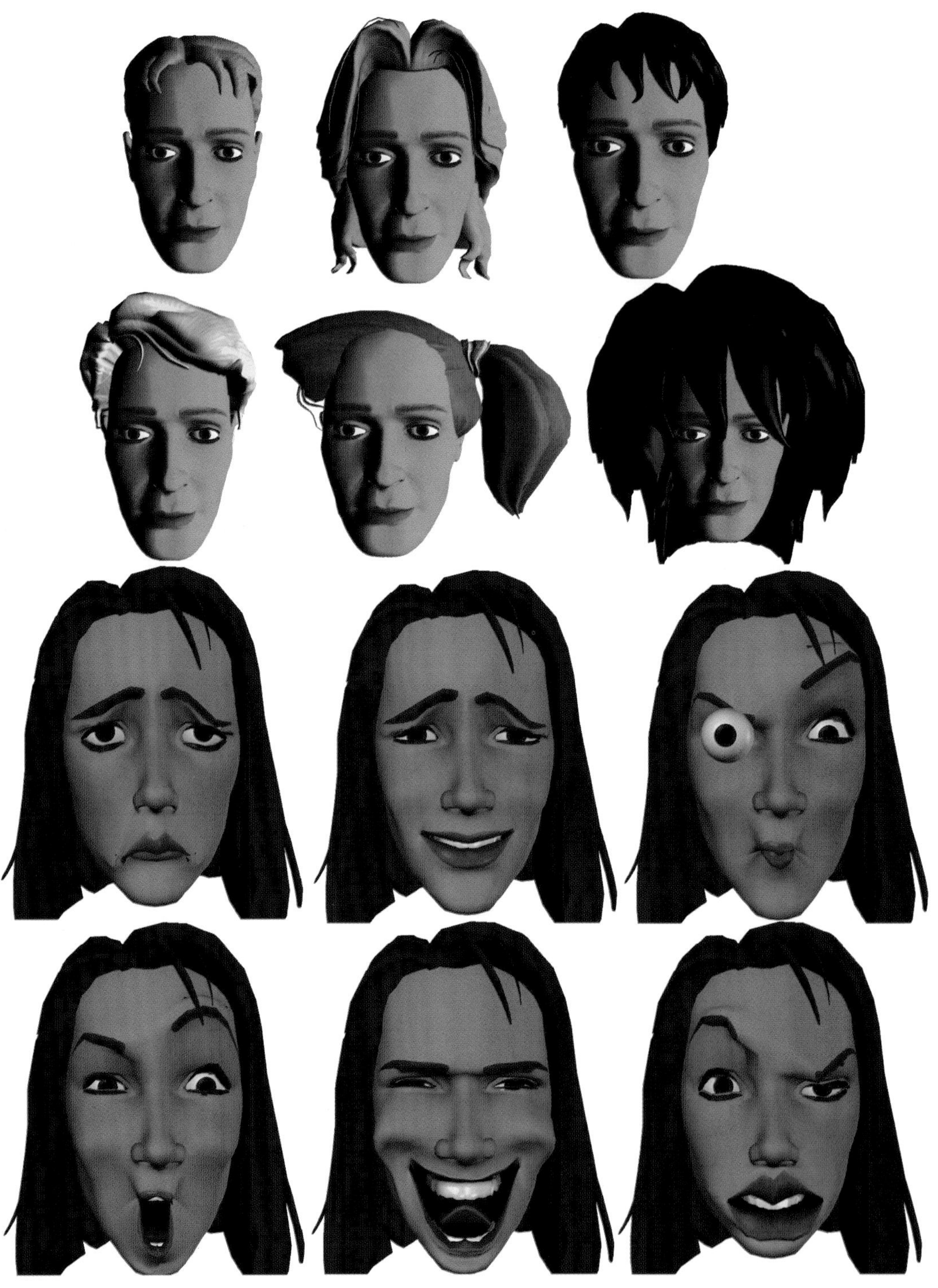

Color Plate 8. Top: Altering the hair on the same figures creates very different personality types. Bottom: The Parameter Dials allow you to dial in specific emotions and facial contortions.

CHAPTER 5

Creating Expressive Faces

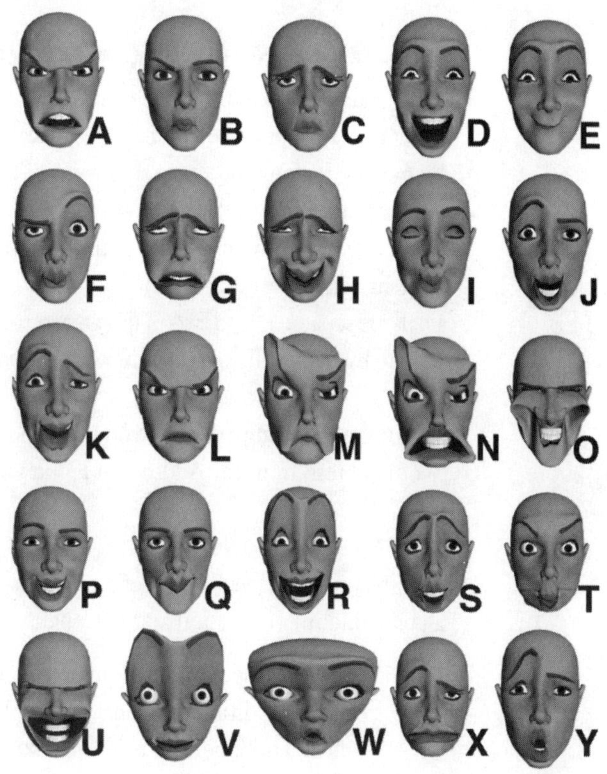

Emotive Power

If the eyes are the window to the soul, as the philosophers tell us, then the face is the house that surrounds those windows. The human face is the central subject of the majority of works of art. The face is so powerful that we look for signs of faces in the natural world as omens and symbols of life. Driftwood, rocks, trees, mountain sides, anything that emulates the features of a human face is revered and assumed to have spiritual powers. The faces on Mount Rushmore are just one example of how the structure of the face overwhelms our senses and touches upon our ancient symbol systems. It is said that the most present and powerful element in the world for children is the shape and power of eyes and mouths, first the mother's, and later others' eyes and mouths.

Two Methods for Face Modification

Poser 3 allows you to mold the expressions of a face in two ways. First, you can select either eye and scale it or rotate it. Scaling the eye is usually accompanied by moving it along the Z axis, in or out of the surrounding face. Otherwise, it will just be scaled inside the head.

The second way that Poser 3 allows you to adjust the seeming emotional content of the face is to alter the Parameter Dials associated with the Head. The Dials are separated into two major areas, Controls for the Mouth and Controls for the Eyebrows. In concert, these two capabilities allow you to cover a wide range of expressive options.

For the following exercises, you should know how to load either the Man or Woman Head from the Additional Figures library.

The Eyes Have It

Manipulating the Eyes in a Poser 3 face is a simple matter to master, and it adds a good amount of emotion and personality to a face. Do the following:

1. Load either the Man or Woman head to the Poser 3 Document window from the Additional Figures library. View the scene through the Head Camera, and Zoom in as needed so that the Head fills the Document space (see Figure 5.1).
2. Click on the Left Eye. When the Left Eye's Parameter Dials appear, use the Side-to-Side Dial to set a value of -40. Do the same for the Right Eye (see Figure 5.2).
3. Repeat the same exercise, but this time, set both Left and Right Side-to-Side Dials to 40 (see Figure 5.3).
4. To cross the eyes, set the Right Eye Side-to-Side to 40, and the Left Eye Side-to-Side to -40 (see Figure 5.4).

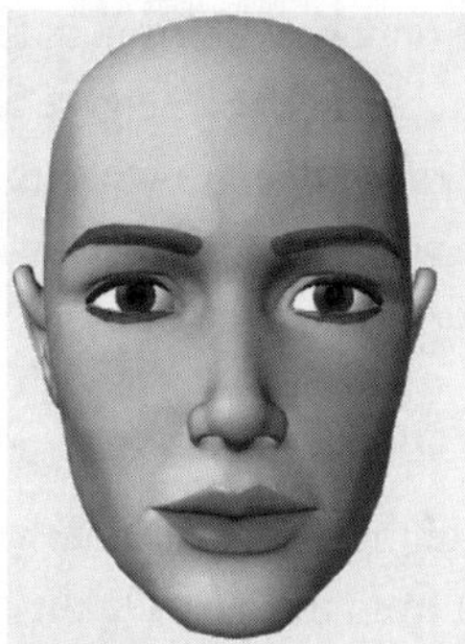

FIGURE 5.1 *The Woman Head as it appears when brought into the Document window.*

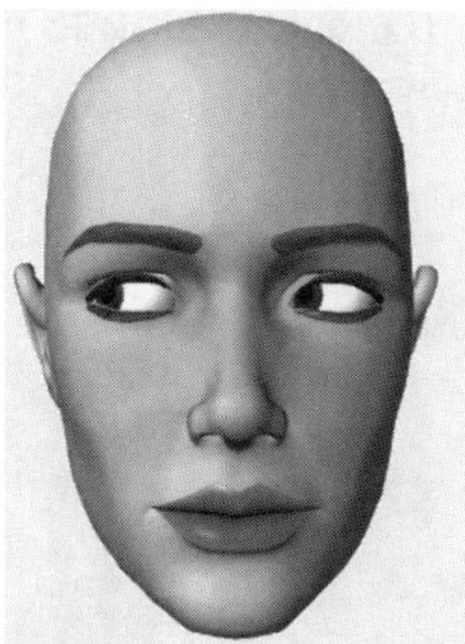

FIGURE 5.2 *The eyes look to the Left in response to Parameter Dial Side-to-Side settings.*

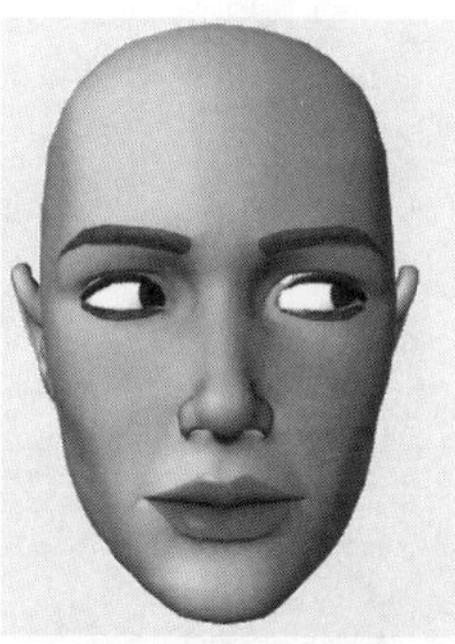

FIGURE 5.3 *Now the eyes shift their view to the opposite side of the face.*

5. Move the eyes in the opposite direction as their cross-eyed values to create extreme wall-eyed behavior (see Figure 5.5).
6. The eyes can also be rolled up or down, either together or opposite each other. Just adjust the values on the Up-Down Parameter Dials for the effect you want (see Figure 5.6).

Size Matters

When you enlarge the size of the eyes (or just one eye), you won't see any results until you move the eye out from the face. Do the following:

1. Select the Left Eye. Set the Scale at 270, and Z Translation at 0.006. Do the same with the Right Eye (see Figure 5.7).
2. If you increase the Z Translation too much, the eye will jump out of the Head. Then it can even turn back to look at the place it came from (see Figure 5.8).
3. Use the X, Y, and Z Translation Dials to place the enlarged eye in the center of the head (see Figure 5.9).

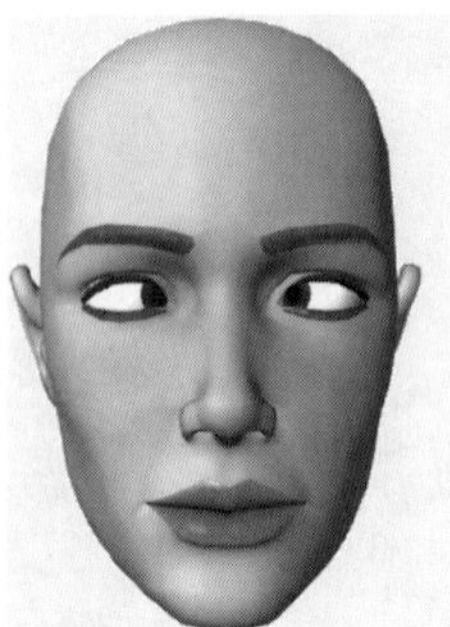

FIGURE 5.4 *The Side-to-Side Parameter can be used to create crossed eyes.*

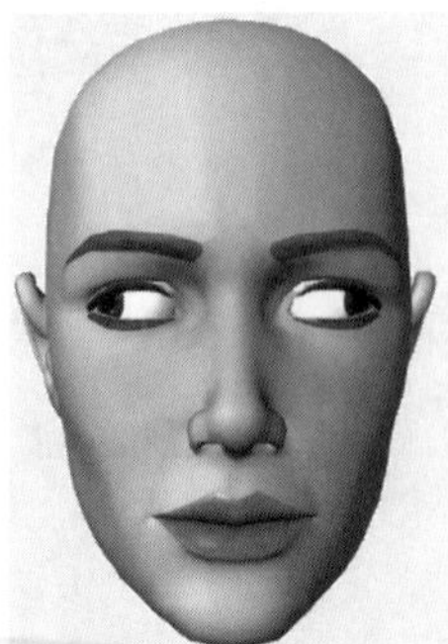

FIGURE 5.5 *The Wall-eyed look.*

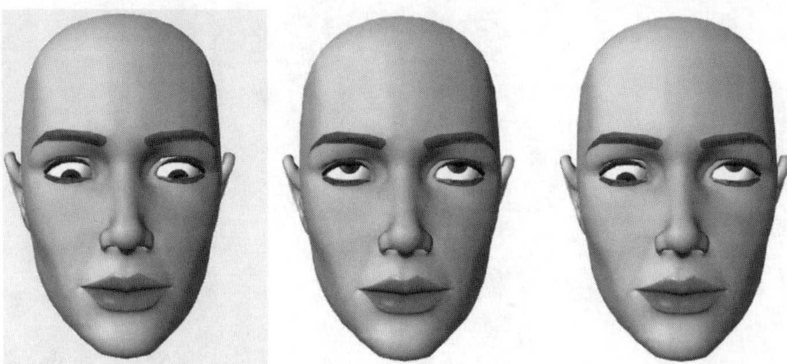

FIGURE 5.6 *The eyes adjusted to look down, up, and opposite each other.*

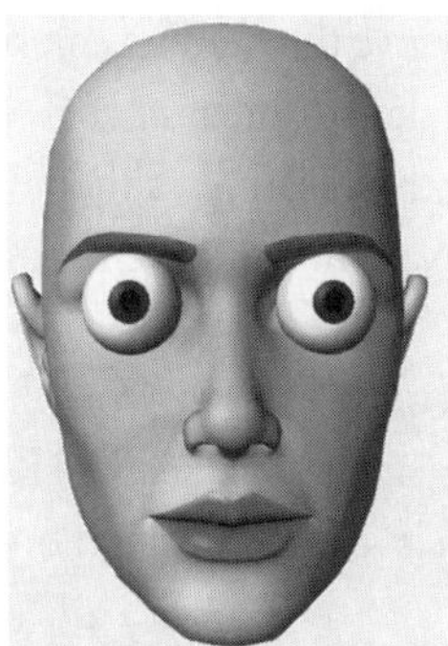

FIGURE 5.7 *The eyes bulge out from the confines of their sockets.*

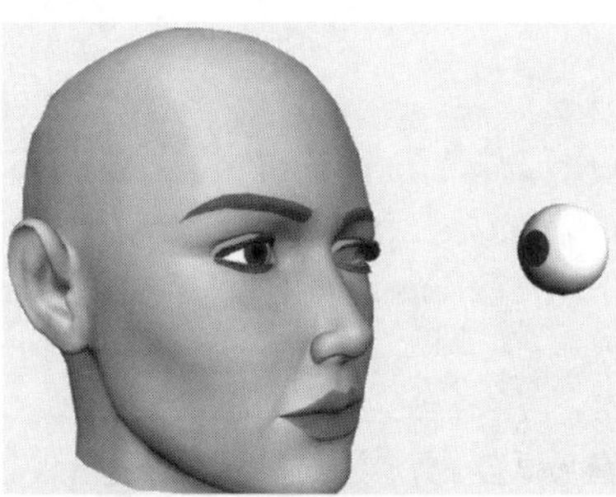

FIGURE 5.8 *Who's looking at whom?*

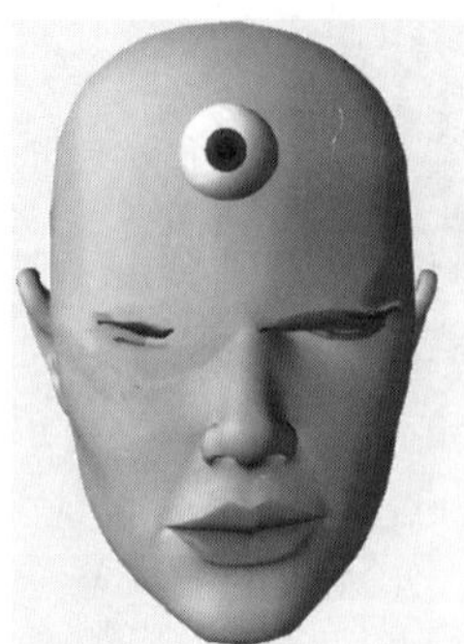

FIGURE 5.9 *The Cyclops lives!*

HEAD PARAMETERS

The Mouth and Eyebrows give the head its emotive capability in Poser 3, because both features can be altered and animated. It is suggested that you leave Limits Off when exploring these features, although you've got to watch the distortions of the face to make sure you haven't gone so far as to warp out the geometry.

Load either the Woman or Man Head (from the Additional Figures library) to your Document window, and let's explore the Parameter Dial settings for the Head. Make sure the Head is selected, and not one of the eyes.

The Eyebrow Dials

Let's look at the Eyebrow Dial settings first. There are three Eyebrow settings types for the Left and Right brow separately. They are Left/Right Brow Down, Left/Right Brow Up, and Left/Right Worry. The Dials can be turned in both negative and positive directions, and the settings can be applied to each brow separately.

Karuna! Note that all Brow settings create emotions by degree and extent, so that smaller variations can make very major differences as far as the emotions that are perceived. Explore a wide range of alternatives, other than the examples presented here.

Left/Right Brow Down Using Negative Brow Down settings tends to create a look of investigation or even a rather haughty expression. Using Positive Brow Down settings creates a look that ranges from extreme concentration to a hint of physical discomfort, or even a touch of sadness (see Figure 5.10).

Note that when both the Left and Right brow settings are equal, you may not get perfect symmetry on the face. Each brow setting stretches the skin and causes wrinkles. You may have to use unequal settings to get a more symmetrical look.

Pushing the Left and Right Brow Down settings to -10 or less creates a severe warping of the skin, and horn-like projections on the head. It also pulls open the eyelids much more, creating a strange menacing appearance. This may be useful information for the creation of certain character types. Setting the Left and Right Brow Down settings to positive values over 4 creates spiky projections that poke through the face (see Figures 5.11 to 5.13).

Karuna! If you need to export and render a model that has been radically warped, like that shown in Figure 5.13, you may have to Triangulate the polygons and/or Adjust the Normals. Otherwise, it may not render correctly. Refer to the documentation in the 3D application you plan to use.

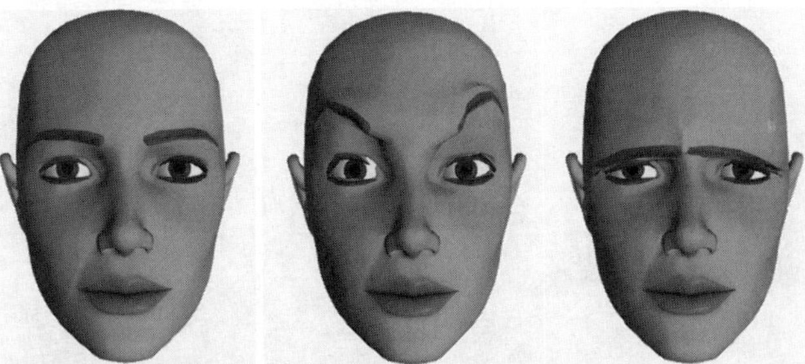

FIGURE 5.10 *Left: Default Brows at 0. Center: Left/Right Brow Down to -4. Right: Left/Right Brow Down to 3.*

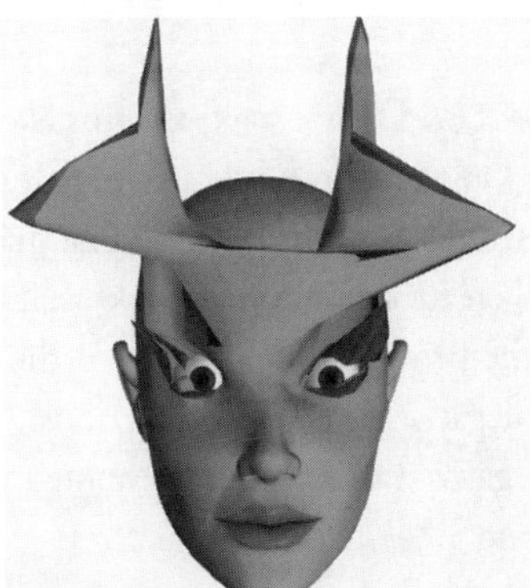

FIGURE 5.11 *Meet Princess Bizarro. Her Right Brow Down setting is -33, while the Left Brow Down setting is -27. The "horns" look symmetrical, even though the settings are different.*

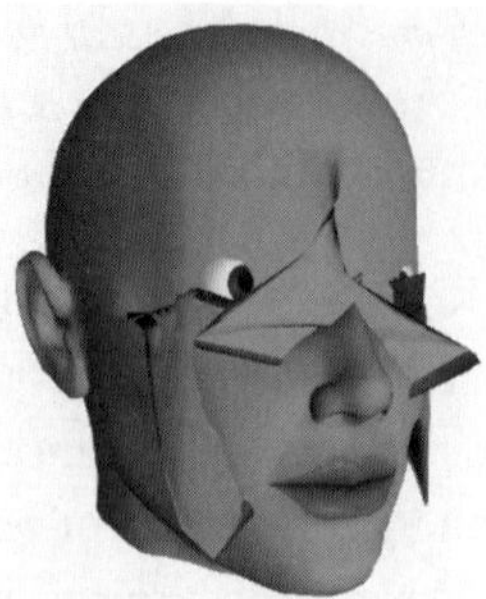

FIGURE 5.12 *No, she isn't very pretty, but could these high settings for the Left and Right Brow Down Parameters (17 and 22) suffice for some alien being in one of your scenes?*

FIGURE 5.13 *In this image, the Left Brow Down setting has been set to 1000. The result is a wall with a face at the upper Right. The mouth and other Parameters still move.*

Left/Right Brow Up Do not make the mistake of thinking that moving the Left/Right Brow Down settings is opposite that of controlling the Left/Right Brow Up settings. They are not related in that manner. In fact, applying variations of both will create unique Brow looks that cannot be achieved by either one alone. Like the Brow Down Parameters, the Brow Up Parameters can be moved in either negative or positive directions. Positive values lend a look of surprise, while negative values tend to give the model an appearance of active listening (see Figure 5.14).

A more radical warping of the skin occurs when the Brow Up Values are pushed below -2 or above 4. This can be useful in creating alien or monstrous characteristics (see Figures 5.15 and 5.16).

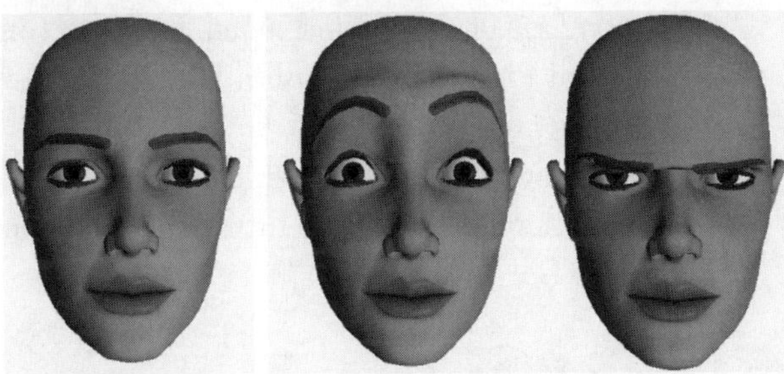

FIGURE **5.14** *The default eyebrow positions. Center: Left/Right Brow Up of 3. Right: Left/Right Brow Up of -3.*

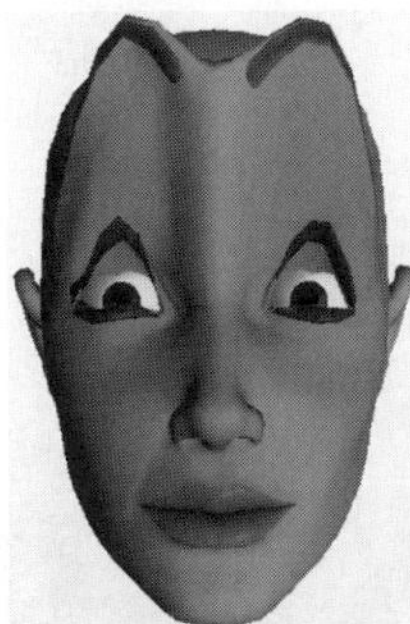

FIGURE **5.15** *A Right Brow of 10 and a Left Brow of 9 were used to generate this head. Note how the Brow Up Parameter pulls on the eyes at higher values.*

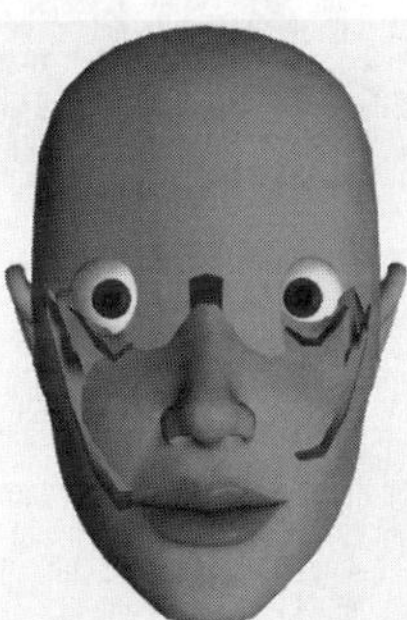

FIGURE **5.16** *Changing the Left/Right Brow Up values to -10 creates a strange result that pulls the skin away from the eyes, and weds it to the cheeks, exposing the eyeballs.*

Karuna! If you radically warp the skin on the head, think about adding a patterned texture to hide the warped anomalies (see Figure 5.17). A reptilian texture works well (see Chapter 17).

Open Lips This is the first mouth Parameter control. It can be used to define standard Parameters, or pushed farther to create stranger results (see Figure 5.18).

Opening the Lips with settings below -1.1 or above 3 pokes parts of the mouth through the face, so these settings may not be too useful for standard models (see Figure 5.19).

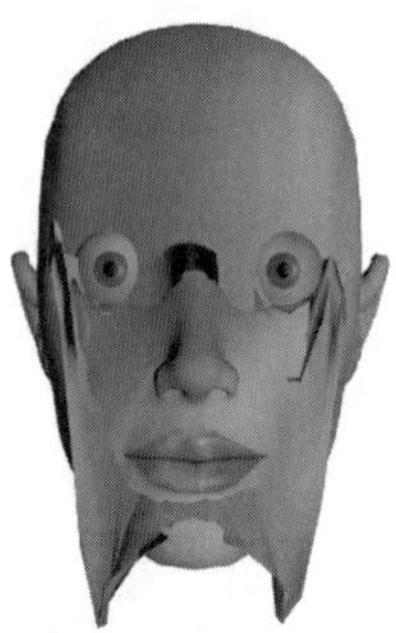

FIGURE 5.17 *Displaced areas of skin look more natural when the head is textured.*

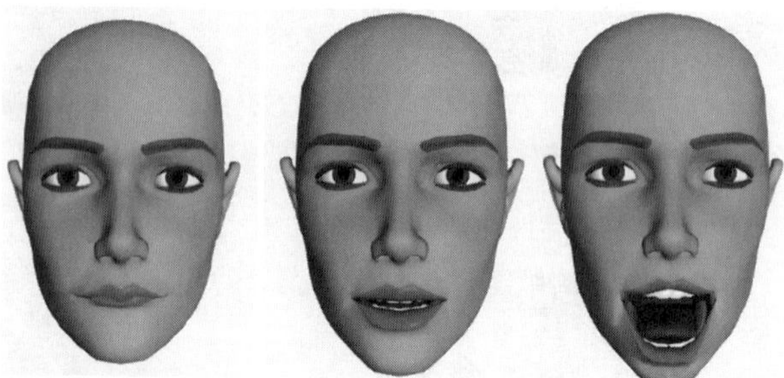

FIGURE 5.18 *A variety of Open Lips settings: -1.1 (pursed lips), .5 (slightly parted), and 3 (maximum without warping).*

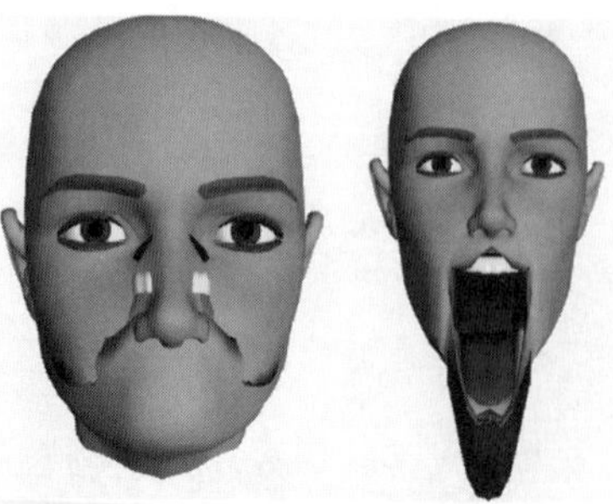

FIGURE 5.19 *Left: With an Open Lips setting of -6, the teeth poke through the face above the bottom of the nose. Right: At a setting of 11, the bottom lip pokes through the chin.*

Smile The Smile Parameter adds a smile at positive values, and a sort of droopy look at negative values. Pushing the Smile Parameter below 1.5 or above (see Figure 5.20).

Pushing the Smile value above 3.2 creates strange deformations (see Figure 5.21).

Karuna! The Smile and Frown Parameters are not opposites. Each deforms very different muscle groups on the face.

Frown The Frown Parameter Dial allows you to create everything from a kissy face (at negative values) to sadness and anger (positive values) (see Figure 5.22).

Mouth "O" Poser 3 allows you to shape the mouth as if it was pronouncing specific vowel sounds, so you can create lip-synching attributes. The Mouth-O Parameter Dial creates a number of different mouth shapes (see Figure 5.23).

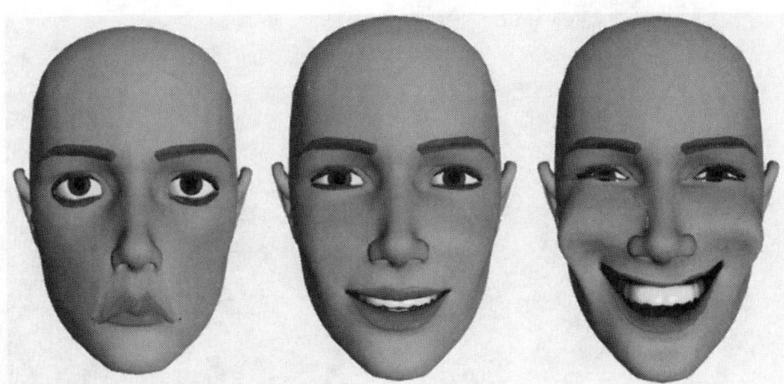

FIGURE 5.20 *Alternate Smile values create different looks. Left to Right: -1.5, 1, and 3.2.*

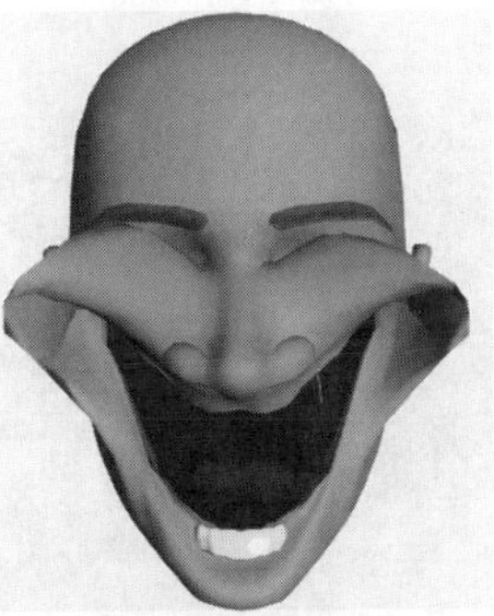

FIGURE 5.21 *The Smile setting at 8.5. The severe warping might serve for the creation of a character like the Joker.*

Mouth "F" The Mouth "F" controls mouth shapes from a thicker bottom lip to a visual representation of the "F" sound. "F" settings above 1 tend to be rather useless by themselves, since it pokes the bottom teeth through the lower lip (see Figure 5.24).

Mouth "M" The Mouth "M" settings create looks from a larger mouth to the visual pronunciation of the letter "M" (see Figure 5.25).

Tongue "T" Phonemes are shaped by a combination of tongue and mouth alterations. This is the first of two Tongue Parameters, the "T" sound. Say the letter "T," and feel what your tongue does (see Figure 5.26).

Tongue "L" This is the second of two Tongue Parameters, the "L" sound. Say the letter "L," and feel what your tongue does (see Figure 5.27).

Worry This is a special Parameter that can be applied to either the Left or Right brow. It's the only Parameter defined as a specific emotion instead of a facial feature. Settings below -2 or higher than 2.5 interfere with the placement of the eyes (see Figure 5.28).

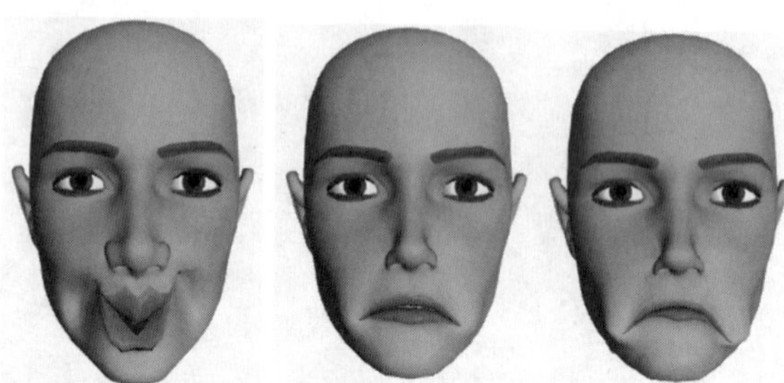

FIGURE 5.22 *From Left to Right, the Frown values are -4, 2, and 3.3 (notice the jowls that are caused).*

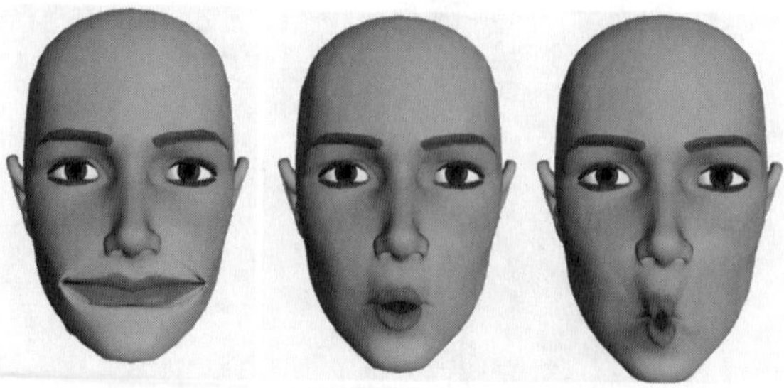

FIGURE 5.23 *From left to right, the Mouth "O" Parameter Dial settings are: -1.2 (horizontally elongated mouth), 1 ("oh"), and 1.8 ("ooh").*

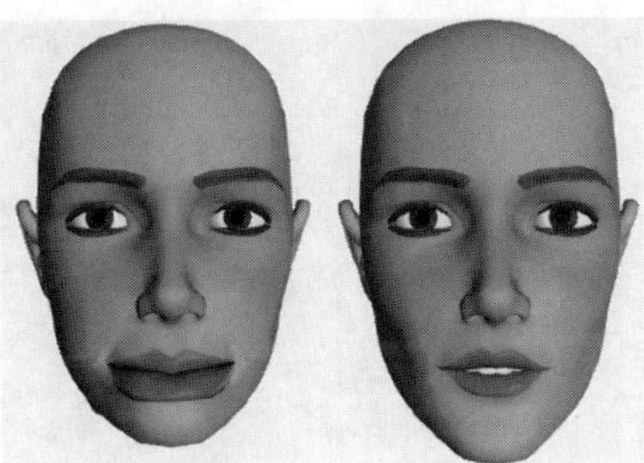

FIGURE 5.24 *From Left to Right, Mouth "F" Parameter settings: -2 (a thicker bottom lip), and 1.*

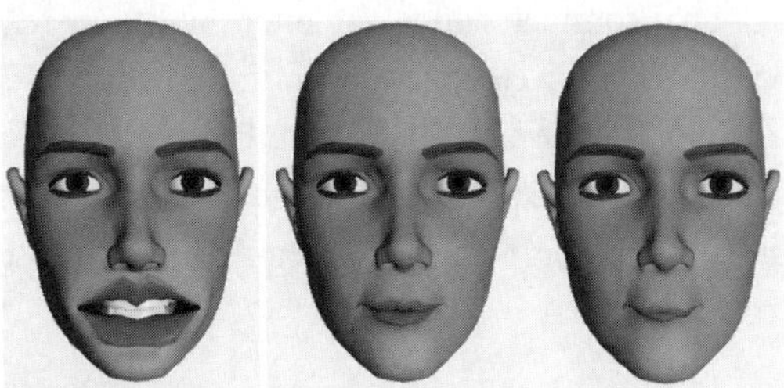

FIGURE 5.25 *Mouth "M" settings of -4, 2.2, and .3.6.*

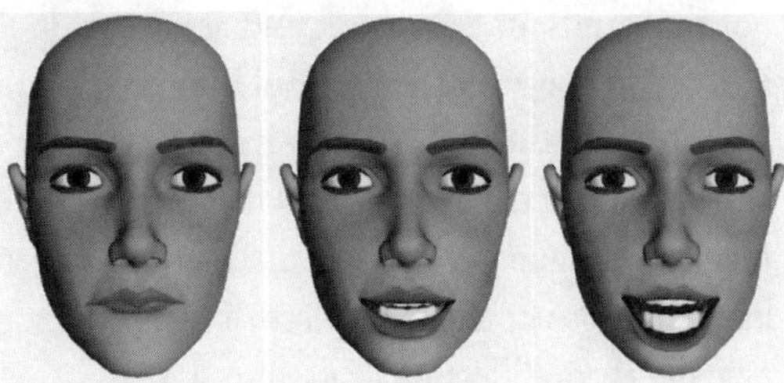

FIGURE 5.26 *From Left to Right, the Tongue "T" settings are -1.7, 1.2, and 3.*

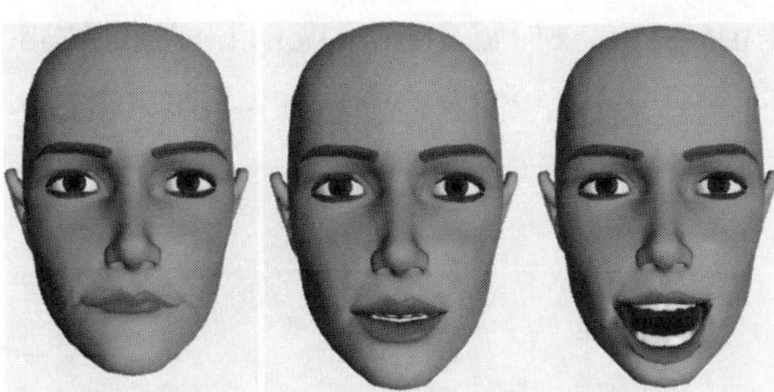

FIGURE 5.27 *From Left to Right, the Tongue "L" settings are -1.3, .4, and 2.6 (singing the sound "la").*

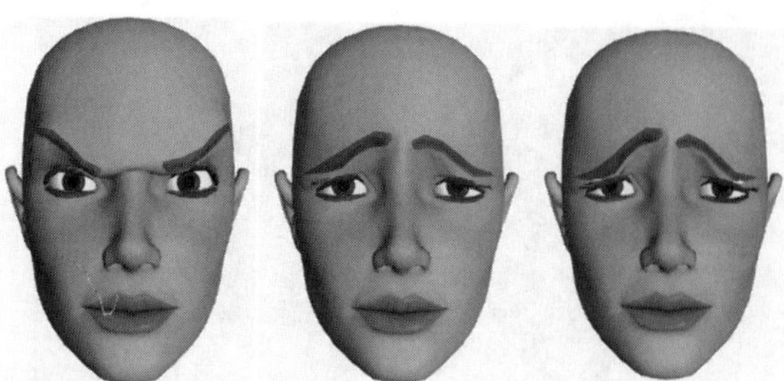

FIGURE 5.28 *From Left to Right, the Worry Parameter Dials were set to -2., 2, and 2.5.*

That completes a look at all of the Parameter Dials for the Head as single events. If you were to use any of the settings described, you could create hundreds of unique facial looks. But that is only the start of facial shaping possibilities. The real expressive fun begins when you use different Parameter settings in combination with each other. As the next section shows, your options become limitless.

PARAMETER DIAL COMBINATIONS

If this book were to detail and display all of the Head Parameter Dial combination settings you can achieve in Poser 3, it would have to have hundreds, if not thousands, of extra pages. What we can do, however, is to give you some idea of just how variable the Head Parameter settings can be when used in combination with each other, and what different combinations lead to. To do this, we've devised a table (Table 5.1) that lists the settings as keyed to the faces represented in Figure 5.29. Apply these settings as detailed to develop the intended looks, and also be sure to explore settings not represented here to develop your own library of different facial expressions.

Moving Along

If you have worked through this chapter, you have mastered the Posing and Customizing of facial expressions in Poser 3, and you're well on your way to mastery of the software. In the next chapter, we'll look at the Posing and Customizing of Poser 3 Animals

Table 5.1 These Parameter Dial combinations detail how you can create specific emotional and personality styles for Poser 3 Heads. See Figure 5.29 for the visual display of the 25 key letter descriptions in this table.

Figure Key	Description	Open Lips	Smile	Frown	Mouth	Tongue	Brow Down	Brow Up	Worry
A	Antagonistic	1.26	.58	2.84	0	0	0	0	2.75 L&R
B	"Well, I never!"	0	0	0	O=1	T=1	0	0	–1.3 Right
C	"Not a good day today . . ."	0	–1.4	0	0	0	0	–1.4 L&R	2 L&R
D	"Yippie!"	2.5	1.9	0	0	0	0	3.5 L&R	0
E	Innocence	–.3	2	0	M 3.7	0	0	3.8 L&R	0
F	Whistler 1	0	–1.5	-3	0	0	–.6 Left	1.4 Right 3 Left	0
G	Seasick (eyes rolled up)	.4	0	2.6	F –.28	L .37	0	0	1.7 L&R
H	Drunk (eyes rolled up)	.4	1.5	–2.9	F –2.8	L.37	0	0	1.7 L&R
I	"Gimmee a kiss . . ." (eyes closed by using a -.02 Z translation)	–1	–.2	–3	O .5 F .2	L.4	0	.2 L&R	0
J	"It's you!"	0	–1.1	–2.7	0	L 2.8	0	3.6 R	.9 R
K	"Heh-heh . . . guess I goofed"	0	.1	–2.7	0	–4.5 T 4.5 L	–1 L	3.6 R	.9 R 2.5 L
L	"Grrrrrr!"	0	0	2.19	0	0	0	0	2.8 L&R
M	Deformed by anger	0	.–7	3.8	0	0	–3.6 R 1.7 L	6.4 R 3.1 L	–4.9 R –3 L
N	Deformed by anger #2	0	–.7	3.8	–11 M	0	–3.6 R 1.7 L	6.4R 3.1 L	–4.9 R –3 L
O	Snapper	0	4.9	–10	0	–6.5 T	0	–1.7 L&R	0
P	"Hello there."	0	.6	–2.3	0	–1.4 T	0	1.3 R	0
Q	Unilip	1.2	–1.5	–4.6	–1.5 O 2.2 F .5 M	–10 T 2.75 L	0	0	0
R	"Holy Moley!"	1.4	0	–2.8	1 O	2.5 L	0	8 L&R	0
S	"Golly Gosh."	–1.7	–1.9	–1.6	0	3 T 1.6 L	0	2.7 L&R	2.4 L&R
T	Canary Head	–.5	–1.9	–1.6	–3.7 F 4.8 M	3 T 1.6 L	0	2.7 L&R	2.4 L&R
U	Whacko Fatmouth	0	3.1	0	–7M	0	0	–2.6 L&R	0
V	Ta'ak (taper added to head, and eyes adjusted at Y and Z Translations values of .004)	–.9	0	0	–1.6 F	1.8 T	0	11.6 R 10.2 L	0
W	Peter L. (Taper used on the Head, and eyes adjusted Z Translations values of .003)	.5	–1.2	0	.7 O 2.3 F	.6 L	0	3.5 L&R	0
X	Sad Clown	1	–1.2	0	–1.5 O –1.9 F	0	0	2.5 R –1 L	1.6 L&R
Y	Opera Singer	0	0	0	2.09 O –4.2 M	0	0	4.2 R	2.6 R .7 L

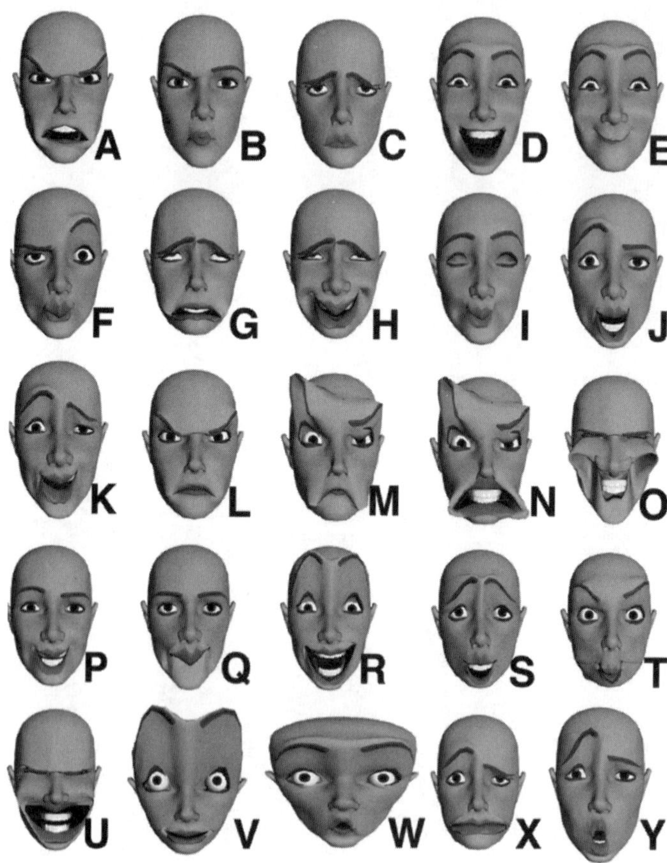

FIGURE 5.29 *These 25 keyed faces are detailed in Table 5.1.*

CHAPTER

6 Posing and Customizing Animal Models

One of the most excitedly anticipated aspects of Poser 3 is the incorporation of animal models. Poser 3 animals are fully articulated, so they can be interactively posed with ease. Five Animal Models ship with Poser 3: Cat, Dog, Dolphin, Horse, and Raptor. The Zygote Media Group was responsible for the design of these models, and they also offer a larger addendum collection of Animal Models on one of their extras CD-ROM collections. The extra Animal Models include: Chimp, Lion, Frog, Cow, Zebra, Penguin, Grizzly Bear, Buck Deer, Gray Wolf, Killer Whale, and Shark. In addition, Zygote provides a Doe model on its Sampler CD. In this chapter, we will explore the customization and posing of all of the Poser 3 Animal Models, both those that ship with the software and the extras collection marketed by Zygote.

Poser 3 Internal Animal Models

The Internal Animal Models consist of the Cat, Dog, Dolphin, Horse, and Raptor. The parameter Dials for each Poser 3 Animal may be configured differently, especially for different species. The Horse, for instance, has controls for all four feet, while the Dolphin (which has no feet) has Parameter Dials for the fins. The Internal Animal Models are found in the Additional Figures directory in the Figures Library.

POSING THE INTERNAL ANIMAL MODELS

There are two ways to think about posing the Animal Models. The first is to pose them naturally, taking advantage of the ways that the targeted animal moves in real life. The second way to work is to think of the Animal Models as cartoon figures, so that their poses become more related to humans than to the animals in question. Both are possible in Poser 3.

Real Life Posing

Remember that the body can communicate emotion as well as the face can. This is certainly true of animals like the Poser 3 Cat, Dog, Dolphin, Horse, and Raptor. Each of these animals has certain features, controlled by specific Parameter Dials, that allow them to display basic (and sometimes quite subtle) emotions. Each Animal Model is different in this regard, with some able to display a wider range of emotions and some a more bounded range.

Posed Cat Bodies The Poser 3 cat is a house pet with possibilities (see Figure 6.1).

You can body-pose the cat model into any number of evocative positions. Just a few of them are shown in Figure 6.2.

FIGURE 6.1 *The Cat model in Poser 3.*

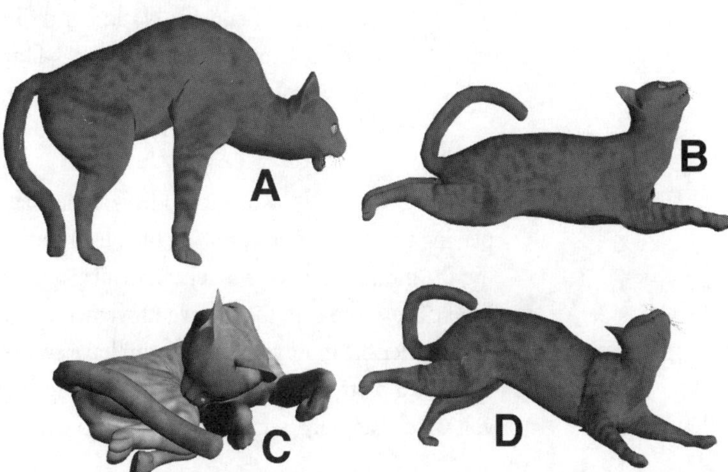

FIGURE 6.2 *A. Angry; B. Begging; C. Sleep Curl; D. Stretching.*

A. **Angry.** Mouth 1.12; Waist Bend -19; Shoulders: Twist -5, Side to Side -12, Bend -44; Tail 1 Bend -47; Forearms: Y-Scale 121, Twist -18, Side to Side 14, Bend -17; Thighs: Bend -22.

B. **Begging.** Mouth .35; Neck Bend -10; Shoulders Bend -30; Forearms Bend -67; Wrists Bend 25; Hands Bend 24; Tails bend (1 to 4) 67, 53, 61, 33; Thighs Bend 51; Legs Bend 23; Shins Bend 34; Feet Bend 2.

C. **Sleep Curl.** Eyes .6; LEar Turn .45; REar Back .28; Chest: Side to Side -48, Bend -2; Feet: Bend 11, Side to Side -9; Forearms: Twist 16, Side to Side -15, Bend -60; Hands Bend 78; Legs: Twist -2, Side to Side -6, Bend 23; Shins: Side to Side 49, Bend 14; Shoulders: Twist 11, Side to Side 14, Bend -21; Thighs: Twist 22, Side to Side -42, Bend -67; Wrists: Twist 10, Side by Side -2, Bend 144; Neck: Twist -6, Side to

Side -21, Bend 107; Tail 1: Twist 10, Side to Side 45, Bend -3, Curve .9; Tail 2: Twist 3, Side to Side 14, Bend -48, Curve 1; Tail 3: Twist 0, Side to Side 0, Bend -34, Curve 1; Tail 4: Twist -1, Side to Side -2, Bend 13, Curve 1.

D. Stretching. LEar Turn .45; REar Back .28; Abdomen Bend 18; Chest: Bend -13; Feet: Bend -40, Side to Side 5; Hips Bend -5; Forearms: Twist 18, Side to Side -14, Bend -31; Hands Bend 31; LLeg: Twist -2, Side to Side -7, Bend 16; RLeg: Twist -2, Side to Side -7, Bend 23; Shins: Side to Side 5, Bend 39; Shoulders: Twist 10, Side to Side 12, Bend -52; Thighs: Twist 0, Side to Side -8, Bend 54; Wrists: Twist -10, Side by Side 3, Bend 11; Neck: Bend -39; Tail 1: Twist 0, Side to Side 0, Bend 36, Curve .9; Tail 2: Twist 0, Side to Side 0, Bend 79, Curve 1; Tail 3: Twist 0, Side to Side 0, Bend 75, Curve 1; Tail 4: Twist -1, Side to Side -2, Bend 13, Curve 1.

Posed Cat Heads The cat model is somewhat limited when it comes to displaying emotions by customizing the Head parts. Aside from opening and closing the mouth, the Cat Model can display a limited range of emotions by Eye Open/Close (no side-to-side eye movements) and Ear movement. Ear movements offer the most variation. If you have ever observed a cat, you realize that it shows a pretty full range of emotions or feeling by the way its ears move, if you watch carefully (see Figures 6.3 to 6.5).

Posed Dog Models The Poser 3 Dog Model is capable of a wide range of looks (see Figure 6.6).

The Poser 3 Dog Model has a wider range of emotional possibilities than the Cat Model. This is mainly due to the fact that the Mouth and Ears have much more variation options. Instead of Eye controls to open and shut the Eyes, however (like the Cat has), the Dog Model has movable Eyebrows. Create the following Dog Model poses by inputting the Parameters given (see Figure 6.7).

A. Ambling Along. Chest Bend -13; Head: Side to Side and Bend -34; Mouth .68; Hip Default; LEar (1, 2, 3) Default; REar (1, 2, 3) Default; Eyebrows Default; LFoot Bend 27; LForearm Bend -57; LHand Bend -35; LLeg Bend 27; LShin Bend -50; LShoulder Bend 46; LThigh Bend -13; LWrist Bend 56; RFoot bend 58; RForearm Bend -57; RHand Bend -2; RLeg Bend 28; RShin Bend -48; RShoulder Bend -1; RThigh

FIGURE 6.3 *Cat Eye settings, left to right: Wide open at -.5, partially open at .5, and closed tight at 1.*

FIGURE 6.4 *Cat Mouth settings, left to right: Closed at 0, partially open at .7, and wide open at 2.*

FIGURE 6.5 *Cat Ear settings, left to right: Ears turned at 1.5, Left Ear Back 1 and Right Ear Side 1, Left Ear Back 1 and Right Ear Side 1 with both ears Turned .6.*

FIGURE 6.6 *One variation of the Poser 3 Dog Model.*

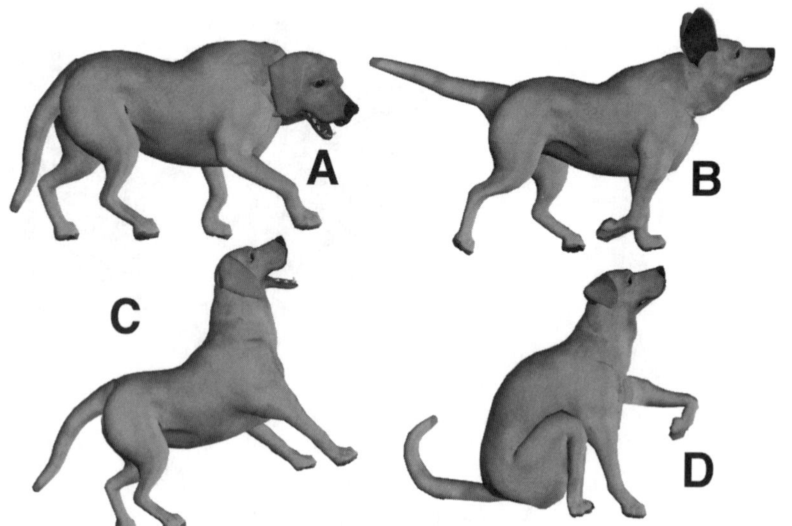

FIGURE 6.7 *A. Ambling Along. B. Sniff Air. C. Bark Jump. D. Sit Beg.*

Bend -52; RWrist Bend 56; Neck1 Bend 94; Neck2 Bend -21; Tail (1, 2, 3, 4) Bend -47, -25, -11, 19; Waist Bend 9.

B. Sniff Air. Chest Bend -13; Head: Bend -47; Mouth 0; Hip Default; LEar1 (Twist, Side to Side, Bend) 29, 15, 79; REar1 (Twist, Side to Side, Bend) 0, 8, -79; Eyebrows Default; LFoot Bend 66; LForearm Bend -24; LHand Bend -33; LLeg Bend 28; LShin Bend -48; LShoulder Bend 26; LThigh Bend -47; LWrist Bend 22; RFoot bend 28; RForearm Bend 20; RHand Bend -41; RLeg Bend 28; RShin Bend -17; RShoulder Bend 5;

RThigh Bend -6; RWrist Bend 65; Neck1 Bend 64; Neck2 Bend -14; Tail (1, 2, 3, 4) Bend -13, 7, -2, 0; Waist Bend 9.

C. **Bark Jump.** Chest Bend -13; Head: Bend 0; Mouth 1.15; Hip Default; LEar (1, 2, 3) Default; REar (1, 2, 3) Default; Eyebrows Default; LFoot Bend 43; LForearm Bend -57; LHand Bend 19; LLeg Bend -57; LShin Bend -48; LShoulder Bend 34; LThigh Bend -34; LWrist Bend 15; RFoot bend 40; RForearm Bend 15; RHand Bend -2; RLeg Bend 28; RShin Bend -48; RShoulder Bend -34; RThigh Bend -46; RWrist Bend 23; Neck1 Bend -2; Neck2 Bend 0; Tail (1, 2, 3, 4) Bend -30, -25, -11, 19; Waist Bend -13.

D. **Sit Beg.** Chest Bend 61; Head: Bend 0; Mouth 0; Hip -79; LEar1 Bend 6; REar1 5; Eyebrows Default; LFoot Bend -6; LForearm Bend -10; LHand Bend 61; LLeg Bend 87; LShin Bend 68; LShoulder Bend -91; LThigh Bend -75; LWrist Bend 115; RFoot Bend -17; RForearm Bend 14; RHand Bend 27; RLeg Bend 112; RShin Bend 37; RShoulder Bend -19; RThigh Bend -74; RWrist Bend -5; Neck1 Bend 16; Neck2 Bend -25; Tail (1, 2, 3, 4) Bend 90, 35, 42, 55; Waist Bend 11.

Posed Dog Heads The Poser 3 Dog Model has a wider range of motion and emotion related to its Head than does the Cat. The Eyebrows do more than just open or close the eyes, they also add a range of expressions. The Ears are separated into three parts, and each can be manipulated separately. The mouth can open and close as expected, and it can also Snarl both front and back. See Figures 6.8, 6.9, and 6.10, and try these and other settings on your own.

CAUTION

Karuna! You should explore variation of the settings presented in Figures 6.8 to 6.10, and keep track of new emotive possibilities you discover for the Dog Model. Save out the best poses.

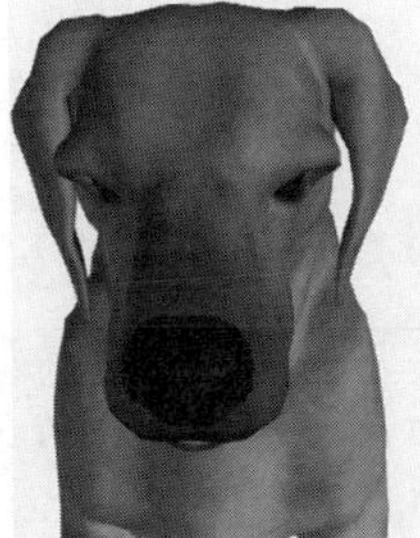
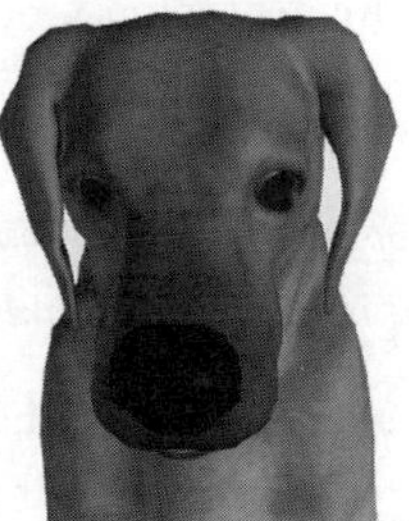
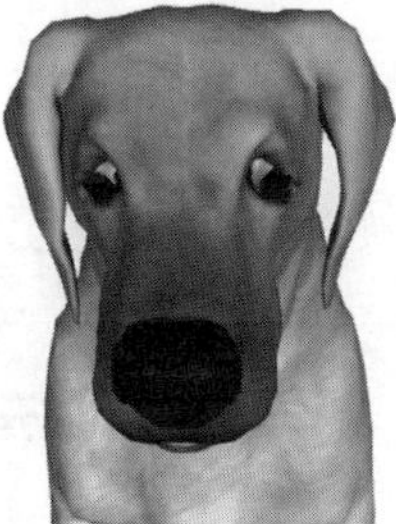

FIGURE 6.8 *A range of Eyebrow settings, left to right: -2, 0, 1.5.*

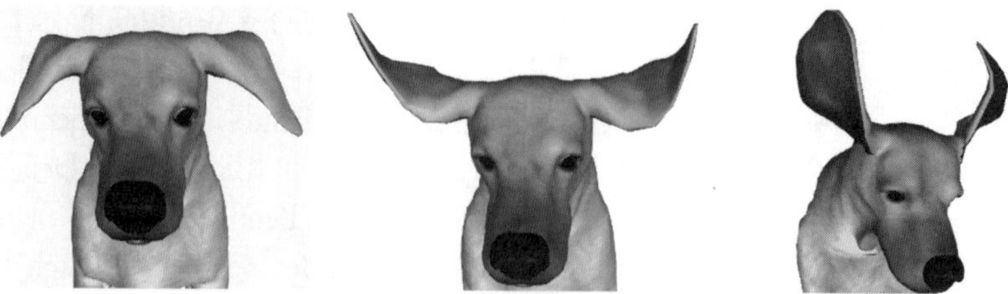

FIGURE 6.9 *Ear movements, left to right: REar and LEar #1 Bend 12 and -12. All three Ear sections Bent at the same angles; both Ear #1 sections Twist/Side-Side/Bend set to 50/15/50 and resized to 150%.*

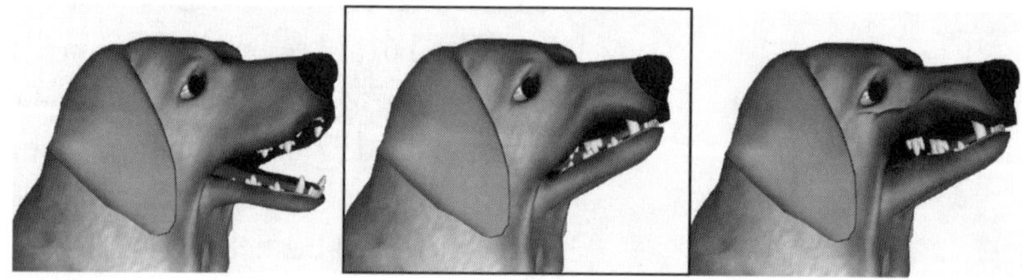

FIGURE 6.10 *Mouth options, left to right: Mouth Open .7, Front Snarl .9 with Mouth Open .05, Rear Snarl of 1.9 added.*

Posing Dolphin Models The Dolphin has always been a friend of the fisherman (see Figure 6.11).

Of all of the animals we share space with on the earth, the Dolphin remains one that evokes both mystery and admiration. It has always been a symbol of freedom, playfulness, and excitement. Dolphins actually have brains that exceed human brains in body weight ratio, and so their intelligence is also something we admire. The Poser 3 Dolphin Model can be posed according to its movable parts, which are far different than the animal models we have explored thus far. The Dolphin Model in Poser 3 communicates its personality through movements of its mouth and tongue, in addition to its body poses (see Figure 6.12).

Copy the settings to generate the poses in Figure 6.12, and then explore your own customized pose Parameters.

A. **Swim Fun.** Chest Bend 13; Head Bend 9; Mouth .5; Tongue .25; Hip Bend -38; Left Pectoral Fin: Twist -21, Bend -13; Right Pectoral Fin: Twist -15, Bend 8; Tail1 -5; Tail2 -10; Tail3 -10; Tail Fins Bend -18.

FIGURE 6.11 *The Poser 3 Dolphin has been modeled with exacting detail.*

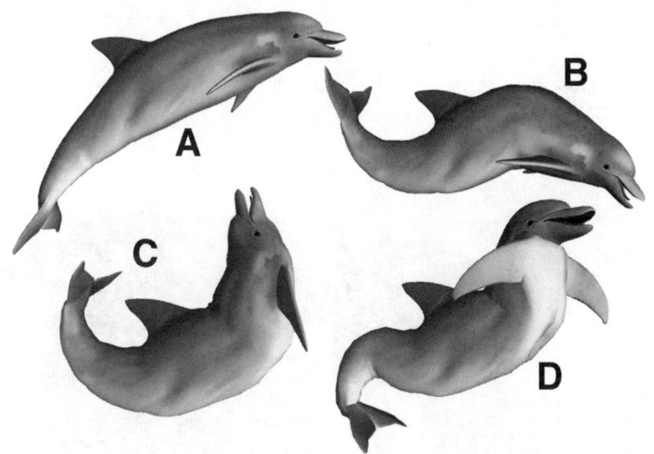

FIGURE 6.12 *A. Swim Fun. B. Tail Up. C. Loopy. D. Contortion.*

B. **Tail Up.** Chest Bend 50; Head Bend 9; Mouth .5; Tongue .25; Hip Bend -38; Left Pectoral Fin: Twist -21, Bend -13; Right Pectoral Fin: Twist -15, Bend 8; Tail1 30; Tail2 -30; Tail3 30; Tail Fins Bend 30.

C. **Loopy.** Chest Bend 13; Head Bend -40; Mouth .5; Tongue .25; Hip Bend -38; Left Pectoral Fin: Twist -21, Bend -13; Right Pectoral Fin: Twist -15, Bend 8; Tail1 40; Tail2 40; Tail3 40; Tail Fins Bend 40.

D. **Contortion.** Chest: Twist -33, Bend -56; Head Bend 68; Mouth .5; Tongue .25; Hip Bend -25; Left Pectoral Fin: Twist 31, Bend -42; Right Pectoral Fin: Twist 31, Bend -40; Tail1 40; Tail2 -57; Tail3 -41; Tail Fins Bend -60.

Posed Dolphin Heads Opening and closing the Dolphin Model's Mouth and adjusting the height of the Tongue are the adjustable Parameters for the Dolphin's Head (see Figure 6.13).

Posed Horse Models The Poser 3 Horse Model is a magnificent steed (see Figure 6.14).

The Horse Model in Poser 3 cannot be altered as far as Head attributes, because no features on the Head are customizable. Except for Twisting, moving Side to Side, or bending, the Head remains as it is (tapering and resizing is also possible, but we'll cover those alterations later). So posing the Horse Model concerns itself with body poses alone (see Figure 6.15).

Explore the settings detailed for the poses in Figure 6.15, and then create your own poses for the Horse Model. When you create poses that you like, be sure and save them to the Poses library.

FIGURE 6.13 *Dolphin Mouth and Tongue settings, left to right: Mouth at 0, Mouth 1 and Tongue .5, Mouth 1.6 and Tongue 1.5.*

FIGURE 6.14 *The Horse Model is deftly crafted and ready for placement in a pasture, race track, or a mounted battle.*

A. **Munch.** Chest Bend -5; Lower Neck Bend -82; Upper Neck Bend -14; Head Bend -48.
B. **Kneel and Drink.** Abdomen Bend 33; Chest Bend -23; Head Bend -48; Ankles Bend 9; Feet Bend -18; Forearms Bend 109; Hands Bend -23; Shins Bend -47; Shoulder Bend 28; Thigh Bend -12; Upper Arms Bend -75; Wrists Bend 17; Lower Neck Bend 51; Tail 1 Bend -45; Upper Neck Bend -28.
C. **Fast Trot.** Abdomen Bend 13; Chest Bend -5; Head Bend -44; LAnkles Bend 67; RAnkle Bend 67; LFoot Bend -20; RFoot Bend -20; LForearm Bend 19; RForearm Bend 95; LHand Bend -38; RHand Bend -38; LShin Bend -82; RShin Bend -82; LShoulder Bend 32; RShoulder Bend 32; LThigh Bend -7; RThigh Bend 43; LUpper Arm Bend -86; RUpper Arm Bend -84; LWrist Bend 13; RWrist Bend 53; Lower Neck Bend -31; Tail 1 Bend 66; Tail 2 Bend 27; Upper Neck Bend -9.
D. **REar Up.** Abdomen Bend -33; Chest Bend -5; Head Bend 6; LAnkles Bend 67; RAnkle Bend 67; LFoot Bend -20; RFoot Bend -20; LForearm Bend 95; RForearm Bend 95; LHand Bend -38; RHand Bend -38; LShin Bend -82; RShin Bend -82; LShoulder Bend 32; RShoulder Bend 32; LThigh Bend -41; RThigh Bend -41; LUpper Arm Bend -84; RUpper Arm Bend -84; LWrist Bend 53; RWrist Bend 53; Lower Neck Bend -13; Tail (1, 2, 3, 4) Bend -45, -13, 23, 33; Upper Neck Bend -32.

FIGURE 6.15 *A. Munch. B. Kneel and Drink. C. Fast Trot. D. REar Up.*

Posed Horse Head There are no controls that affect the Horse Head's features.

Posed Raptor Models The Raptor is a nasty beast, with claws that tear and teeth that feast (see Figure 6.16).

The Velociraptor was unknown to the general public until Stephen Spielberg immortalized it in the film "Jurassic Park." Now it's known the world over as an ancient dragon with a voracious appetite and the means to get what it wants. The Poser 3 Velociraptor is extremely posable, with both body and head parts that can be moved to communicate all of the sinister messages you can think of (see Figure 6.17).

Explore the settings detailed for the Raptor poses in Figure 6.17, and then create your own poses for this exquisite Model. When you create poses that you like, be sure and save them to the Poses library.

A. **Haunch Sit.** (Claws and Fingers not altered for this example). Abdomen Default; Chest Bend 24; Head Bend -30; Mouth 1.2; Hip Default; LFoot Bend 9; LForearm Bend -121; LHand Bend 59; LShin Bend 124; LShoulder Bend 28; LThigh Bend -93; LToes (1 and 2) Default; RFoot Bend 9; RForearm Bend -121; RHand Bend 59; RShin Bend 124; RShoulder Bend 28; RThigh Bend -93; RToes (1 and 2) Default; Neck 1 Bend -53; Neck 2 Default; Tail (1, 2, 3, 4) Bend 27, 27, 60, 60.
B. **Sniff.** (Claws and Fingers not altered for this example). Abdomen Default; Chest Bend -67; Head Bend -30; Mouth 0; Hip Default; LFoot Bend 9; LForearm Bend -121; LHand Bend 59; LShin Bend 124; LShoulder Bend 28; LThigh Bend -93; LToes (1 and 2) Default; RFoot

FIGURE 6.16 *Dinosaur lovers will spend a lot of time posing the Raptor Model.*

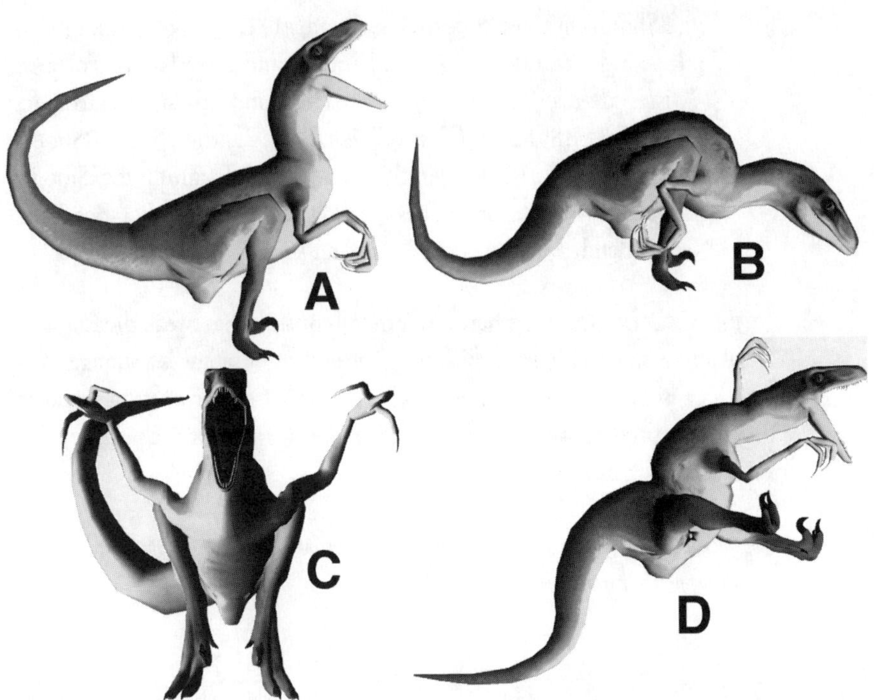

FIGURE 6.17 *A. Haunch Sit. B. Sniff. C. Prepare Pounce. D. Rear Up.*

Bend 9; RForearm Bend -121; RHand Bend 59; RShin Bend 124; RShoulder Bend 28; RThigh Bend -93; RToes (1 and 2) Default; Neck 1 Bend -53; Neck 2 Default; Tail (1, 2, 3, 4) Bend -39, 27, 60, 60.

C. **Prepare Pounce.** Abdomen Default; Chest Bend 24; Head Bend -63; Mouth 1.35; Hip Default; LFoot Bend 9; LForearm Bend -121; LHand: Bend 59, Side to Side 26; LShin Bend 124; LShoulder Side to Side 41; LThigh Bend -93; LToes (1 and 2) Default; RFoot Bend 9; RForearm (Twist, Side to Side, Bend) -80, 40, 30; RHand: Bend -59, Side to Side -26; RShin Bend 124; RShoulder Side to Side -41; RThigh Bend -93; RToes (1 and 2) Default; Neck 1 Bend -88; Neck 2 63; Tail (1, 2): Bend 27, 27 and Side to Side of 60, 60.

   Use the Right Hand Camera to open claws and fingers on the Right Hand, and then use Symmetry Right To Left to pose the left Hand.

D. **Rear Up.** (Claws and Fingers not altered for this example). Abdomen Bend -68; Chest Bend -47; Head Bend -68; Mouth 1.4; Hip Bend -18; Feet 0; LForearm (Twist, Side to Side, Bend) 45, 7, -81; LHand (Twist, Side to Side, Bend) -6, -2, 18; LShin (Twist, Side to Side, Bend) 0, -5,

20; LShoulder (Twist, Side to Side, Bend) -141, -42, 6; LThigh (Twist, Side to Side, Bend) 11, 29, -71; LToes (1 and 2) Default; RForearm (Twist, Side to Side, Bend) 45, -7, 81; RHand (Twist, Side to Side, Bend) -6, 2, -18; RShin (Twist, Side to Side, Bend) 0, 5, 20; RShoulder (Twist, Side to Side, Bend) -78, 14, 47; RThigh (Twist, Side to Side, Bend) 0, -50, -83; RToes (1 and 2) Default; Neck 1 Bend 35; Neck 2 Bend -37 ; Tail (1, 2, 3, 4) Bend 42, 20, 48, 32.

Posed Raptor Heads There aren't many controls that tweak the Raptor's facial options, in fact there are just two: Jaw and Mouth. Jaw is a strange control. It causes the jaw to elongate and jut upward at negative settings, and at positive settings as well. Mouth controls the opening and closing of the mouth (see Figure 6.18).

Leave the Raptor Jaw setting at .5 to 1, because a little overbite displays the gnashing teeth much more clearly.

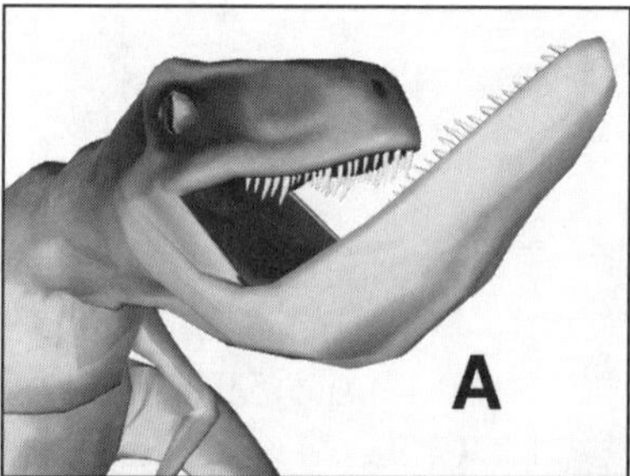

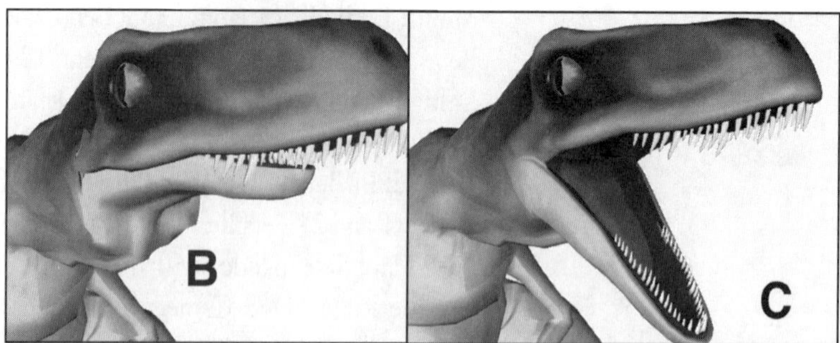

FIGURE 6.18 *With the Jaw setting at -7, even though the Mouth setting is 0, the Jaw rotates upward and out. B. A Jaw value of 4 is just as strange, making the lower Jaw shorter, giving the Raptor a serious overbite. C. .75 is about the best large open mouth setting. Negative Mouth settings do nothing.*

Posed Raptor Hands and Feet The Raptor is one of the few animal models that has posable hands. There are three Claws and three Fingers on each hand that can be posed. Unfortunately, there is no control that allows you to Grasp, with all appendages working at the same time, so you have to pose each Finger and Claw separately (see Figure 6.19).

You should spend some time trying to create different poses for the Raptor's Hands, saving the ones that might be useful in later projects to the Poses library. You'll find that the Bend Parameter is the most useful control in posing the Fingers and Claws.

Although the Raptor has three toes on each Foot, the Parameter only lists two controls: Toes 1 and Toe 2. Toe one controls the two main toes, while Toe 2 controls the terrible tearing claw on the Foot (see Figure 6.20).

Poser 3 External Animal Models

The Zygote Media Group, the same developers responsible for the design of all of the models in Poser 3, offers an addendum CD bursting at the seams with alternate Poser 3 content. One of those libraries contains a wealth of new Animal Models, a collection that greatly extends the professional capacity and the sheer enjoyment of working in Poser 3. That being the case, we would be

FIGURE 6.19 *Three different poses of a Raptor Hand, with Fingers and Claws set to different values.*

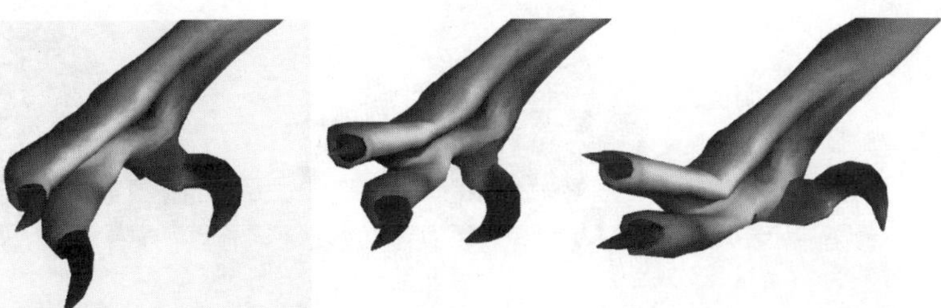

FIGURE 6.20 *here are three views of the Right Foot with its three clawed toes, set to different Bend values.*

remiss not to dwell on the Zygote extra Animals in this chapter. I can't imagine any dedicated Poser 3 users not wanting to add the Zygote Animals and other items to their Poser 3 creative reservoirs.

The Zygote CD is called "Stuff for Poser 3." It contains Human and Animal Models, Motion Files, and Props and Accessories. The CD comes with the Sampler already open, allowing you to unlock the other libraries as you pay to do so and receive a key code in return. For information on pricing and availability, contact Zygote at http://www.zygote.com. You can also contact Zygote at 801-375-0553, or 888-3DMODEL.

THE ZYGOTE ANIMALS

The Zygote Animals Models include the Bass, Bear, Buck, Chimpanzee, Cow, Doe, Frog, Killer Whale, Lion, Penguin, Shark, Wolf, and Zebra. This greatly expands the possibilities for Animal scenes and animations in Poser 3. It also adds a number of additional customized Animal options, as we shall detail later in this chapter.

Karuna! If you have the Zygote Animal Models, use the detailed posing information that follows as a guide for posing. After that, explore your own customized settings, saving poses that look good to your Poses library.

Posing the Zygote Bass

The Zygote Bass Model consists of five Fins, three Body parts, and the Head. The only Head features that can be manipulated are Mouth Open and Mouth Closed. Mouth Closed works like the Jaw parameter on the Raptor, elongating or shortening the lower jaw. To explore the poses for the Zygote Bass, adjust the Parameter Dials for each of these items (see Figure 6.21).

FIGURE 6.21 *A. Mouth Open 1.0 (other elements at default). B. Body 3 Bend -38, Body 4 Bend -23, Tail Fin Bend -23, Head: Twist 40, Side to Side -34, Bend 56.; Mouth Open 3.5, Mouth Closed 4.7.*

Posing the Zygote Bear

The Bear Model can be both Body and Head posed. The Head includes Parameter Dials for controlling the Snarl as well as the openness of the mouth. You might be better off applying just a color instead of a texture map when posing the Bear with stretched out limbs, since this can cause strange anomalies in the texture map (see Figure 6.22).

Karuna! Use the following settings to pose the Zygote Bear Model and save the poses to the Poses library, in a new folder called Animals. Then customize the settings in order to create new poses of your own.

A. **Bear Stand.** Neck Bend 88; Head Side to Side -25; Snarl 2; Mouth 0; L&R Thigh Bend 65; R&L Shoulder: Side to Side and Bend are -37, 60 and 37, 60; L&R Forelegs Bend -62; LFrontFoot Bend 0; RFrontFoot Bend 125 ; Abdomen Bend 15. All other parts at defaults.
B. **Bear Sleep.** L&R Shoulder Bend -77; L&R FrontFoot Bend 83; Head Side to Side -12; Mouth Open -3; L&R Thigh -70; L&R Shin 122; L&R BackFoot Bend 52. All other parts at defaults.

Posed Bear Heads

The Bear's Head can be posed to communicate a small range of emotions by using the Parameter Dials to Open and Close the Mouth, and to set the value of the Snarl (see Figure 6.23).

Note that the larger the Snarl Value, the more closed the eyes of the Bear. Negative value Snarls opens the eyes and also drops the jowls.

FIGURE 6.22 *A. Bear Stand. B. Bear Sleep.*

FIGURE 6.23 *From left to right: Snarl 2 and Mouth Closed .75; Snarl -2 and Mouth Open 1; Snarl -3, Mouth Open 2, and Mouth Closed -1.*

Posing the Zygote Buck

The Zygote Buck model has legs and body sections that can be modified. As far as the facial features, only the ears and eyes can be altered. The Buck is perfect for adding interest to a Poser 3 woodland scene (see Figure 6.24).

TIP

When you are bending the front of an animal, such as making it bend to drink or eat, leave Inverse Kinematics on for the front feet. This way, when you bend the front part of the body, the front legs will respond naturally. You can turn IK off later for more freedom in posing other parts of the body.

Posing the Zygote Chimpanzee

The Zygote Chimp is a model that many Poser 3 users will overuse, because it is crafted so realistically. The Chimp is also perfect for Walk Designer sessions, since its body shape so closely resembles the human shape and appendages (see Chapter 14 on the Walk Designer). The Chimp has fully articulated hands and feet that can splay apart and grasp items. The Head can be posed by altering the Mouth Open and Closed settings, as well as by adjusting the eyes (see Figure 6.25).

A. **Threatening.** Leave IK on, and move body down from waist. The knees will bend automatically. Right and Left Shoulder, Bend -60 and 44. Right and Left Forearm, Bend -53 and 40. Mouth Open 4.2.
B. **Knuckle Walk.** Abdomen Bend 90. Head Bend -75. Right and Left Shoulder Front To Back 50 and -88. Right and Left Forearm Side to Side, -24 and -30. Left and Right Thigh and Shin Bend -15 and 70. Right and Left Foot Bend -44 and -12.
C. **Sitting.** Abdomen Bend 90. Right Thigh/Shin/Foot Bend -40, 70, -25. Left Thigh/Shin/Foot Bend -46, 77, -12. Right Shoulder: Twist -27,

FIGURE 6.24 *From left to right: Close-up of the Buck's Head with a Bend of -50 and ears altered by Side to Side of 30; Head Side to Side -50 and Bend -3, Ears Side to Side 30 and Bend 75; Front Legs bent naturally by leaving IK on, neck Low/Mid/Upper Bend 75, 20, 35. Head Bend 35.*

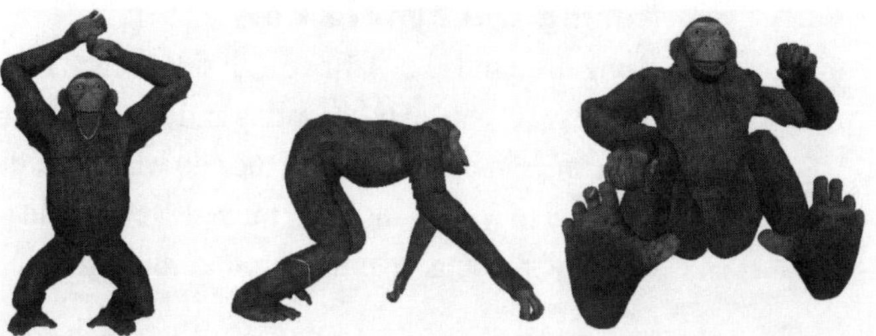

FIGURE 6.25 *From left to right: Threatening, Knuckle Walk, and Sitting.*

Front to Back 50, Bend 46. Right Forearm: Twist -47, Side to Side 54, Bend 30. Right Hand: Twist -117, Bend 47. Left Shoulder: Twist -72, Front to Back -64, Bend -122. Left Forearm: Twist 31, Side to Side -43, Bend -91. Left Hand: Twist -6, Side to Side 30, Bend 3.

Posing Chimp Hands

The Chimp's hands are super-posable, with all of the finger and thumb joints included. But the most startling feature concerning posing the Chimp's hands are that they respond suitably well to being automatically posed by assigning them Hands from the Hand Poses library. Because the Chimp has some finger and thumb dimensions that are different from human hand proportions, you may have to tweak the results after assigning a posed Hand. But that beats having to pose the Chimp's Hands one digit at a time (see Figure 6.26).

Posing Chimp Heads

You don't have a lot to work with when you want to manipulate the Chimp's facial expressions. All that's possible is to open or close the Mouth and to move the

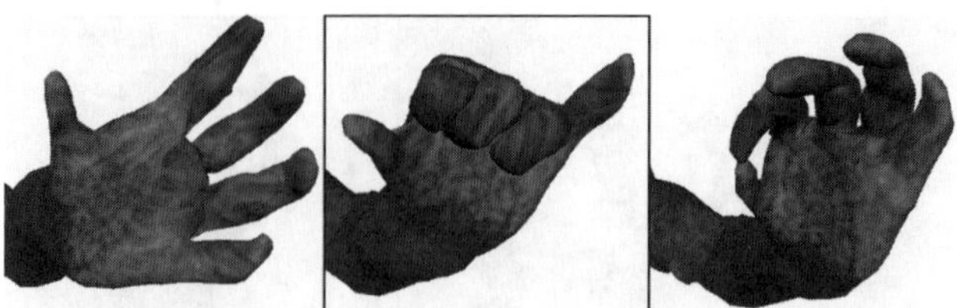

FIGURE 6.26 *From left to right: Splayed Fingers using the Side to Side controls, "Call Me" from the Hand Poses library, and "OK" from the Hand Poses library.*

Eyes. Surprisingly, these limited alterations can still create a number of expressions. Try the settings in Figure 6.27, and then explore your own alternatives.

Posing the Zygote Cow

Being surrounded by farms on all sides where I live, I can attest to the fact that cows have two main poses: eating and standing around. The only other pose that sometimes intervenes is what they do when rain threatens, which is to lie down wherever they are. This being the case, you should work to master the three main cow poses: Eating, Standing Around, and Lying Down (see Figure 6.28).

NOTE

Unique among the Poser 3 Animal Models, the Zygote Cow has seven Tail sections. This allows for some fancy tail posing.

CAUTION

Karuna! You can usually get away with stretching an Animal's neck on the Z axis up to 130%, if its Head has to be closer to the ground while foraging.

Posing the Zygote Doe

Refer to Figure 6.24, the Zygote Buck, and the settings detailed in the caption, to pose the Zygote Doe. Most of the same settings are used here (see Figure 6.29).

FIGURE 6.27 *Left to right: Closed Mouth and Eyes rolled upward 23 degrees as if musing; Eyes Side To Side -40, and Mouth Closed -2.7 creates a look of semi-surprise; left and Right Eyes Side to Side -40 and 40, Mouth Open 2.2, and Mouth Closed 2.4. The result is this rather silly look.*

Posing the Zygote Frog

The Frog is the only amphibian in the Zygote Animal Models collection. It's a big fat bullfrog, so make sure to place it on a lilypad, or maybe along the edge of a murky swamp (see Figure 6.30).

FIGURE **6.28** *The three main cow poses: Eating, Standing Around (with the Tail in a strange loop), and Lying Down. Using these images as examples, pose your Zygote Cow Model accordingly.*

FIGURE **6.29** *From left to right: Close-up of the Doe's Head with a Bend of -50, and ears altered by Side to Side of 30; Head Side to Side -50 and Bend -3, Ears Side to Side 30 and Bend 75; Front Legs bent naturally by leaving IK on, Neck Low/Mid/Upper Bend 75, 20, 35. Head Bend -60.*

FIGURE **6.30** *The Zygote Frog, posed as detailed left to right: Head Bend -35, Mouth Open 3.6, Mouth Closed 3.9, Eyes resized to 150%; Head Bend -35, Mouth Open 7, Mouth Closed 19, Eyes resized to 250%; Head Bend -35, Mouth Open 0, Mouth Closed 5, Eyes resized to 75%.*

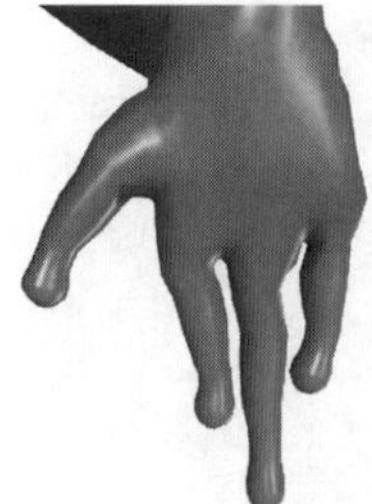
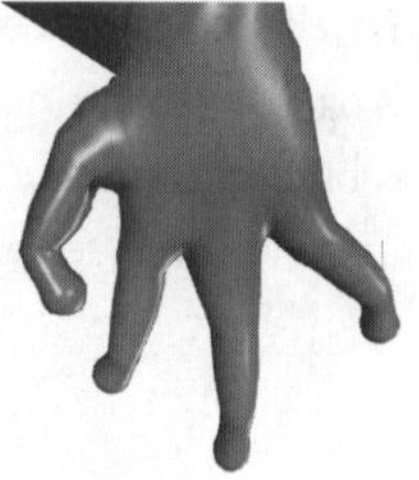
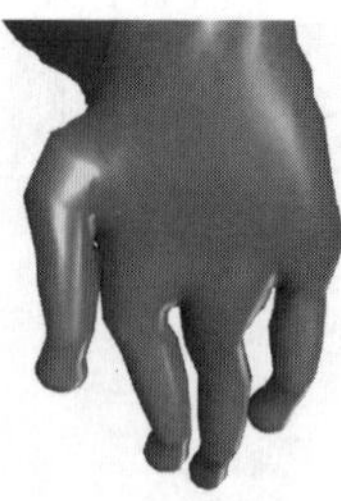

FIGURE 6.31 *Using the Side to Side and Bend Parameter Dials, the Frog's Fingers and Toes can be individually posed.*

Input these settings for the Zygote Frog Model to get these poses. Then alter them to explore other useful poses.

Be sure to explore posing the Frog's Hands and Feet, since fingers and toes can be manipulated (see Figure 6.31).

- Use the Side to Side Parameter Dials when you need to splay the Fingers or Toes.
- Use the Bend Parameter Dials to open and close the Fingers or Toes.

Posing the Zygote Killer Whale

To pose the Killer Whale, you need only alter any of the four body sections, the Head, and three Fins. The Head has posable Mouth Open/Mouth Closed settings. Always use the Killer Whale's texture map, unless you want it to look like another creature altogether (see Figure 6.32).

FIGURE 6.32 *From left to right: Mouth Open 1.2, Mouth Closed -9.5, and a Body 3 Bend of -21; Body 1 and Head Bend of 40, Mouth Open 2, and Mouth Closed 6; Body 1 Side to Side -24, Body 2 Default, Body 3 Side to Side -47, Body 4 default, Head Bend 30 and Side to Side -50, Mouth Open 4, Mouth Closed 6, Tail Fin Bend -45.*

NOTE

Consider using the Killer Whale in a composite scene with the Dolphin, or even with the Shark.

Posing the Zygote Lion

The Lion is indeed King of the Beasts, and the Zygote Lion is as regal as they come. The Head has open and closed Mouth Parameters and a Snarl. The Tail has four sections, and a separate Parameter for the Tuft at the end. Use the settings detailed to pose the illustrated figures, and then explore your own Lion poses (see Figure 6.33).

A. **Roaring.** Head Bend -63. Mouth Open 3.
B. **Sitting.** Head Side to Side -38 and Bend 34. Mouth Open 3. L&R Thigh/Shin/Ankle/BackFoot -5, -52, 160, 0 and L&R Shoulder 18. (front and back appendages are Symmetrical).
C. **Rear Up.** Head Bend 2. Snarl 2. Mouth Open 3. Four Tail section Bends 31, 34, 38, 40. Tuft Bend 30. Abdomen Bend -45. Chest Bend -33. Right Thigh Bend -32. Left Ankle Bend 34. Left RearFoot Bend -25. Right Shoulder Bend 35. Right Forearm Bend -8. Other settings at their default position.

Posing the Zygote Penguin

The penguin has gotten a lot of commercial attention recently, appearing in a number of TV ads as the spokes-animal for this or that product. The Penguin reminds us of ourselves because it walks upright and looks like it's always wearing a tuxedo (see Figure 6.34).

A. **Look Down.** Head Bend 63; LShoulder: (Twist and Side to Side) -138, 35 (LShoulder at Symmetry); Abdomen Bend 60.

FIGURE 6.33 *A. Roaring. B. Sitting. C. Rear Up.*

B. Look Up. Head: (Side to Side and Bend) -46, 59; Abdomen Bend 39; LRShoulder Side to Side 26 (LShoulder at Symmetry).

C. Sit. Head Bend -49; Abdomen Bend 66; Chest Bend 72; LRShoulder: (Twist and Bend) -88, -105 (LShoulder at Symmetry).

Posing the Zygote Shark

The Shark is a symbol of aggression for human beings. The Zygote Shark Model (see Figure 6.35).

FIGURE 6.34 *Look Down, Look Up, and Sit.*

FIGURE 6.35 *A. Attack. B. Swimming. C. Bite Tail.*

Input these settings for the Zygote Shark Model to get these poses. Then alter them to explore other useful poses.

A. **Attack.** Head Bend -31, Mouth Open 3.
B. **Swimming.** Tail Fin Side to Side ; Body (4, 3, 2) Side to Side 31, -9, -26, 27.
C. **Bite Tail.** Tail Fin Bend -56; Body (4, 3, 2, 1) Bend -39, -68, -60, -3; Head Bend 51; Mouth Open 1.75; Mouth Closed -1.

Posing the Zygote Wolf

The Zygote Wolf can't be manipulated as finely as the Dog Model, but it can be posed enough to emote some powerful features. The Head offers only the Ears for posing (see Figure 6.36).

Input these settings for the Zygote Wolf Model to get these poses. Then alter them to explore other useful poses.

A. **Grrrrr!** Neck 1 Bend 77. Head Bend 73, Tail 1 Bend -50, Mouth Open 1.
B. **Howl.** Neck 1 Bend -17. Head Bend -69, Tail 1 Bend -30, Mouth Open -.3, Mouth Closed .09, R Thigh Bend -30, L&R Shoulder Bend -2, -28.
C. **Sniff.** Neck 1 and 2 Bend 81, 31. Head Bend -66, Tail 1 Bend -30, Mouth Closed .8, R Thigh Bend -14, Waist Bend 6, Chest Bend 12 (IK on for L&R Front Legs).

FIGURE 6.36 *A. Grrrrr! B. Howl. C. Sniff.*

Posing the Zygote Zebra

CAUTION

Karuna! Without a texture applied, you can use the Zebra as another Horse Model.

The Zygote Zebra can be placed in a scene with the Lion, as long as it's far away enough not to become the Lion's breakfast. As with other Animals, its main Head posing feature is the Ears, which, along with the Tail, can be forced to twitch to ward off the flies (see Figure 6.37).

NOTE

Input these settings for the Zygote Zebra Model to get these poses. Then alter them to explore other useful poses.

A. **Looking Your Way.** Tail bend (1, 2, 3, 4) -28, 0, -21, -29. Lower/Upper Neck Side to Side -39, -11. Head Twist/Side to Side/Bend -13, -29, -15.
B. **Grazing.** Tail Bend (1, 2, 3, 4) 60, 60, 50, 40. Head Bend -63. Lower/Upper Neck Bend 83, -7. Increase the Z Scale of both the Upper and Lower Neck to 135, so the Head reaches closer to the ground.
C. **Resting.** Tail Bend (1, 2, 3, 4) 60, 60, 50, 40. Head Bend -6. Right Shoulder/UpperArm/Forearm/Hand Bend 60, -117, -143, 58. Left Shoulder/UpperArm/Forearm/Hand Bend 2, -120, 75, 58. R&L Thigh/Shin/Ankle/Foot Bend 0, -79, 165, 0.

FIGURE 6.37 *A. Looking Your Way. B. Grazing. C. Resting.*

Assigning Human Characteristics to Animals

If you are creating a cartoon for a children's show or art for a children's storybook, posing animals as if they were mimicking humans might be of high interest to you. In all cases, because of the way that the Animal Model is articulated, there is no global guarantee that you can simply select a pose from the Poses Library and apply it to an Animal. Sometimes this works, and sometimes it causes bizarre results.

In general, there are two ways to transform animal poses into a more human look:

1. Use a pose from the People Poses library on the animal. Note that you will have to tweak the results by hand, because animal anatomy is probably going to warp a bit in the attempt to fit the pose.
2. Resize or rescale one or more of the animal's appendages or extremities to mimic human arms and legs. This is sometimes very effective, though it works for some animals and not for others.

Whatever human pose you assign to an Animal Model, rest assured that you will have to fine-tune it by hand (see Figure 6.38).

FIGURE 6.38 *Human poses assigned to the Chimpanzee Model, and then fine-tuned a little by hand. From left to right, top to bottom: Model Stance, Superhero Landing, Yess Masster, Flying Kick, and Lunge.*

Animals that have some similarity to the human anatomy and can be made to easily stand upright are the best choices for emulating human characteristics. These Poser 3 models include the Raptor, Chimpanzee, Penguin, and to some extent the Bear, Cat, and Dog. The Dolphin is in a special category because of its historical symbol as a guide of the sea.

CUSTOMIZING ANIMAL MODELS

At first glance, even after purchasing the Zygote Animal Models, it seems that you will have a total of eighteen Animal Models to populate your Poser 3 scenes. You actually have a lot more than that, because each Animal Model can be customized. In Chapter 7, we'll explore ways to customize models by compositing them with other models, but there's even a simpler way to create customized models, as we already started to explore in Chapter 3 with the human figure. Animal Models can also be customized by using two basic Parameter Dial ranges or Editing Tools: Tapering and Resizing. Add some rotation when it's called for, and you can expand your Animal collection by a multiple of 10 or more.

Using these two parameter attributes, you'll be surprised at how many Animal Model variants you'll be able to create. True, some will be fantasy creatures, but all will differ from the original Animal represented. As we present some examples for each of the eighteen Animal Models, we are not suggesting that our examples exhaust the possibilities. On the contrary, after following our illustrated examples, you should strike out on your own. Save your new creations to an Altered Animals library for future use.

All Poser 3 models, including Animals, can also be customized by mapping alternate textures to them or using just a color map. See Chapter 17 on Handshaking for more details on this and related possibilities.

In all of the customized Animal Models shown in the illustrations that follow, we will use three modification tools in succession: Tapering, Resizing (globally or along a singular axis), and Rotation. The exact parameter Dial values will not be given, because by now you should be quite familiar with the principles involved. You should be able to look at the illustrated examples, read the basic caption, and apply the parameter changes shown for each customized Animal Model. The object here is to test your knowledge of all of the material that we've covered so far, especially the Parameter Dial modifications. Look at the altered models and see how well you can match them by adjusting the body part values. If you find something even more interesting along the way, so much the better. Save your new models to the Figures library in a new folder.

Karuna! It is very important that you realize that setting extensive tapering, rotations, or resizing will deform your models. The trick is the do it just enough to get what you want without causing the model to become a chaotic jumble. You can only master this technique through experimentation, experience, and by watching the model views carefully.

The Customized Cat

The Cat Animal Model is very cute, representing a friendly tabby pet. Some of the modifications that can be applied however, will definitely alter the Cat's personality (see Figure 6.39).

The Customized Dog

See if you can figure out how the standard Dog Model was transformed into these other dog types. Save the customized Dogs you discover along the way (see Figure 6.40).

FIGURE 6.39 *From left to right: Snagglefooted Catwallah, Snaprax, Tabbis (mapped with Chimp texture).*

FIGURE 6.40 *From top left to bottom: Poochus, Daaschund, Foohound.*

The Customized Dolphin

The Dolphin Model is related to all of the strange fish shown here. Look at the illustrations and try to emulate these forms (see Figure 6.41).

The Customized Horse

You might think that there's nothing much you can do with the horse, but take a look. Study these illustrations, and try to develop the figures (see Figure 6.42).

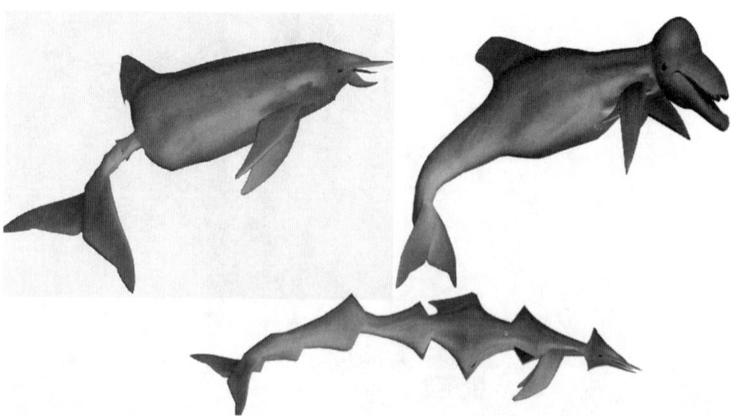

FIGURE 6.41 *From top left to bottom: Wormtailed Thrasher, Gray Brainwhale, Cambrian Rivergar.*

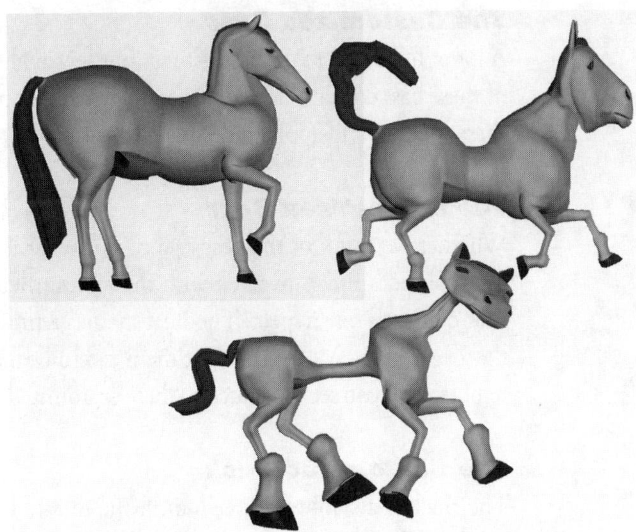

FIGURE 6.42 *From top left to bottom: Trojanus, Hobart's Equimax, Horzee.*

The Customized Raptor

The Raptor may be one of our dim ancestors. At any rate, it has a definite disposition and dislikes being ordered around. All manner of related beasties can be shaped from its parts. Look at the illustrations and try to shape a Raptor like the versions represented (see Figure 6.43).

FIGURE 6.43 *From top left to bottom: Scissorsaur, Spider-armed Spoonbill, Kangasaur.*

The Customized Bass

A lot of folks love to go Bass fishing, but few anglers would want to catch any of these bass cousins. See if you can tell what Parameters were altered to create these models, and apply the changes to your Zygote Bass (see Figure 6.44).

The Customized Bear

Whether we think of the bear as a cave dweller in the deep woods, or as the more placid animal involved with the circus, there is little question that the bear demands our respect. The Bear models represented here are variations of the Zygote Bear Model. Look at them carefully and try to make your bear resemble what you see illustrated in these customized variations (see Figure 6.45).

The Customized Buck

The Buck is a symbol of freedom in the forest. The variations we can create from the Zygote Buck Model are numerous, with the illustrated figures being a few examples. Investigate customizing the Buck model, using these figures as a beginning blueprint (see Figure 6.46).

The Customized Chimpanzee

The Zygote Chimp is the Animal Model closest to the human form and one of the most fun to customize. See if you can discover how the parameters were

FIGURE 6.44 *From top left to bottom: Jim's Gooberskark, Northern Clampmouth, Headerfish.*

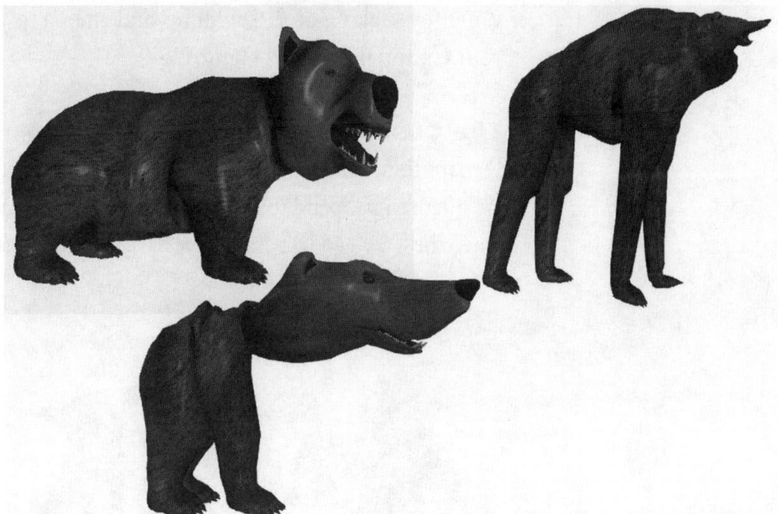

FIGURE 6.45 *From top left to bottom: Piggy-bear, Giant Bear-sloth, Miniature Shagbear.*

FIGURE 6.46 *From top left to bottom: Beaver-Tailed Naxod, Pink-eared Sloof, Horned Ebex.*

varied by looking at these figures and then applying the same alterations to your Chimp model (see Figure 6.47).

The Customized Cow

Perhaps these customized Cow Models only appear in dream pastures, but they are interesting. Spend some time looking at the figures and then apply what you see to the Cow Model parameters. Save the creations you enjoy (see Figure 6.48).

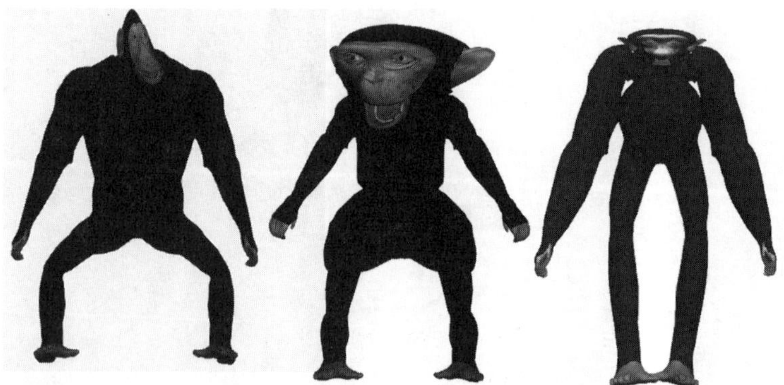

FIGURE 6.47 *From left to right: Gorillax, Bavarian Troll, Furry Hedrus.*

FIGURE 6.48 *From top left to bottom: Monrovian Flat-faced Bovus, Mouse-nosed Harg, Russian Mousecow.*

The Customized Doe

Even the gentle Doe can undergo a personality overhaul when customized with the Parameter Dials. See exactly how in these examples and then apply what you see to the Zygote Doe (see Figure 6.49).

The Customized Frog

The deep-throated frog can be heard in the spring, croaking its song to the night. But what does it really look like? We think we know, but maybe it resembles one of these Zygote Frog variations. After looking at these illustrations, see if you can tweak the Parameter Dials to create similar creatures (see Figure 6.50).

The Customized Killer Whale

The Killer Whale model from Zygote is as real as models can get, especially with its texture applied. But there are other modified creatures waiting to be born from this form. Here are a few. Look at them and try to figure out how these results were achieved by altering the Parameter settings (see Figure 6.51).

The Customized Lion

If the Lion decides to wear another personality, who is there to argue with it? Take a look at these customized Zygote Lion Models and see if you can create them (see Figure 6.52).

FIGURE 6.49 *From top left to bottom: Mule-faced Cameray, Upright Thamper, Wing-eared Rooney.*

FIGURE 6.50 *From top left to bottom: Common Bulgix, Martian Sandfoo, Shapiro's Egophibian.*

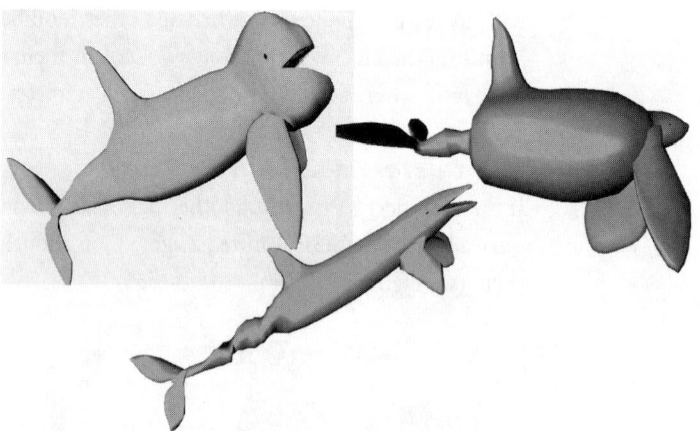

FIGURE 6.51 *From top left to bottom (with no killer Whale texture applied): Bulbous-headed Seapoot, Western Blobwhale, Torpedo Fish.*

The Customized Penguin

There are just a few animals that can live in the cold reaches of the planet. Polar bears and penguins come to mind as the two most well known. The penguin has always been seen as a proxy human being, since it walks upright with a decidedly Charlie Chaplin gait. The Zygote Penguin Model for Poser 3 captures all of the lovable characteristics that the penguin possesses. We've taken more than a few liberties to customize the penguin model into a wider range of creatures. See if you can tell how these new models were constructed from the standard Zygote penguin and then apply your learning to the Zygote Penguin on your system (see Figure 6.53).

FIGURE 6.52 *From top left to bottom: Irish Swamplion, Giant Lionarg, Lionette.*

FIGURE 6.53 *Note that the penguin texture was not used on these customized models. From left to right: Wrenthrax, Eastern Blue Pigeon, Samoan Jily-Jily.*

The Customized Shark

The shark rules the sea, intimidating most of the other inhabitants. Just look at the variety of customized creatures born from the Zygote Shark Model. Try to customize your Shark model in the same ways that are illustrated here (see Figure 6.54).

The Customized Wolf

The wolf is a dog with a serious attitude. These canine cousins of the wolf were customized from the Zygote Wolf Model. Investigate the illustrations, and when you're ready, customize your own Wolf model in the same manner (see Figure 6.55).

The Customized Zebra

CAUTION

Karuna! Strong patterned textures, like that of the penguin and the zebra, sometimes work against you when you're customizing a model. That's because we recognize these and other strong patterned creatures by their pattern as well as their shape. Explore other patterns as textures, or just use color. See Chapter 17.

FIGURE 6.54 *From top left to bottom: Needle Shark, Bubblehead, Posersaurus.*

FIGURE 6.55 *From top left to bottom: Bat-eared Lubock, Wild Fragdog, Brazilian Rock Camel.*

FIGURE 6.56 *From top left to bottom: Longfaced Fragus, Two-footed Equiz, It-Ain't-Trigger.*

The Zebra is known for its stripes. Underneath those stripes is a beautiful equine animal, a wild cousin of the horse. Customizing the Zygote Zebra Model is similar to customizing the Horse. Try your hand at applying customization modifications that cause the Zebra to resemble the customized Zebra figures shown here (see Figure 6.56).

Moving Along

If you have followed all of the examples presented in this chapter carefully, and have applied the detailed Parameters to each Animal's figure elements, then you are well on your way to mastering animal poses and alterations in Poser 3. In the next chapter, we'll detail the compositing methods that you can apply to all sorts of models, creating some interesting hybrid characters in the process.

CHAPTER

7 Composited Figures

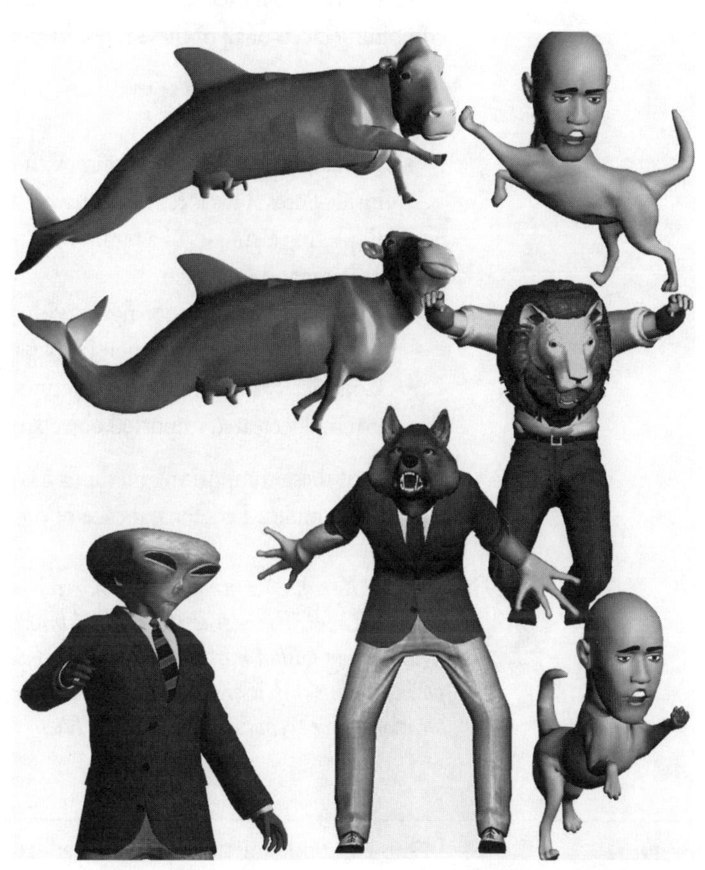

What Is a Composited Figure?

When you were born, all of the genetic material that makes up the parts that are now you was taken from two sources, your mother and your father. That's how most of life works on this planet. Is it the same law for everywhere in the universe? We just can't be sure. Now imagine that you exist on a planet with a more multifarious life-generating law, one that admits multiple contributing parents in the procreation of the species. Well, that might mean that you would have father number seven's nose, mother thirteen's left eye, mother twenty's right eye, and so on. This is exactly what we mean by composited figures in Poser 3, because Poser 3 is its own planetary system with its own laws.

Composited Figures in Poser 3 can be created in several ways, including combining facets of all of these ways. In general, composites can be created by:

- Combining one or several parts from Poser figures into one amalgamated whole.
- Replacing elements of a figure with other figure elements, drawn from inside Poser. This is especially useful in creating cross-species composites.
- Replacing elements of a figure with other elements, drawn from outside of Poser and imported.
- Modifying elements of a figure with morphed elements (used mostly for Heads, but possible for their body parts as well).
- Completely replacing all of a figure's parts with either internal props or externally created imported objects.

Each of these compositing methods has rules and cautions and moves from simple to complex. Let's look at each of them in turn.

Karuna! Karuna! Karuna! When you create a composited figure and want to save it out, DO NOT save it to the Figure library! All that will be saved is the selected figure, along with a misleading image of the composited whole, and not the composited figure(s) that are unselected. When you want to save out your Composited creations, save them as Poser 3 Project Files.

Internal Amalgamated Composites

In this composite method, items are added to the selected figure, without removing any of the elements of the figure itself.

SINGLE PROP COMPOSITES

What is a Prop? A Prop is any element in your Poser 3 scene that is not a part of any Poser figure. A Prop can be a sphere that acts as a ball, or a staircase that the figure navigates. There is also a more specific type of Prop, one that is attached via a hierarchy to a Poser 3 figure. If you attach the spherical ball to a figure's right hand, for instance, every time the figure moves its right hand the ball will move with it. If you attach the figure to the stairway, other things are possible. You can set a walk motion in which the figure walks up the stairs without any problem. If the stairs are moved from one side of a room to the other, however, the figure will move along with them. All sorts of things are possible when Props are either the child of a figure element, or the parent. The first thing you need to do is to know how to add a Prop to the Document window.

To add a Prop to your Document window, do the following:

1. Go to the Props folder in the Library List (accessed by clicking on the list toggle at the right of the screen). See Figure 7.1.

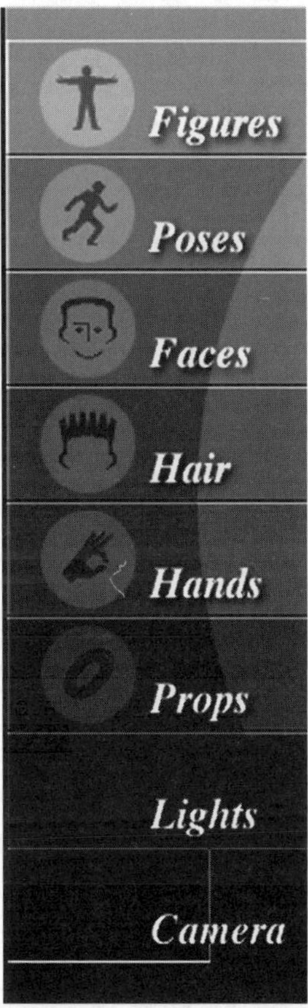

FIGURE 7.1 *The Library List.*

2. Click on the Props item in the list. When the Props library folder appears, make sure the Prop Types listing is selected from the drop down list. See Figure 7.2.
3. Double-click on the Ball to add it to the Document window. After it's added, double-click on the "Box" Prop below it to add it as well. Move the Box above the Ball in the Document window. Your Document window will now contain both Props, with the Box above the Ball, as displayed in Figure 7.3.
4. With the Box selected, bring up its Properties dialog (Edit/Properties). Click on Set Parent and make the Ball the Parent of the Box. See Figure 7.4.

The Ball is now the Parent of the Block. Rotate or Move the Ball, and the Block moves and rotates with it. Move or Rotate the Block, and nothing happens to the Ball, because it is not the Parent of the Ball.

Note that you cannot cross-parent objects, so that they are each other's parent. This would be highly incestuous, anyway.

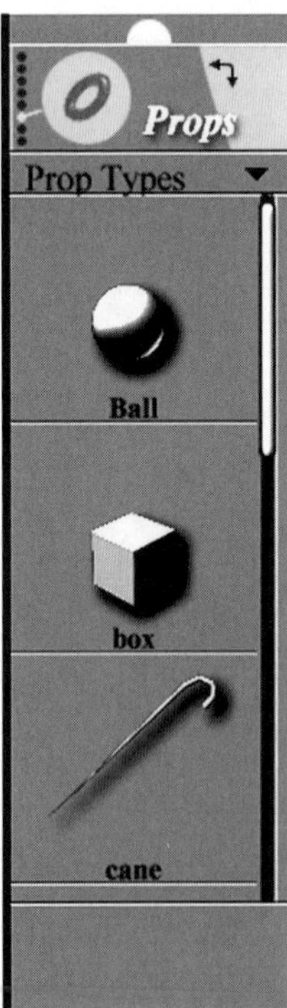

FIGURE 7.2 *The Prop Types listing shows the "Ball" as the first Prop object in the list.*

FIGURE 7.3 *Your Document window now contains the Ball and the Box Props.*

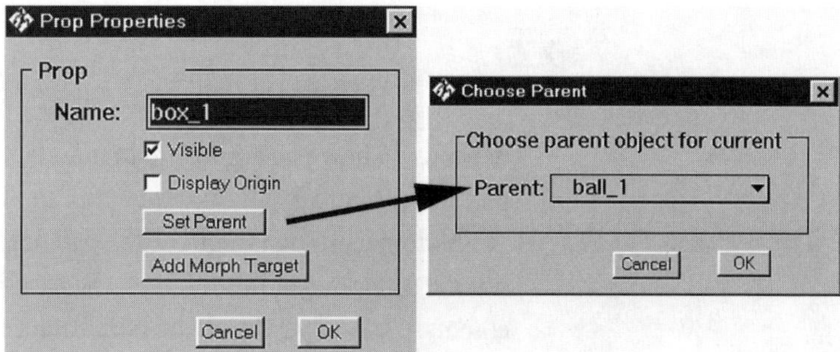

FIGURE 7.4 *Make the Ball the Parent of the Box.*

Congratulations! You have now mastered parenting a hierarchy, so anytime we simply say "Parent this object to that object," we will assume you know exactly what to do.

Basic Geometric Props

Basic Geometric Props include the Ball, Box, Cone, Cylinder, Square, and Torus in the Prop Types folder inside of the Props library. Make sure you know how to access this location and that all of these items are located there. With any human figure loaded in your Document window, do the following:

1. Add a Torus Prop to the Document window and move it so that it rests over the waist of your human figure, like a belt. Resize the Torus as needed (see Figure 7.5).
2. Now for parenting. What part of the figure's body should be the Parent of the Prop? What part of the body should control the Torus? That all

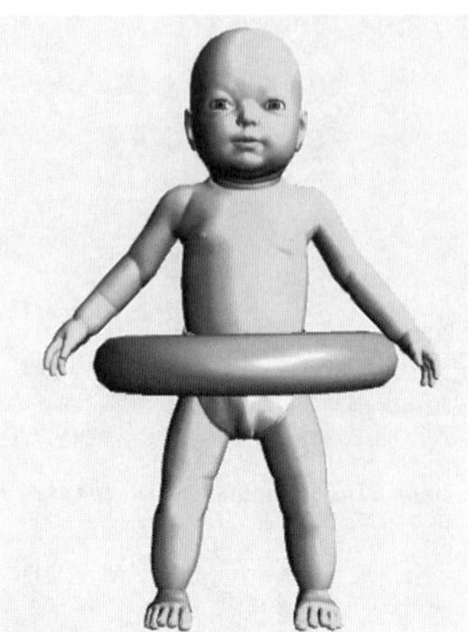

FIGURE 7.5 *The Torus Prop covers the waist of the figure (in this case, the Zygote Baby) like a belt.*

depends on how you're going to manipulate the figure, and also on what part of the figure is closest to the Prop. In this case, the Prop is closest to the Abdomen, so that might be the parent to select. But the Abdomen is not the core element in the figure, the part that moves all of the other elements. That duty is left to the Hip. Parent the Torus to the figure's Hip. Now rotate or move the Hip, and the whole figure as well as the Torus should move and rotate along with it (see Figure 7.6).

Now do this exercise all over again, but this time, move the Torus Prop over the Head like a hat. Parent the Torus Prop to the figure's Neck, because the

FIGURE 7.6 *Rotating and/or Moving the Hip moves and rotates the whole figure, as well as the attached Torus Prop.*

Neck controls Head movements. We could also Parent it with the Head, but usually the neck is adjusted to control the Head. Now, moving any other parts of the body that are Parents to the Neck (Chest, Abdomen, Hips) will also move the Torus Prop (see Figure 7.7).

Any of the basic Props can be used in this same manner. You can even construct Prop "clothes" to encase most of a figure (see Figure 7.8).

Hair Library

Hair is a Prop that comes into the scene already parented with the figure's head. You can only add one hair Prop at a time from the Hair library, but hair Props in the Zygote "Hair and Hats" Props library allow you to add as many hair objects as you like. Note that Hair is automatically parented to the Head only

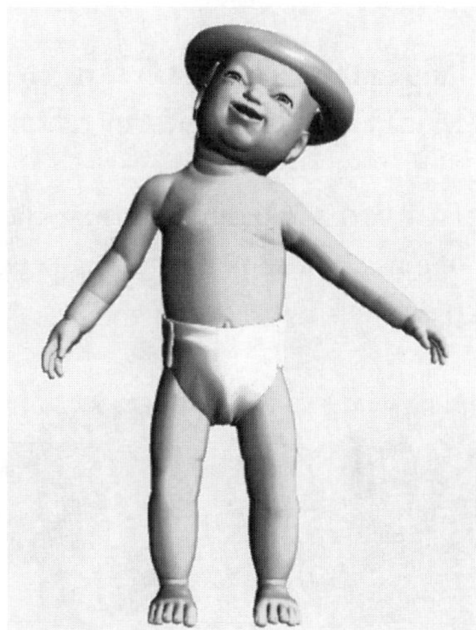

FIGURE 7.7 *The Torus Prop is now an attached Hat. The Torus moves and rotates with the Neck.*

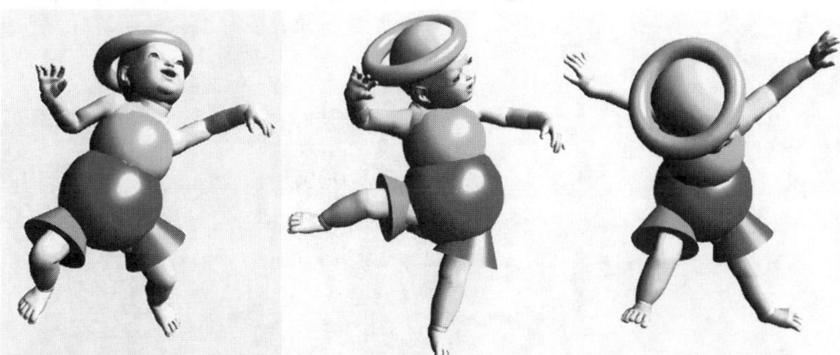

FIGURE 7.8 *Multiple basic Props used to encase the figure, with each one parented to appropriate parts of the body.*

when it is added from the Hair library, and not from the Zygote "Hair and Hats" Props library.

CAUTION

Karuna! It is highly recommended that you purchase the Zygote Extras libraries, so that you can add the new "Hair and Hats" Props and also the new Hair folder to the Hair library.

Open the Hair library and click on one of the Hair objects. In a matter of seconds, it will appear in your Document window and may come in perfectly in place on the figure's head.

NOTE

The way to guarantee an instant placement of the Hair on the Head of your figure is to avoid moving the figure around until after the Hair is placed. Use the Head Camera to make fine-tuned adjustments to the position of the Hair.

Each Hair Prop can be resized on any axis, so in effect, you have dozens of unique hair styles made possible by these modification methods (see Figure 7.9).

Strange Modifications You can try turning the Hair upside down or tilting it on the side of a head for some interesting personality transformations (see Figure 7.10).

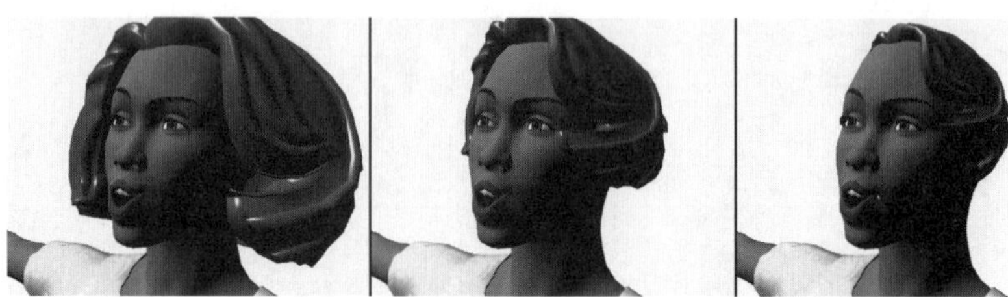

FIGURE 7.9 *Any Hair element from the Hair library can instantly be altered to produce a series of unique hair styles by simply resizing it on any axis or globally. The Zygote African American Casual model is depicted here.*

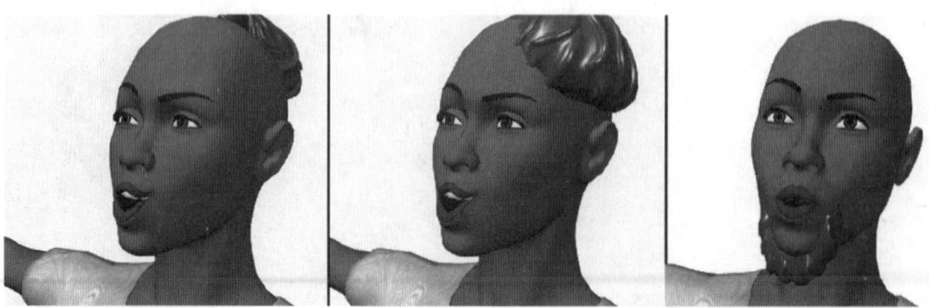

FIGURE 7.10 *Left to right: Hair sized at 30% and moved to the back of the head; Rotated and placed over left ear; Flipped around and used as a beard.*

Hair from the Hair and Hats Folder in the Props Library

The main difference in using Hair from the Hair and Hats Props library is that you can use as many selections as you like. Not being limited to one clump of hair makes the creation of all kinds of alternate looks and effects possible (see Figure 7.11).

NOTE

Note that you must manually make the Head the parent of the Hair that comes from the Hair and Hats folder in the Props library.

Zygote Hat Props

First, let's look at the Zygote Hair and Hats folder in the Props library again. If you have not purchased the Zygote extras, then you can use a basic geometric Prop as a stand-in. This time, instead of focusing upon hair, we'll look at hats. There are six hats in the Zygote Hair and Hats folder of the Props library: Baseball Cap, Baseball Helmet, Cowboy Hat, Helmet, Police Hat, and Top Hat. Any hat you select has to be positioned in place, and the Head has to be selected as the Parent (see Figure 7.12).

FIGURE 7.11 *Left to right: Female Hair 3 from the Zygote Hair and Hats folder in the Props library; Hair 3 and Hair 2 used together to create a double tinted look; Female Hair 1, 2, and 3 used together for a triple tint.*

FIGURE 7.12 *From left to right: A jaunty placement of the Baseball Helmet; The Cowgirl; Law Enforcer.*

Other Single Zygote Prop Composites

The difference between using a Prop and creating a Prop Composite is that the Prop in a Composite has a Parent element that is one of the elements of a model. A standard Prop might be a chair. A Prop Composite would be a hair or hat object, or any other Prop, attached by a Parental hierarchy to the selected figure. You can attach any Prop to a figure to make a Composite, although attaching a chair to a head may seem a little unusual to some viewers. A Zygote Mop Prop, on the other hand, can make a fine head of hair when turned upside down (see Figures 7.13 and 7.14).

Note that you will often have to bury part of the Prop used in a composite in the figure itself, so take care how the figure bends so as not to expose the Prop.

FIGURE 7.13 *The Zygote Mop Prop, from the Zygote Samples folder in the Props library, makes a fine head of hair on this Zygote Alien figure (from the Sampler Characters collection).*

FIGURE 7.14 *Another interesting Prop Composite uses the Zygote Pitchfork to add a quadruple antennae to the Alien's head.*

MULTIPLE ELEMENT COMPOSITES

When we start to multiply the number of items, as well as the kind of items, that can be used to develop a Composited creation, the geometry of possibilities goes right through the roof. No more do we see Poser 3 as a simple application with a limited number of character sets, but instead are made to realize that the only limit to our capacities are the barriers we ourselves place on our creative intent and our openness to possibility. This is what good creative software (and creativity in general) is supposed to do, to move us beyond the restrictions of our own limited belief systems, to push at the "rules."

Multiple Figure Composites

This section of the chapter introduces the use of Invisible Properties into the Composite mix. This is the most important of the Multiple Composite techniques, since you can use it to create some pretty spectacular beings without even using any Props. The general idea is simple: Combine the elements (or an element) of more than one Poser figure. To do this effectively, we'll have to introduce another option: Invisibility. Any selected element of a Poser 3 figure can be made invisible, simply by checking the Visibility box in its Properties dialog (see Figure 7.15).

A Vital Preparation If it is your intention to combine multiple Poser 3 figures (models) into one, then you would do well to make some preparations beforehand. More than likely, you will be most interested in transposing the head, and possibly hands or feet, of one figure onto another, to form an interesting composite. To do this, the figure whose head you want to use should have all of its other elements made invisible (usually, you leave a Neck in place as well). Instead of doing this rather tedious task each time you create a multi-

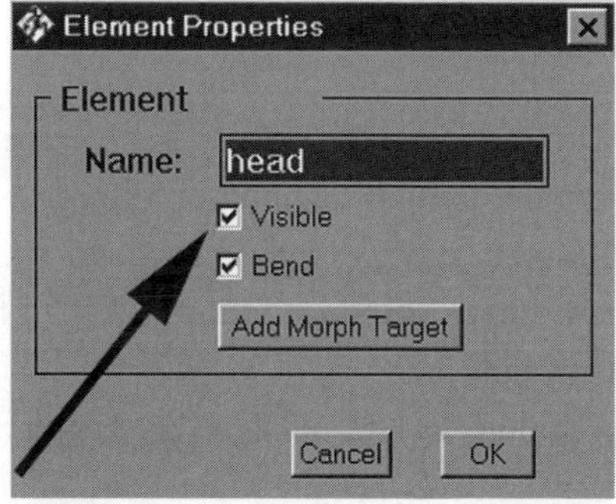

FIGURE 7.15 *By unchecking the Visibility box in any element's Properties dialog, that element is made invisible in the Document window.*

ple figure composite, you can save a lot of effort by putting in some necessary preparatory work beforehand. Here's an approach that I took, because creating figure composites in Poser 3 is one of my favorite endeavors.

I looked at every head of every figure, People and Animal, that I found interesting. One at a time, I brought that figure into Poser 3 and proceeded to make Invisible (Properties dialog) all elements but those I wanted to work with. In the case of a figure's Head, I kept the Head, Eyes, and Neck parts. Everything else was marked as not visible. Then I created a separate directory in the Figures library called "Headz." After each figure was treated for visible/invisible elements, I saved out the Head and associated parts as a separate figure in my new Headz folder. This took about five hours, but in return, I now have a library collection of heads that can be used to replace the head of any other figure. I did this with all of the internal models whose Heads I was interested in, and also with all of the Zygote extras. In my "Headz" folder are visible Heads for the following models: African American Casual Man and Woman, Alien, Asian Casual Man and Woman, Baby, Bass, Buck, Chimp, Dog, Dolphin, Frog, Heavy Man and Woman, Horse, Killer Whale, Lion, Old Man and Old Woman, Penguin, Raptor, Shark, Skull, Sumo, Wolf, and Zebra. This is quite a collection of heads!

When you have done the same thing with the models whose heads you want to use in composited figures, the steps to take for doing the actual compositing are simple to follow and remember. Do the following:

1. With a selected figure already in your document window (a figure whose body you will use in the composite), bring in the head from your Headz folder that you want to use. Normally this will be loaded as Figure 2.
2. Make the Head, Neck(s), and Eyes (if there are any Eyes listed separately) of Figure 1 invisible (Properties dialog).
3. Making sure that Figure 2 is highlighted in the Figures list, select Figure 2's "Body" element. This is because the Body must be selected (though it is invisible) for moving and rotation.
4. Move and Rotate the Head of Figure 2 (the figure whose Head you are using in the composite) until it is placed over the body of Figure 1 (the figure whose body will remain in the composite mix) in the correct orientation on its axis. Resize the new Head if necessary to suit the composited whole.
5. Select the lowest Neck of Figure 2, or select the Head if there is no Neck, and activate the Set Figure Parent command in the Figure menu. When the dialog comes up, select Figure 1 for the figure and then whatever el-

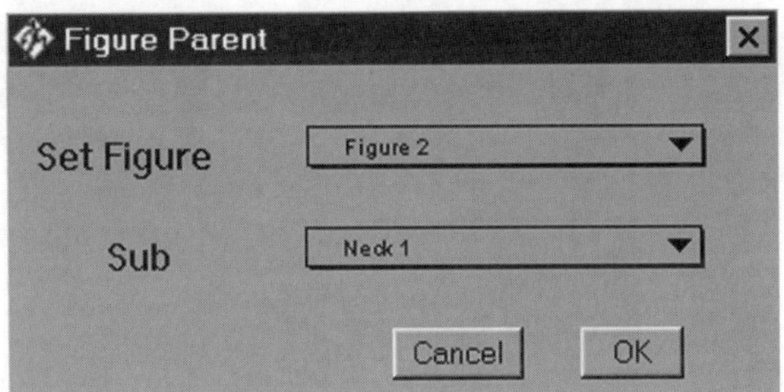

FIGURE 7.16 *To attach the figures together, you have to set the Parent hierarchy in the Set Figure Parent dialog.*

ement is going to act as the parent. For instance, if the Neck of the Head (Figure 2) needs a parent, it is best to select the Neck of Figure 1 (the body). Note that a Parent does not have to be visible to still control the child element (see Figure 7.16).

You can use the same technique to create a separate Figure library for Hands, Feet, and miscellaneous body parts such as tails and ears.

Multiple Basic Prop Composites

We have already introduced the idea of Multiple Basic Prop Composites in Figure 7.8. Now let's push it a little farther. There are two ways to use Props in a composite relationship. The first is to simply parent a prop to a hand, as if the hand were holding it. This is good for shields, weapons, and utensils of every kind. For instance, you could use this method to attach a broom to a figure's hands, and then pose the figure to sweep the floor. A sword could be parented to one hand and a shield to the other for a battle scene. The second way to utilize a Prop in a composite is to force it to substitute for a body part. One of the Heads from our Headz library could replace the head of a skeleton figure, creating a rather strange but definitely audience-attracting image (maybe just right for Halloween). See Figure 7.17.

TIP

If you want the Skeleton figure to show up more clearly on a white or light backdrop, color it a medium gray instead of its default cream-white.

If we take Figure 7.17 and add a cane parented to the right hand, a ball parented to the left hand, and a cube parented to the Head, we have created a true multiple composite, using both the Head from an alternate source and three basic Prop sources (see Figure 7.18).

FIGURE 7.17 *The Zygote Heavy Man Head replaces the Skeleton Head on a Skeleton body, using the methods described previously.*

FIGURE 7.18 *A more complex composited creation results when several different Props and another Head is used.*

Two More Figure Choices In the Additional Figures folder in the Figures library are two more figure types that we haven't covered yet, the Mannequin and the Male, Female, and Child Stick figures. You might think that these optional models are useful only for setting up poses, which they are, but they are also very useful when it comes to crafting composited models. Both the Mannequin and the Stick Figures are already composed of basic geometric elements, so modifying them by combining their geometries with more realistic elements, especially Heads, gives them a unique character. Use either the Mannequin or Stick Figures with a more realistic Head when you want to both call attention to the Head, and also when you want to mystify your audience. Both of these options as bodies would also be great for crafting posed images for a children's storybook (see Figure 7.19).

An advantage in working with the Mannequin and Stick Figures is that they render lightning fast. This makes them great for posing, and when your project is OK for it, also useful as body elements.

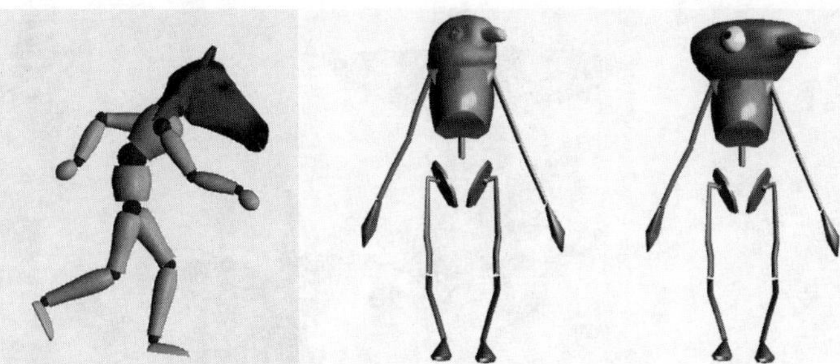

FIGURE 7.19 *Left to right: The Mannequin with a Horse's Head attached; A Penguin Head attached to a Female Stick Figure; taper of -175 added to the Penguin's Head, with the Eyes resized to 700%.*

Multiple Zygote Prop Composites

Karuna! The Zygote Animals, People, Props, and more are mentioned continuously throughout this book. If you don't have them, you can substitute other basic figure elements in their place. It is highly recommended, however, that you purchase the whole Zygote Extras collection at the earliest date possible, since it expands the uses that Poser 3 can be put to ten times over.

CROSS-SPECIES COMPOSITES

If you have been following along with the material on Composite Figure creation, then it's time for some visual learning. The next three pages display some of the myriad of inventive creatures that are possible when you use these separated parts to build multiple figure composites. By now, you should be able to look at these figures and understand how they are constructed. Most use the Zygote figures, so you will be somewhat at a creative loss if you don't have them yet. Look at the figures carefully for study and also use them as a relaxing moment of eye candy (see Figures 7.20 to 7.22).

USING EXTRA HEADS AND HANDS

In the Additional Figures folder in the Figures library are four very important models that can play a large role in helping you create novel composite figures. There are two Heads, Male and Female, and two Hands, Left and Right. These are stand-alone elements, so no invisibility has to be applied. When you need to add a basic hand or Head to another figure in the Document window, this is the place to shop for it.

FIGURE 7.20 *There is no limit to the virtual genetic engineering that you can accomplish in Poser 3.*

FIGURE 7.21 *It's doubtful that your local zoo features any of these fine specimens.*

FIGURE 7.22 *Poser 3 is an excellent resource when it comes to developing cross-species models.*

What other types of scenarios might benefit from these elements? Well, there is no stopping you from adding as many Hands or Heads from this folder as your system memory will allow, remembering that each one can be posed separately. You can spread a number of posed Heads out on a table, stack them one on top of the other, or blend them together front to back. The same thing can be done with the hands from this folder. Any multiple or configuration of these elements can be added quickly to your Document (see Figure 7.23).

INCORPORATING EXTERNAL FORMS

By *external forms,* I mean any 3D element created in any non-Poser 3 application. Since Poser 3 can import 3D Studio, Wavefront, DXF, QuickDraw 3D, and RayDream formatted objects, you can use just about any 3D application to construct Poser 3 figure elements and/or Props. All 3D applications save out data in one or more of the formats that Poser 3 can import.

CAUTION

Karuna! When possible, stay away from DXF content. It's a format every 3D application understands, but it's difficult to texture map correctly, and often it responds poorly to smoothing operations, leaving you with faceted object elements.

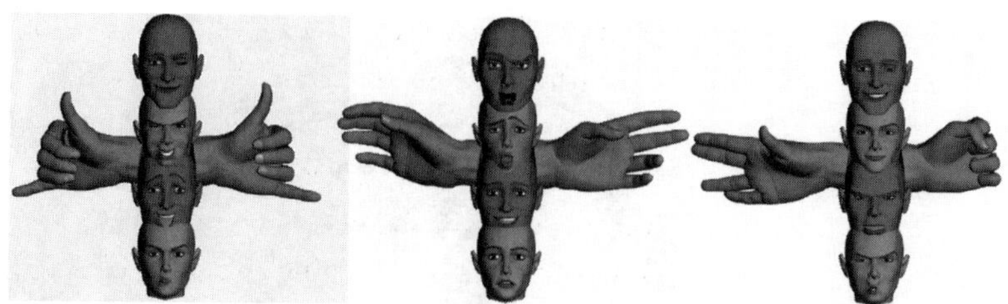

FIGURE 7.23 *This sculptured creation uses nothing but the generic Heads and Hands found in the Additional Figures folder in the Figures library.*

It's obvious that you can use a 3D program outside of Poser 3 to create Props such as chairs, pillars, and other environmental elements. We're confining our discussion here to composited figures, however, so that calls for some special attention in the 3D application you're using.

Note that we are not spending time in this chapter talking about Poser 3's ability to handshake with Ray Dream Studio. That will be detailed in Chapter 17 on handshaking techniques and tips.

SEEING DOUBLE

With your Headz library folder filled with Head elements, you can easily assign multiple Heads, all separately controllable, to any figure in your Document (see Figure 7.24).

CREATING POSER 3 ELEMENT CONTENT

I am of the opinion that you will use Poser 3's native tools to create most of the bodies and heads you will need, and that any elements generated outside of

FIGURE 7.24 *Creating a Raptor with multiple Heads is easy when you've saved out its Head-only element and read it back in, attaching the clone to the Raptor body.*

Poser 3 will be mostly addendum Props and somewhat mechanical replacement parts for Poser figures. Added to this might be costuming elements, like suits of armor, headgear, and the like. This is not to say that you can't or shouldn't create organic elements outside of Poser, it's just that those elements will not be posable like Poser's native body parts (at least not without a tremendous amount of hassle setting up complex Blend Zones). So let's focus our attention then on a project that you can handle in any 3D application for Poser 3 import.

RULES FOR BASIC ELEMENT DESIGN

There is no limit to the potential complexity of the elements that can be used to replace parts of a Poser 3 figure. Using an external 3D application, you can design as many customized parts for the Poser 3 figure as it has figure elements. In this way, you would import the parts into Poser 3 and then place them over the existing body elements. The original elements would be invisible, but they would act (and be assigned) as the Parents of the imported parts. Your beginning explorations in this area need not be this complex, however. All that you have to do is to minimize the number of elements used to replace the Poser figure's elements. How many unique parts, at a minimum, should you consider creating? Here's a simple solution:

- Create a unique Head. The Head is always the focus of attention, so it should always stand out as a figure element. As a second, and sometimes better option, use a posable Poser 3 Head as part of the new composite.
- Create one element to act as both the Chest, Abdomen, Collars, Hands (but not the fingers), and Hip. This element can be resized so that it can be cloned and act as each of these three body parts.
- Create one element that will act as all of the Arm parts (including hands and Fingers) and all of the Leg parts (excluding the Feet).
- Create another element that will serve as the Feet.

That's it! By creating four basic 3D forms in your favorite 3D application and porting them to Poser 3, you can create your own basic Poser 3D posable figure.

A Total Figure Element Replacement Project

Here is one example of testing out the basic figure element design method we just discussed. Follow along, using your own favorite 3D application as the design environment. Do the following:

1. Create a Head for your new model, or skip this step and add a Poser 3 Head once you're back in Poser 3.
2. Create one element that can be resized cloned to use as the Chest, Abdomen, Collars, Hands (but not the fingers), and Hip. It can be as basic or as complex as your RAM will permit.
3. Create one element that can be resized and cloned for the Arm and leg parts, including the fingers.
4. Create an object that can be used as the Feet. This same object can also be cloned to use as the Toes if need be.
5. Save out all of the elements in a format that Poser 3 can import (preferably as a Wavefront OBJ file, if your 3D application supports that format). See Figures 7.25 to 7.27.

I used Organica, a MetaBlock 3D design application from Impulse for this project. Organica is available for both the Mac and Wintel systems.

6. In Poser 3, import each of the elements you just created.
7. Import a figure whose Head you want to use, import a previously saved Head from your Headz folder, or import a Head from the Additional Figures folder in the Figures library.

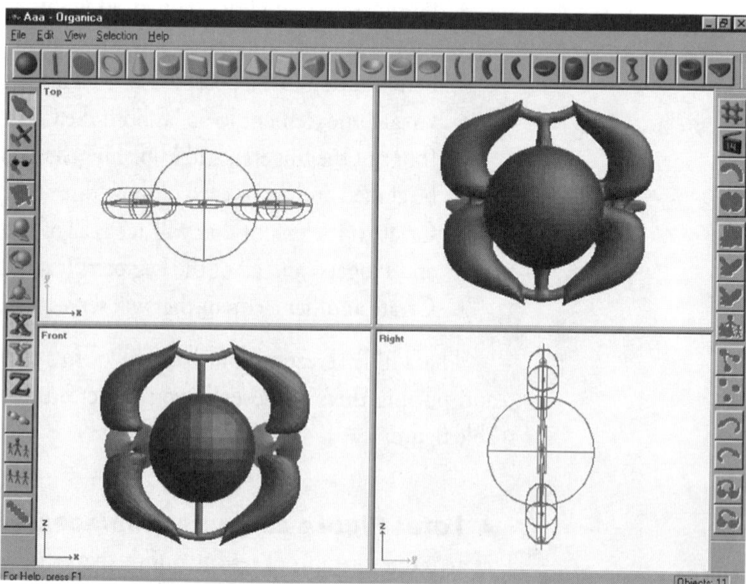

FIGURE 7.25 *The main body element is created and saved as a 3D Studio format object.*

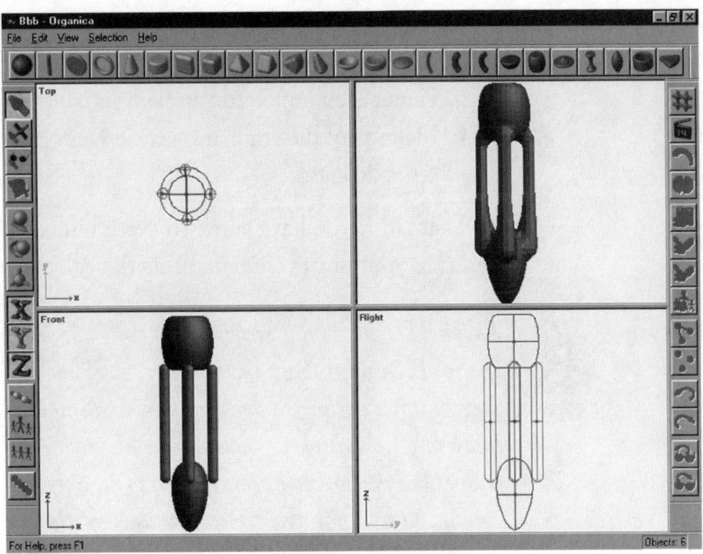

FIGURE 7.26 *The Arm and Leg element is created and saved as a 3D Studio format object.*

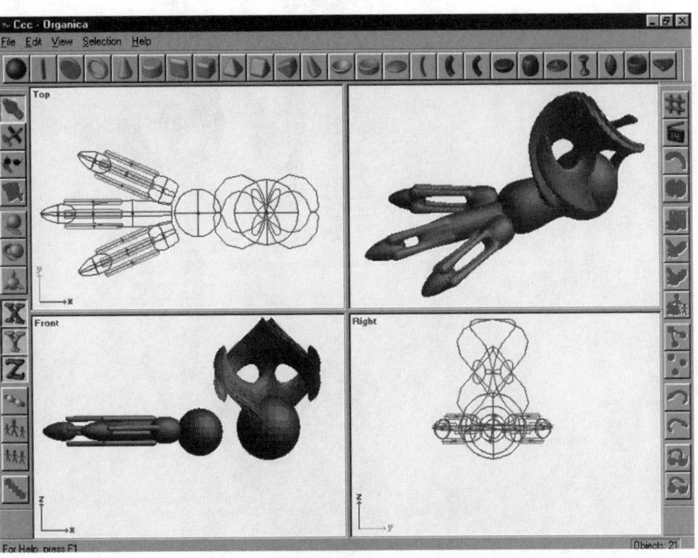

FIGURE 7.27 *The Foot element is created and saved as a 3D Studio format object.*

8. Import all of the other elements as many times as necessary to use as elements for all of the figure's parts. Place each part in its proper orientation.
9. Parent each imported part with its control element on the Poser figure.
10. Make all of the original Poser elements invisible in their respective Properties dialogs.

That's it! If you have parented everything correctly, you can pose this new model to your heart's content, using the Parameter Dials (see Figure 7.28).

CAUTION

Karuna! Do not try this exercise unless you have at least 128 MB of memory on your system. Even with that much memory and more, you may still run into trouble. Poser 3 is not optimized for large files, and importing objects seems to make them much larger. Multiple imported object files can severely tax your system, and it may crash. One way to conserve memory is to use only limited imported objects to do this exercise, so that one object might be used for the Chest, Abdomen, and Hip combined. Perhaps another might be used for the Shins, leaving the original figure's Thighs in place. Poser 3 will warn you when memory is low.

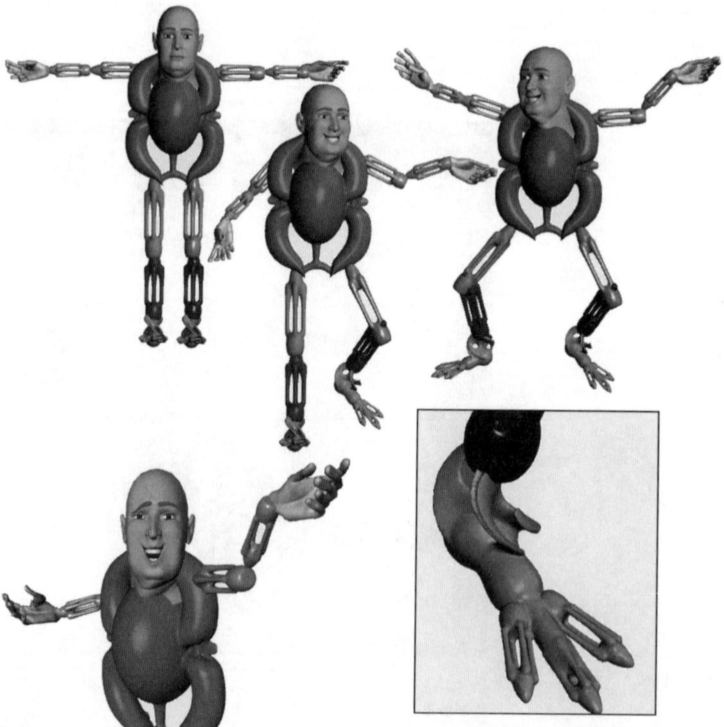

FIGURE 7.28 *Your new model with its imported elements can be posed by using the familiar Parameter Dials. Total weight of this file as a Poser 3 project is almost 18 MB.*

RIDERS

Another type of Composite is any two or more figures that are connected to each other, but not blended together. A perfect example of this is a horse and rider, or any figure with another figure riding it (it could be a horse riding a person for variety). The most important consideration here is how the parenting takes place, from what part to what part. This has important considerations for animation work, which we'll look at in Chapter 13.

As far as developing an interesting graphic composite that shows the Rider situation, there are a few cautions to observe:

1. Make sure the Rider is posed so that none of its parts are immersed inside of the transporting figure. This means posing legs more than anything else so that they are opened wide enough and at the correct angles. It's a good idea to place the Rider above the transpiration (Y axis) and to adjust the pose from there. That way, you can test the composite by dropping the Rider down until everything looks OK.
2. Think about using IK on both of the Rider's legs, and parenting one or both feet to the body part of the Transporter that the feet are closest to. That way, you can make the Rider separate from the transport every once in a while to make it seem as if the Rider is bouncing. More on this in Chapter 13.
3. Give the Rider a little slouch, no matter if the transportation is an Animal or a Vehicle. Nobody sits up straight except robots, so a slouch looks more natural (see Figure 7.29).

TAIL TALES

Don't be restricted by what you think a stand-alone element is, and how it must or must not be used. Instead, try and look at all elements as having no defined purpose, and you'll be surprised what novel ideas come to mind. In Zen, this is called Beginner's Mind, and to be creative in Poser, to push it to the edge, you have to approach your work with Beginner's Mind.

Let's assume that you have saved out an animal's Tail, making all of its other body parts invisible. You could apply the Tail to anything—another Animal, a human model, or a Prop. But there is yet another use for Tail object—many uses, in fact—that have nothing to do with its being called a "Tail" at all. Instead of thinking of its name, think of its geometry, its shape. Of course, the Animal Tails you have saved out might be slightly different. The Raptor's Tail is very smooth and conical, while the Lion and Zebra Tails have tufts on the end. What do all of the Tails have in common? They are long elements that

FIGURE 7.29 *Baby Sumo loves the Bear. Because the Bear has thick fur, it's OK to allow Baby Sumo to sink into it a bit.*

move from slightly wider at one end (in most cases) to thinner at the other, and they can be posed in a curve.

Can you think of any Animals that are long and shapely like the Tail and have the ability to shape themselves in a curve? If you answered "snakes," you have just seen the Tail with Beginner's Mind. Tails make very interesting Snake-like objects, and you can put any Head on the wider end that you prefer (see Figure 7.30).

FIGURE 7.30 *Snake-like creations can be generated quite easily if you use a Tail as the Snake's body.*

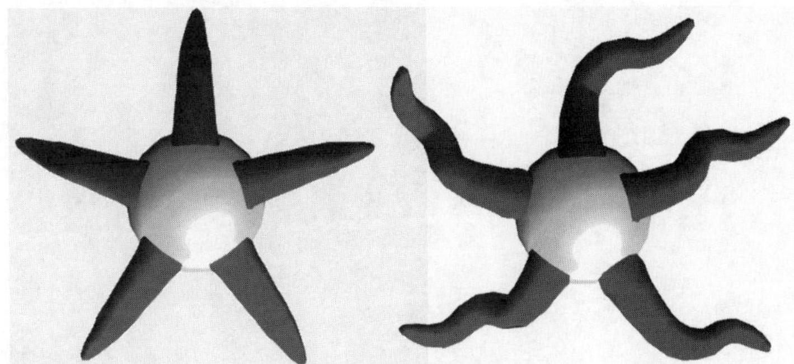

FIGURE 7.31 *A Starfish created from Dog Tails is another example of a unique composite model in Poser 3.*

A Starfish of Tails

One unique model you can create quite easily from the Dog's Tail is a starfish. Here's how:

1. Import the Dog and make everything invisible except for its Tail parts. Save this as a figure called "Dogtail1" to a new folder in your Figure library called "Other."
2. Select New from the file menu, and import the Dogtail five times.
3. Go to the Top View and rotate four of the Starfish arms at increments of 72 degrees (72, 144, 216, and 288) on the Y axis. This forms a star shape made of Dog's Tails.
4. Place a Ball Prop in the center and squash it on its Y axis, so that it flattens out. Make the Ball the Parent of all five Starfish arms. You can shape the arms by selecting any of the sections but the first one and rotating it (see Figure 7.31).

Moving Along

In this chapter, you were invited to explore the creation and modification of composited figures. In the next chapter, we'll look at backgrounds and Props in detail.

CHAPTER 8

Backgrounds, Props, and Rendering

When you create a Poser 3 animation or image, it looks rather naked if just placed against a single color backdrop or if it stands alone in an otherwise empty environment. Backgrounds and props add more than interest to your Poser 3 work: They add emotional and narrative context. Remember that if a picture is worth a thousand words, than a well thought out picture, with other graphics elements in proximity to your main actors, are worth a million words. A story can be told in seconds by the visual content alone, so having control of all of the possible content in your Document is a necessity.

The Ground Plane

The Ground Plane is a singular rectangular plane that acts as the recipient for objects shadows and also as the base upon which the actors play. The Ground Plane is toggled on or off by selecting it from the Display menu under the Guides listing. If Ground Plane is checked, it's on. If unchecked, it's off.

QUESTIONS AND ANSWERS ABOUT THE GROUND PLANE

Here is a listing of general questions and answers that refer to the Ground Plane and its uses.

Can I See the Ground Plane from All Camera Views?

No. The Ground Plane remains hidden in the Front, Left, and Right Side Camera Views, but is visible in all other views.

Can the Ground Plane Be Rotated?

Yes. The ground Plane can be rotated in all Camera Views in which it can be seen. Use the Turn Parameter Dial to rotate the Ground Plane on its Y (vertical) axis. When in the Dolly, Posing, Left/Right Hand, and Main Camera views, you can use the Trackball to rotate the whole scene, and the Ground Plane along with it. There are no independent controls for rotating the Ground Plane left or right, or back to front. For this reason, you can't use the Ground Plane as a wall, except if you reorient the whole scene after using the Trackball.

Can Items Emerge from beneath the Ground Plane?

Yes! If you have a Ground Plane textured like water or colored blue, for example, you can place the Dolphin beneath it and have it jump in and out of the virtual "water." To move something beneath the Ground Plane, move it on its negative Y axis. The only stipulation is that you must ***Turn Shadows Off,*** because objects below the Ground Plane cast shadows on the Ground Plane itself, leading to strange confusion for the viewer. When an object is placed below the Ground Plane, its shadow looks like a hole, colored in the shadow color, that sits on the Ground Plane.

Can the Ground Plane Accept Textures?

Yes. The Ground Plane will accept any single picture textures in any of the formats that Poser 3 can read. In a future version of Poser 3, it would be nice to be able to assign movies to the Ground Plane.

Can the Ground Plane Be Resized?

Yes. It can be resized on its X (horizontal) and Z (in and out) dimensions. It has no thickness, so it can't be resized on its Y (vertical) axis. The Ground Plane can also be resize-animated (see Section II).

CREATING PATTERNED GROUND PLANES

Karuna! Karuna! Karuna! The following information is not available in the documentation, but only in this book. Using this information will enable you to create some optical illusions in Poser 3.

You are not limited to the single Ground Plane Poser pretends to give you. With a simple trick, you can create an infinite array of multicolored or multitextured Ground Planes. Here's how:

1. Go to the Top Camera view. Check Ground Plane in the Guides listing in the Display menu.
2. With the Ground Plane selected, color and resize it until it covers about one-fourth of your Document Window. Paste it to the Background.
3. Recolor, resize, and relocate it somewhere else. Paste it to the Background again.
4. Do this until you have created an interesting pattern of multi-colored rectangular shapes. Render the composition (making sure Background Picture is selected in the Render Options dialog) and save to disk (see Figure 8.1).

Using Paste to Background techniques is one of the only ways you can use Poser 3 as a painting application to create bitmaps that can be applied to other Poser 3 elements.

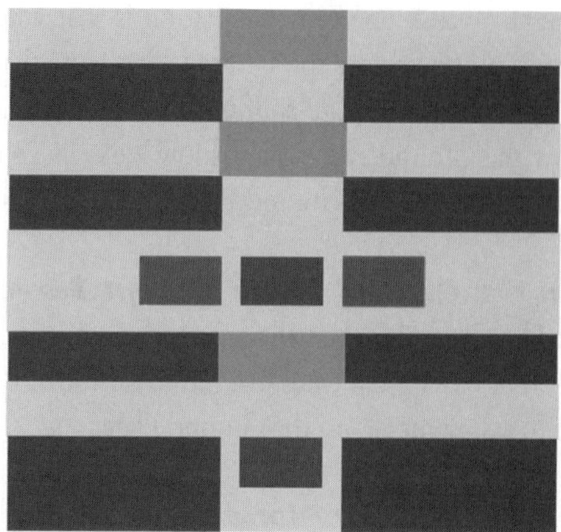

FIGURE 8.1 *The result of your pattern explorations might resemble this image.*

OBLIQUE ABSTRACTED PATTERNS

The method above creates horizontal/vertical grid-like patterns. If you want to create oblique patterns using a version of the same method, do the following:

1. Make sure the Dolly Camera is selected. Turn on the Ground Plane from the Guides listing in the Display menu.
2. Use the Dolly XYZ, Yaw/Pitch/Roll, and Scaling parameter Dials to adjust the view so that you create an oblique view of the Ground Plane. Paste it into the Background.
3. Do this as many times as needed to create a series of oblique trapezoids, as seen from the Dolly Camera view.
4. When you get something you like, render and save it to disk. Make sure Background Picture is selected in the Render Options dialog (see Figure 8.2).

One Step Farther

When you've finished creating your patterned backgrounds, you can use them as texture maps for the Ground Plane (see Figures 8.3 and 8.4).

SHADOW F/X

Optical Illusions sometimes add viewer interest, because the eye and mind are puzzled and attracted to seeing the impossible. Shadow effect can contribute to optical illusion constructs.

FIGURE 8.2 *Here's an example of oblique pattern development, using the technique described.*

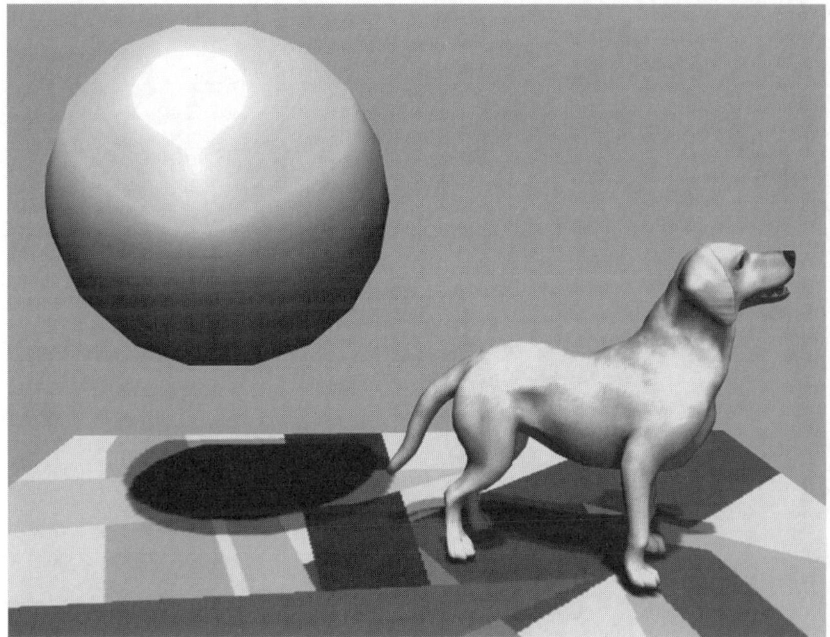

FIGURE 8.3 *The oblique pattern is shown here lapped to the Ground Plane.*

Shadow Letters and Logos

Construct a letter prop out of cube Props, or import a letter object in one of the formats that Poser 3 accepts. Make sure shadows are on. Turn on Shadows in the Render dialog as well. Place the object out of view on the Y (vertical) axis, so all you can see in the Document is its shadow. Try rendering this image with a dark shadow on a light Ground Plane, and as a light shadow on a dark Ground Plane. If you explore the placement of the elements carefully, you'll be able to cast a shadow of a word or even a logo on the Ground Plane and anything else that's resting on it. See Figures 8.5 and 8.6.

Rendering an object profile as a Silhouette and pasting that to the background does basically this same thing.

Shadow Spotlights

When does a Shadow suffice as a Spotlight? When it is much lighter than the Ground Plane and the other elements in a Poser 3 Document. There is a way

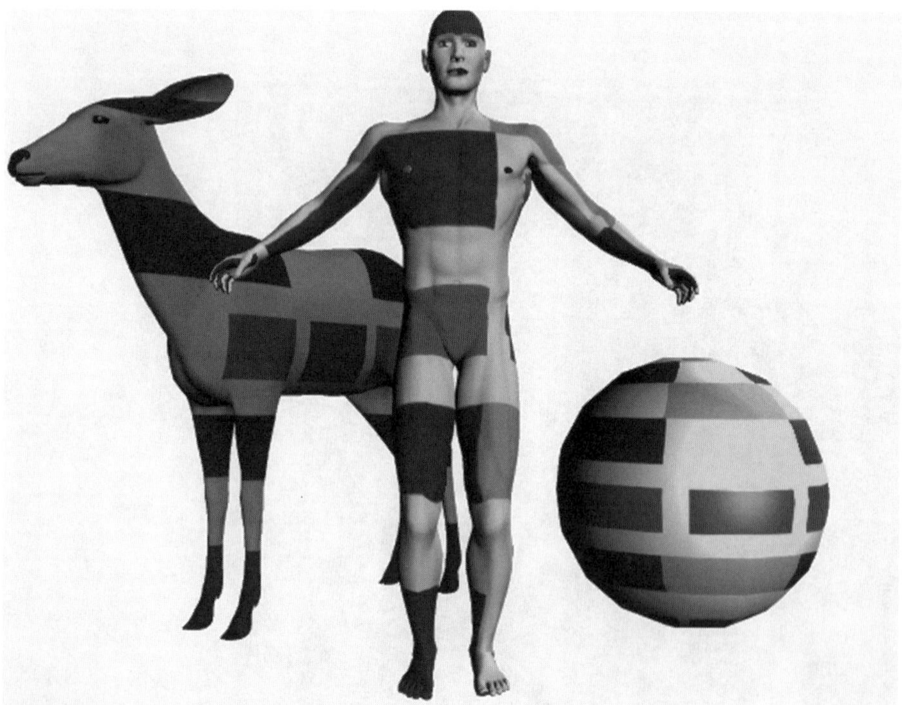

FIGURE 8.4 *The rectangular pattern is shown mapped to a Deer, a Heroic figure, and a Ball Prop.*

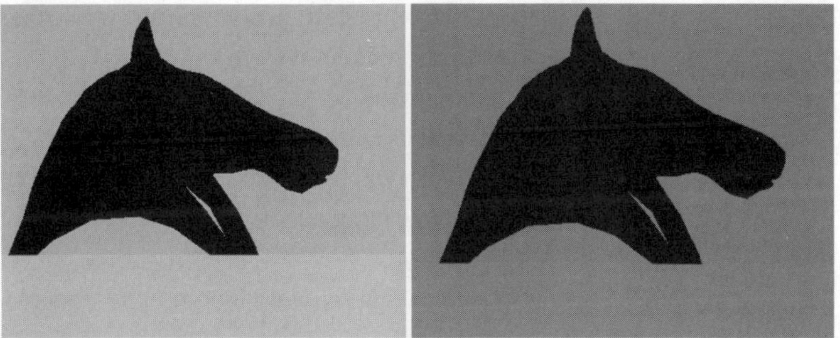

FIGURE 8.5 *Here is the Zygote Bullhead Prop, casting a shadow on a Ground Plane. The view was Pasted to the Background and the Prop removed. Poser 3 can be used to develop logos using this same shadow method, and the saved images can then be mapped to figures or Props. On the right the saved image is mapped to a Ball Prop.*

FIGURE 8.6 *We can paste the new logo into the background as many times as we like, using it to texture a Ground Plane or any other selected item later on. The image on the right shows a Zygote Lion figure, surrounded by elements mapped with the texture we just developed.*

that you can achieve this effect in Poser 3, remembering that the Displayed image does not show what light and shadows really look like when rendered, so a screen capture application is sometimes needed if you like what you see in the Document Display. Do the following:

1. Create a Ground Plane colored black.
2. Place a large ball over it, so that the ball is centered out of sight at the top.

3. Make sure Shadows are turned on in the Display menu and that the Shadow Color is set to white.
4. Move the lights so that they shine down from above the scene. You should see a white oval on a black ground.
5. When you have the view you want, use your screen capture application to grab just the Document window, avoiding any outlines of the window itself.
6. From your capture application, save out the image in a format that Poser 3 can read.
7. Import the image into Poser 3 as a Background. Place any figure you want over it, and the figure will appear to be in a spotlight (see Figure 8.7).

There are a number of screen capture applications that you can use to grab a portion of a screen. Flash comes to mind for the Mac and PaintShop Pro for Windows systems. Search them out on the Web by looking up "Grab" or "Capture," or ask your friends what they use and recommend.

Backgrounds

Imagine that you are standing in front of the painting of the Mona Lisa. There is a certain impression you take away when viewing this painting, caused by all of the elements in the image, including its background composition and col-

FIGURE 8.7 *Using the technique described above, we have forced a Ball object (out of view at the top) to cast a white shadow on a black Ground Plane, and then the Document window was captured and saved. The figure was rendered over the image after it was read back in.*

oring. Now imagine that the background is a scene of New York traffic. Her smile just doesn't seem the same, does it. Perhaps it has changed from an impression of satisfaction to a more sardonic look. But nothing in the smile has changed at all. It is the alteration of the background that has lent a whole new emotion to the image.

An image excites emotion because of the proximity and content of all of the elements contained within it. Backgrounds are not arbitrary, but play a large role in how we interpret the deeper meaning of the image as a whole. See Figure 8.8.

SINGLE COLOR BACKGROUNDS

Just use the eyedropper attached to the Background Color button to bring up a system palette, select a color, and that's it. A few things to remember about what color to choose will serve you well:

- Select white if you plan to print your work, since that saves on ink used for the background color.
- Select black for work to be transferred to tape, since it pops out the images better for video and multimedia and also lends a better 3D look to the composition.
- Select a color NOT present in your Document elements if you plan to use Alpha compositing to drop the background out.
- If you want to emphasize the colors in the rest of your Document, select a background color that is the compliment of the dominant color in your work. For instance, if you have a lot of pink, red, or brown skin tones, use a green background color. If you have blue tones that dominate your composition, the complimentary color would be orange. The basic Complimentaries are red/green, blue/orange, and violet/yellow.

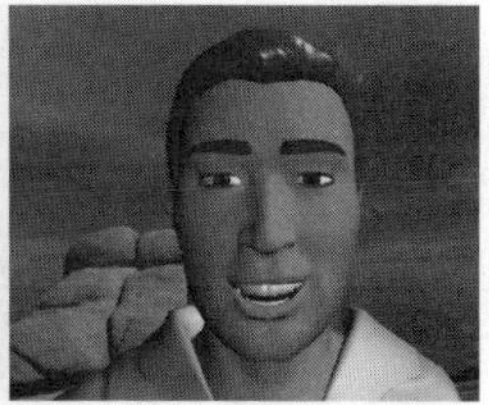

FIGURE 8.8 *Here, the same foreground Poser 3 face is superimposed over different backgrounds, allowing you to experience how important a role background content can be.*

COLOR GRADIENT BACKGROUNDS

There is no way to create gradient backgrounds in Poser 3 directly, so it means developing them in an outside application. Use any bitmap painting application that offers gradations (Photoshop, PhotoPaint, Paint Shop Pro, Painter) and create a gradient with the size and resolution that fits your Poser 3 project. Then simply import it as a background Picture.

Karuna! NEVER use a gradient background if you plan to Alpha composite your Poser 3 output.

PHOTOGRAPHIC BACKGROUNDS

You can add an amazing amount of realism to your Poser 3 work if the background is photographic. Your audience may well wonder if the figures they are seeing are virtual or real. Select your photographic background imagery to enhance the mood you're trying to create. One of my favorite background themes is clouds, which seems to enhance almost any foreground pose or animation. There are hundreds of stock image CD collections that feature just about any theme you can imagine.

Karuna! When using images that come from a purchased CD collection, make sure that they are not copyrighted, and that they say in clear bold type that you may use them on your own projects without paying a fee.

MOVIES AS BACKGROUNDS

Poser 3 allows you to select an AVI (Windows) or a QuickTime (Mac and Windows) movie file as the background for your compositions. Sometimes, the foreground doesn't have to move at all to create an interesting final composite using this alternative. If you face your figure so that its back is facing the camera, for instance, and it is rotated so that it seems to be flying into the screen, you can use animated footage in the background to give the scene a real sense of flying motion. This is, in fact, the exact way superheroes take flight in film work, by being composited against a background in motion.

It's very important to remember that any animation that you create in Poser 3 can itself become a background animation for use with additional foreground figures and props. Doing this several times in a row results in very complex animations with several layers of interest. See Section II for more details on the animation process.

USING YOUR DIGITAL CAMERA, SCANNER, AND VIDEO CAMERA

You have at your disposal some awesome graphic power if you own a scanner and/or a digital still or video camera. Remember that the whole idea behind computer graphics and animation is to integrate them seamlessly with the video medium. Computer graphics and animation began as a way of initiating interactive television.

If you plan to use your video sequences as a Poser 3 background, you'll need all of the devices that allow you to connect your camera to the computer. This usually consists of an interface that reads in the analog video signal on one end and outputs digital video to the computer on the other. Check with your camera manufacturer to get the details and pricing.

Using your scanner to develop Poser 3 background footage is a simpler matter, since it is already connected to your computer. Just make sure you resize the images captured so that they fit the Poser 3 Document size you're using.

Karuna! When using images that are scanned from printed copy, make sure they are not copyrighted. The best assurance you have of this is to scan in photos you have taken yourself.

Props

We've already looked at props in some detail in Chapter 7, especially concerning their ability to modify a figure. In this chapter we'll stretch your knowledge of ways to use and modify Props in your Poser 3 compositions.

HATS AND THEIR MODIFICATION

What is a hat? Instead of defining a hat as a Prop that is shaped like a commonly accepted geometry of a hat, let's open it up a bit. For creative purposes, a hat is anything you can place on the head of a figure. Some Props, like a chair, will create a rather bizarre hat, so there is degree and extent. Other Props, like a Box or a Ball, may suffice as hats in certain circumstances (see Figure 8.9).

Composited Hats from Basic Props

You can use any number of Props to create your own composite hats (see Figure 8.10). Just make sure the parenting is in the correct order. The lowest member of the group should have the Head as its Parent, and the other members of the hat group can then be parented to each other.

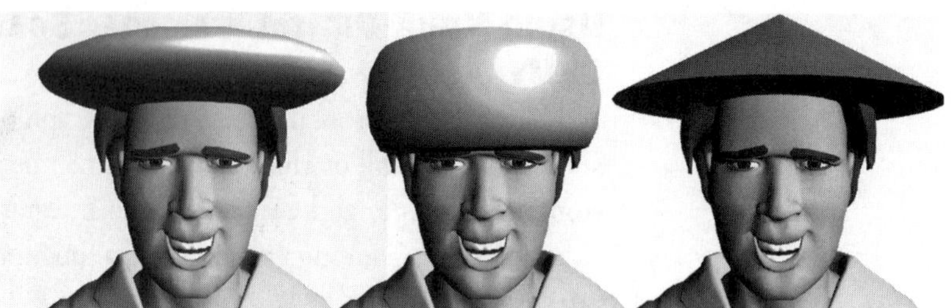

FIGURE 8.9 *Various basic Props, resized, and placed as hats (Ball, Torus, and Cone). The Head is selected as the Parent of the Prop.*

FIGURE 8.10 *Left to right: Top hat created from two cylinders; Wizard's hat from a Cone and squashed Torus; hat created from two Stairs Props, a Ball, and a Torus.*

CREATING STRANGE HAIR PROPS

In Chapter 7, we've already looked at how Hair Props, from the Hair library or the Zygote extras CD, can be resized and composited with other Hair Props. There are yet other ways we can create Hair Props from non-Hair Props. In Chapter 17, when we look at exporting Poser 3 elements to Ray Dream, we'll discover even more radical ways to develop hair Props.

Internal Props for Hair

It's easy to create the famous Marge Simpson look in Poser 3. All you need to do is to stack a series of balls on the head of a figure, making sure that each is parented to the next and that the bottom one has for its Parent the head of the figure (see Figure 8.11).

Hair from Zygote Not-Hair

In the Zygote Extras Props library, in the Sampler folder, is a Prop called House Plant. It makes interesting, though radically contemporary, Hair (see Figure 8.12).

FIGURE 8.11 *Marge, eat your heart out! A single, double, and quadruple beehive hairdo*

FIGURE 8.12 *The Zygote House Plant Prop presents a more radical hairpiece.*

If we can use a plant as a Hair substitute, can a tree be far behind? In the same Sampler folder is a Prop called Tree. It too can be used as a rather alien-looking Hair Prop (see Figure 8.13).

BUILDING PROP VEHICLES FROM INTERNAL ELEMENTS

You can import all manner of Props from external sources in any format that Poser 3 recognizes. But you can also challenge your creative potential by constructing Props from elements in the standard Poser Props libraries. Here are just a few examples.

FIGURE 8.13 *The whole Zygote Tree Prop can be used as a strange hair element.*

The Wagon

You can construct basic composite Props using the simplest of elements from the Prop Types folder in the Props library. This wagon uses three Boxes, four Cylinders, and two Canes. Look at Figures 8.14 and 8.15 and see if you can construct this wagon to closely match the illustrations. As a hint, the wheels are Cylinders whose X dimension has been resized to 15%.

The wagon may be pretty basic, but once you add an animal pulling it and a rider and include a background image, the whole scene looks almost photorealistic. The Zygote Zebra and Heavy man have been added here, and the Zygote Cowboy Hat Prop sits on his head (see Figure 8.16).

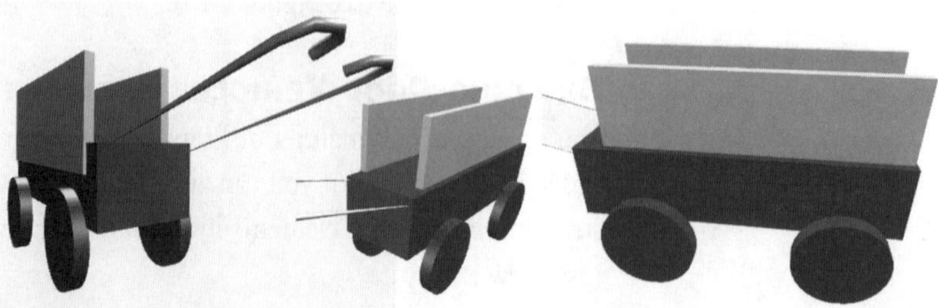

FIGURE 8.14 *All of the parts of the wagon use the main body as the Parent.*

FIGURE 8.15 *One last touch might be to add two elongated Cylinder Props as wheel axles.*

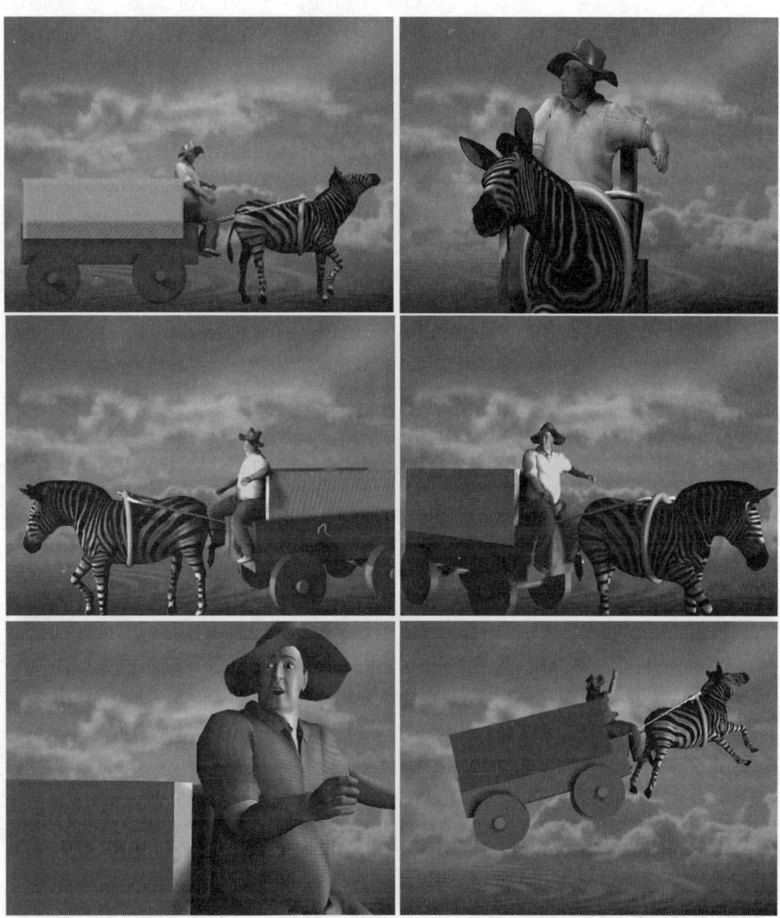

FIGURE 8.16 *Adding a rider and a transport animal, the basic wagon Prop blends into the image quite well.*

The Basic Biplane Composite Prop

CAUTION

Karuna! When you are using multiple Props to build a composite model, the very first thing you should do, before altering any dimensions or rotating the Prop, is to attach it to its correct Parent. Otherwise, if you alter it first, it will warp out when parented later.

It's amazing what one Prop can provide. Resizing it on its various axis allows you to construct an infinite number of shapes. This is what was done to create the Biplane Composite Prop. Only the Cylinder Prop was used. The main fuselage is the parent of everything except the propeller. The parent of the propeller is the hub on which it sits, so it can be animated to spin in space. Different views of the Cylinder-constructed Biplane are provided in Figure 8.17. Study this illustration, and use it to construct your own version of the Biplane Prop.

After you've finished the Biplane Prop, place a Poser 3 Head (from the Additional Figures folder) in the cockpit and render a few images (see Figure 8.18).

The Ear-Boat

See Figure 8.19.

FIGURE 8.17 *Study these illustrations carefully and use them as a blueprint to construct the Cylinder-based Biplane Prop.*

FIGURE 8.18 *Adding a Head and a Background image completes the scenario.*

INTERNAL REPLACEMENT PROPS

You can replace every body part of a figure with a prop. All you have to do is to place as many Props on the screen as there are parts of the figure and put them in position over the body element they are to substitute for. Next, with each body part selected in turn, go to Replace Body Part With Prop in the Figure menu. When the dialog appears, simply select the Prop that will be replacing that body part (see Figure 8.20).

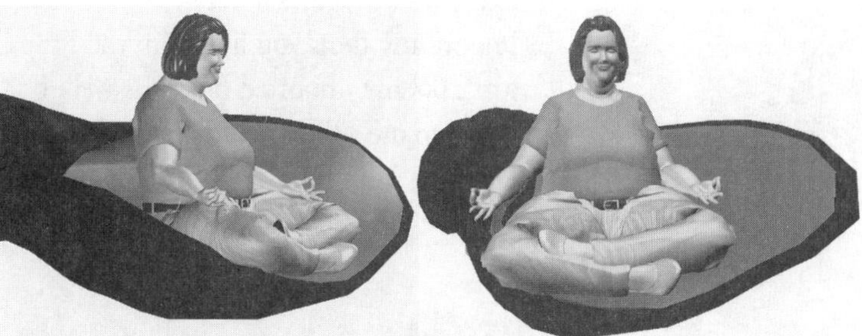

FIGURE 8.19 *The Zygote Heavy Woman model sits in meditation inside of a Cow's Ear boat.*

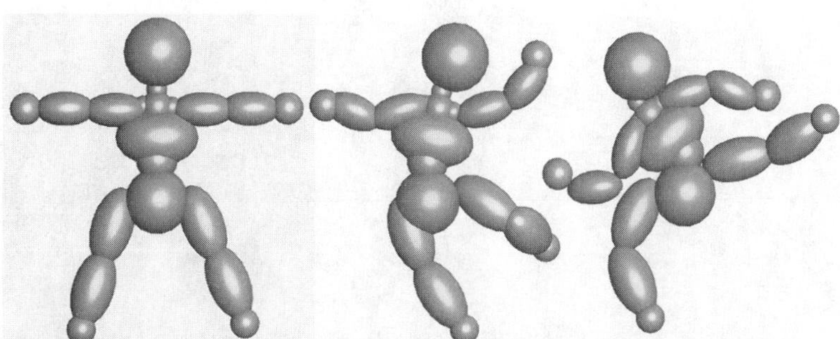

FIGURE 8.20 *This Sphere being was created by replacing all of the body parts of a Stick Figure with Ball Props. It can be posed like any other figure.*

NOTE

If you plan to replace all of the body parts with Props, make sure to use the Stick Figure or Mannequin figures as a base. Neither have finger joints, so the replacements are simpler. Of course, if you plan to use Posed hands, then you'll have to use an initial figure that has finger joint elements.

CAUTION

Karuna! Karuna! Karuna! What could be so important that it deserves a Triple Karuna notice? Just this . . . under normal circumstances, when you bring a Prop into your Document, you cannot use the Taper operation on it. This is too bad, since it robs you of a way to create some interesting new shapes. However, when you use any Prop to replace a body part, it can now be tapered. This can lead to all sorts of new figure looks! See Figure 8.21.

How to Use Taper on Any Stand-alone Prop

Here's a way to do the impossible, to use the Taper operation on any Prop you import. Just do the following:

1. Place a Head in your Document window (from the Additional Figures folder in the Figures library).
2. Import any Prop you like from the Prop library. You can force this to work on any imported object as well, but the results are often erratic. Better to use a Prop already in the Props Library.
3. Place the Prop directly over the Head, covering it. Click on the Head,

FIGURE 8.21 *When a Prop is used to replace a body part, you can use the Taper operation on it. This is not something you can do on an ordinary Prop. All of the elements you see here are tapered Ball Props.*

and select Replace Body Part With Prop from the Figure menu. Replace the Head with the named Prop from the list.

4. Make both Eyes invisible. Select the Prop, which is now called Head, and use the Taper Parameter Dial to taper it as you like. See Figures 8.22 and 8.23.

FIGURES (AND PARTIAL FIGURES) AS PROPS

Just as you can use Props to replace body parts and give the Props movement and poses, so too you can perform the reverse action. Body parts can be used as interesting Props in your compositions. Here are a few ways to do it.

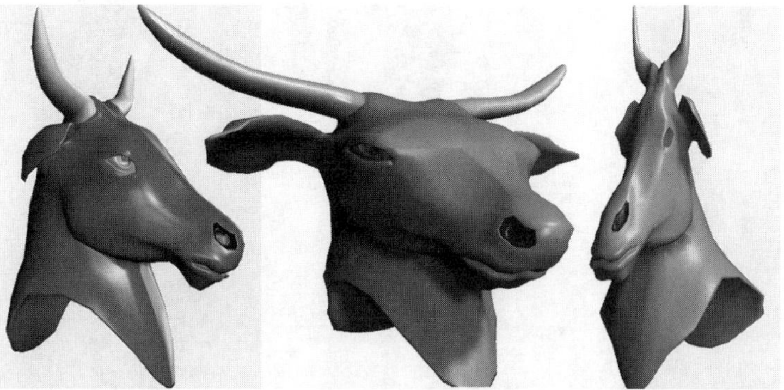

FIGURE 8.22 *Any Prop can be customized with a Taper by using the method described. The Zygote Bullhead Prop is on the left, and its Tapered versions on the right.*

FIGURE 8.23 *The tapered Bullhead Prop used over a nude male model, replacing the Head. Different Tapers create different personalities.*

Statues

Take any figure, pose it, and put it on a Cylinder or a Box, and you have an instant statue. Remove the figure's texture map, and colorize all of its parts with the same color (see Figures 8.24 and 8.25).

Hand Chairs

One of the most popular contemporary pieces of furniture in recent years has been the molded hand-chair from Sweden. Poser 3 allows you to create your

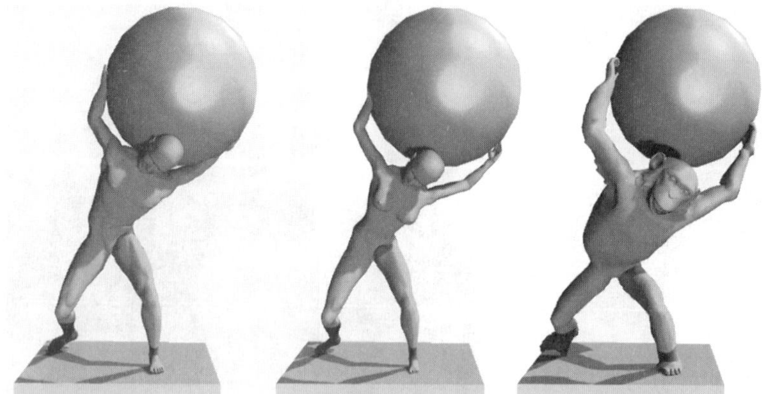

FIGURE 8.24 *Any figure can be used as a posed Prop Statue.*

FIGURE 8.25 *Imported into Bryce as an OBJ file, the statue can be cloned and textured.*

own. Simply import a hand from the Additional Figures folder in the Figure library, pose it, and place a seated model on it (see Figure 8.26).

Table Legs

If the museum you visit has an Egyptian or a medieval furniture collection, you're bound to see some tables with carved animal legs. Poser 3 allows you to create this furniture style as well. Just select the animal you want and make everything invisible but its legs and feet. Save it to disk and then import another pair. Place as needed and attach a Prop table top (either a squashed Box or Cylinder). See Figure 8.27.

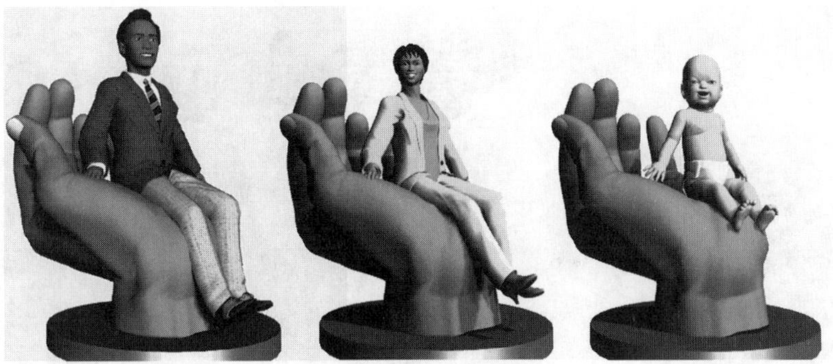

FIGURE 8.26 *The Hand Chair is a comfortable place to rest.*

FIGURE 8.27 *A table with carved animal legs.*

Doorway

In the same manner used to develop the table in Figure 8.27, we can develop a doorway frame by using the arms of a human or animal model. See Figure 8.28.

The Oracle

One of the most evocative fables in mythology is that of the severed head that lives to prophesy the future. Sometimes, the head is embedded in a rock or a crystal, and sometimes it sits alone on a table. Poser 3 has all the tools you need to create this mythic object. Just import a Head from the Additional Figures folder in the Figures library. Decide whether you want to embed it into a Box or Sphere, or another Prop, and make that Prop the parent of the Head. See Figure 8.29.

FIGURE 8.28 *The arms of a Zygote Chimpanzee model were used to create this doorway.*

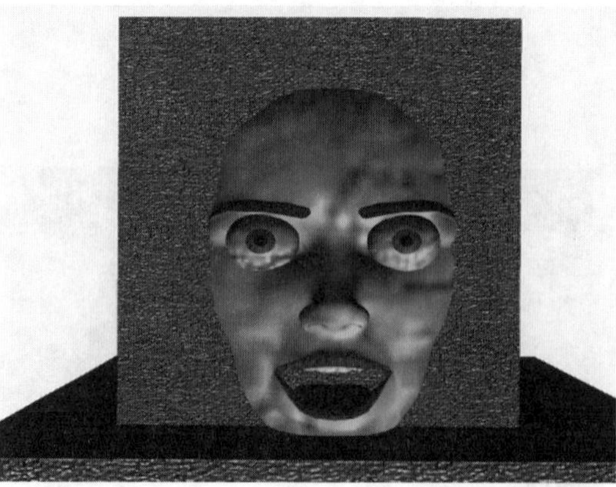

FIGURE 8.29 *The talking head is a marvel to behold. Everything uses the Ground Default texture. The Eyes are resized to 280% and moved forward on the Z axis by .005.*

CREATIVE RENDERING

NOTE

When rendering to disk, especially for multimedia sizes (320 × 240), your Display Renders will look just about as good as the Render Settings renders. The difference is that Display Renderings often render 3 to 5 times faster. Just make sure that the Display render selection is on its highest option. Keep this in mind when time is a consideration.

USING RENDER STYLES

Refer to Table 8.1 for ideas on where to use various Render Styles. Also see Figure 8.30.

NOTE

You can only render these styles in three ways: You can use the Make Movie operation with Display Settings selected, you can grab the image with a screen grab application, or you can Export the image from the File menu. No other rendering method will allow you to render in these styles.

FINISHED RENDERING

When you are ready to render final images to a file, the Render dialog offers you a number of options. We present these options in Table 8.2, along with their uses.

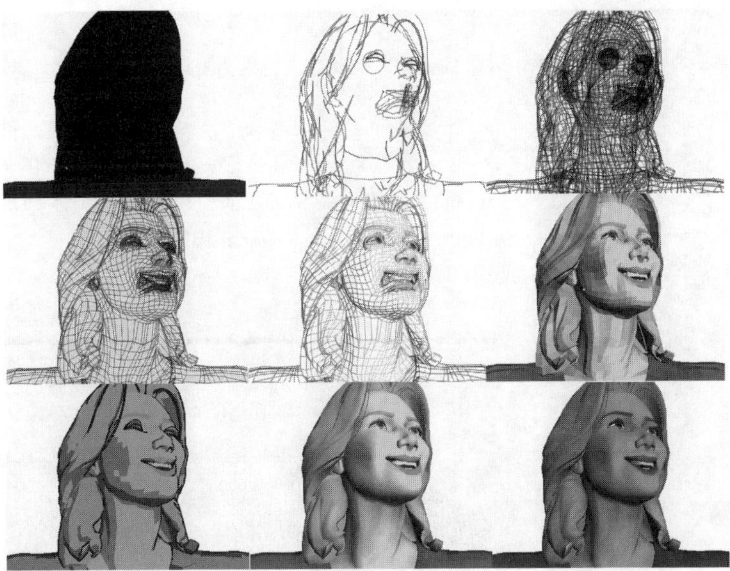

FIGURE 8.30 *Figure 8.30 left top to right bottom: Silhouette, Outline, Wireframe, Hidden Line, Lit Wireframe, Flat Shaded, Sketch, Smooth Shaded, and Texture Shaded Render Styles of the same image.*

Table 8.1 You can select from amongst Render Styles to create looks for different uses in Poser 3.

Rendering Style	Media Look	Uses
Silhouette	Filled-in Silhouette	Use this style when you want to see just the silhouette of the image or animation. This is the option to use when you want to create an Alpha matte of the Document, useful in After Effects and other media effects applications.
Outline	Quick Pencil Sketch	This style resembles what animators call a "pencil test." It's also useful for exporting to a paint application and applying color or textures there.
Wireframe	Complex Ink Sketch	This style allows you to see all of the data on all of the layers of the Document. Use it when you want to create a structural blueprint of the image.
Hidden Line	3D Ink Sketch	This style drops out data hidden by the frontmost layers. Use it to create a more eye-friendly structural image than the Wireframe style.
Lit Wireframe	Colored Pencil	This style creates beautiful colored pencil Rotoscopes of the data for use in single images or animations.
Flat Shaded	Faceted 3D Look	When you want a faceted look, this is the style option to select.
Sketch	Very Cartoony—Looks Like a Wash Media	This is the style to target when you want to create a 2D cartoon look.
Smooth Shaded	Default 3D	This is the default Display style.
Texture Shaded	Textured 3D	Click on this style to get a pretty authentic preview of the textures applied to your Document elements.

Table 8.2 Finished Rendering options and uses.

Rendering Options	Uses
Main/New Window	Most of the time, you'll want to render in a New Window, because that allows you more options for size and resolution. You can do quick test renders by selecting Main Window.
Width/Height	The width and height of your rendered output is based upon a proportional size related to your display size. Pixels is the standard measure, though you may also select Inches or Centimeters (only when New Window is selected).
Resolution	Select 72 DPI for video and multimedia, and at least 300 DPI for print purposes.
Antialias	As a rule, leave this checked on. Jaggies are bad news, and Poser 3 renders fast enough to warrant Antialiasing even for previews.
Use Bump Maps	If you have Bump Mapped Textures in the Document, check this option.
Use Texture Maps	If you have Texture Maps in the Document, check this option.
Cast Shadows	This is the one option that can slow down your rendering dramatically. Check it for more realistic output that displays the shadows related to the three light sources and their blended colors.
Background Options	Your three choices are Background Color, Black, or Background Picture. If you have a Background Picture (or animation) loaded, select this choice. Black makes video output look a lot more three dimensional. Printed images should have a light or white backdrop as a Background Color.

Moving Along

In this chapter, we have explored backgrounds and Props and how to customize and modify their parameters. We also looked at Render Styles and options in the Render dialog. The next chapter of the book begins Section II, which is dedicated to animation in Poser 3.

SECTION

Poser 3 Animation

Poser has evolved from a 2D graphics utility in Poser 1, through a user friendly animation toy in Poser 2, to a full professional art and animation masterpiece in Poser 3. What began as an application dedicated to supporting 2D painting, but allowing you to import 3D posed figures into Photoshop and Painter so they could be painted on, has risen far from its roots. Not that you can't use Poser 3 renders for that very same purpose, but Poser 3 boasts animation capabilities no other software at any price can compete with. All of this has been accomplished in a creative environment with a very easy learning curve, so that beginners and professionals alike can create startling animated figures in just a few minutes. Chapters 9 to 15 are dedicated to various animation options and techniques.

Animation Controls

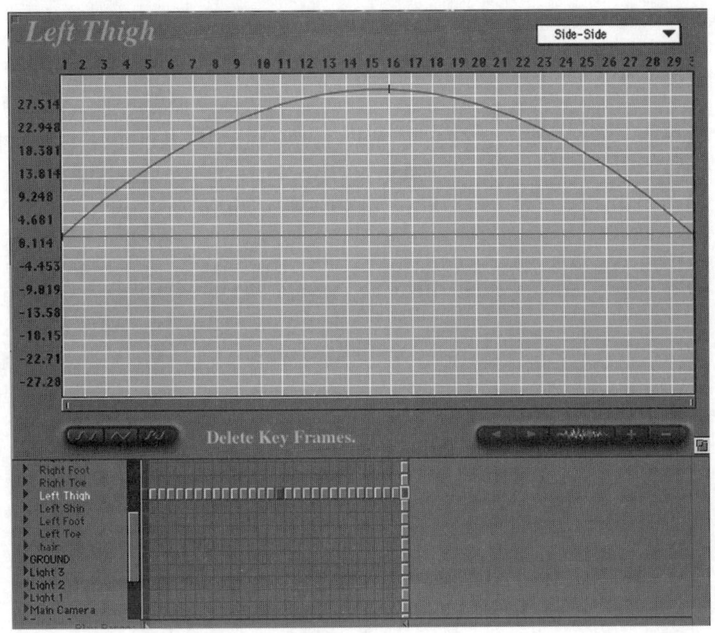

The Idea behind Keyframing

The terms *keyframe* and *keyframing* are buzz words heard a lot around animation studios. Traditionally, there are two classes of animators: Keyframers and Tweeners. A Keyframer is an artist who draws the main poses in an animated sequence, while the Tweener fills in all of the frames, the "in-betweens," from one keyframe to the next. Both take a lot of work and a lot of thought. When the computer came on the animation scene, everyone began to realize that the manual labor of tweening was about to be replaced by a non-human approach. As a number cruncher and data analyzer, the computer rules. In a computer animation application, all that the computer needs is an indication of where the keyframes, the main poses, are. From there, all of the in-betweens can be interpolated mathematically, so there is smooth motion from one keyframe to the next. The main job of the Poser 3 animator, then, is to set up the keyframe poses. This is not always as easy as it sounds.

A walk cycle is the most common example of this. In a walk cycle, several things are happening at the same time. Legs are in motion, joints are bending, arms are swinging, the torso may be bending or swaying from side to side, and the head may be bobbing around. The best way to handle keyframes is to get the gross movements under control first, and then move to the finer motion attributes. In a walk cycle, the simplest way to do this is to set keyframes that show the left leg at its forward most position, and the right arm at its backward most position at the first frame. Then set the middle keyframe with the right leg at its most forward position, and the left arm at its most backward position. The last keyframe would be a repeat of the first frame, so that the animation could loop and show the cycle repeating (see Figure 9.1).

We'll have more information on walk cycles in Chapter 14, when we take a detailed look at the Walk Designer, and when we explore the uses of IK (Inverse Kinematics) later in this chapter. For now, let's look at the modules that allow us to set keyframes and associated animation menu commands in Poser 3.

FIGURE 9.1 *The standard keyframe poses in a walk cycling animation.*

CAUTION

Karuna! The trick behind good keyframing is to use only enough keyframes to accomplish the movement you want. Keyframing every frame makes it very difficult to edit a frame, because it can lead to jumpy movements in the surrounding frames.

Two Animation Control Environments

Poser 3 features two separate but linked control environments in which animations can be composed and edited: the Animation Controller and the Animation Palette.

THE ANIMATION CONTROLLER

The Animation Controller is located at the bottom of the Poser 3 screen and is brought up by clicking on its control bar (see Figure 9.2).

Let's spend a little time looking at each element on the Animation Controller interface, describing what each of the components does.

At the top left are the VCR controls. These are used to locate any frame in an animation sequence, and to play/stop a Preview Animation (see Figure 9.3).

At the center are two input areas: a Frame counter that tells you what frame you are at and the total number of frames in the sequence. To set the number of total frames in a sequence just click in this second area and type in the number of frames you want. By the way, if you attempt to enter a number in the frame field that is higher than the number of frames in the animation, you will get an error message that states that your number is out of range. The very first thing you should do when starting to configure an animation is to set the total number of frames you want. Remember that the Frame Rate (frames per second) will determine how much time the animation will take to run once through (see Figure 9.4).

At the top-right of the Animation Controller are controls for setting and maneuvering keyframes (see Figure 9.5).

FIGURE 9.2 *The Animation Controller.*

FIGURE 9.3 *The VCR controls, left to right, are First Frame, Last Frame, Stop, Play, Previous Frame, and Next Frame.*

FIGURE 9.4 *The Frame Counter and Number of Frames indicators.*

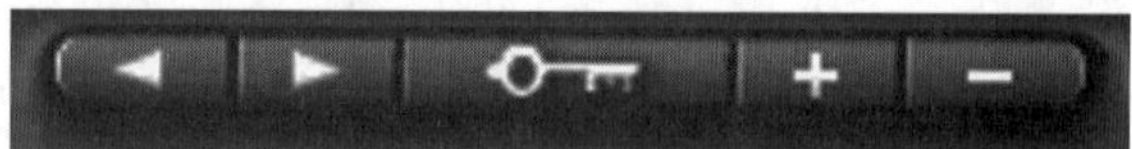

FIGURE 9.5 *These controls, from left to right, do the following: Previous Keyframe, Next Keyframe, Edit Keyframes (brings up the Animation Palette), Add Keyframe, and Delete Keyframe.*

Note that Previous and Next Keyframe will take you to the frame for the selected element. If that element has no keyframes, you will not move to another frame.

At the bottom left the word "Loop" appears. There is a small light next to it. Clicking on this area turns the light on or off. When on, your preview animation will play over and over again until manually shut off. If the light is off, the preview will only play once (see Figure 9.6).

In the center is the Interactive Frame Slider. Moving the frame indicator arrow allows you to go to any frame on the timeline. The Frame Number Indicator above displays the frame number (see Figure 9.7).

Last, the Skip Frames Indicator is on the bottom right (see Figure 9.8). This toggle allows the preview to play the keyframes or every frame in the sequence.

FIGURE 9.6 *The Loop Indicator.*

FIGURE 9.7 *The Interactive Frame Slider.*

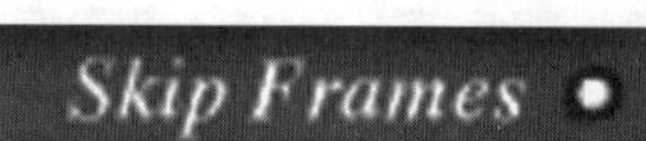

FIGURE 9.8 *The Skip Frames Indicator.*

Animation Controller Hints and Tips

When using the Animation Controller, here are some things to keep in mind:

- Always set the number of frames first, realizing that the number, when divided by the frames per second rate, gives you the runtime of the animation.
- As a default, keep looping on. When a preview runs a few times, you can see flaws more clearly, then find the offending frame(s), and make necessary corrections.
- You seldom have to use the "+" key to create a keyframe, as every time you adjust an element in the document window, a keyframe is created automatically. I sometimes use it as a "paranoid factor," just to make doubly sure that a keyframe has been made at a certain frame. Using the "-" key, however, is a different matter, since removing offending keyframes is often necessary to get the exact movements you want.
- Assign your gross movements first and preview the results. Then add finer motions, previewing as you go. Set the Skip Frames to off so you can see the details in the preview.

THE ANIMATION PALETTE

Clicking on the Key Symbol in the Animation Controller brings up the Animation Palette, which has its own definitive controls for editing the animation (see Figure 9.9).

Karuna! This section on the Animation Palette is a refresher that points out some of the important elements. It is not a substitute for reading and working through the Poser 3 documentation and tutorials on this topic.

Just as we did with the Animation Controller, let's walk through each of the elements that makes up the Animation Palette.

Our first stop is at the bottom of the palette. You should see a green line with an arrow on each end. This represents the Play Range of the animation. You can move the right arrow to the right until it reaches the last frame in the sequence and to the left to any frame before that. You can move the left arrow to the right to any frame before the right arrow, and to the left as far as the first frame. Limiting the play range allows you to preview a sequence of any length, which is very useful for catching and correcting unwanted glitches (see Figure 9.10).

Our next stop on the tour of the Animation Palette is the center area. You will notice a long list of items on the left, representing every element in your

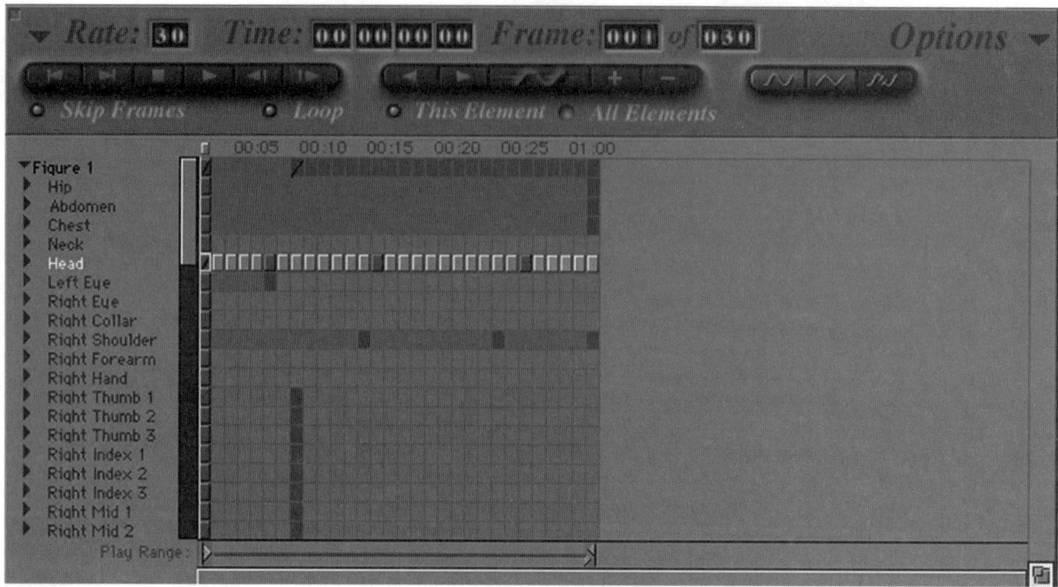

FIGURE 9.9 *The Animation Palette.*

FIGURE 9.10 *The interactive Play Range indicator.*

Document window. Highlighting any element by clicking on its name will also highlight all of its frames to the right of the name, which turn white. Green frames indicate that there are some keyframes already set for that element and that they are Spline Interpolated. Red frame indicators tell you exactly where the keyframes are located. Pinkish frames indicate that a Linear Interpolation is going on. You can click on any frame to highlight it, and the resulting vertical highlighted column tells you exactly what each element is doing at that particular frame. If any element in the vertical stack is red, it is a keyframed element. If it is green, it is an element in motion between keyframes (a tween). If it is white (or gray when not selected), it is stationary (see Figure 9.11).

Right above this frame area are four text-based controls: Skip Frames, Loop, This Element, and All Elements. The first two, Skip Frames and Loop, have already been adequately covered in our look at the Animation Controller. This Element and All Elements are two sides of one control, since selecting one in-

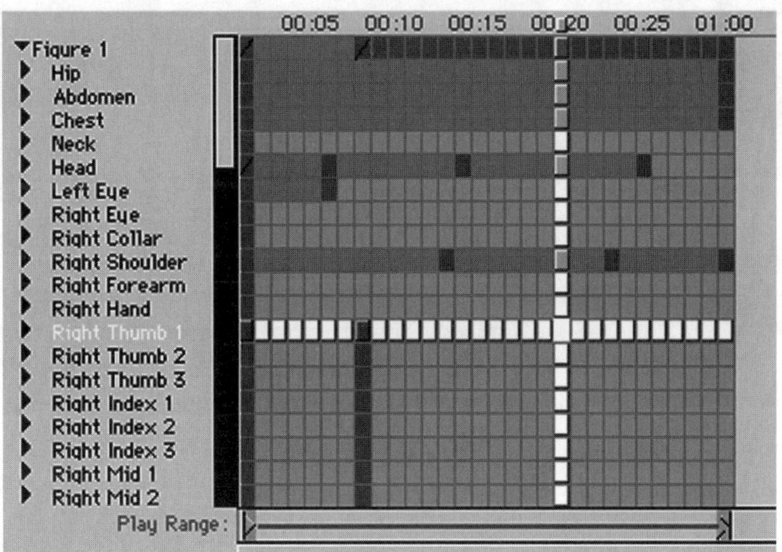

FIGURE 9.11 *The element list on the left and the frame indicators on the right.*

hibits the other. What are they used for? If you select any element frame in the frame area below, you will see a vertical highlighted stack, showing each element in your Document at that point in time. If you wanted to hit the plus key to make that frame a keyframe, or the minus key to delete it as a keyframe, it would matter if either This Element or All Elements were chosen. Selecting This Element would act to add or delete a keyframe for just that element. Selecting All Elements would add or delete keyframes for every element in the highlighted vertical stack (see Figure 9.12).

Above the text-based controls are three rows of buttons. The first is the familiar VCR controls already covered under the Animation Controller. The second row is also familiar, with the exception of the center button, which is unique to the Animation Palette. This center button, with the symbol of a squiggly line on top, is the Graph Display Toggle, which we'll detail in a few paragraphs. The third row contains three Interpolation buttons and is better left untouched, because these same three Interpolation buttons also appear in the Graph Display. They make more sense to use there. See Figure 9.13.

Skip Frames Loop This Element All Elements

FIGURE 9.12 *The most important commands here are the last two: This Element and All Elements, and how they each address keyframe alterations.*

FIGURE 9.13 *The three control groups of buttons: the VCR controls, the Keyframe controls, and the Interpolation controls.*

At the very top are the time and frame displays and the Options menu. The displays address Frame Rate (frames per second), Timecode indicator (Hour / Minute / Second / Frame), present Frame, and total number of Frames. This is a display, not meant to be altered. The Options list includes the following items that can be selected or deselected, simply by accessing them: Display Frames or Timecode, Loop Interpolation, and Quaternion Interpolation. Selecting either Frame Display or Timecode Display will use that system as a rule of measurement over the frame selection area. Loop Interpolation and Quaternion Interpolation are separate items, and both can be selected or deselected individually. See Figure 9.14.

The Graph Display

Clicking on the Graph Display button brings up the Graph Display for whatever item is selected in the hierarchy list. Readjusting the display via a Splined or Linear curve allows the selected element to have whatever priority is selected animated according to the shape of the curve. The properties include: Taper, Scale, Xscale, Yscale, Zscale, Twist, Side-to-Side, and Bend. If the Head is selected, all of the animatable elements can be edited via a motion graph. It takes practice to configure animations with the Graph Display of specific elements, so be prepared to spend some time learning the techniques. See Figure 9.15.

The best way to learn to configure animations with the Graph Display is to avoid setting any movement with the Animation Controller at first. Simply set the number of frames, jump onto a selected elements Graph Display, and modify the graph. Preview the animation to see what you've accomplished.

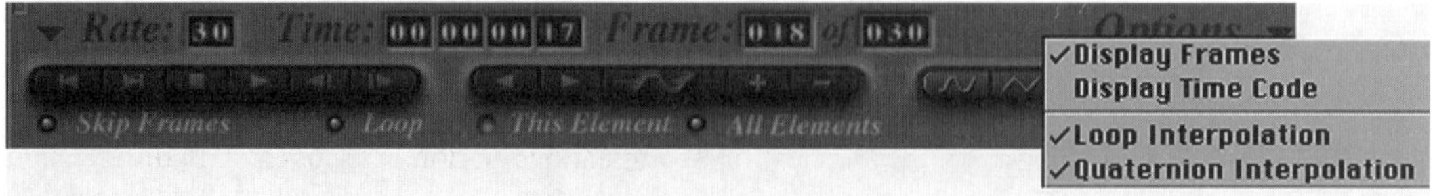

FIGURE 9.14 *The top row of display items and the Options menu.*

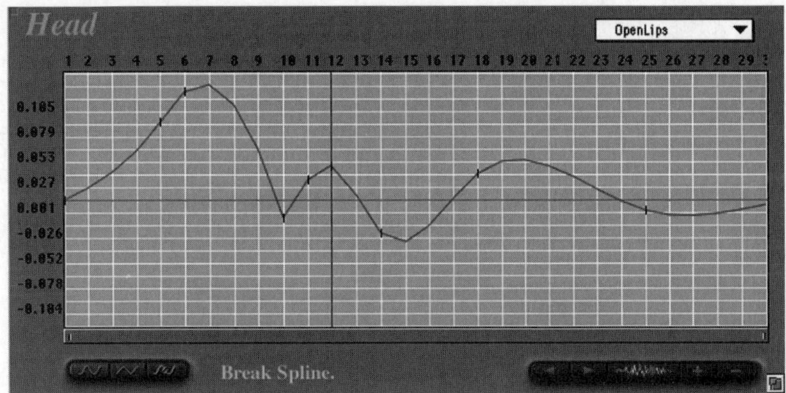

FIGURE 9.15 *The Graph Display modified to animate Lip Movements on a human model's Head.*

Using the Graph Display and altering Mouth attributes and Eye Blinks leads to more realistic movements and is 1000% faster than accomplishing the same animated poses via parameter dials.

Animating to Sound

If you will notice, the bottom right row of buttons on the Graph Display shows what appears to be a sound wave. Clicking on this button will bring up a visual display of a sound file, if one is loaded into the Document. By following the amplitude shape of the wave (where it is higher and lower) you can edit the motion curve of any selected element to move accordingly. In this manner, you can accomplish lip synching and other choreography.

The Animation Menu

The Animation menu at the top of your screen contains essential items that you must be aware of in order to creatively interact with your Poser 3 animations. Let's look at each of the listings in some detail. See Figure 9.16.

ANIMATION SETUP

This is where you configure the animation output settings, including Frame Rate, Output Size, Frame Count, and Duration. It's a lot easier to do this all in one place, rather than to address these parameters in a series of different locations. See Figure 9.17.

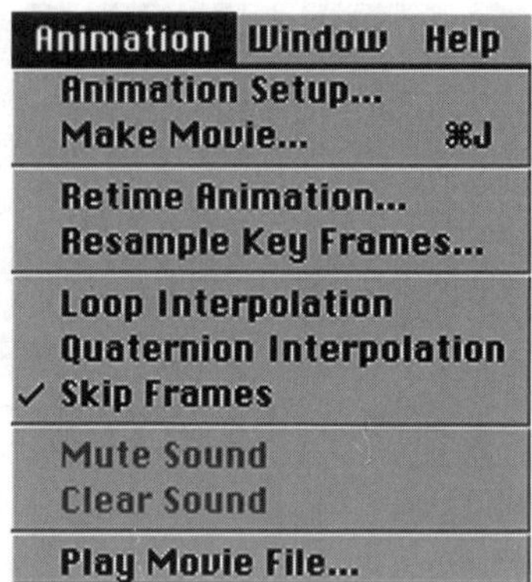

FIGURE 9.16 *The listings in the Animation Menu.*

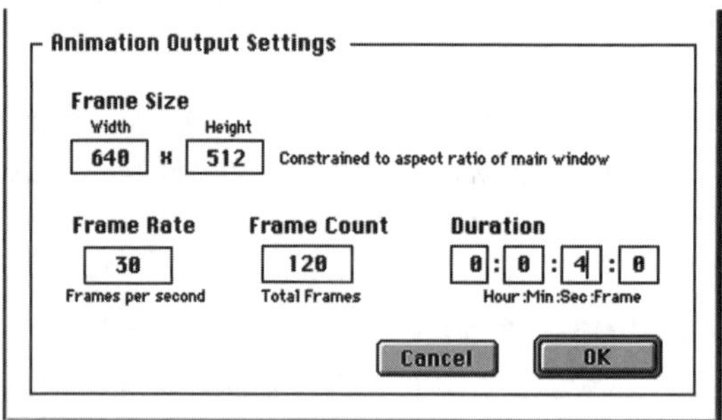

FIGURE 9.17 *The Animation Output Settings dialog.*

MAKE MOVIE

When you are ready to record your masterpiece, this is the doorway to enter. You'll be taken through three separate steps, each with its own dialog: Movie Parameter Settings, Compression Settings, and the Save Path dialog. When using compression, I prefer Cinepak at full quality, but you can explore other options. See Figure 9.18.

RETIME ANIMATION

You may decide that the animation has to fit into a different time slot and that you can't spare the time to reconfigure all of the keyframes. In that case, you can use this simple process to retime it from one length to another. See Figure 9.19.

RESAMPLE KEYFRAMES

When would you need to resample the keyframes? If you've done a lot of editing on separate elements in the animation and you notice that there are places

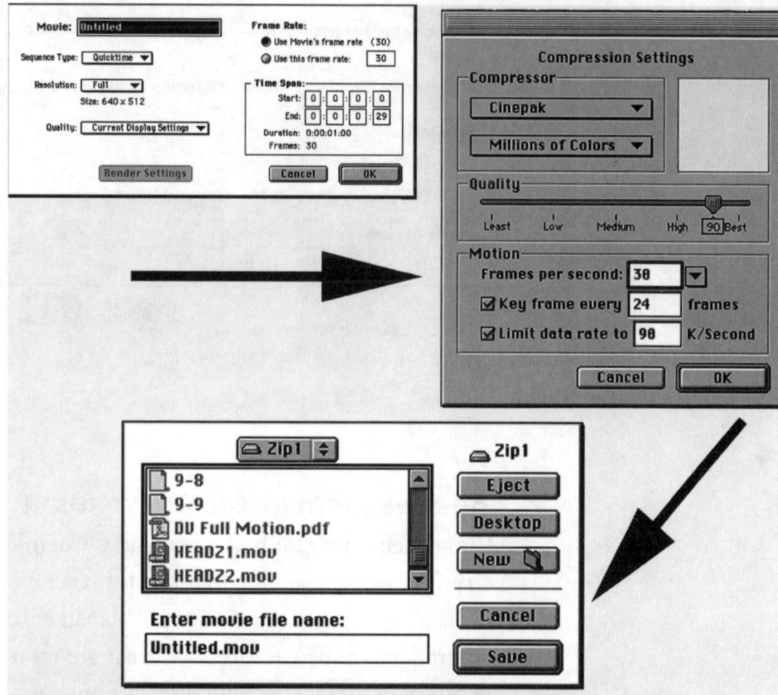

FIGURE 9.18 *When you select Make Movie, these three dialogs allow you to adjust all of the parameters you need.*

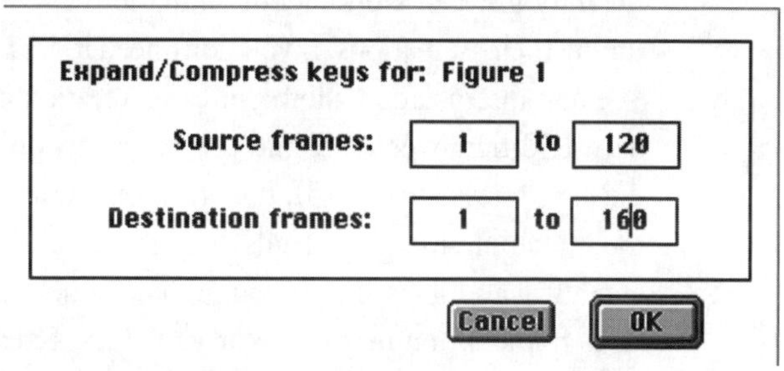

FIGURE 9.19 *The Retime Animation dialog.*

in the preview that look less smooth than you would have hoped, Resampling the Keyframes might help. You can either resample the animation by giving the computer the power to select where resampling should occur, or set resampling to force the addition of keyframes every nth frame. There's no guarantee that this will solve all of your concerns, but it may be worth a try. See Figure 9.20.

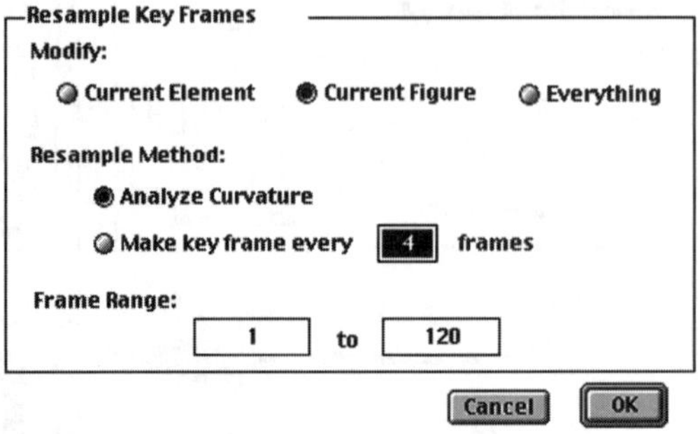

FIGURE 9.20 *The Resample Keyframes dialog.*

LOOP INTERPOLATION/QUATERNION INTERPOLATION

Here are definitions for both Loop and Quaternion Interpolations, written by Larry Weiner, the main programmer for Poser 3.

Quaternion interpolation is a special mathematical interpolation technique that produces in-between motions that are more predictable between poses, but can cause strange-looking discontinuities when you look at the graphs of individual rotation parameters. The interpolation happens by using all three rotation channels at once, instead of simply interpolating each one individually (which is the default). It's only useful for animators who are really getting into the nitty-gritty of working out animations and are having trouble with fine-tuning their animations. If you don't need it, it's probably easiest not to use it.

Loop interpolation allows for easier creation of cycling animations. If you have a 30-frame sequence and put keyframes only at frames 1 and 15 (introducing some change at 15), then turn on loop interpolation, you will see that the animation smoothly blends through frame 30 back to frame 1. Viewing the graph will also show this. If you put keyframes near the end that are not similar to frame 1, you may get some very unexpected and strange in-betweens in the frames just before these because the last frame is essentially the frame before the first frame. Viewing the graphs really helps make it clear what is going on.

SKIP FRAMES

This is a menu repeat of the same item shown in the Animation Controller.

MUTE SOUND/CLEAR SOUND

These commands work when you have an audio file loaded as part of the animation.

PLAY MOVIE FILE

Play AVI (Windows) or QuickTime (Windows and Mac) movies inside of Poser 3. This is useful when previewing an animation you just rendered, and also for previewing an animation you are considering for use as a background.

IK

IK means Inverse Kinematics, and Poser 3 has a powerful IK engine. Kinematics itself refers to the movement of chained elements. The best example as far as the human body is concerned is comprised of the links between the Shoulder, Upper Arm, Lower Arm, and Hand, or those between the Thigh, Shin, and Foot. Many Human and Animal models come into Poser 3 with two or four limbs IK enabled by default. I usually disable it for most animations, but your work habits may incline you to leave it assigned.

I prefer to use IK when there is no looping of the animation involved. Using IK on a looped sequence can lead to some run-ins with chaos, because a lot of adjustments have to be made to make the last frame equal to the first as far as the modification of the elements. You can think of IK as glue. With IK enabled for a limb, the end element of that limb will remain glued to the spot if any elements higher in the chain are moved or rotated. This is great when a figure is to do push-ups, since the hands (if the arm is IK enabled) will remain on the floor. It's even OK if the figure is to throw a ball, as long as you maneuver the hand and not any other part of the arm. It is less useful if the throwing motion is to be repeated over and over in a continuous loop, because the position of all of the elements will have to be returned to their original orientation, by using either the parameter dials or the Motion Graph.

Preparatory Movements

Just a word or two about preparatory movements in an animation. Before an actor participates in an action, there is usually some hint about what is to occur. Think of a tiger about to leap on its prey. The tiger's body tenses, it goes into an anticipatory crouch, and its powerful muscles ready for the jump. A warrior is about to cast a spear. The spear hand is brought back slowly, and a concentrated look zeroes in on the target. The spear arm is brought back on a line to the target. The release is sudden, compared to the preparation. Preparatory motions create more realistic animations. Compared to actions, like leaping or throwing, preparatory motions take up to three or four times (and sometimes more) what the action will take. Actions are sudden, so that the keyframes set up for a quick action are very close together. Preparatory movements, on the other hand, take a lot longer. The keyframes are widely spaced apart, leading to

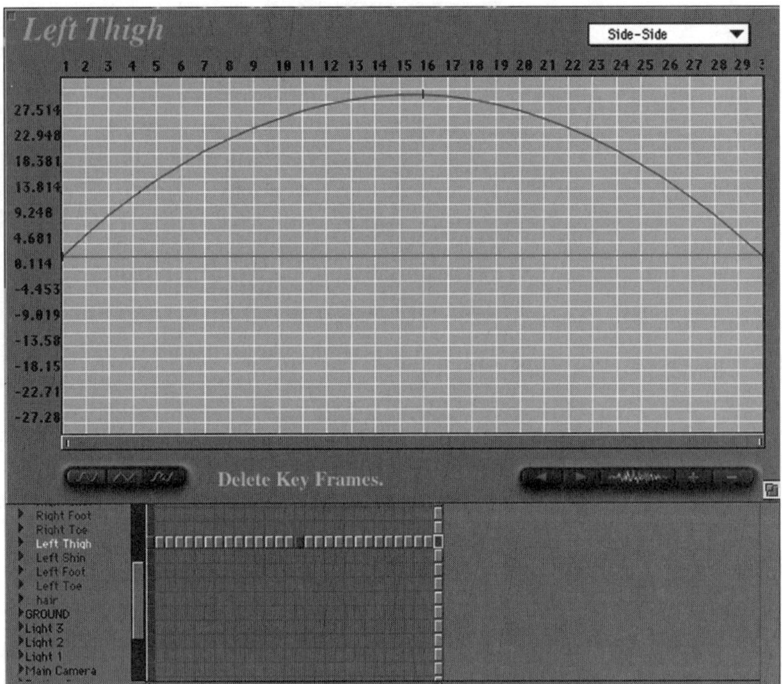

FIGURE 9.21 *A motion curve for side-to-side movement of the Left Thigh.*

slower and smoother motion overall. It is this preparatory movement that lends an air of anticipation and suspense to an animation. See Figure 9.21.

Moving Along

This chapter opens the door to configuring animations in Poser 3. In the rest of the chapters in this animation section, we'll explore how various elements in a Document can be readied for animated output.

CHAPTER 10

Animating Articulated Hands

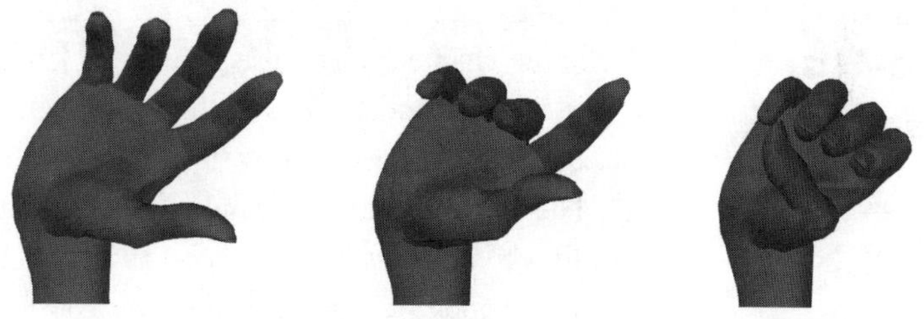

One of the most spectacular attributes of Poser 3 is both the sculpted excellence of the Hand elements and the ability to animate all of the digits. The sculpted quality owes its existence to the modeling masters at the Zygote Media Group. In previous editions of Poser, hands viewed from close up looked terrible, more like a childish attempt at drawing. In Poser 3, all of that has changed for the better. The hands are of such high quality that they can appear photographic under the right lighting. Hands exist as two types of objects: connected to figures and stand-alone constructs. Each type has its uses.

Pre-Attached Hands

In this chapter, when I use the word "Hands," I am speaking about the hands on human models. Some of the animal models have front paws or claws that are called "Hands," but we'll leave animal model animation for Chapter 12. The term Pre-attached Hands, then, refers to the hands that come as part of a human model when you import that model into your Poser 3 Document. As such, hands are animated whenever you move any body part that causes the hand to tag along in some movement. The simplest and most common case would be any movement of the arm parts to which the hand is attached. To make a model wave hello, for instance, is to animate the forearm to which that hand is attached. See Figures 10.1 and 10.2.

Rule number one for animating a hand is to use either the Left or Right Hand Cameras. See Figures 10.3 and 10.4.

MANUALLY ANIMATING A HAND

Having zoomed in on a Hand with either the Left or Right Hand Camera, you are set to animate its separate parts.

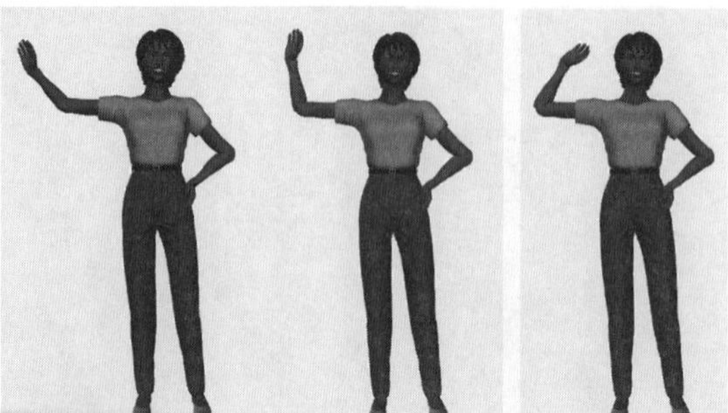

FIGURE 10.1 *The Hand in this sequence can be seen waving, because the forearm to which it is attached is set to animate from side to side.*

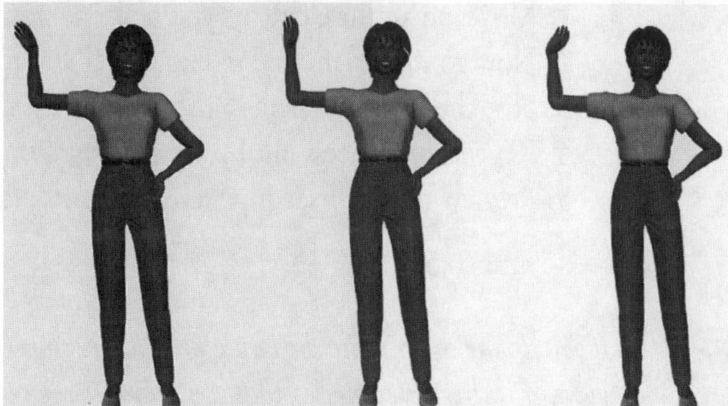

FIGURE 10.2 *In this sequence, the hand itself is seen waving side to side, while the forearm remains stationary.*

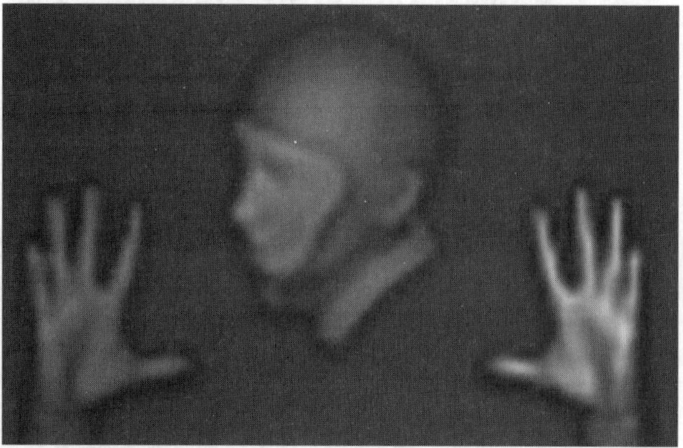

FIGURE 10.3 *The Hand Cameras zoom in on the hands.*

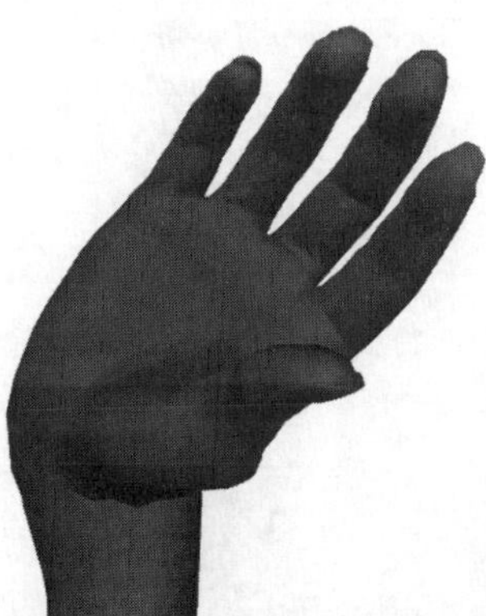

FIGURE 10.4 *The Right Hand in Figure 10.2 is zoomed in on using the Right Hand Camera.*

1. Move any of the elements you desire to pose.
2. Now go to the Animation Controller and move to another frame.
3. Pose the Hand elements again.
4. Repeat this process until you have posed the elements at the last frame.
5. Preview the results, edit where necessary, and save to disk.

See Figure 10.5.

If you decide to animate the hands on a figure that is also to be animated in other ways, it is strongly suggested that you animate the rest of the figure first, saving the hands until last. That way, you can animate the hand elements and also adjust whatever positions in space the hand is to be at the same time.

A SIMPLER WAY OF ANIMATING HANDS

There is a far simpler method to use when it comes time to animate hands. Instead of starting from scratch, use one of the pre-set poses from the Hands Library as a start, and tweak the elements as necessary. Go to the last keyframe in your sequence, select another pose from the Hands library, and tweak that into position. This can be up to ten times faster than trying to shape the poses manually. See Figure 10.6.

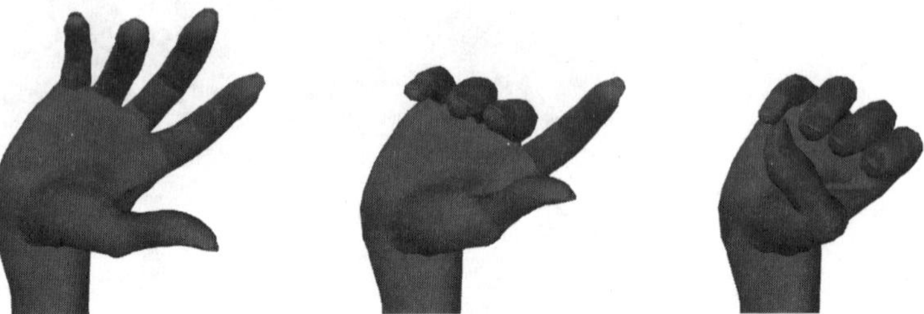

FIGURE 10.5 *By selecting any of the movable elements of a Hand, while in the appropriate Hand Camera mode, you can keyframe animate the Hand with the Rotation Tool.*

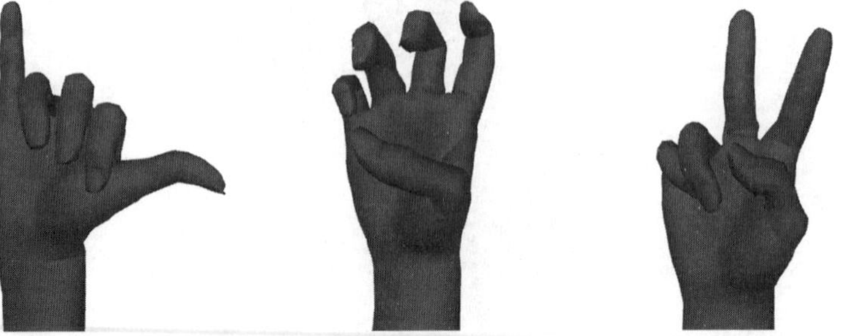

FIGURE 10.6 *These three poses from the Hands library can be used as keyframes, so you can animate from one to the other.*

Stand-alone Hands

There are two stand-alone hands, left and right, in the Additional Figures folder in the Figures library. These hands float in air and can be used when you need just the hand in a scene, without the rendering or storage overhead of including other body elements (see Figure 10.7). As we'll see in Chapter 13, they can also be used to create some unique animated effects.

HAND POSING STAND-ALONE HANDS

You can use all of the techniques available to you for animating Pre-attached Hands to animate the Stand-alone Hands. Just select the element you need to adjust, go to the keyframe you want, and use the Rotation Tool to reposition it.

ANIMATING STAND-ALONE HANDS WITH THE HANDS LIBRARY

You can also use all of the techniques available to you for animating Pre-Attached Hands to animate the Stand-alone Hands, using the Hands Library method. Just select the element you need to adjust, go to the keyframe you want, and select a new Hand pose from the Hands library. Tweak as needed.

Animated Hand Projects

There is an infinite variety of situations in which you might focus upon animating the hands of a model, or other situations where using the stand-alone hands might suffice. Here are just a few ideas that challenge your Poser 3 interactions.

1. **The Balinese Dancer.** Balinese ritual dances are known throughout the world for the intricate and animated hand movements required of the practitioners. If you want this animation to be authentic, it will require a lot of research on your part, either from books or from detailed videos, or both. Make sure you are zoomed in close enough to allow the viewer to appreciate all of your detailed Hand posing if you take this project on.
2. **Pebble Pickup.** This is a project that can use either hands attached to a figure, in which case you'll also have to animate the figure stooping

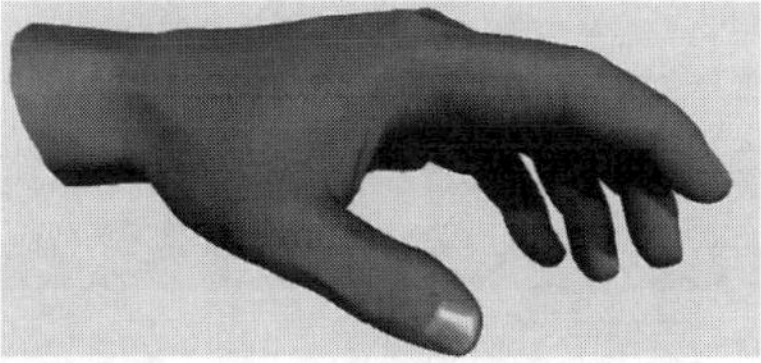

FIGURE 10.7 *The stand-alone hands float free of any body element connection.*

down, or with a stand-alone hand. Prepare for this animation by observing your hand, or a friend's hand, doing this task. Watch the way that the hand prepares to close on the object (which can be a Ball from the Props library) and observe how each finger plays a part in the action. You can do all the keyframing manually. Use the Grasp parameter when the Hand is over the Ball, and use it again (negatively) when the Hand is to release the Ball.

Karuna! If you notice that your hand model is shaking in the animation, which makes you think the hand has the shivers, you can correct this in the Motion Graph. Just select the offending finger elements, and go to the Bend option in the list. If the motion curve jogs up and down, simply straighten it out in the frames in which there is to be no bending. You will probably have to break the curve as well at those keyframe points. See Figure 10.8.

Karuna! Be aware that the Grasp Parameter places a keyframe at every tween, so editing may take a while.

HAND JEWELRY

Using a few simple props creates hand jewelry, which can be animated itself.

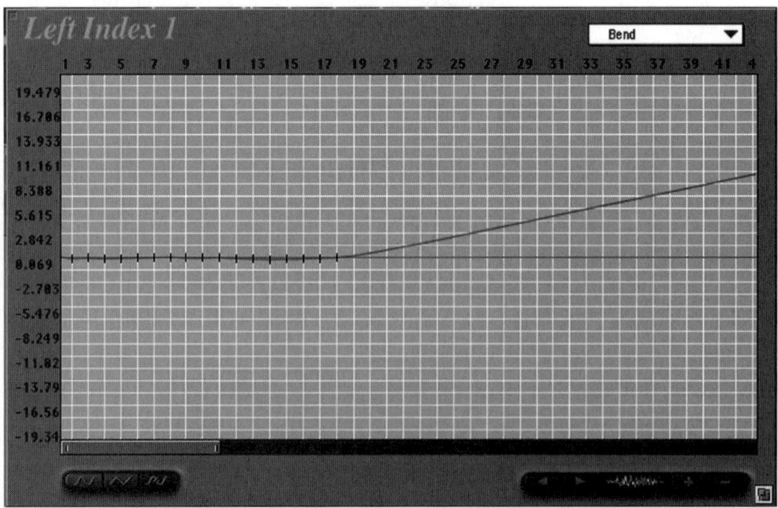

FIGURE **10.8** *If there is shaking going on that you want to stabilize, open the offending elements Motion Graph and straighten out the keyframes. The keyframes on the left have been straightened out.*

STRANGE HAND

Resizing and elongating the elements of a Hand on various axes leads to some strange hands, like those used in a horror movie, as the actor transforms into a creature less than human. Using a resizing animation, you can also make a thumb throb, as if hit by a hammer. See Figure 10.9.

TALKING HEAD RING

Using a Torus for a ring, you can easily attach a free standing Head to it. Once the Head is attached, it can be animated, providing the viewer with an eerie apparition. See Figures 10.10 and 10.11.

SHARP WARRIOR WRIST BANDS

In the movie "Ben Hur," the chariots are outfitted with sharp blades. You can easily place a wristband that has retractable knives around a hand. Just use cone props and elongate them in a keyframe animation to create this effect. See Figure 10.12.

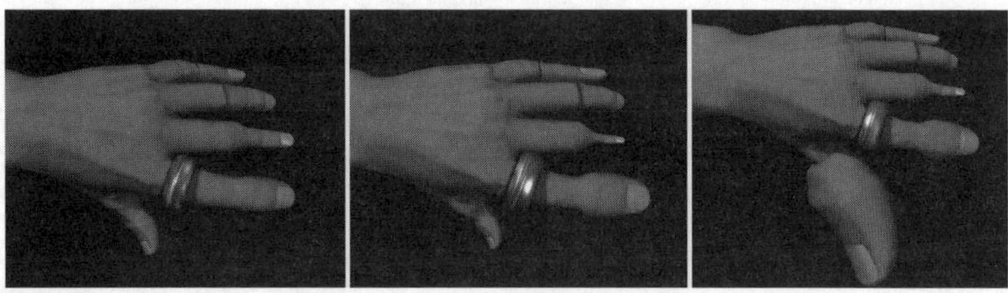

FIGURE 10.9 *Hands may be animated to throb and morph.*

FIGURE 10.10 *The Talking Head Ring sits on an animated hand.*

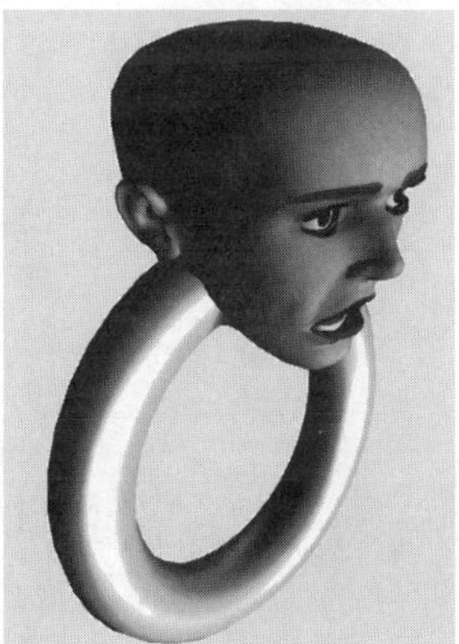

FIGURE 10.11 *The Talking Head Ring close up, ready to slip on a finger.*

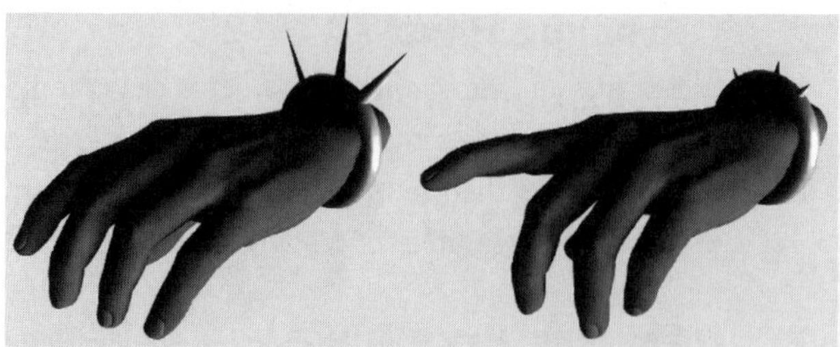

FIGURE 10.12 *A dangerous animated wrist band.*

Study Your Body

When you need a special animated hand gesture, you have the best modeling tool at your disposal—your own hands. Open your hand and slowly make a fist. Watch how each finger and your thumb moves, some parts moving faster than others, and some at different angles. The animator has two friends, his or her own body and a mirror. Using these two readily available study items, any body part can be animated realistically.

Moving Along

We've looked at animating Hands in this chapter. As we move to the next chapter in the animation section, we'll be studying facial and eye animation.

CHAPTER 11

Facial, Mouth, and Eye Movements

Compared to all of the other methods that computer animators have had when it came to the difficult task of animating faces, Poser 3 is a miracle. Gone are the tedious manipulations of "bones" or the construction of countless morph targets. Instead, with just a few turns of a set of Parameter dials, the targeted head of a model is reshaped into a new expression, or a whole new being. This opens up the craft of character development and animation to everyone, young to not-so-young, novices to professionals. Even if you have no interest in animating anything else in Poser 3, you're sure to spend hundreds of hours staring at the screen as your animated characters' faces come to life.

Animating the Mouth

The mouth of any person we meet, along with the eyes, tells an immediate story about that person's intentions and the motives. Not a word need be spoken for this to occur. Think of the times that you have met someone new and the way that the pose of their lips suggested either an invitation to deeper communication, or a warning that you had best maintain your distance. This is obviously true in romantic encounters, but it reaches far beyond that specific intent. The other night, while watching a news program on television, I was struck by the downward turn of the mouth of a high government official. It turned out that his views matched the message his mouth transmitted before he even uttered a world. Animation is about observation, because you can't shape a story for anyone else until you are well aware of all of the ways that stories can be told.

ANIMATING WITH MOUTH CONTROLS

Poser 3 offers you three main ways to shape the mouth with Parameter controls for keyframe animation purposes: Open Lips, Smile, and Frown. The Parameter dials that control these feature-warping options can be adjusted in either a positive (right) or negative (left) direction, resulting in some very different looks. In addition to this, a nearly infinite variety of mouth shapes can be created by combining two or all of these Parameter settings. Expanding upon the Mouth Parameters even farther, there are also Parameter dials that control the shaping of the lips for the sounds "O," "F," and "M," and Tongue controls for "T" and "L."

Karuna! Be aware that the following parameter settings may differ slightly, depending upon the model you are working on. This is because different models deform according to their own unique structures.

Open Lips

As a stand-alone Parameter, the effective range of Open Mouth lies between –.9 to +2.5 (see Figure 11.1). Higher or lower values begin to cause severe distortion of the face, from poking the teeth through the lips (values lower than –.9) to poking the lips through the upper head and chin (values higher than 2.5). For all but the strangest types of animated figures, stay within these suggested limits. When combined with the other Mouth Parameters, however, you will find that you can stretch these limits a bit.

Practice Session Create an animation, keyframing nothing but the Open Mouth Parameter at different settings. Use the Face Camera. Using just the Mouth Open Parameters, you can simulate a chewing action.

Smile

The textbooks say that the act of smiling is actually based upon an archaic aggressive display, a baring of the teeth. This explains why some smiles look absolutely frightening, while others seem sanguine. Use a range from –1.5 to +2.2 for the most common parameter values (see Figure 11.2). Ranges lower or higher create facial distortions, because Smile also pulls and pushes on the skin below the eyes. Negative settings create a pouty sad look (the lower lip

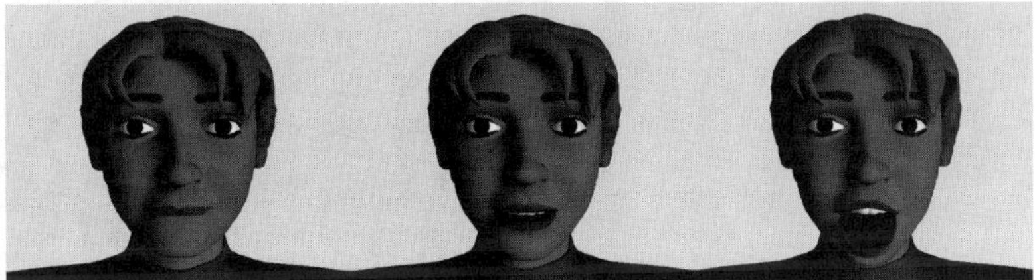

FIGURE 11.1 *From left to right, Open Mouth settings of –.9, .5, and 2.5.*

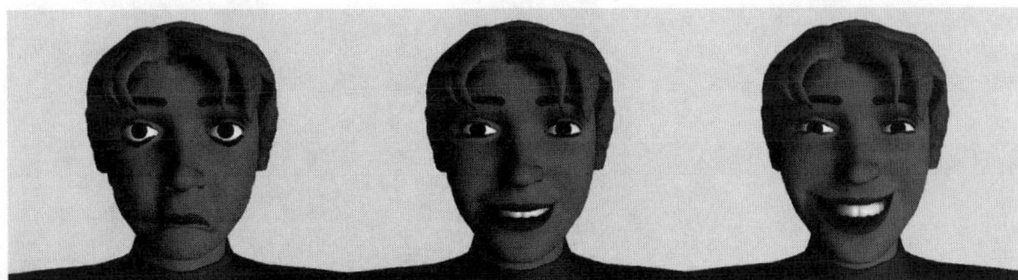

FIGURE 11.2 *From left to right, Smile values of –1.5, 1, and 2.2.*

actually starts to tuck under the upper lip), while higher settings light up a face with a smile.

Adding Mouth Opens to a Smile makes it a laugh, and adding negative Mouth Opens to a negative smile emphasizes the sadness.

Practice Session Create an animation, keyframing nothing but the Smile Parameter at different settings. Use the Face Camera. Using just the Smile Parameters, you can simulate an emotional rollercoaster.

Frown

At first glance, you might think that a Frown parameter is just the opposite of a Smile, and that since a sad countenance can be generated with a negative Smile, why bother to have a Frown Parameter? This is not the case, however. A Frown pulls on different areas of the face, so using a Frown negative alone creates a different quality of smile, and using a positive Frown creates an alternate sadness component. A standard range is from –2 to +1.5 (see Figure 11.3). A –2 value creates the smile of a naive simpleton, complete with dimples. A +1.5 value creates a caricature Frown, like that of a sad clown.

The Smile and Open Mouth Parameters can either moderate or accentuate the Frown parameter, depending if its value is set negatively or positively. See Figure 11.4.

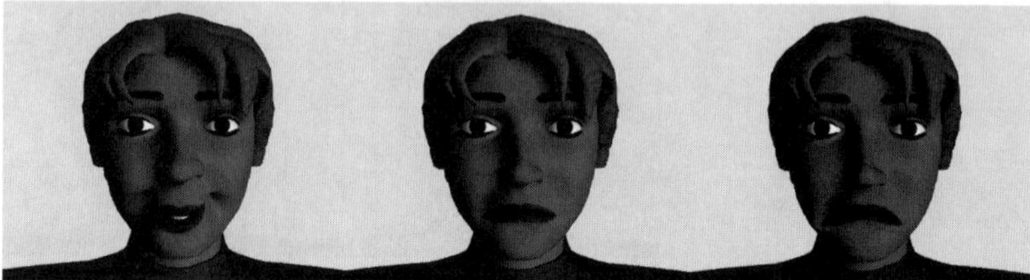

FIGURE 11.3 *From left to right, Frown values of –2, .9, and 1.5.*

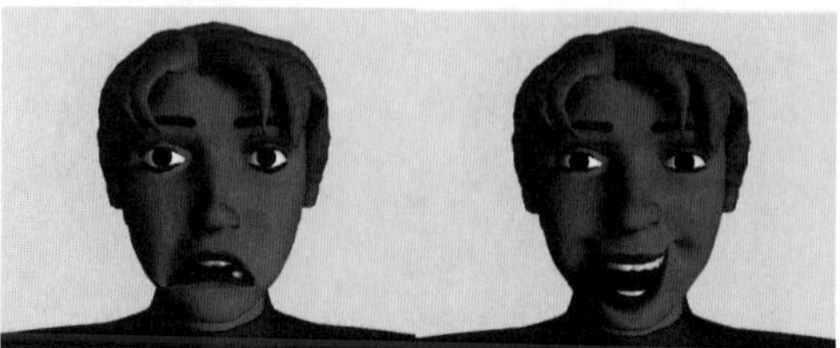

FIGURE 11.4 *Left: Frown of 1, Open Mouth of –.5, and Smile of 1.8. Right: Frown of 1, Open Mouth of 1, and Smile of –1.5.*

Practice Session Create an animation, keyframing nothing but the Frown Parameter at different settings. Use the Face Camera. Using just the Mouth Open Parameters, you can give your figure a dimpled smile at negative values, or a clown-like frown at positive values.

Combining the Three Basic Mouth Parameters

By using different Parameter combinations of Open Mouth, Smile, and Frown, you can create some startling keyframes that morph from one emotional expression to another. See Figure 11.5.

Mouth Shapes for Phonemes

To shape a mouth as if it is pronouncing a word, you'll have to take the syllables of the word and shape the word from those mouth structures. You can explore phonemes in Poser 3 in two ways. One is to experiment with the Mouth Letter Structures (O, F, and M), and one by one, with nothing else animated, see what happens when you alter their parameters. See if you can hear the imaginary sound being made. Write down your observations. See Figures 11.6 to 11.8.

Karuna! Shape the mouth into a kiss-ready pucker by a Mouth Open setting of –1.2 and a "O" setting of 2.3.

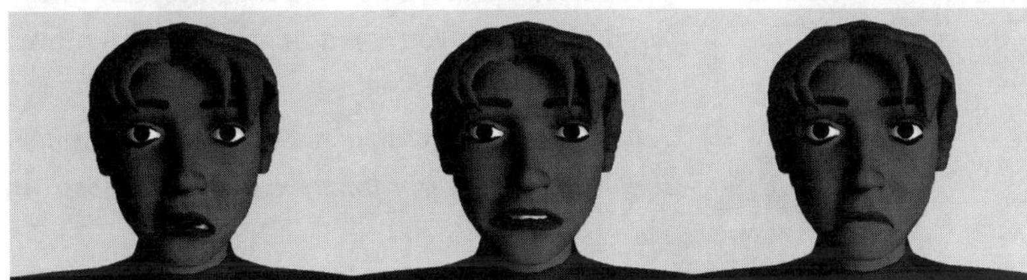

FIGURE 11.5 *Left: Chagrin—Open Mouth of 1, Smile of -.8, and Frown of .8. Center: Uh-Oh—Open Mouth of .325, Smile of .09, and Frown of 1.116. Right: Guilty—Open Mouth of –.130, Smile of –1.027, and Frown of .8.*

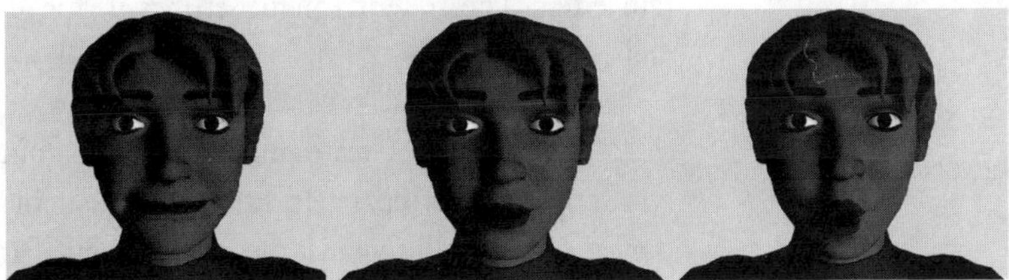

FIGURE 11.6 *Parameter Values for "O" from left to right: –.9, .5, and 1.5.*

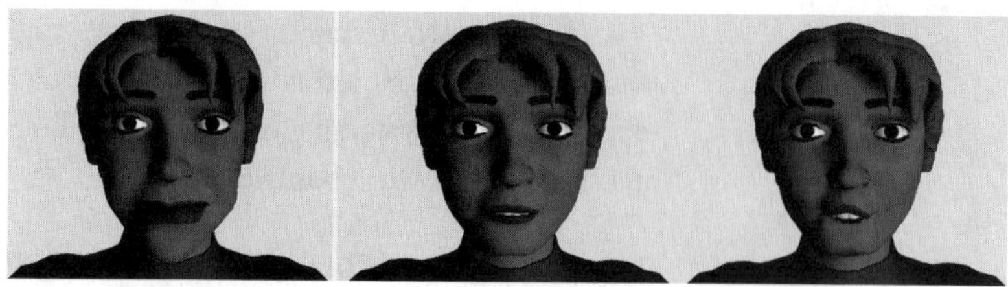

FIGURE 11.7 *Parameter Values for "F" from left to right: –2 (puffs out lower lip), 1, and 3 (best for "F" look). Values higher than 3 push the teeth through the chin.*

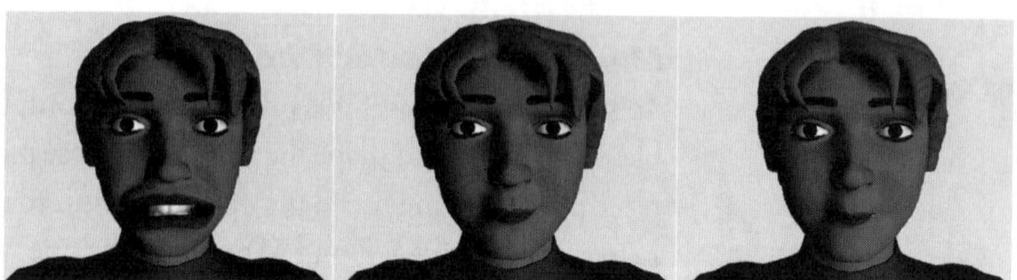

FIGURE 11.8 *Parameter Values for "M" from left to right: –5 (open lips and clenched teeth, great for that "G-forces look", or letter "I" if mouth is opened), 2, and 2.7 (maximum without facial distortion).*

Practice Session Create three animations, keyframing nothing but each of these three Mouth shapes separately, adjusting the Parameter to different settings. Use the Face Camera. Using just these three Mouth Parameters, see what words or sounds you can hear as the mouth moves.

Karuna! Don't forget that you can apply phoneme mouth shapes very quickly by simply assigning them from the ready-made poses in the Phonemes folder in the Faces library.

The Tongue

The placement of the tongue plays a large role in producing sounds, and the Tongue Parameter dial settings in Poser 3 help you create the look of certain letters. The present Tongue settings are for "T" and "L." See Figures 11.9 and 11.10.

Practice Session Create animations, keyframing nothing but each of these two Tongue shapes separately, adjusting the Parameter to different settings. Use the Face Camera. Using just these two Tongue Parameters, see what words or sounds you can hear as the mouth moves. The Tongue Parameters act as interesting modifiers to other Mouth Letter Parameters. Using a series of alternate

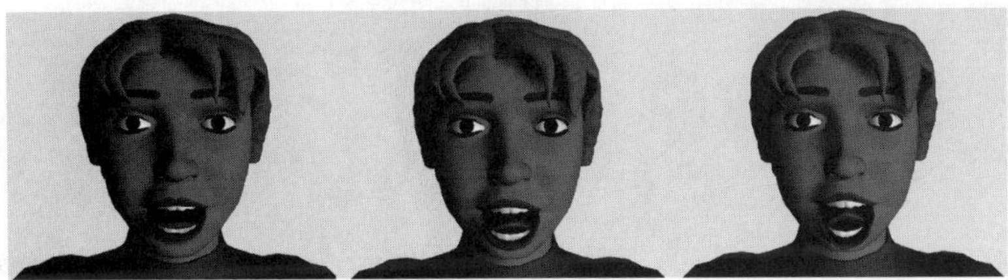

FIGURE 11.9 *Parameter Values for Tongue "T" from left to right (all with Mouth Open of 1.5): .5, 1.1, 1.8. You can see the effect of the T Tongue best when the mouth is open, except when it is used to modify and deform other Mouth settings.*

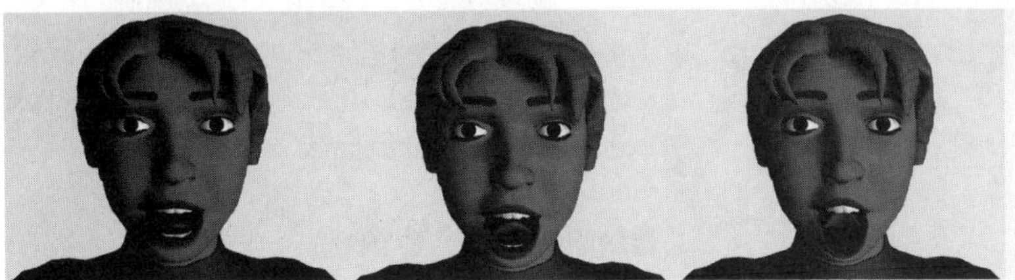

FIGURE 11.10 *Parameter Values for Tongue "L" from left to right right (all with Mouth Open of 1.5): .5, 1.1, 1.8. You can see the effect of the T Tongue best when the mouth is open, except when it is used to modify and deform other Mouth settings.*

Parameter settings for the Tongue "L" shape, with the mouth open at 1.5, you can create a character that is singing "La" sounds, just right for caroling on the holidays.

Animating the Eyes

The ancient proverb says that the eyes are windows to the soul. When we want to know if someone is lying, or what that person's real intentions are, we look deep into his or her eyes. The way that eyes dart around or remain focused and steady indicates a lot about the personality of their owner. Everything that the eyes do has a powerful effect on the total personality.

SIZE MATTERS

Small beady eyes, like those of the rat, are interpreted by us as denoting a sneaky or conniving character. Large wide eyes, like those of the doe, are interpreted by us as a sign of docility or child-like consciousness. You can alter the size of a model's eyes in Poser 3 (Figure 11.11).

Vampires, villains, and addicts are usually depicted with small beady eyes. Heroes and lovable characters are many times depicted with large eyes, though when they bulge out excessively, the personality types become more bothersome.

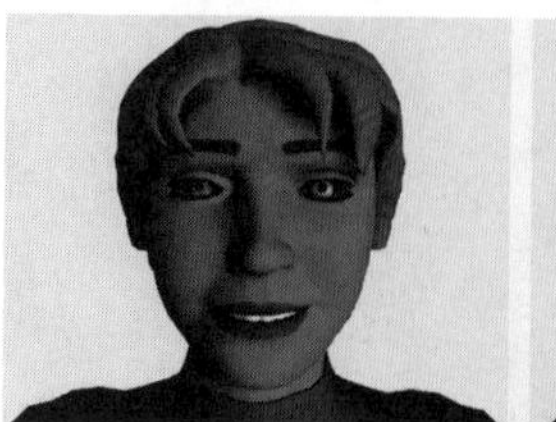

FIGURE 11.11 *The same model with small beady eyes (40%), large-sized eyes (122%), and large bulging eyes (122%, with a Ztrans of .002).*

NOTE

The difference between large eyes and bulging eyes is their placement on the Z (in and out) axis. To keep large eyes without making them bulge, move them on the Z axis a distance of from –.002 to –.004.

Blinks and Winks

A Blink works on both eyes at the same time, while a Wink works on only one eye. Use the Left and Right Blink parameter dials to animate either. Using a negative value opens the eye very wide and can be useful for emotional responses like surprise or shock. See Figure 11.12.

NOTE

If your character's eyes are to blink during an animated sequence, do not time them too symmetrically. Instead, add some randomness to the timing of the keyframes for a more natural look.

Sproing!

By using the Z Trans Parameter dial with higher values, you can move the eyeballs right out of the head for a pretty startling animated effect. See Figure 11.13.

FIGURE 11.12 *Blink Parameters set to create the following, left to right: Sleepy Eyes (values of .6 for each Blink, with opposite eyebrows raised and lowered); Blink Right; Negative Blink value of –1.25 for each eye (eyebrows also raised up).*

FIGURE 11.13 *Using higher and higher Z Trans values, you can pop the eyes out of and away from the head.*

NOTE

An interesting variation on this effect is to make the eyes smaller (40%) in the first frame, and larger as they leave the eye socket (200% for the last frame).

ATTENTION TO EYEBROWS

You should always think about adding animation to the eyebrows to enhance whatever animated expressions your model is invoking. The eyebrow movements in Poser 3 also pull at the skin around the eyes, further enhancing any animated eye movements. Eyebrow Parameter dials exist for three separate movements: Up, Down, and Worry.

Left/Right Eyebrow Down

Positive settings move the eyebrows down, and negative up. Do not conclude, however, that the negative settings are the same as using the Eyebrow Down Parameters, since different areas of the face are stretched. See Figure 11.14.

NOTE

Explore animating each eyebrow with its own unique parameters to create some very subtle emotional variations.

Left/Right Eyebrow Up

Positive settings move the eyebrows up, and negative down. Do not conclude, however, that the negative settings are the same as using the positive

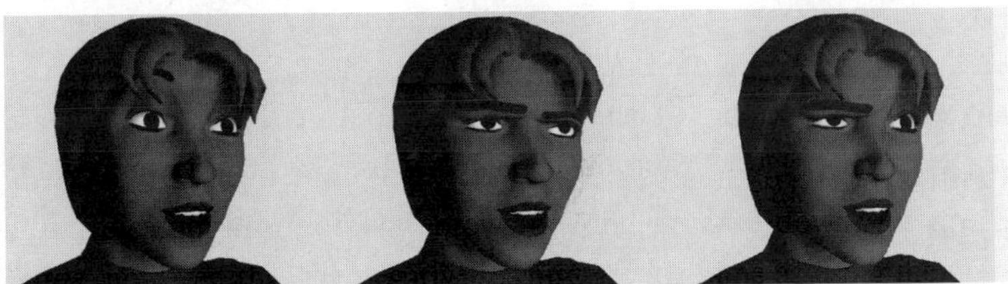

FIGURE 11.14 *Left to right, Eyebrow Down Parameters: -3.1 (surprise or awe); 2 (concern); separate settings (Left -2.8, and Right 2.5, an investigative look).*

FIGURE 11.15 *Left to right, Eyebrow Up Parameters: –1.3 (sad concern); 1.5 (mild surprise); (Left –2, and Right 2.5, probably physically impossible).*

FIGURE 11.16 *Left to right, parameter settings for Worry: -2 (Anger); 1.6 (Worry); Verge of Tears (Worry of 2.2, Smile of 1, and Frown of 1.3).*

Eyebrow Down Parameters, since different areas of the face are stretched. See Figure 11.15.

Left/Right Eyebrow Worry

Negative settings create an angry countenance, while positive values create worry and guilt. See Figure 11.16.

Practice Sessions Create animations, keyframing nothing but each of these three Eyebrow Parameters separately, adjusting the values to different settings. Use the Face Camera. Used in conjunction with animated eyes, a wide range of emotions can be indicated.

Two Approaches to Animating Facial Characteristics

There are two main approaches to animating faces. One is to animate the distortions of the face caused by altering tapers and sizes. The second is to animate the mouth, eye, and eyebrow features. A third option, morphing, will be reserved for Chapter 15. Actually, you can consider all of the options to be morphing based. Using tapers and resizing, as well as animating features (because distortions are involved), can be considered internal morphing. All of these methods can be used singly or in combination, depending upon your needs and goals.

FACIAL DISTORTION ANIMATIONS

You can alter the tapering of the head, positively or negatively, to create interesting facial animations. The eyes are not included in tapering the head, so they will have to be treated separately, unless you want to leave them as they are. The eyes are included when you alter the head's size. Any Prop attached, like Hair, has to be treated separately in these modifications.

Size-wise

You can use any of the axis parameter dials to resize the head, which will also distort the face. Shortening the Y axis and widening the X axis creates a character that can be used as a bully. Other axis modifications create different characters. Animating size modifications creates a head that bulges in and out, useful for cartoon or science fiction projects. See Figure 11.17.

NOTE

You will have to resize the neck when modifying the size of the head on any axis.

Practice Session Create an animation that starts with a head Y axis globally sized to 0%, and ends with a Y axis globally sized to 125%. Watch the head grow on the neck like a melon.

Tapering Reality

A positive Taper on a Head creates a conehead figure, while a negative Taper creates a figure wider at the bottom of the face. Alter between the two for a bizarre face-warping animation. See Figure 11.18.

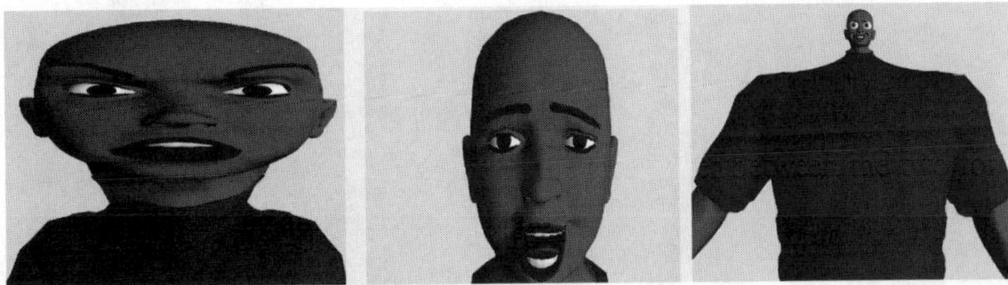

FIGURE 11.17 *A collection of head resizes, left to right: Y of 82, and X of 227; Y of 137, and X of 110; Pinhead displays a head resized to 25%.*

FIGURE 11.18 *A Taper of 160 and –100 used on the same figure.*

FACE LIBRARY KEYFRAMING

Every time you create a face that displays an interesting emotion, or a distortion that you appreciate, save it to the Faces library in your own custom folder. Faces can be applied as instant keyframes later on, to any figure, saving you a lot of time and energy.

Moving Along

In this chapter, we have explored how Poser 3 faces can be customized using controls for the mouth, eyes, and eyebrows. We also looked at the application of phonemes and the tapering and resizing of heads, all as animation techniques. In the next chapter, we'll explore the animation of animals.

CHAPTER

12 Animal Animation

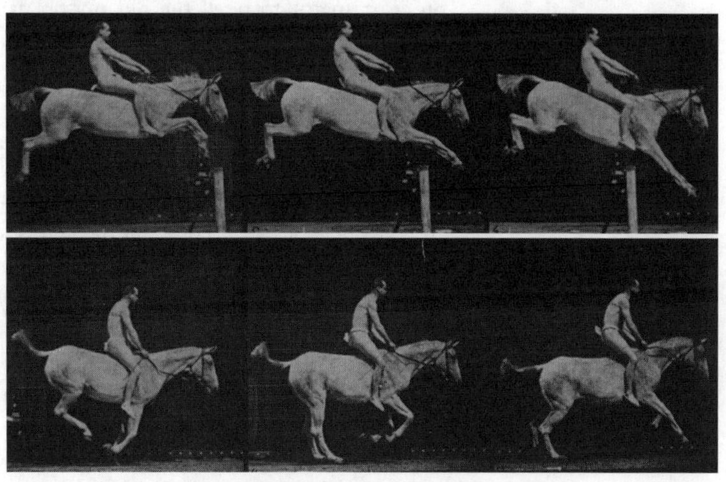

We share the world we live on with a myriad of other creatures, creatures with personalities and lives very different from ours. For the animator, animals represent a unique opportunity to tell stories. Disney Studios keeps the animal mythic tradition alive by introducing films every year that allow animals to speak as stand-ins for human characters and personality types. This tradition is worldwide, since animals have always played a major role in children's fables and teaching stories. Every culture has its favorite animal myths, from the Trickster Raccoons of native America to the Tigers of India. The animal models included with Poser 3, and the additional models offered on the Zygote Extras CD, provide new resources for the computer animator to retell the old myths, as well as to create new integrated human and animal model productions.

Where are the Poser Animals?

The Poser Animals can be found in your Figures directory, in the Animals folder. If you have purchased the Zygote Animals collection, then they can be found in the same directory in a folder called Zygote Animals. The standard animals included with Poser are the Cat, Dog, Dolphin, Horse, and Raptor. The Zygote Animals include the Doe, Bass, Bear, Buck, Chimpanzee, Cow, Frog, Killer Whale, Lion, Penguin, Shark, Wolf, and Zebra (Figure 12.1).

There is no way this book can walk you through definitive animation controls for all of the animals involved. Learning how animals move requires a lifetime of study and attention to detail. At the end of the chapter, we will suggest a unique way that you can tap into one resource for studying animal movements. In addition to that, if you are interested in creating realistic animations for your Poser 3 animals, it is highly recommended that you observe animals in motion every chance you get. Many of you probably have house pets, which is a good place to start. Cats and dogs are always on the move. Carry a sketch book with you and jot down the major points that determine their movement, where their feet are, what their heads are doing, and what bends first and in what order when they walk or run or recline. After that, the next best thing to do is to take a trip to a local zoo, carrying along the same sketch book. Look at the animals that match those offered in Poser 3, or included on the Zygote CD. Spend a day sketching their movements and how their movements reflect their attitudes. If you do this five or six times, you'll be amazed how much your observations will be translated into your digital animation skills. Another way to study animal movement is to watch, and even purchase, a collection of the nature shows offered on public television, or other suitable TV channels. Those of you who have the appropriate hardware can even digitally capture frames of an animal's movements, so you can study them more closely. And then there is one

FIGURE 12.1 *The full complement of Poser 3 Animals, from the standard shipping models to those contained on the Zygote Extras CD.*

of my favorite ways of studying animal movements, by accessing the Muybridge *Complete Animal and Human Locomotion* volumes.

Eadweard Muybridge

If you've never heard or seen the name Eadweard Muybridge before ("Eadweard" is pronounced "Edward," by the way), then you haven't explored the history of animation. Muybridge was one of the founders of the principles of animation, and his work still holds a sacred place amongst the texts that beginning animators are required to study.

The story of how Muybridge got into animation in the first place is fascinating. Reportedly, someone made a bet with him that a running horse always has its feet on the ground. This was in the late 1800s, and photography was just in its infancy. Muybridge set up an ingenious experiment to prove once and for all if the running horse ever had all of its feet off of the ground at any point. He set up a series of cameras at a race track, with each one connected to a trip wire. The rest is history. When the photos were developed, they showed clearly that at one point in the horse's stride, all of its feet leave the ground. After this experiment, Muybridge spent the rest of his life filming motion studies of humans and animals.

Since the last copyright on Muybridge's work was filed at the turn of the century, his books and photos are now totally copyright free. This means that you can use his extensive single-frame animation studies any way you want to, even republishing them on your own. I have checked this out thoroughly. He has three volumes published, and lately republished. They aren't cheap ($75.00 a volume), but for any animator, they are a must-have. The three-volume set ($225.00) is sold by Dover Press,* order numbers 23792, 23793, and 23794. See Figure 12.2.

USING THE MUYBRIDGE BOOKS

The Muybridge books are packed with single-frame sequences taken from Muybridge's movies. The sequences depict various animals and humans in different kinds of motion. Many of the animals are ones not yet addressed as Poser models, though the list of available animal models is sure to expand in the future. Because they are copyright free, you can scan in the pages and put the animations back together as a movie if you like. Their real value for Poser studies, however, comes after you scan the pages in and use the separated animation frames. Here's how:

1. Scan in a page from a Muybridge volume that depicts an animal in motion that resembles one of the Poser 3 models you have. The horse might be a good example.
2. In a suitable paint application, cut out and save each frame separately. Make sure that each frame is saved in the same size.
3. Open Poser 3, and load in the Animal figure that is represented in the Muybridge files you saved. Import the first frame of those files as a Poser 3 background, and place the animal in the same position and size as that indicated by the imported frame.
4. Turn off IK. Rotate the animal's limbs until they match the background

---

* Dover Publications, Inc.
31 East 2nd Street
Mineola, NY 11501
(516) 294-7000
(no e-mail address)

FIGURE 12.2 *The Muybridge volumes published by Dover Press are all called* Human and Animal Locomotion. *The two-volume set pictured here is an older release from my private collection, separately configured for humans and animals.*

pose as closely as possible. Save this Pose in a separate folder in your Poses library.

5. Load in the second frame, and go through the same process. Repeat this process for every frame you have to pose.
6. Delete the Figure and start a new Poser Document. Configure an animation with a length equal to the movie you will create. To determine the length, multiply the motion frames you will be importing by 15. For example, if the Muybridge motion frames number eight, then the length of your movie will be $8 \times 15 = 120$. At 30 frames a second, this works out to a 4-second animation.
7. Load in your figure again. At every 15th frame, starting with frame #1, load in the poses you saved out. These will be the keyframes in the animation, and your computer will create the Tweens. When you are finished, you will have a real-world animal animation study.

See Figures 12.3 to 12.12 for some examples of the Muybridge Animals in Motion sequences.

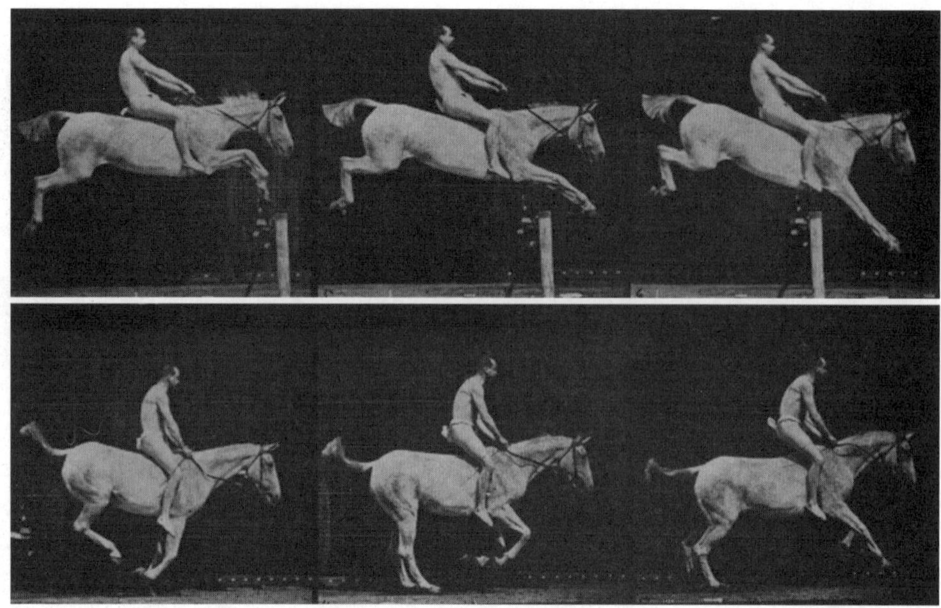

FIGURE 12.3 *Horse jumping an obstacle. Start with the gallop, then keyframe the jump, and keyframe the gallop again. You'll have to tweak some of the tweens.*

FIGURE 12.4 *Mule kicking. This could also be a horse kicking, or any other suitable animal.*

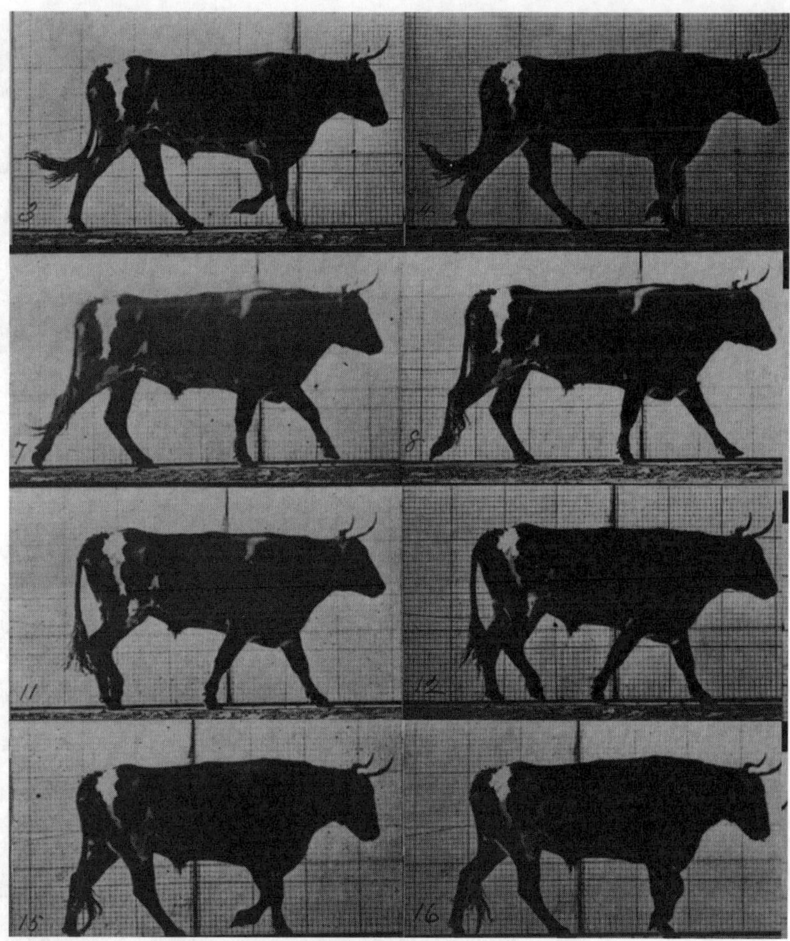

FIGURE 12.5 *Cow walking. This could also be a Bear, or other suitable animal.*

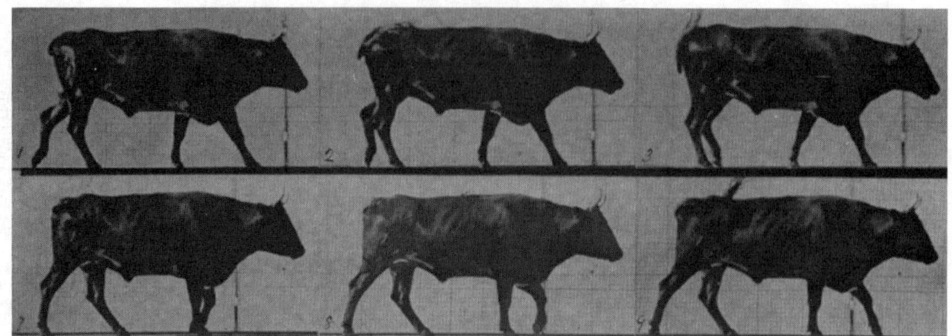

FIGURE 12.6 *Another Cow walk.*

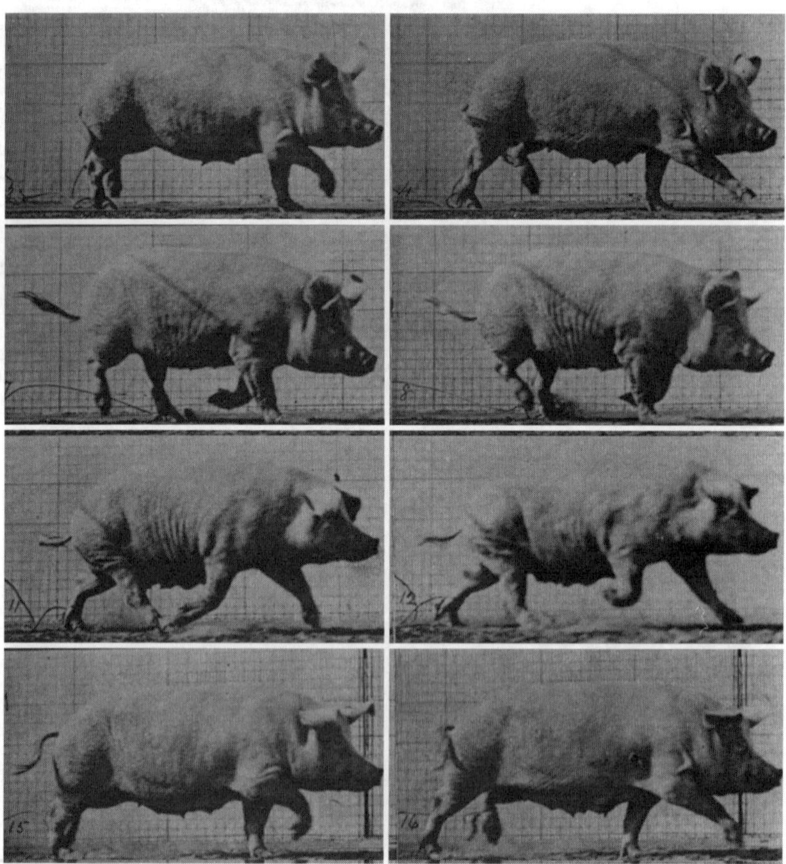

FIGURE 12.7 *Pig running. These poses work great for the Bear, or any other lumbering animal.*

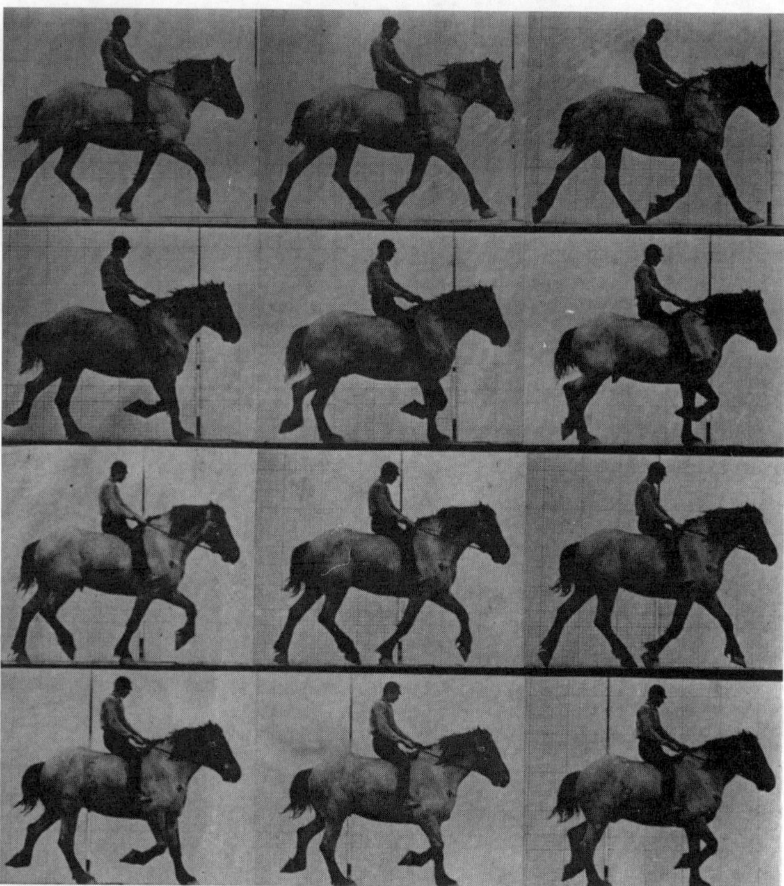

FIGURE 12.8 *Horse trotting. Use this with a rider atop your steed and pose the rider's bounce as well.*

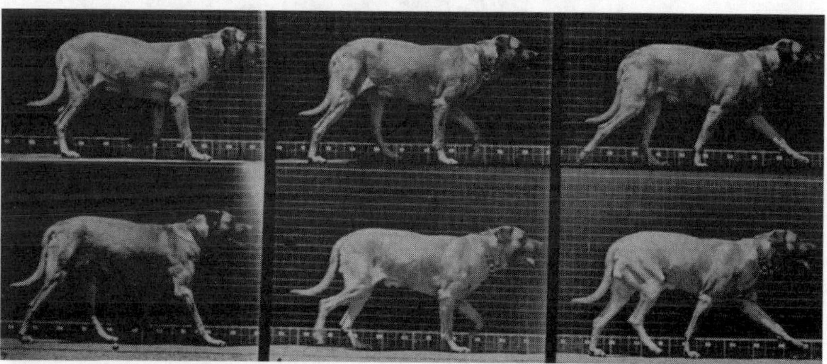

FIGURE 12.9 *Dog running.*

FIGURE 12.10 *Dog running faster.*

FIGURE 12.11 *Cat run and pounce.*

FIGURE 12.12 *Horse jump.*

Karuna! All of the Muybridge studies are in various stages of completion, so to use the poses in a finished animation, you'll have to adjust and add keyframes. You can apply the poses to any model, though when animal poses are applied to a human model, be ready for comical surprises.

The following figures display a few of the human motions in the Muybridge volumes. You can go through the same process described and apply the animated poses to the Chimpanzee and the Raptor, because their body parts have some similarity to the human body. See Figures 12.13 to 12.17.

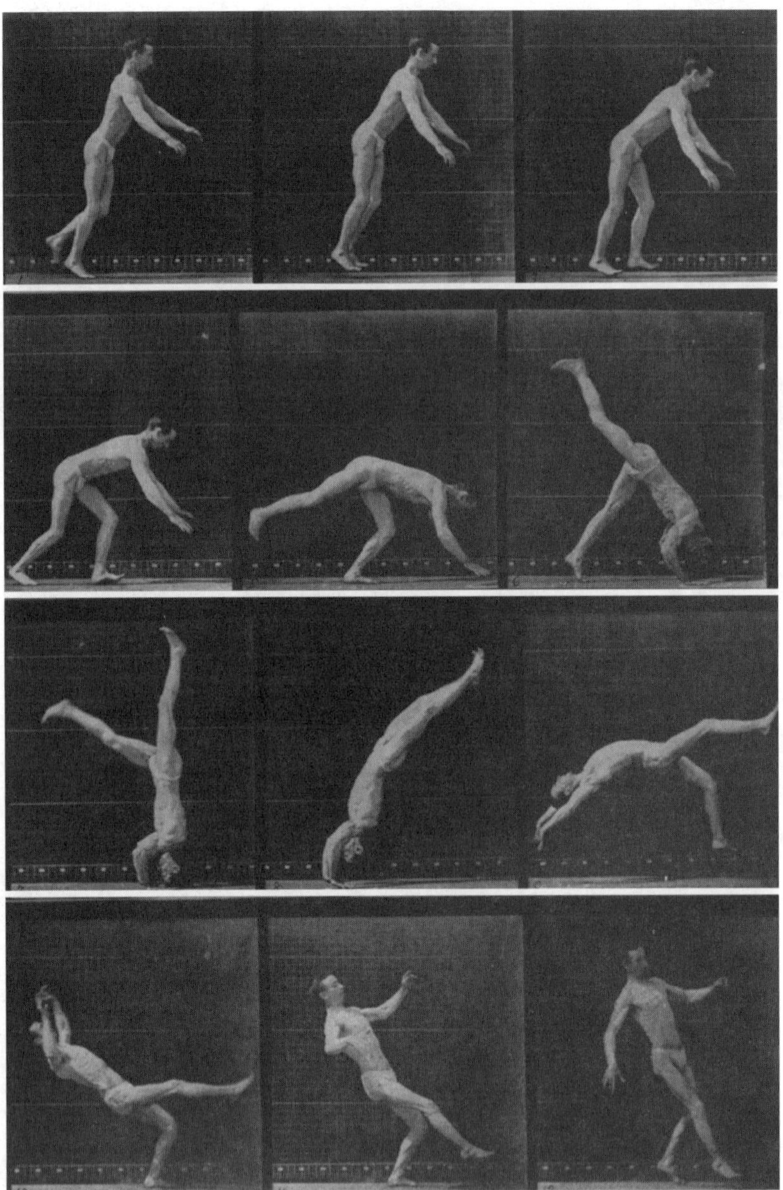

FIGURE 12.13 *Somersaulting. This is interesting applied to the Chimpanzee.*

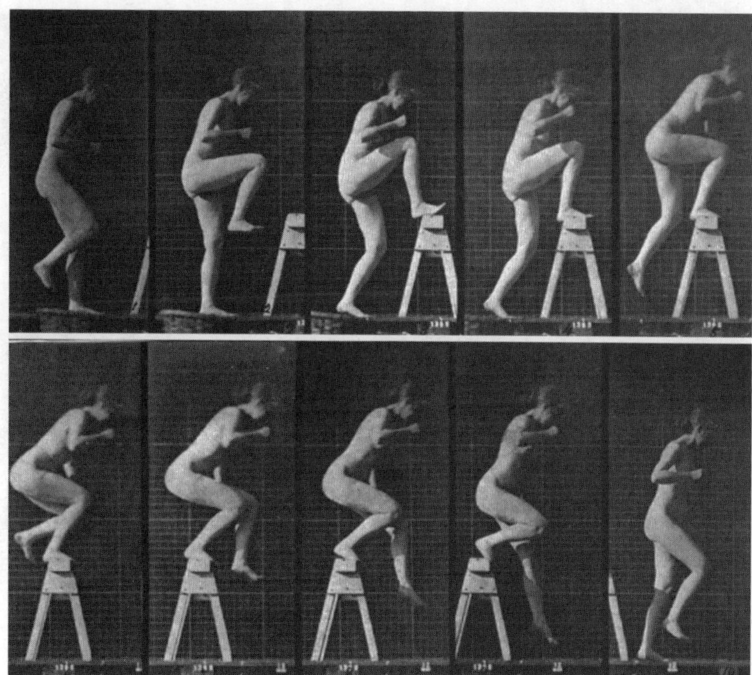

FIGURE 12.14 *Climbing over an obstacle. This could be used to depict the Raptor climbing over a rock, on its way to the prey.*

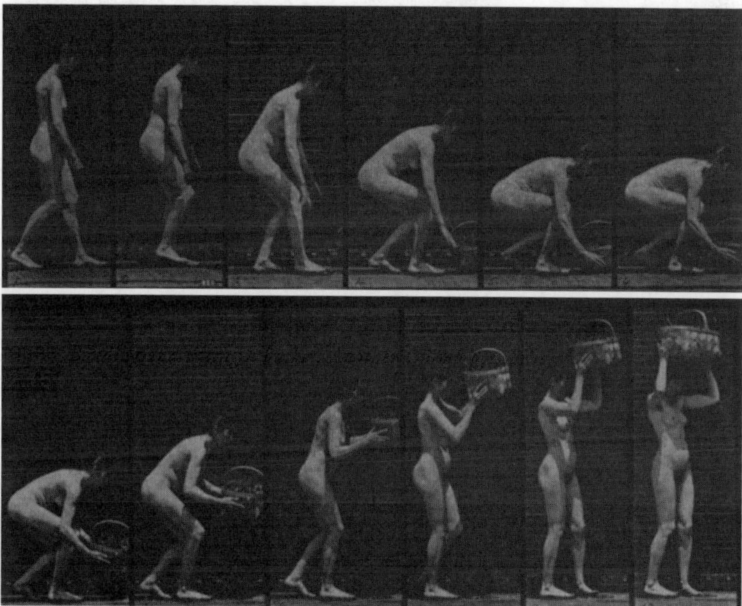

FIGURE 12.15 *Bending and lifting a basket. Another Chimp possibility.*

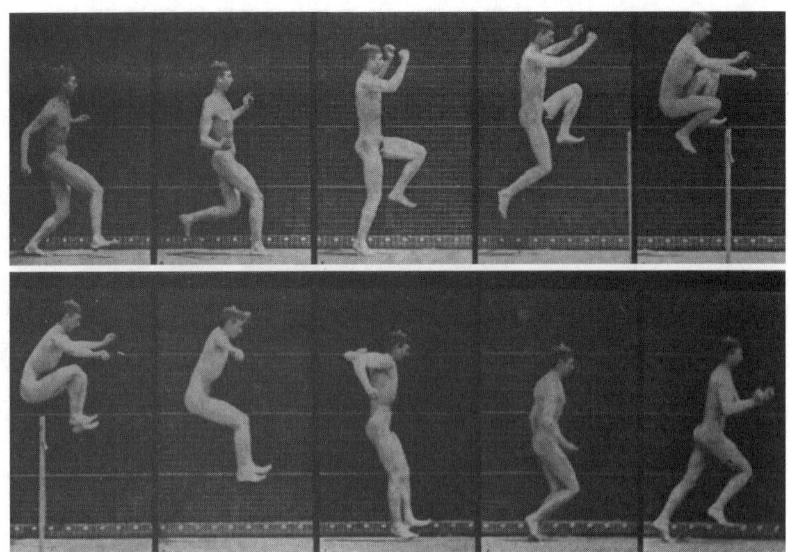

FIGURE 12.16 *Run and jump. Very funny when applied to the Raptor.*

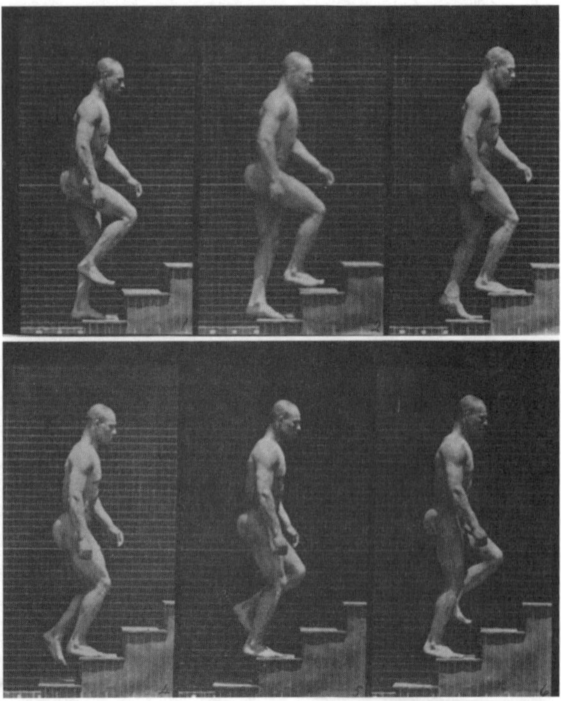

FIGURE 12.17 *Walking up stairs. This would make the Chimp look part human.*

Tips on the Poser Animals

There are some things to be aware of when animating the Poser and Zygote animals.

THE CAT

Aside from animated whole figure poses, like running, stalking, and leaping, the cat's personality is best defined by close-ups of the head. The best stories cats can tell are with their ears and eyes. The ears especially determine emotion on the cat. Try to observe a cat and watch as its ears tell you how it feels. When the ears are back and straight up, the cat is usually saying "I am not comfortable with this situation." When both of the cat's eyes blink, it is often a sign of love and appreciation.

THE DOG

The dog's personality is often determined by the position of its tail, whether up in friendliness or tucked between the legs in anger. The most telling sign of aggression is when the head is down and the shoulders higher than the neck. To set the dog on a walk with this pose is very effective for stalking. The Poser Dog model can be posed on two legs like a human, so various human poses can create animated dog cartoons.

THE DOLPHIN

When you animate the Dolphin's tail moving from side to side, as if swimming, move the head in the opposite directions. This provides interesting animated

contrast. Animate the Dolphin's tongue moving up and down when you want to create the impression that it is speaking.

THE HORSE

The Muybridge volumes are especially useful when it comes to configuring animated poses for the horse, since there are so many plates devoted to the horse in different motion studies. When the horse is simply standing in the background in your animations, make its tail flick from side to side. This simple technique is very effective and lets the viewer know that the horse is alive.

THE RAPTOR

The most interesting parts of the Raptor are its teeth and claws, the very same body parts that are frightening. No matter what the Raptor is doing, whether standing or in motion, keep these parts in motion. Even a slight opening and closing of the jaw, coupled with a twitching movement of the claws, is enough to give your viewers a chill. Try applying various human poses to the Raptor for more comedic effects. Don't forget to animate the claws on the feet. When the Raptor starts to run, its tail should be straight out, or even up a little.

THE DOE

As the gentlest of creatures, animate the Doe's movements to be subtle and slow. The Doe tends to move its head side to side frequently to search for possible predators when they're in the area. When the Doe runs, it should leap every once in a while.

THE BASS

All that needs to be animated on the Bass when it is swimming peacefully in the river are the belly fins and the mouth, and both very little. Of course, when it's caught on a hook, the whole body thrashes wildly.

THE BEAR

The Bear lumbers as it walks. When it runs, it tends to leap a little, with its front half leaving the ground, followed by its back half doing the same. Poser

provides the necessary parameters for you to give the Bear a great animated snarl, especially effective for close-up head shots.

THE BUCK

You can use many of the horse sequences from the Muybridge volumes to animate the Buck. Animate it running with head down for a dramatic effect. Try your hand at animating two Bucks in combat, locking their horns.

THE CHIMPANZEE

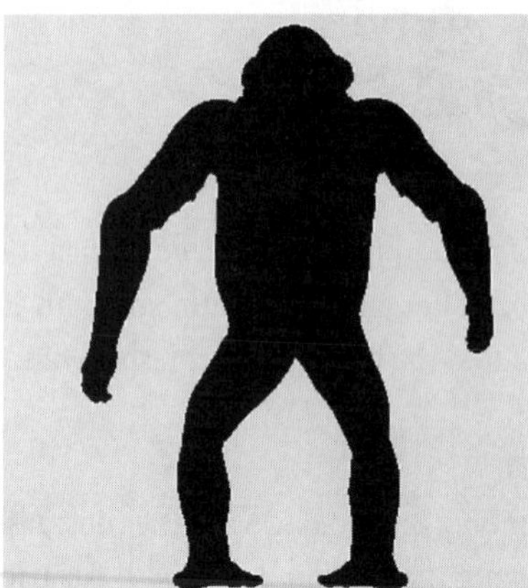

More than any other animal, the Chimp responds very effectively to any human pose, though sometimes comically. Use standard human poses as keyframes to animate the Chimp, especially the dramatic poses like the karate kick. When we explore the Walk Designer in Chapter 14, we'll see that the Chimp also can be animated through this alternate method.

THE COW

Cows usually move with their heads down, and they seldom run. Consequently, to show a complete cycle of a Cow's walk, you have to have a larger animation (ten seconds is adequate). If you want to add horns and show the Cow as a Bull, animate the head up and down and side to side to show the aggressive horn movements.

THE FROG

When leaping, the Frog's back legs go from a folded position to straight out. To emphasize the animated explosiveness of a leap, make the legs longer when stretched out and shorten their length when folded. When the Frog opens its mouth, bulge the eyes out.

THE KILLER WHALE

Except for a slight movement from side to side of the tail sections, all you have to do to animate the Killer Whale is to set it on a path that takes it in and out of the water. Curve its body to make the motion look more fluid.

THE LION

The Lion should always raise its head skyward when it roars. Except when chasing prey, the Lion walks rather leisurely. Its tail flicks regularly to keep flies away.

THE PENGUIN

Make sure that the penguin rocks from side to side as it waddles along. Its wings should also flap while this is happening.

THE SHARK

The most frightening aspect of the Shark is that it shows little movement while gliding along, so animating it is rather simple. When it bites prey however, it tends to spin wildly to tear away what it wants.

THE WOLF

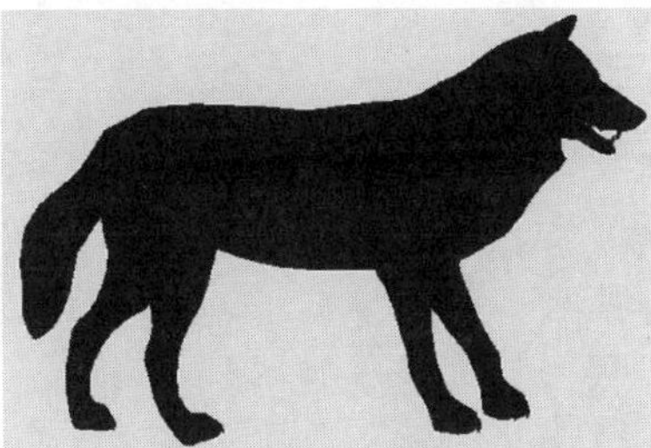

Animate the Wolf much as you would the Dog. The most effective animated pose for the Wolf is to show it in silhouette, baying at the moon.

THE ZEBRA

Animate the Zebra much as you would the horse, making the Muybridge volumes a good resource. When standing around, animate the tail flicking a lot, along with the ears.

Moving Along

In this chapter, we've explored some of the aspects of animating animal models in Poser. The next chapter looks at composite models and how they can be animated.

CHAPTER 13

Composite Character Animation

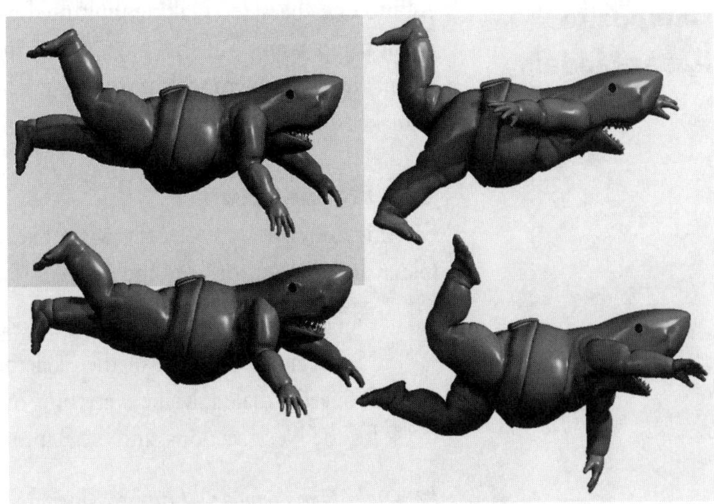

Having already covered the development of composite characters in Chapter 7, it is important to spend some time exploring how to animate your composited creations. Depending upon the type of composited model you are working with, there are some problem areas that may arise when you try to animate it. In this chapter, we'll look at how to animate three different types of composites: Multiple Composite Poser Models, Prop Composites, and Composites that combine models and props.

Multiple Composite Poser Models

As you saw in Chapter 7, it is very possible to combine two or more Poser models into one character, making unwanted parts invisible. So that's what we are about to do again, but this time, animating the composited character. So to begin, we'll use two models from the standard sets that ship with Poser 3, just to make sure everyone has them and can follow along.

THE RAPSKELION

For this exercise, we'll use the Male Skeleton from the Additional Figures folder, and the Raptor from the Animals folder. Do the following:

1. Open Poser and load in the Male Skeleton and Raptor models. Make the Neck, Jaw, and Head of the Skeleton invisible in the Male Skeleton's Properties dialog. Make everything on the Raptor model invisible except for the Neck sections, and the Raptor's Head. See Figure 13.1.

Karuna! Always remove all Inverse Kinematics from all models used to construct a composited figure.

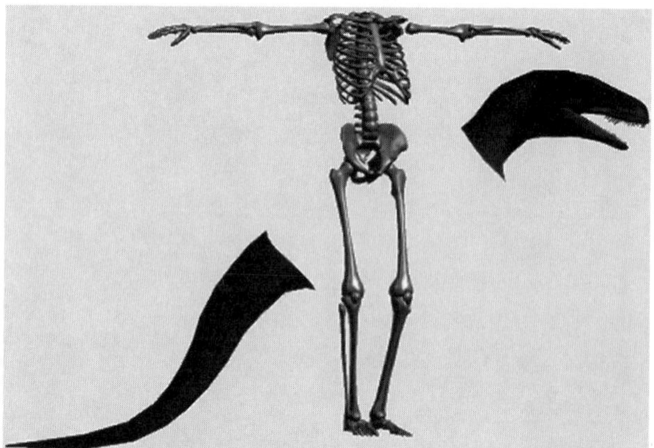

FIGURE 13.1 *The composited figure starts with these components.*

2. Turn both models so they are facing in the same direction. You will have to adjust the Skeleton so it is larger, and the Raptor so it is smaller as we go along, so the parts look like a natural fit. Select the Raptor Body from the list, and carefully move the Raptor Body until the Head sits on the Male Skeleton's upper Chest. See Figure 13.2.
3. As shown in Figure 13.2, you can see the way that I bent the body as a standing pose. I did this because the head is large, and I wanted to adjust the spine so it looked like it was accommodating the weight of the head. You should look at the figure and make the same adjustments.
4. In the list, if the Skeleton was added first, it shows up as Figure 1 and the Raptor as Figure 2. When you want to move body parts of the Skeleton, make sure Figure 1 is selected. Select Figure 2 when you want to animate the Raptor's Head parts.

Karuna! Make sure that you save this figure as a Poser 3 Document file and not as a library figure. The reason is that if saved as a figure, only the selected half of the model will be saved.

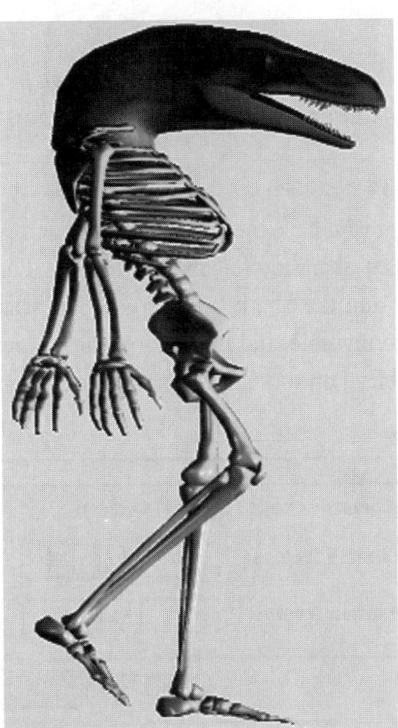

FIGURE 13.2 *The Raptor Body is moved so the Raptor Head sits on the Skeleton Body.*

5. Go to the Animation Sets folder in the Poses library and double-click on any of the walking or running sets. You'll see how many frames it takes below its name. Change the number of frames in your animation to 120 at 30 FPS (that's four seconds).
6. The animated pose has been added starting at frame 1 of your animation, but the whole animated pose only covers part of your 120 frames, so you have to expand the animation to address all of your frames. Open the Retime Animation dialog in the Animation menu on the top toolbar. See Figure 13.3.
7. The first row asks you for the number of frames you want to expand, and the second row asks what you want to expand the animated frames to. In the first row, input the number of frames in the animated poses you loaded in. If that number was 24 for instance, the first row should read 1 to 24. You shouldn't have to do anything in the second row, as that lists the total number of animated frames, in this case 1 to 120. Hit OK. The animation is now retimed. You can also compress animated frames in the same manner.
8. Preview the animation. Tweak where necessary, and when satisfied, render to disk.

Karuna! Make sure you check out the animation from different angles before rendering. You may even want to render more than one angle for later editing together.

SHARKBOY

Those of you who have the Zygote Sampler and Animals libraries can try this one. It's called Sharkboy for obvious reasons. Load in Baby Sumo from the Sampler set and the Shark from Zygote Animals. Make everything but the Shark's Head invisible, and make Baby Sumo's Head invisible. Carefully place the Shark's Head on top of Baby Sumo's neck in a vertical position (select the

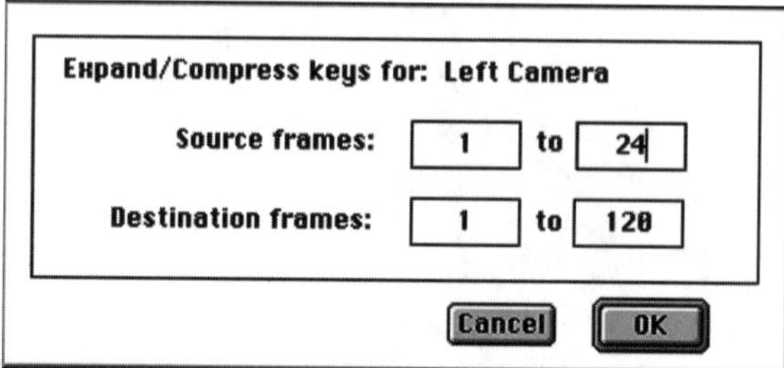

FIGURE 13.3 *The Retime Animation dialog.*

Shark's Body to move it and rotate it on the X axis). Make Baby Sumo's Neck the Parent of the Shark Head. Rotate Baby Sumo's body so that it is horizontal.

This is important. Many times, when you create a composite out of two or more models, it is important not to use either model's texture. Instead, use the Paint Tool to color both models so the parts match hues. This makes the finished composite look less like two separate models. It's also effective to use colored lights to blend the seam where the models meet.

See if you can animate the arms and legs of Baby Sumo so they look like they are flapping in water. Set the first and last keyframe of your animation first, making them the same. This allows you to loop the animation as many times as you like. See Figure 13.4.

Prop Composites

There may be times when you want to create an animation in Poser that has no human or animal models in it. It may be that you need a background animation, or perhaps an animation for a non-Poser project. You can use Poser to animate any Props in the Props library, or any 3D objects whose file format Poser can import. Poser's keyframe animation capability is far more variable than addressing human and animal models alone. See Figure 13.5.

Take a close look at the objects being animated as displayed in Figure 13.5. They are all very simple objects. The best way to learn how to animate complex scenes is to start with simple objects. That way, your interest is centered upon

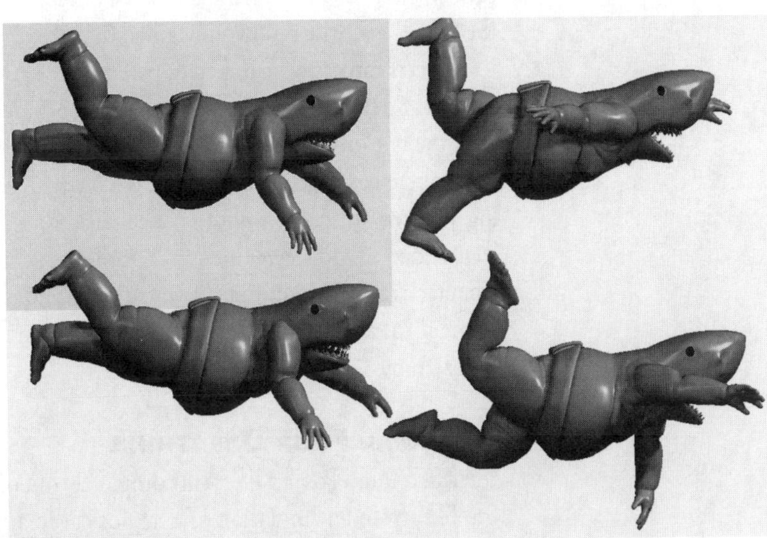

FIGURE 13.4 *Sharkboy is a combination of Zygote's Baby Sumo and the Zygote Shark.*

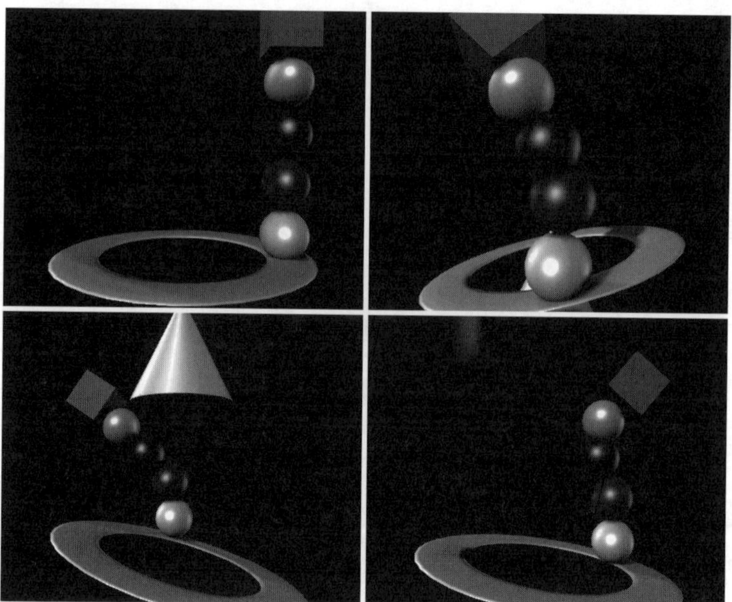

FIGURE 13.5 *Here is a selection of frames from an animation, all of whose elements are basic 3D models from the Props library.*

the animation, not the allure of the objects. The same principle is applied to movie-making in general. If you can tell a story with basic objects, think how much more you can do when it comes to developing themes with more complex objects. Basic objects are seen as symbols anyway and can sometimes force the viewer to create his own imagined dialog.

Objects can easily be linked or parented to each other in Poser. The stack of spheres and the top cube shown in Figure 13.5 are all hierarchically connected, with the bottom-most object set as the parent of the object above it. The bottom sphere has the flattened Torus as its parent, so as the Torus tilts, the moving stack of objects tilts with it. The background sphere and the rising cone were added to add viewer interest, but they are dispensable to the main action. The stack rotates around the flattened torus and is also affected by the motions of the torus itself. Take a look at this animation on the CD-ROM. It's called Props1.mov.

EXTERNAL PROP CREATIONS

You can create a Poser 3 lifeform completely out of Props. It can take any form you like, from an emulation of a dog or cat to a more otherworldly creature. No human or animal models are involved, but you can use the Props Parameter dials for rotational and positional movement. In a composited Prop char-

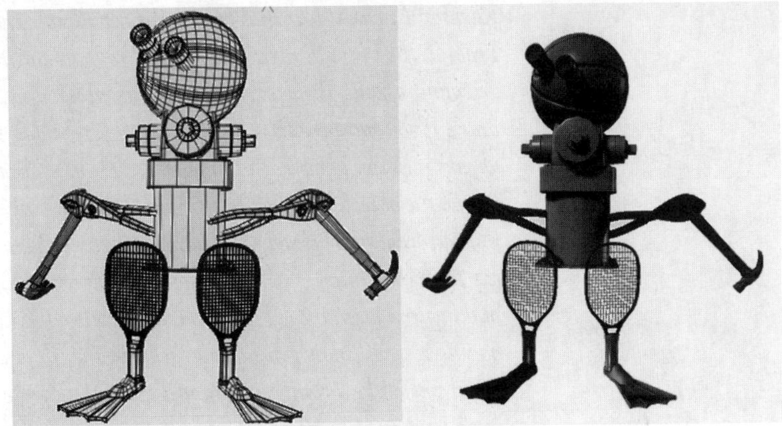

FIGURE 13.6 *Each of the elements of this figure consists of a Tool or Sports Prop from the Zygote Prop libraries. Here, the Fire Hydrant is the central Parent figure.*

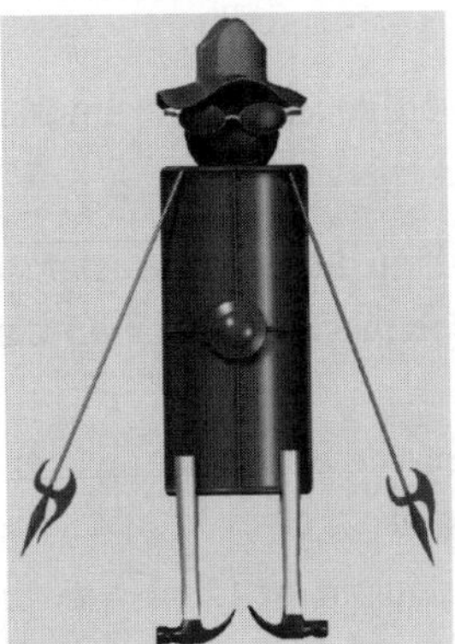

FIGURE 13.7 *Hammers for legs, Spears for arms, a Shield for a body. All this topped by a Basketball for a head, wearing Sunglasses, and covered by a Cowboy Hat. This figure can be animated by rotating any of its Zygote Props parts.*

acter, each of the Props is linked in a series of parental chains. See Figures 13.6 and 13.7.

Mixed Composite Combination Animations

In addition to replacing a figure element with a Prop, you also have the option of parenting the Prop and any selected element of the model. Using a Sword Prop, for instance, you can move it into position over one of the hands of the model, and use that same hand as the Prop's Parent. The Prop still has independent movement on its own when it is selected, but any additional movement of its parental model element will also animate the parented Prop.

Karuna! Karuna! Karuna! Here is an invaluable tip for working with the Zygote Props in the Props library. The Zygote Props are written to the document in a tilted orientation, with their Origin Points messed up, and their icons missing from the library. If you have the time and patience, here's what to do to fix them. First, set the object's rotation to zero after importing. Then, move its Origin Point so that it centers on the object. Use the Outline Display Mode when moving the Origin Point so you can see it more clearly and jump between views to center it. Last, delete the object from the library (but not from the Document). Now add it to the library again, making sure to hit the OK button on the dialog and not the Return key on your keyboard. You will now have a color icon in the library. That fixes everything. Now, when you make a composited model using the Zygote Props, they will come in perfectly, and rotating them will do what you expect. Do this for each Zygote Prop.

RULES FOR USING PROPS WITH HUMAN AND ANIMAL MODELS

Whether attaching a sword to an animated musketeer or a hat to a horse, here are some suggested rules to attend to:

- Always move the Prop into position before posing the model. Use the orthographic views to make sure the Prop is positioned exactly where you want it.
- Turn off IK, so that necessary editing later avoids having keyframes assigned to every frame.
- Turn on Full Tracking in the Display menu when positioning Props, so you are aware of the exact position of the Prop as related to the body of the model when moving it.
- When placing a Prop in the model's hand, leave the hand open. After it is placed, close the hand on the Prop by using the hand's Grasp Parameter.
- If you are creating an animation with more than one human or animal model in it, you might explore (when possible) fully animating the first figure before loading the next one in. Otherwise, the edits can get very tricky, and you will definitely have to be adjusting the motion curves.

See Figures 13.8 to 13.10.

Once the Props have been positioned and parented, you can use the model's rotational Parameters to animate the character. See Figure 13.11.

FIGURE 13.8 *The unaltered Zygote Heavy Man model, surrounded by the Props before their placement. While placing the Props, leave the model in its defaulted position.*

FIGURE 13.9 *The Props are placed in position, related to the model. The Hat is Parent to the Knife, and the Head is Parent to the Hat. The Saw and Shovel are Parented by their respective Hands.*

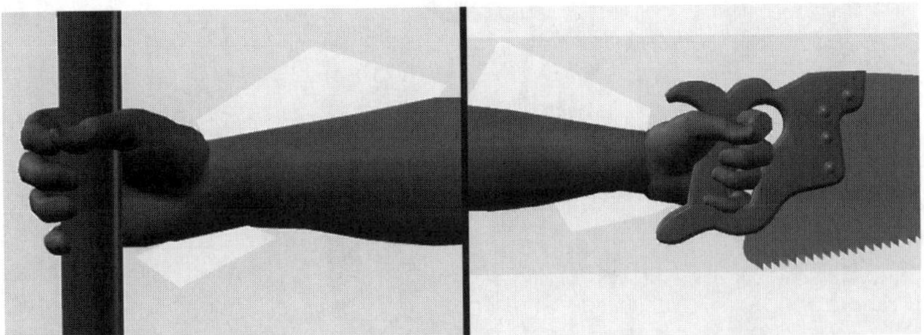

FIGURE 13.10 *Close-up cameras of the hands display the use of the Grasp Parameter Dial to "hold" the Props.*

COMPLEX COMPOSITES TO ANIMATE

Just how complex a scene can be animated in Poser 3? Look at Figure 13.12 for just one example. The head and hands of the large figure were replaced by spheres. A Zygote Police Hat is parented to the large head sphere, and a sword to the left hand sphere. A Zygote Alien model, with an enlarged head, sits on the right hand (sphere) of the large model. On the Alien's head is a parented Zygote Female Hair Prop. There are thousands of possible animations that can be created from just this one composited composition.

Shooting a Cannonball

One of the Props in the Zygote Tools and Weapons folder is a wonderful cannon, ready to play a part in your movies. To do this exercise, you will need to

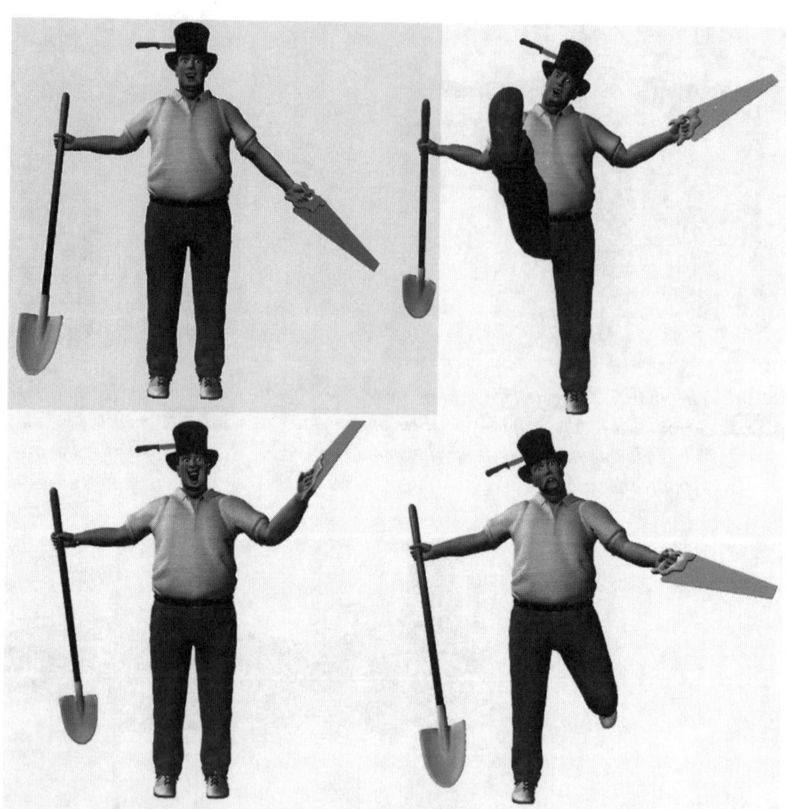

FIGURE 13.11 *Selected frames from the animation of the PropGuy model.*

FIGURE 13.12 *One example of a fairly complex composite that can be keyframe animated.*

have the Zygote Props folder installed in your Props library. Use the frames in Figure 13.13 as a reference. Do the following:

1. Load the Zygote Sumo Baby, or any other model you would like to use as the cannoneer. Load the Zygote Cannon Prop. Face them both away from the camera.
2. Make this a 150-frame animation. Move the cannoneer's arms at frame 1 so they are up in the air, and down at the side in frame 100. This is the "Fire" command.
3. You will be adding two Ball Props. One is for the cannon explosion and the other for the cannonball. Place the Ball Prop to act as the explosion around the front of the cannon and set its size to zero at frame 1. Set its size to .001 at frame 99, and to 400% at frame 101. Set its size to zero again at frame 106. Color it red.
4. For the cannonball, resize the Ball so that it fits comfortably in the barrel of the cannon and color it dark blue. Place it just inside of the cannon barrel at frame 1 and set its protrusion to .001 from the barrel in frame 107. In frame 150, set its distance from the cannon on a straight trajec-

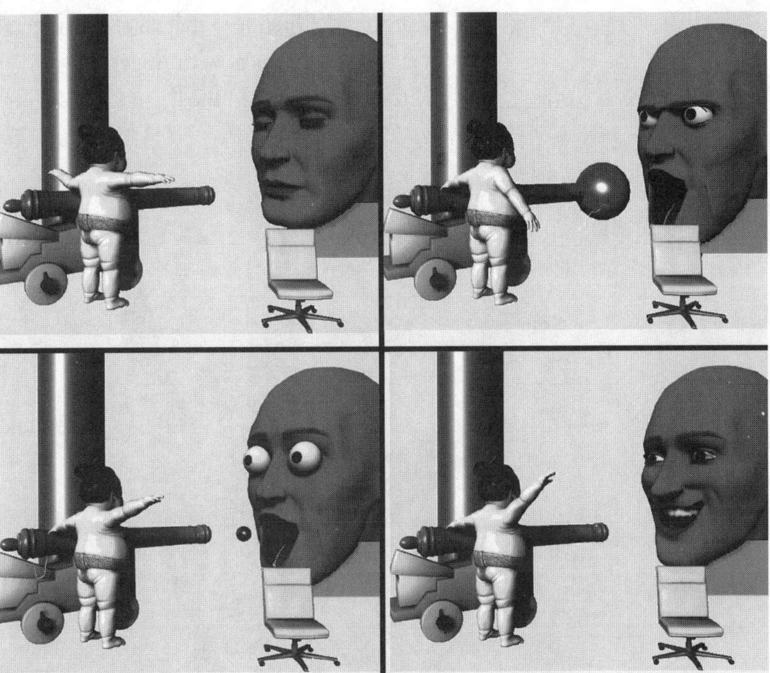

FIGURE 13.13 *Selected frames from the Cannonball animation, displaying the items described in the tutorial.*

tory off the screen. If you've done this right, the preview will show an explosion followed by the cannonball flying straight out of the barrel of the cannon.

5. Within plain view in your Document window, load one of the heads from the Additional Figures folder. Set it up so the mouth is in a direct line in front of the cannon. Set frame 1 and 80 to keyframe the mouth closed and keyframe 105 to a wide open mouth. Add some expression to the eyes and eyebrows at this same point.
6. The cannonball should head right into the wide open mouth. At frame 125, close the mouth and give it a smile. Return the mouth to no smile and closed at the last frame, so the animation can loop.
7. If you like, you can add some other Props in the scene just for interest. Save the animation to disk after you render it.

Hand 'O Heads

In this final animation walkthrough in this chapter, we will create an animation that would be nearly impossible to design with anything else but Poser 3. I call it "Hand 'O Heads," and you'll see why. Do the following:

1. Load the Left Hand from the Additional Figures folder. This is a stand-alone hand. Open it so that all of the fingers are pretty straight and rotate it so that it is vertical with fingers upward as seen by the camera. Create a little space between the fingers. See Figure 13.14.

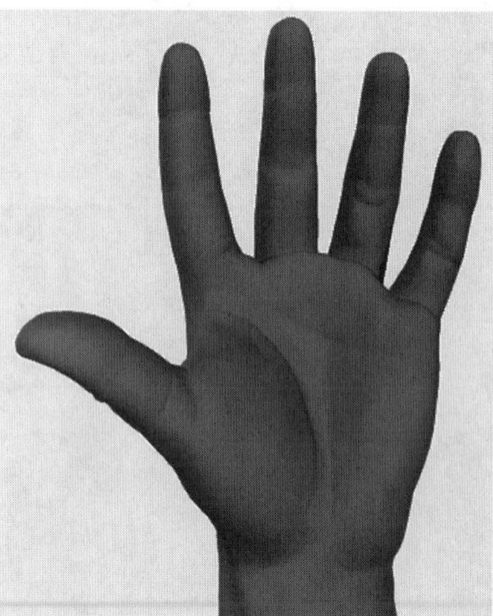

FIGURE 13.14 *The Left Hand is loaded to the Document window.*

2. Now load five stand-alone Heads from the Additional Figures folder. They can be any mix of the male and female Heads.
3. Resize each Head so it looks natural on top of a finger of the hand, and place each Head on the four fingers and the thumb. Each Head should be parented to the third finger or thumb part which it sits on. See Figure 13.15.
4. Place some Props, Hair and/or Hats, on each of the Heads. Parent the Hats and Hair to the same finger part that each respective Head is parented to. Give each of the faces a different expression. See Figure 13.16.

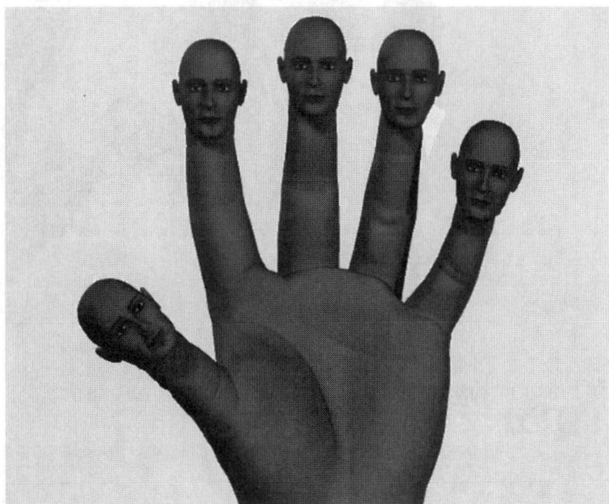

FIGURE 13.15 *The Heads are in position on each of the fingers of the hand.*

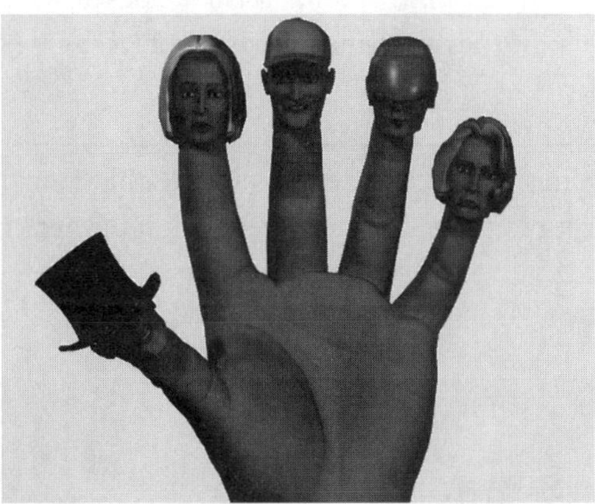

FIGURE 13.16 *Each of the Heads now has a Hair or Hat Prop, and a unique expression.*

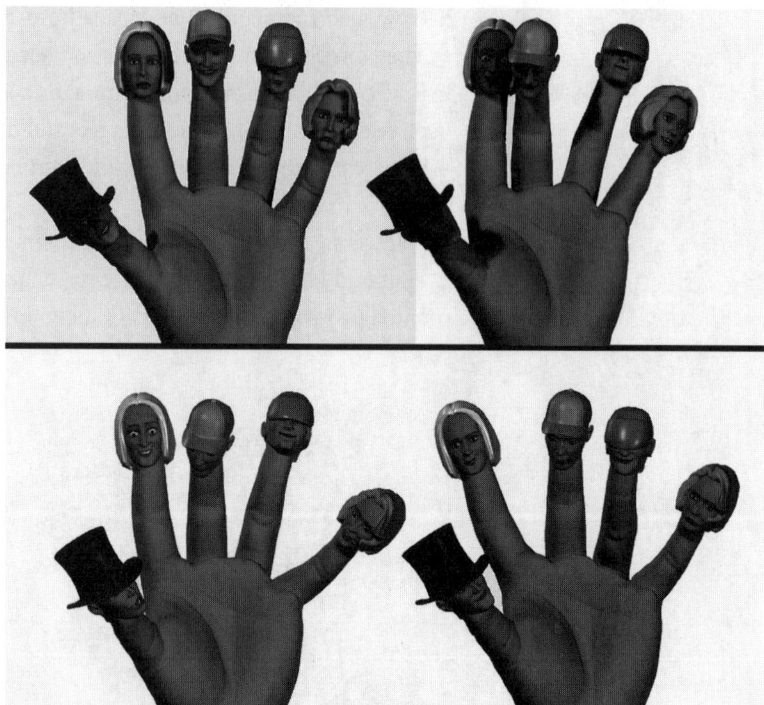

FIGURE 13.17 *Frames from the Hand 'O Heads animation.*

5. Keyframe animate each of the Heads, altering their expressions and rotations, and animate a slight movement into the finger each sits on. Make this a 180-frame animation. Render, save to disk, and amaze your friends and family. See Figure 13.17.

Moving Along

In this chapter, we have explored creating composited animations of different types. In the next chapter, we'll look at the miraculous Poser 3 Walk Designer.

CHAPTER

14 The Walk Designer

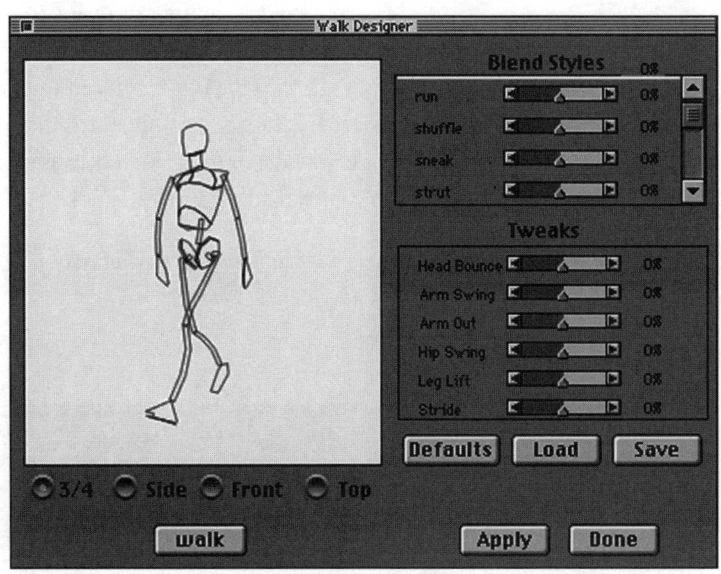

Poser 3 addresses one of the most complex and often supremely annoying tasks that an animator faces: how to create a realistic walk pattern for a targeted character. In Poser 3, the targeted character has to be bipedal, but future versions of Poser may address quadripeds as well. The Walk Designer is one of the most powerful features of Poser 3, though it is quite simple to use and master.

The Walk Designer Control Dialog

The Walk Designer Control Dialog is an interactive display that shows you exactly what the various parameter dials do as you adjust them. See Figure 14.1.

Let's take a quick tour of this dialog (refer to Figure 14.1). On the left is an animated display that shows you exactly what your walk looks like as you adjust the dials on the right. You can watch the walk from a 3/4, top, side, or front view. It is highly recommended that you switch among all of these view options before designing a walk, because that enables you to catch any anomalies in your walk design that might be hidden from one view alone.

Karuna! Make sure the Foreground color is very dark in order to see the animated preview in the Walk Designer.

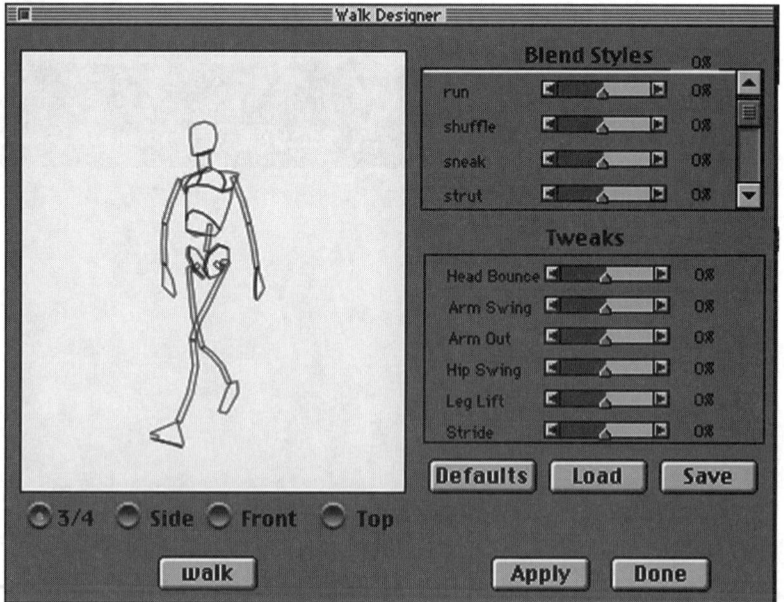

FIGURE 14.1 *The Walk Designer Control Dialog, accessed from the Window menu.*

On the right are two groups of walk design parameter dials: Blend Styles and Tweaks. Think of Blend Styles as the major parameters, and Tweaks as adjustments within those parameters. In Table 14.1, we will look at each of the Blend Styles and Tweaks in detail, describing what various parameter settings do.

Below the Tweaks Parameter Dials are three buttons: Default, Load, and Save. Hitting Default zeroes out all of the Parameters. Anytime you design a walk that you like, you can Save it to disk by first clicking on the Save button, and then selecting a name and target drive path. Click on Load to import previously saved walk designs.

The bottom row of buttons includes Walk, Apply, and Done. Click on Walk (which then becomes Stop) to activate the mannequin walking with your adjusted walk style, and Stop to cease its motion. Apply brings up the Apply dialog, with another list of specific parameters to decide upon before committing the walk to the target model. After modifying all of the Apply parameters as you want them, you are returned to the Walk Designer Control Dialog to click on Done.

THE APPLY DIALOG

After the walk has been designed to your liking, clicking on Apply is the next step. This brings up the Apply Dialog. See Figure 14.2.

Refer to Figure 14.2 as we explore each option in the Apply Dialog. At the very top of the dialog are two input areas, one for Start Frame and one for End Frame. The simplest way to configure the frames being addressed is to leave these settings at their defaulted indications, as this represents the total length of your frame settings, beginning to end. But as we'll see a little later in this chapter (under Non-Sequential Walks), there are reasons for selecting other than the defaulted frame number references here. Leaving this at the defaulted numbers results in the walk being applied to every frame in your present sequence.

Under the frame settings is a list of the Figures (models) in your Document window. Select the model from this list that you want to apply the present walk to. The walk remains resident in the Walk Designer, so you can apply the same walk to another model after applying it to the one selected, though it's always safer to save your customized walks before applying them to the model.

The next setting down consists of a checkbox for Walk in Place. Walk in Place is most useful when you are going to export the animated sequence to RayDream and set the figure on a path in that environment. Walk in Place is also useful when it's enough to show the figure walking in place for the project you're creating (perhaps a project that doesn't even require showing all of the

Table 14.1 Parameter setting conditions for Blend Styles and Tweaks. Note that these are examined here as unitary options, with all other settings defaulted to zero.

Parameter Setting	All the Way Down	1/2 Down	Defaulted at Zero	1/2 Up	All the Way Up
Run This setting differentiates between walks and runs.	Creates a wacky bouncing motion that can seriously jumble appendages like arms and hand positions.	Creates a skipping motion.	Creates a normalized walk.	Creates a bounding run, good for a fast race.	Creates a chaotic bouncy run and can cause overlaps in arm swings and positions.
Shuffle A Shuffle is defined as a walk with a relaxed attitude.	Creates a jumbled disorganized skip.	Creates a hubristic walk, as if the model were self-satisfied beyond criticism.	No effect on the walk.	Creates a plodding shuffle, as if the figure were looking at the sidewalk and just ambling along.	Creates an erratic shuffle, making the figure look like something is physically wrong with the legs.
Sneak Defined as a walk that remains unexpected when practiced.	Jumbles the entire upper body in a tangle.	Still pretty radical since it distorts other body parts.	No effect.	A caricature of a sneak, more like a New Orleans strut.	A cartoony strut, with the body bending back and forth radically at the Hip.
Strut A Strut is a display of pride, sometimes used to attract the opposite sex to one's importance.	Creates a movement in the arms reminiscent of dancing, or what some communities call the "Hand Jive."	Creates a Strut that makes the arms look like they're swatting flies when the Arms are extended outward.	No effect.	A real determined Strut.	A Strut that makes the arms look like they're shadow boxing.
Head Bounce The head bounces naturally to compensate for rhythmic impacts suffered by the lower body.	Makes the head shake violently, which would break the neck.	Creates a head bounce that makes the head shake as in signifying "yes."	No effect.	Reverse of –50%.	Reverse of –100%.

Arm Swing There is always arm swing in a walk, so this parameter setting just emphasizes it to various degrees.	Arms swing rather limply.	Arm swing a little less limp.	No effect, normal arm swing.	Arms swing a little more purposefully.	Arm swing is very purposeful, as in a march.
Arm Out This parameter forces the arms away from or closer to the torso (definitely move the arms away from the torso in a walk if the model is heavy).	Arms crossed in front of chest for the whole walk.	Arms crossed in front of pelvis for the whole walk.	No effect.	Arms pushed away from body, as if the model had very muscular arms.	Arms radically pushed away, forming a cross with the torso.
Hip Swing Used to emulate a seductive feminine walk.	Hips sway radically.	Moderate hip sway.	No movement.	Hip sway opposite of –50%.	Hip sway opposite of –100%.
Leg Lift This parameter sets the height of the legs at their maximum.	Legs sort of slide along the ground.	Legs off the ground a little.	Normal height above ground during walk.	Legs lifted up noticeably.	Legs lifted off ground as in a march.
Stride This represents the distance covered with each step.	Walk in place.	Short stride.	Normal stride.	Above normal stride.	Very long stride, like Grouch Marx.

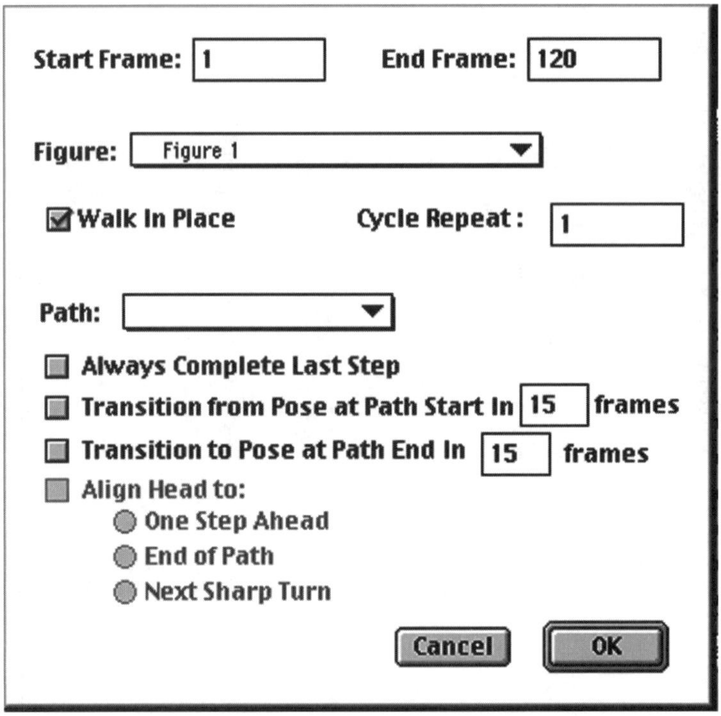

FIGURE 14.2 *The Apply Dialog.*

foot movements). Walking and running in place over a moving backdrop is an old movie trick, and this can be duplicated in Poser 3. Another Walk in Place use comes about when you are going to map the animation file to a moving plane in another 3D application and set the plane in motion. Most professional 3D applications allow you to do this, dropping out the background color. This is a way to export Poser 3 animation files to most every 3D application around, making no difference if Poser directly supports that application. On the right is another input area that remains ghosted out unless Walk in Place is checked, called Cycle Repeat. If a model is walking in place, without moving on a path, you can set the Cycle Repeat to any whole number. The higher this value, the faster the walk will seem, since the walk has to be stuffed in a finite number of frames. The number placed here is in direct proportion to speed, so 2 will create a walk speed 2X as fast as 1, and 3 would be 3X, and so on.

If you have designed a path in your document window, it will appear in the Path selections and can be chosen from there. Obviously, you cannot set the model on a path and have it walk in place at the same time. There is an interesting optical illusion possible, however, as follows.

Out of Body Experience

1. Create two figures exactly the same and have them occupy the same exact space in your document. Create a Path for one (covered later under Paths if you need a refresher), but not for the other.
2. Apply the same Walk Design to both, except make the one with no path Walk in Place. The path for the other should be circular.

Can you guess the result? The figure will walk out itself like a ghost, and return to itself in perfect harmony. Use this to create an "out of body experience" animation.

THE APPLY DIALOG (CONTINUED)

At the bottom half of the Assign Dialog is a series of checkboxes.

Always Complete Last Step

If the animation is to loop, then this should be checked. If it is to be part of a patched sequence, then it need not be.

Transition From Pose/To Pose

Your model may be sitting at the start of an animation, then get up, assume a pose, and walk away. In this case, the model will need some number of frames to complete its initial movements. Checking Transition From Pose and inputting a number in the associated area (a path has to be assigned for this to make any sense) allows you to reserve frames for the initial pre-walking movements. In the same manner, Transition To Pose allows a model to end a walk by assuming another pose not associated with that walk. You have to carefully explore each of these options. Do not expect to get what you want on the first try. The main caution is to allow enough frames at the start and/or end of the walk sequence for the changes in action. The more radical the poses are from each other, the more transitional frames you will need.

Align Head To

If you have set the walk on a path, then you may command the model to look in specific directions while it is moving on the path. There are three options: One Step Ahead, End of Path, and Next Sharp Turn. The model's head will then move according to your selection.

CAUTION

Karuna! Do not assign any Head Bounce to the walking model when using the Align Head To options, or at most, very small values. It is disconcerting to see the model looking in a direction while its head is also bobbing up and down, unless you are trying to emulate a serious nervous condition.

Walk Design Parameters

Table 14.1 details what each of the Blend Styles and Tweaks accomplishes when set to five different values: All the way down, halfway down, defaulted, halfway up, and all the way up. Note that the Blend Styles range from –200 to +200, while the Tweaks range from –100 to +100. Settings in between those indicated moderate the detailed results.

Walk Design Parameter Combinations

The real magic of the Walk Designer comes when you combine more than one Blend Style and Tweak. These combined parameters lead to all sorts of unique walk looks. We have detailed some of them in Table 14.2.

Paths

Poser 3 is not as enabled a 3D Path animation environment as are other more robust applications, but it does offer you the chance to set objects and models in motion on a path. To draw a animation path in Poser, do the following:

1. Click on the model to be animated and go to the top camera view.
2. Under the Figure menu, activate the Create Path mode by selecting it.
3. You will see a path line extending out from the figure in the top view. Clicking on the line activates the path creation options. The Nodes that are displayed can be moved. Clicking on the path where no node is pre-

Table 14.2 How various combined parameter values create six unique walk styles. Input these values and see if you would name them the same as the author did, then explore your own settings. Save the Walk Designs you like.

Settings	Leaping Run	Max Pronging	Creepy Monster	Oh Yeah!	Tromp Romp	March
Run	83	–120	–3	0	3	0
Shuffle	0	0	0	0	–18	0
Sneak	0	18	25	0	25	0
Strut	0	0	0	0	0	0
Head Bounce	23	0	0	49	0	0
Arm Swing	20	–74	–100	0	–100	100
Arm Out	–38	100	100	0	38	0
Hip Swing	0	100	0	–100	0	0
Leg Lift	0	0	0	0	56	100
Stride	100	100	–70	0	–52	30

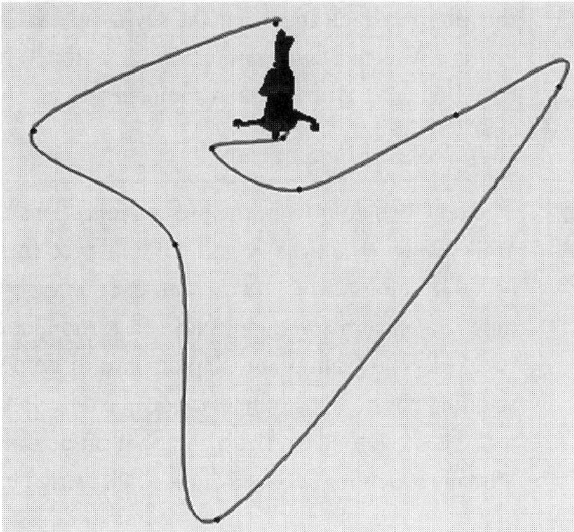

FIGURE 14.3 *Use the mouse to place and move path nodes in the top view.*

sent places a node at that point. Explore these options. When you are finished, simply stop customizing the path. See Figure 14.3.

4. Human and animal figures can be assigned a path in the Walk Designer, but Props cannot. Props have to be keyframe animated. Whenever you design a path, it is given a sequential numerical name (Path 1, Path 2, and so on).

NOTE

Note that a Path cannot be moved in the Y axis (up or down) and that it always rests upon the ground plane.

5. Clicking on a Path activates it, and brings up its parameter dials, where it can be scaled and/or translated along its X or Z axis, and rotated on the Y axis.

Transitional Walks

By "transitional walk" I refer to a walk assigned from the Walk Designer that targets fewer frames than the total number in your sequence. The extra frames can be at the start, end, or both the start and end of your animation. This necessitates checking the Transition From at Path Start and/or Transition To at Path End. Be aware that transitional walk may require some tweaking of your poses, since movement from one pose to another in a set number of frames may jostle elements you want to remain stable. In that case, simply go into the Motion Graph and delete the keyframes that are causing the problem. Applying a Walk to a figure sets up keyframes for every frame, which often have to be deleted and re-posed when anomalies occur.

Animals and the Walk Designer

The only two animals in the present collections that work very well with the Walk Designer are the Zygote Chimpanzee (best) and the Raptor (second best). To some extent, you can also use the Zygote Penguin, but some frames may render with severe polygonal distortion, and the poses will have to be tweaked. The Chimp and Raptor have to be positioned first to mimic the standing position of a human model, before applying Walk Designer parameters. The Zygote Alien, Baby, and Baby Sumo can also be considered standard human models for purposes of the Walk Designer.

USING OTHER ANIMALS WITH THE WALK DESIGNER

Here is a technique that I discovered that allows you to have varying degrees of success using the Walk Designer to animate other Poser animals (except for fish of course). Do the following:

1. After importing the selected animal from the Figure library folder, go to the right side view camera.
2. Turn off all IK settings. Bend the animal as shown in Figure 14.4.
3. In the Front camera View, use the Side-to-Side parameter to rotate each shoulder 90 degrees as shown in Figure 14.5.

FIGURE 14.4 *Note how the animal model is bent, so that a Walk Design can be applied.*

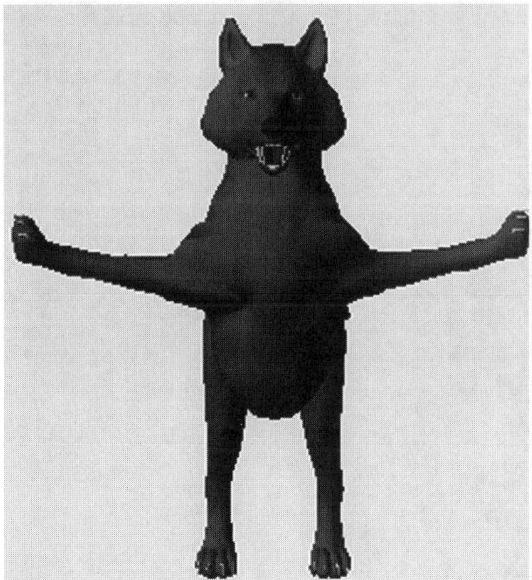

FIGURE 14.5 *The Shoulders of the animal are rotated Side-to-Side as shown here.*

FIGURE 14.6 *After applying the walk, the animal's arms will probably be crossed.*

4. Go to the Walk Designer and apply a walk to the animal. You will notice that most of the time, the animal's arms will be crossed when you preview the walk pose. See Figure 14.6.
5. To fix the arms, go to the keyframe Editor. Place a marquee around the left and right shoulders, and all of their children (upper arms, forearms, and hands). Delete all of these keyframes. See Figure 14.7.
6. Back on your Document window, you can now keyframe animate the arms again, having deleted all of the Walk Designer keyframes. Exploring these options further, and perfecting their technique, you can develop a whole library of animals perfect for fables and fairy stories. See Figure 14.8.

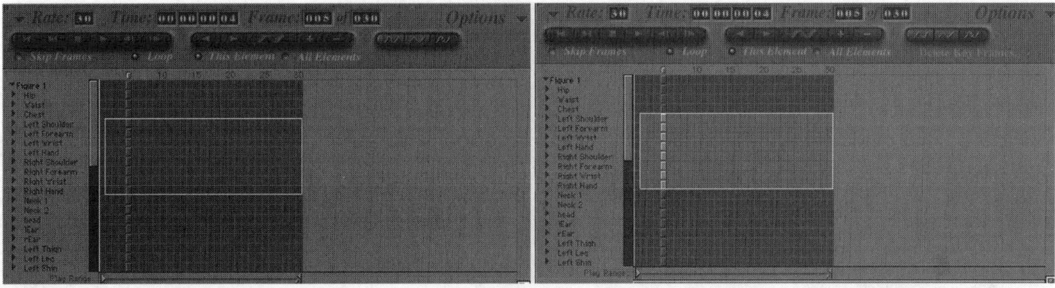

FIGURE 14.7 *The selected keyframes are deleted from the animation.*

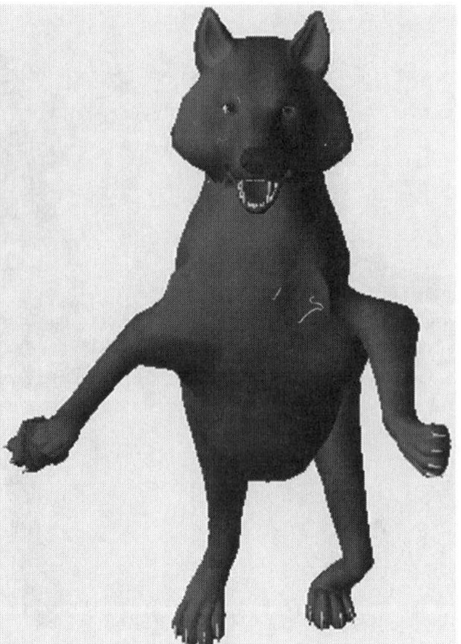

FIGURE 14.8 *The finished animated animal is ready for your own Mother Goose production.*

Using BVH Motion Files

Import a BVH Motion File, and it is instantly associated with your selected figure. I've found that the Z axis option works best when the question comes up on import. I've also found that the standard Poser figures work with BVH files better than many of the Zygote extras models. This is especially true when it comes to hand and arm twists, which if they're pushed too far, distort the model. You'll have to explore BVH files on a case-by-case basis. If you find them useful for your work, you can contact BioVision or House of Moves via their Web sites. They often post freebies that you can download and explore within Poser 3. BVH data works well when you expand the animation to a larger sequence. The motions still appear realistic when the sequence is expanded. See Figure 14.9.

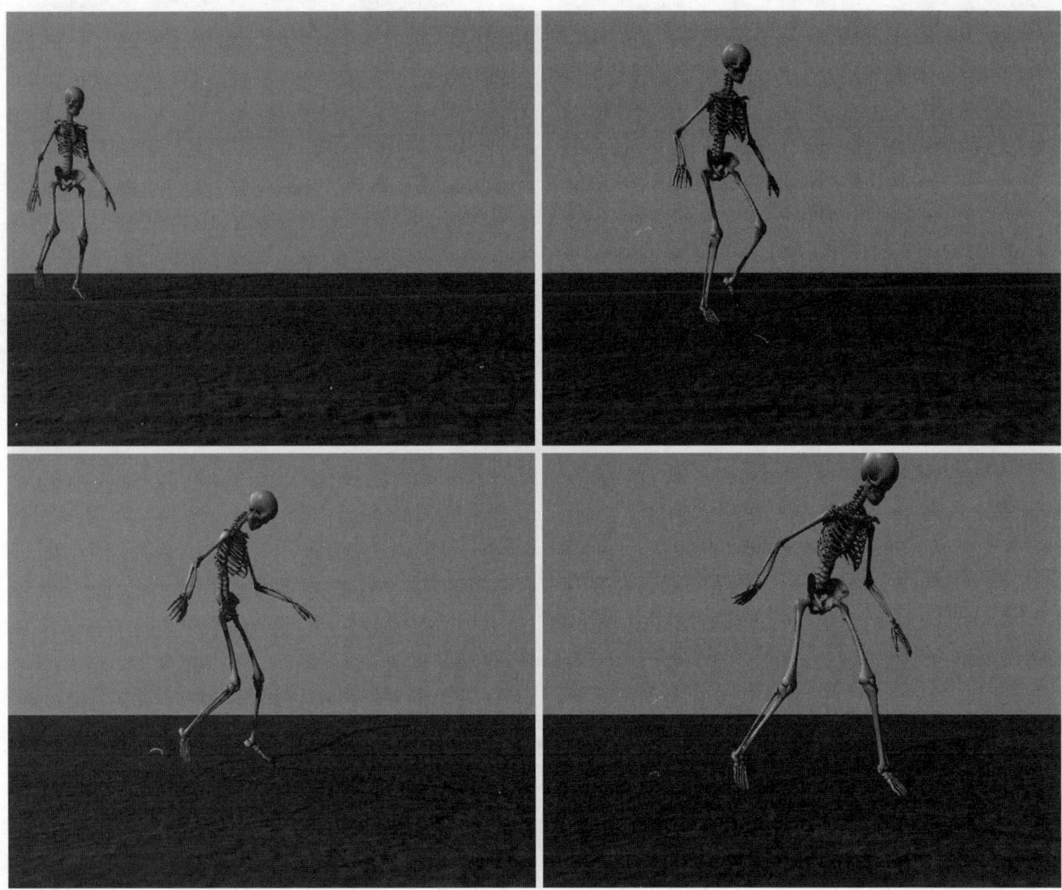

FIGURE 14.9 *This series of frames is from an animated sequence that uses the Poser Female Skeleton as a target for the Drunk.BVH file in the Men's Motions folder, located in the Motion capture directory on the Poser 3 CD.*

Moving Along

In this chapter, our focus has been to explore the intricacies of the Walk Designer, as well as to take a look at the application of BVH motion data files. In the next chapter, we'll detail how morphing works in Poser and what it can be used for.

CHAPTER 15

Morphing Madness

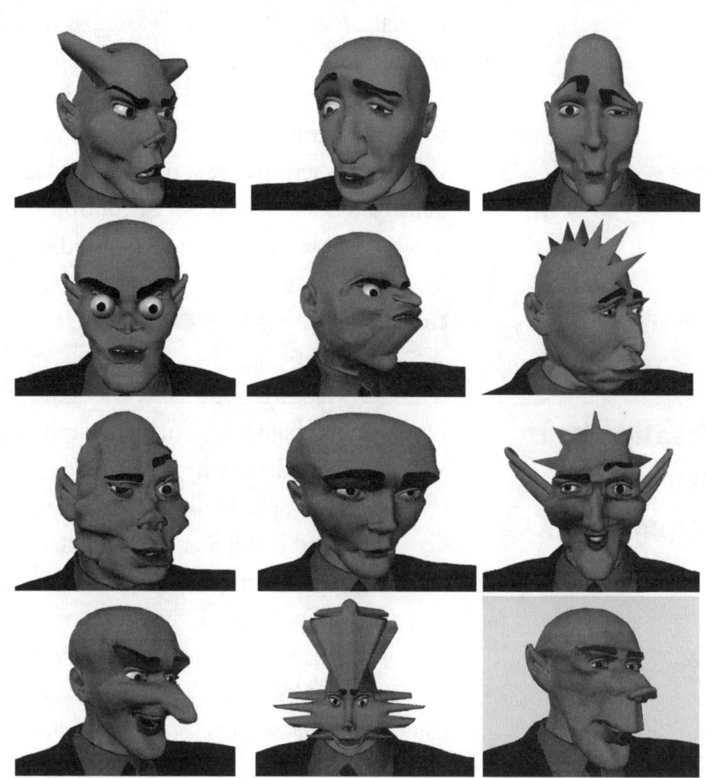

Everywhere you look in Poser 3, you will find tools and modules that are at the very edge of revolutionizing computer graphics and animation. The Morph capacity is another shining example. Actually, every time you tweak a Parameter dial, you are engaging in 3D morphing. A morphing target can be thought of as a target point on an object, and in adjusting a Parameter dial, you are moving toward (or away from) that 3D target point. It is also possible to move beyond a target point, which is where distortions are more likely to occur. Let's take an example to demonstrate.

Let's say that the optimum target point for the Smile Parameter is 2. If you move the Smile Parameter dial so that it reads 1, you have moved 50% of the way towards the Smile Morph target point. Moving the value to 2 will place you at that target point. Increasing the value to 4 will give you a very wide smile, but because you've moved beyond the optimum target value of 2, you will also severely distort surrounding areas of the face. Sometimes this can be quite beneficial, since it can be controlled to create extreme caricatures. Most times, however, you will want to avoid it altogether. This is an example of internal morphing in Poser 3, but you also have the option of adding externally created morph targets.

Creating Your Own Morph Targets

Let's first talk about what external morph targets are and why they are so useful. After that, we'll detail what you need to have and know to create them.

As you have by now discovered in your explorations of Poser 3, parameter dials are limited in number, so their potentials for transforming a targeted body part are also limited by what they address. There are no parameters, for instance, that deal with puffing out the cheeks or for enlarging the forehead. Wouldn't it be useful to have parameter dials for these actions when you needed them? Of course it would, and that's exactly what developing morph targets is for, to accommodate the further customization of selected parameters.

WHAT YOU NEED TO PROCEED

At this time, in order to proceed with the development and customization of morph targets, you need an external 3D application. Poser 3 supports any external 3D application that can save in the WaveFront (OBJ) format when it comes to the development of morph targets, but its central focus is on MetaCreations' Ray Dream Studio version 5 or higher. At the time of this writing, version 5.02 of Ray Dream Studio is available as an upgrade to version 5.0.

It can be downloaded from the MetaCreations Web site (http://www.metacreations.com). You must already have Ray Dream Studio version 5 installed to be able to upgrade to the latest version. The upgrade will automatically install what is needed over either the Mac or Windows versions of Ray Dream Studio 5.0.

The next step, if you haven't done this at the time Poser 3 was initially installed, is to install the specific Poser 3 Ray Dream plugins into Ray Dream Studio. If you are doing this after installing Poser 3, then open the Poser 3 installer, and select Custom. You will see the needed Poser 3 filters listed in your options. Simply check them and nothing else, and the Poser 3 installer will find the proper Ray Dream Studio plugins folder, and install the plugins.

CAUTION

Karuna! It is vital that when updating your Ray Dream application, that you should first remove it entirely. Copy any needed files to a separate storage space. Then reinstall version 5, and only after that, install the updater. This is because the updater is extremely finicky about finding anything extra other than the original Ray Dream Studio 5 application to update. You can replace any extra extensions or other files later, from the stored data you saved. Install the Poser files contained on the CD-ROM by selecting a Custom install of Poser 3.

Install the Poser Browser Files from the Poser 3 CD-ROM as follows:

1. Open Ray Dream 5.02 and go to the Browser. In the Browser menu, select Add Folder.
2. When your path dialog appears, find the Poser Browser Files folder on the Poser 3 CD-ROM and open it.
3. You won't see any files, but that's OK. Click Open Document while the Poser Browser Files folder is open.

Now you will see a collection of Poser 3 models in the new Poser Browser File, ready for use in Ray Dream Studio.

NOTE

Another alternative is to drop the Poser Browser Files in the 3D Clips folder in the Presets directory of Ray Dream Studio.

DEVELOPING POSER 3 MORPH TARGETS

If you have done everything detailed here so far, you have enabled Poser 3 and Ray Dream Studio 5.02 to talk to each other, or to put it more technically, to pass files back and forth. Now you're ready to explore another realm of Poser magic, developing your own Poser Morph targets.

Karuna! If you are using Poser 3 to develop unique characters for animated sequences, then you absolutely must master the Morphing process. Morphing gives you the capability to create thousands of customized characters from the basic figures shipped with Poser 3.

For your first morph target exploration using Ray Dream Studio, after you have successfully upgraded it and transferred the Poser filters over, proceed as follows:

1. Open Ray Dream. Go to the Import selection in the File menu and find a figure you would like to work on in the Poser/Runtime/Geometries library. Import it as a WaveFront (OBJ) file.
2. Double-click on the figure once it is viewable in the Ray Dream Perspective View window. This sends it into the Mesh Form Modeler.

Karuna! Do not move or rotate the figure in any manner, or all will turn to chaos!

3. In the Mesh Form Modeler, double-click on the body part you want to alter. Since the Figure is a grouped creation, that part will be highlighted.
4. Go to the Selection menu and choose Invert. Everything but your selected element will be highlighted. Delete the highlighted elements. Now all that is left is your targeted element.
5. Go to the Left View, or another orthogonal view that allows you to clearly see your selected element. You may want to zoom in (again, **DO NOT** rotate or move the element in any way!). Use the marquee or selection arrow to highlight that part of the model you want to alter.
6. Click on the Sphere of Influence (Magnet icon) in the toolbar. Select one of the four modification options in the dialog (Cubic Spline, Linear, Spiky, or Bumpy). Set the dimensions to 1 mm.
7. With the left mouse button held down, move the circular area that appears on screen over your selected points and vertices, so that you pull them away from their present position.
8. Click on "Done" (lower left corner of the display), which returns you to the preview screen. With the selected element still highlighted, choose Save As from the File menu.
9. Save your altered figure element in the same folder as its parent figure. Call it by a descriptive name and make sure it is saved as a WaveFront (OBJ) file.
10. Open Poser 3. Select the same figure you added morph targets to, and load it to the Document window.

11. Activate the body part that has morph targets and go to its Properties dialog. Click on Add Morph Target, and then on Locate, to locate the folder where the figure and its morph targets reside. Select one of the Morph Targets you created in Ray Dream Studio. Click on OK. Name the Parameter dial and click on OK again.
12. The Parameter dial that controls how much of the Morph target is activated is now resident in the Parameter dials stack and ready for keyframe animating and posing.

See Figure 15.1 for a visual map that shows you the route to take to develop a Morph Target.

The following steps are displayed in Figure 15.1:

1. Poser Figure is imported into the Perspective View in Ray Dream Studio. Double-clicking on it transports you to the Mesh Form Modeler.
2. In the Mesh Form Modeler, double-click on the element you want to work on (in this case, the Head).
3. Select Invert from the Selection menu. Your selection is inverted. Delete everything selected, and only the Head will be left.
4. Zoom in so you can see the mesh.
5. Go to a view that allows you to choose points and vertices. Select the points you want to modify with the marquee or the Selection Arrow.
6. Click on the Sphere of Attraction Tool and choose an attraction type.
7. Hold the mouse over the selected points and drag out the modification.
8. Click on "Done," and you are returned to the Perspective Preview window.
9. Select Save As from the File menu and save the object as an OBJ (WaveFront) file in the same folder as the original figure.
10. Open Poser and load in the original figure.
11. Select the element on the figure (in this case the Head). Go to the elements Properties dialog and click on "Add Morph Target."
12. When the next dialog pops up, click on Locate to find the Morph Target file you created in Ray Dream Studio. Name the Morph Target. Click on OK, then on OK again.
13. You will now see a new Parameter dial in the stack of dials, named accordingly.
14. Turn the Parameter dial to preview the effect on your selected element on the figure.

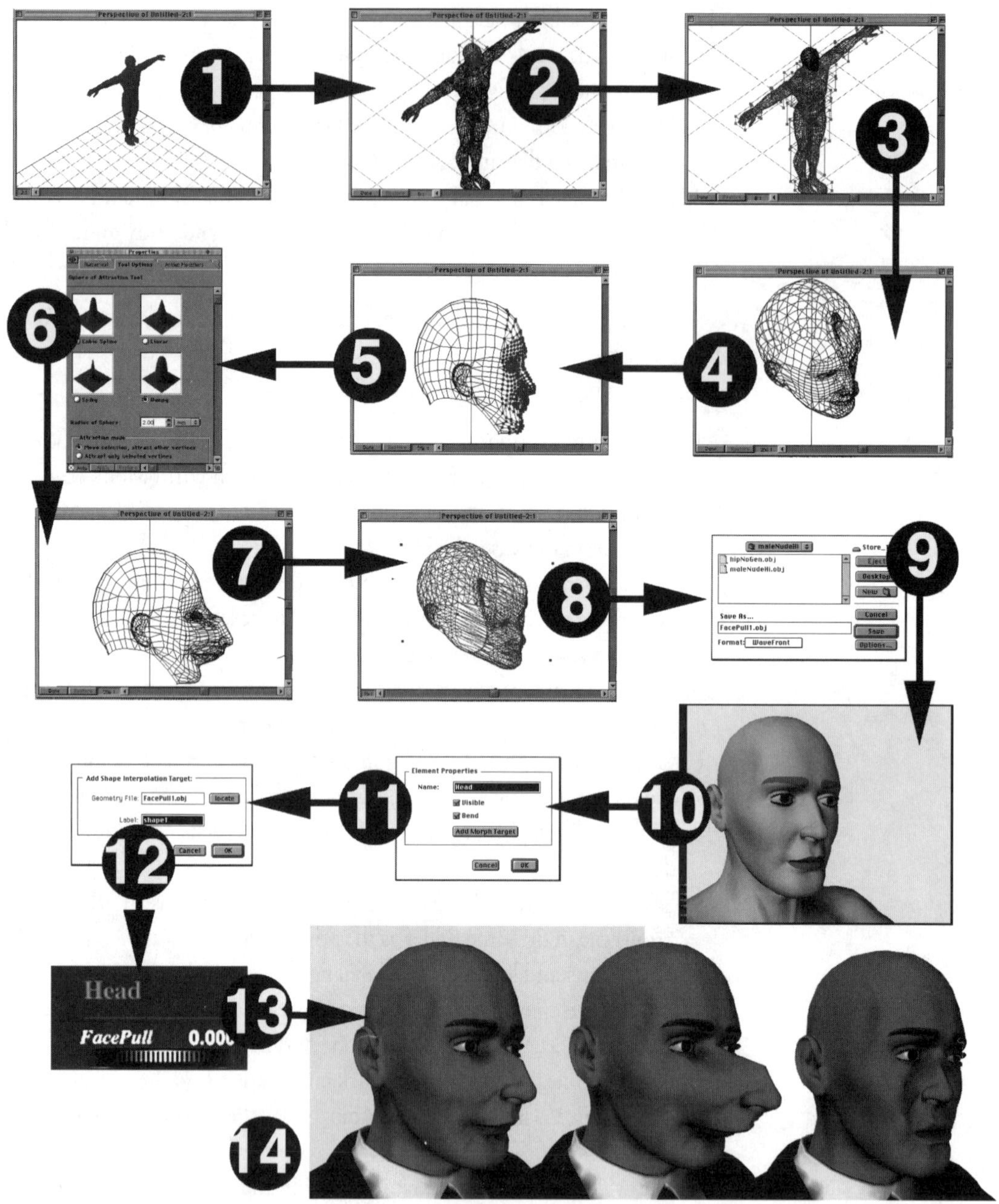

FIGURE 15.1 *A visual depiction of the process of creating Morph Targets with Ray Dream Studio for use in Poser 3.*

TARGET MORPH TYPES

There are as many Target Morph Types as you have the patience to create. Every unique group of points on a targeted element of a figure can be modified in many different ways and each one can be saved as a unique OBJ file for that element. As long as no polygons are added or removed and no rotation or repositioning of the element takes place, you can create dozens of original Target Morph dials for the intended figure element. This opens up Poser 3 as the most variable character creation tool around. Following are some examples of customized head Target Morphs you might like to investigate. All of the graphics examples are based upon the Male Business Suit model, though you may apply variations like these to any model you like.

Earoidz

In this example, the ears are pulled outward and upward to create the Target Morph. The result ranges from *Star Trek*'s Spock to head wings. See Figure 15.2.

Uplift

With this Target Morph, the whole front of the face from brow to lips can slide up or down. This, of course, pulls at the attached skin in either direction. Eye openings and placement may have to be adjusted with a negative Blink Parameter. See Figure 15.3.

FIGURE 15.2 *A series of alternate parameters using the Earoidz Target Morph.*

FIGURE 15.3 *A series of alternate parameters using the Uplift Target Morph.*

Talouse

This Target Morph is named after Toulouse Lautrec, because by elongating the nose and chin of the head, the resulting look resembles a figure in one of his paintings. See Figure 15.4.

Spikes

This simple Target Morph was created by pulling five spikes out of the head. You might even equate it with a Statue of Liberty look. Using negative values pokes the spikes through the face. See Figure 15.5.

Nostril

This Target Morph moves just the tip of the nose, up with positive values and down with negative values. See Figure 15.6.

FIGURE 15.4 *A series of alternate parameters using the Talouse Target Morph.*

FIGURE 15.5 *A series of alternate parameters using the Spikes Target Morph.*

FIGURE 15.6 *A series of alternate parameters using the Nostril Target Morph.*

Wide Nose

This simple Target Morph adjusts the nose width within a narrow range before distortions set in. See Figure 15.7.

Lowface

It's a good idea to develop two Lowface Target Morphs, one that stretches the lower half of the face vertically and the other one that stretches it horizontally. Used together, you can create a large number of diverse characters. See Figure 15.8.

Long Chin

This Target Morph lengthens or shortens the chin. See Figure 15.9.

FIGURE 15.7 *A series of alternate parameters using the Wide Nose Target Morph.*

FIGURE 15.8 *A series of alternate parameters using the two Lowface Target Morphs.*

FIGURE 15.9 *A series of alternate parameters using the Long Chin Target Morph.*

Lips Out

Lips Out was created so that only the lips move, and negative values are discouraged since they expose the teeth (maybe good for a monster). Pushed to extreme values, you have a duck bill. See Figure 15.10.

Two Horns

Growing horns is easy with a Target Morph that does nothing but size two horns on the sides of the head. See Figure 15.11.

Eye Stretch

This Target Morph stretches the eyes very subtly, addressing just a few polygons. The results can be just what's needed for oriental looks, or for more radical deformations. See Figure 15.12.

FIGURE 15.10 *A series of alternate parameters using the Lips Out Target Morph.*

FIGURE 15.11 *A series of alternate parameters using the Two Horns Target Morph.*

FIGURE 15.12 *A series of alternate parameters using the Eye Stretch Target Morph.*

Droop

This Target Morph selects points on the front of the face from nose to just below the lips, so the face can move up or down, stretching other skin along with it. See Figure 15.13.

Dome

The Dome Target Morphs address just the top of the head, making it stretch. So if you plan to use a wig, they're not that useful. With a bald head, however, you can create some neat effects. See Figure 15.14.

ChinJut

There is a lot of character defined by the shape of the chin. In this Target Morph, the chin can either jut out or in. See Figure 15.15.

FIGURE 15.13 *A series of alternate parameters using the Droop Target Morph.*

FIGURE 15.14 *A series of alternate parameters using the Dome Target Morph.*

FIGURE 15.15 *A series of alternate parameters using the ChinJut Target Morph.*

Cheek Puff

Puffing the cheeks is easy. Simply select a cheek section from the left view in Ray Dream Studios Mesh Form Designer and resize it to 200% on the X axis. Save as an OBJ file as usual. See Figure 15.16.

Face Pull

This Target Morph pushes the face backward or pulls it forward, for interesting animation keyframes or character development. See Figure 15.17.

MORPHING MADNESS IN ACTION

The real fun comes about when you combine all of the Morph Targets you have, developing either unique characters and/or keyframe poses. Remember that added to all of the Morph Targets you create, you can add the variations offered by tweaking the standard Parameter dials. All of this together gives you an unbelievable amount of customizing opportunities for altering your figures. As an example, see Figure 15.18, which starts with the Male Business Suit figure as a base, and through applying all of the Parameters developed in this chapter (as well as tweaking the standard Parameters), results in a myriad of unique characters.

FIGURE 15.16 *A series of alternate parameters using the Cheek Puff Target Morph.*

FIGURE 15.17 *A series of alternate parameters using the Face Pull Target Morph.*

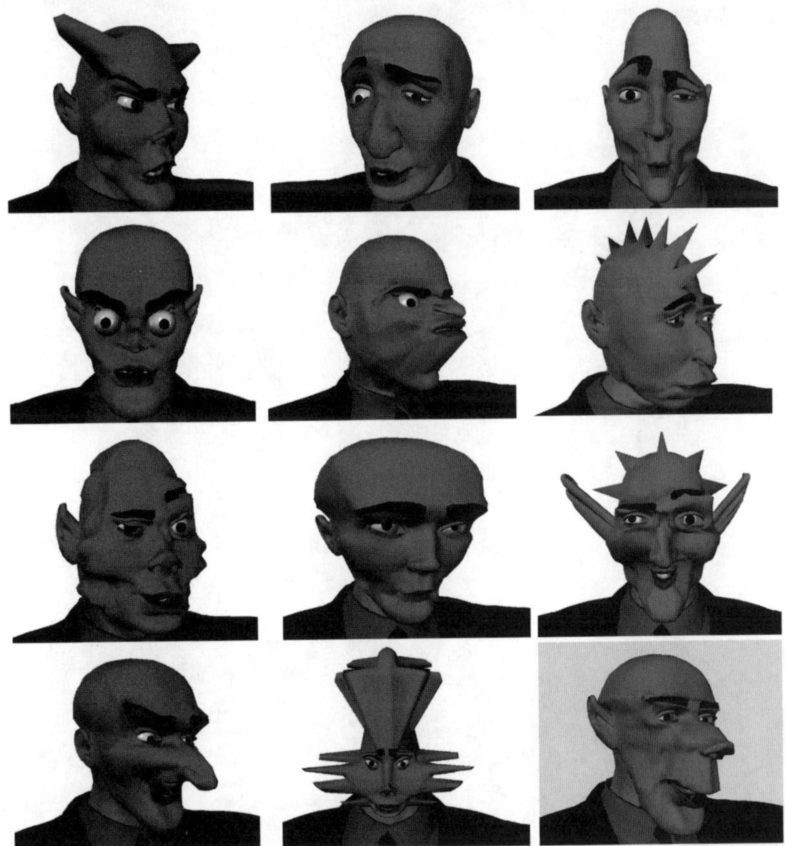

FIGURE 15.18 *This display of diverse characters was generated from the same figure, by altering the polygonal mesh with Morph Targets created in Ray Dream Studio.*

NOTE

We have used heads as a focus for our Morph Target descriptions, because that is the main way most of you will assign Morph Targets. However, you can assign a Morph Target to any figure element you like using the same techniques.

Moving Along

In this chapter, we have investigated the creation of Morph Targets and detailed how they are used to modify and customize figure elements. In the next chapter we begin the Advanced Topics section with a look at hierarchical scripting.

SECTION III Advanced Topics

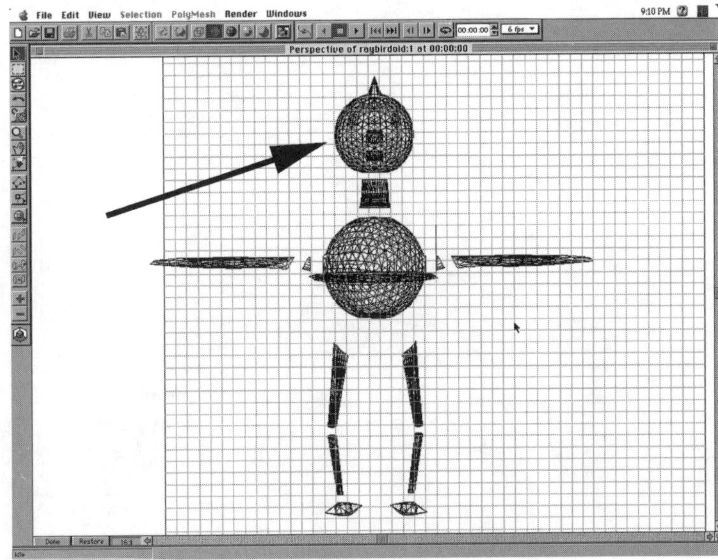

This section of the book should only be read and worked through after you have mastered the basics and all of the previous exercises. Here, you'll learn about creating hierarchies, handshaking with other applications, and new ways to work with Poser from a number of master users.

CHAPTER 16 Creating Hierarchies

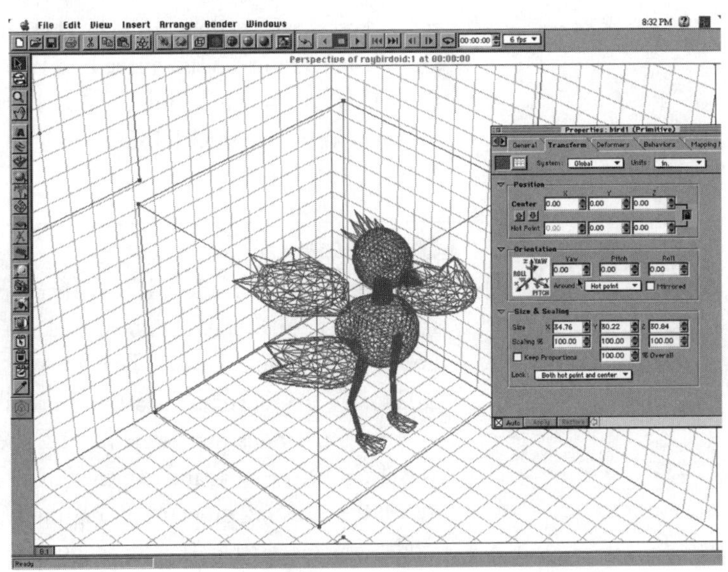

One of the most complex topics in Poser 3 concerns the creation and implementation of hierarchical structures, making it possible for you to create your own models in a 3D application for use in Poser. If the hierarchical procedure is correctly implemented, the models you import into Poser will have their own Parameter Dials, so they can be animated just like any internal Poser model.

CAUTION

Karuna! It is vital that you download and work through the Advanced Poser User's guide from the MetaCreations Web site before working through this chapter.

This chapter includes two detailed approaches for developing figures outside of Poser, creating their hierarchies, and using them as animated elements in Poser 3. Each tutorial was written by a Poser 3 master user, and, coupled with the Advanced User Guide information and tutorials, should enable you to incorporate your own models into Poser 3.

The Red Ant[1]

OVERVIEW

The Ant model was made in Rhino 3D (www.rhino3d.com) as a group of separate parts (head, thorax, abdomen, and legs segments) then exported in Wavefront Object format (.OBJ). That file was imported into RayDream Studio 5.02 for the naming of each part in the Mesh Form Modeler.

After the various parts were named, the file was exported from RDS in Wavefront OBJ format and reopened in text editor—in this case a good quality word processing program. Using the text editor, the various parts of the model were given separate color assignments by typing in material statements for the object groups.

Materials editing complete, the Object file was named "ant1.obj" and saved in a new directory called "Metacreations\Poser3\runtime\geometries\ ant."

A hierarchy file was then created and converted in Poser 3. The newly created "Poser Ant" was then opened in Poser 3 and given color assignments from the surface materials menu. The Joint parameters were then edited and the Ant was added to the figure library.

THE DETAILS

The following text details the exact methods used to develop the Poser file for the Red Ant object. See Figure 16.1.

[1] Text by Jeffrey J. Howarth. The model "ant1.obj" was created and is owned by Ian W. Grey.

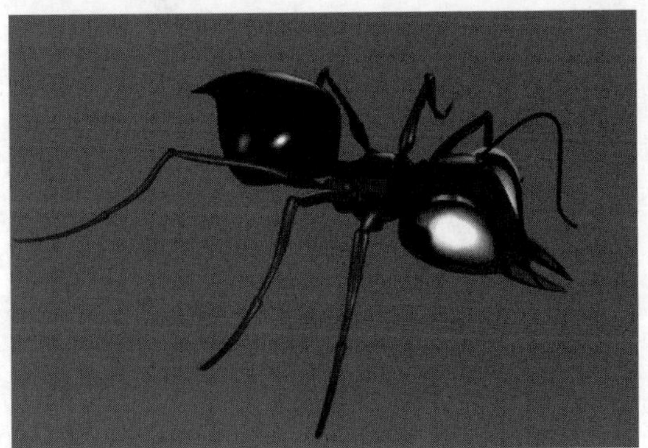

FIGURE 16.1 *The Red Ant, modeled by Ian W. Grey.*

RayDream Studio

To create custom figures for Poser 3 you will need a 3D modeling program that can successfully be used to create and edit models in Alias Wavefront Object format. Wavefront is the base format of Poser figures. For this example, MetaCreation's RayDream Studio 5.02 with the Poser 3 plug-in was used.

Setting up RDS5 and Poser 3 First, make sure RDS5 is updated to RDS 5.02 (the patch can be downloaded from www.metacreations.com/downloads) and have the new Poser 3 plugin installed. The plugin is installed from the Poser 3 CD ROM during CUSTOM installation. If you have already installed Poser 3 but not the Ray Dream plugins, then reinstall from the Poser 3 CD-ROM, unchecking every option other than RDS PLUGINS. You will be asked to locate your RayDream directory to complete the operation.

The Plugin includes updates for the MFM (Ray Dream Mesh Form Modeler), a new WaveFront import/export filter, and a New Poser Modeler addition (the latest update for the Poser Modeler can be downloaded from the MetaCreations web site). A good primer for the next steps would be to read the Poser 3 *Advanced Techniques Manual,* which can be found on the MetaCreations web site in Adobe.PDF format (http://www.metacreations.com/products/poser3/resources2.html).

Importing the Model The Red Ant model was made in separate parts and exported as an assembled whole in Wavefront .obj format. In RDS it was imported with a mesh form "Object for Each Group" selected in the WaveFront import filter dialog. This makes it easier to manage in the MFM.

Naming the Parts Each part of the model was brought into the MFM selected and named using the "Name Polymesh" command from the MENU>POLYMESH. OBJ files are native to the updated MFM.

The head was named "head," the thorax "thorax," and so on. The six legs had three separate parts each and were named as follows: The right front leg parts were called "rfLeg1," "rfLeg2," "rfLeg3." The same pattern was used to name the rest of the legs. The left middle leg becomes "lmLeg1," lmLeg2," "lmLeg3," and so on.

Exporting the Model The various parts of the model were grouped and exported in Wavefront format. In the Filter options dialog all options were checked, including the "Export Textures" option. When this option is checked, each group object of the model will be given surface material statements within the OBJ file.

OBJ Text Editing

Next, the OBJ file has to be edited.

Editing the OBJ File .OBJ model files are basically in plain text format; the materials statements are easily edited in a word processing program (BBEdit is a good choice on the Mac, and a similar text editor can be selected for Windows users). In this case I used MS Works 4.0.

Open the file as a plain text (Windows format) in the word processor that has a word search function; this will be needed to easily find the group statements, which are headed by a "g." Search for all occurrences of the letter "g" to find the groups. They will look like this: "g head," "g lEye," "g lfLeg1," and so on. Above each group you will see a materials statement.

```
usemtl head
g head
```

By "exporting textures" from RDS the "usemtl" statements were placed above each separate group, and now this has to be edited further. These statements are placed between the data sections of text and are the only parts of the obj file that can be edited in this manner.

For the six legs there are eighteen separate parts, thus eighteen different materials were specified during the export. This is too many for convenience in Poser so we will reduce the material used for the legs to one "Legs." Here is an example of what to do:

```
usemtl rfLeg1
g rfLeg1
```

should be changed to:

```
usemtl Legs
g rfLeg1
```

Specify the material as "Legs" for each one of the eighteen leg parts.

Editing the Groups Some parts of the model are separate but need to be part of the same group yet still retain the individual colors. The head is one example here. The eyes and the antennae should be part of the head and need to be edited. The group and materials statements appear this way:

```
usemtl rEye
g rEye
usemtl lEye
g lEye
usemtl lAntennae
g lAntenae
usemtl rAntennae
g rAntenae
```

These statements should be changed to:

```
usemtl Eyes
g head
usemtl Eyes
g head
usemtl Antennae
g head
usemtl Antennae
g head
```

In this form the eyes and antennae will be part of the head, yet retain their individual colors.

Save this in Plain Text to the "runtime\geometries\ant" directory of Poser. The file may save as **ant1.obj.txt** and must be renamed to **ant1.obj**.

Setting up the Hierarchy

Now the Hierarchy file or .PHI must be created. This must also be in plain text form. The first line of the .PHI points to the directory where the "ant1.obj" is located.

```
objFile :Runtime:Geometries:ant:ant1.obj
```

The rest are statements that show the linkage of all the parts, including their rotation order and Inverse Kinematics chains.

```
1 thorax yzx
  2 abdomen yzx
2 head yzx
    3 lMand yxz
         3 rMand yxz
2 lfLeg1 xyz
  3 lfLeg2 xyz
     4 lfLeg3 xyz
2 rfLeg1 xyz
  3 rfLeg2 xyz
     4 rfLeg3 xyz
2 lmLeg1 xyz
  3 lmLeg2 xyz
     4 lmLeg3 xyz
2 rmLeg1 xyz
  3 rmLeg2 xyz
     4 rmLeg3 xyz
2 lrLeg1 xyz
  3 lrLeg2 xyz
     4 lrLeg3 xyz
2 rrLeg1 xyz
  3 rrLeg2 xyz
     4 rrLeg3 xyz
ikChain  LeftFrontLeg  lfLeg1 lfLeg2 lfLeg3
ikChain  RightFrontLeg  rfLeg1 rfLeg2 rfLeg3
ikChain  LeftMidLeg  lmLeg1 lmLeg2 lmLeg3
ikChain  RightMidLeg  rmLeg1 rmLeg2 rmLeg3
ikChain  LeftRearLeg lrLeg1 lrLeg2 lrLeg3
ikChain  RightRearLeg rrLeg1 rrLeg2 rrLeg3
```

Save this file in plain text format as a .PHI. It may save like this "ant.phi.txt" and must be renamed "ant.phi."

Converting the Hierarchy in Poser 3

By now the obj file should be in the proper directory and the .phi should be ready for conversion. Open Poser 3 and select "convert hier" from the file menu. Locate your newly created ant.phi and choose "OK." If everything is as it should be, the file should process within a few minutes and "New Set" dialog should open up. Specify a name for the new figure and choose "OK." The figure should be added to the figure library under "New Figures."

Colors and Joint Parameters

Go into the New Figures library and open the ant. When it first appears on screen it may be off center. Center it in the main camera view. You will notice that the various parts of the model are colored differently. New colors can be chosen from the surface materials dialog to create a "Red Ant." The eye color was achieved by setting the base color to "black," the highlight to "white," then increasing the highlight size to 98%. It almost looks like a lens. Once the colors are chosen, it's time to set the Joint parameters.

1. Disable IK for the legs then change the camera view to TOP and the Figure Style to OUTLINE. Select the head then open the properties dialog and disable Bending. Do this for the Thorax and Abdomen also.
2. Select the head and open the Joint Parameters dialog from MENU>WINDOW. You will see that a Green Cross and a Red Cross appear at the center of the head. Use the mouse to drag the Green Cross to the base of the neck. This will be its rotation origin. Next drag the Red Cross to the tip of the nose. This will be the Limit point. Choose a side view from the Camera menu and continue making adjustments.
3. Select each part of the model and set the center and limits for each, including all the leg segments. Save your new model to the library.

The joint parameters can be adjusted at anytime, but the changes must be saved as a new figure. The knowledge concerning the joint parameters is sparse at this time, experimentation may be necessary. For more information about Poser and Poser creation please visit the Poser Forum Online and

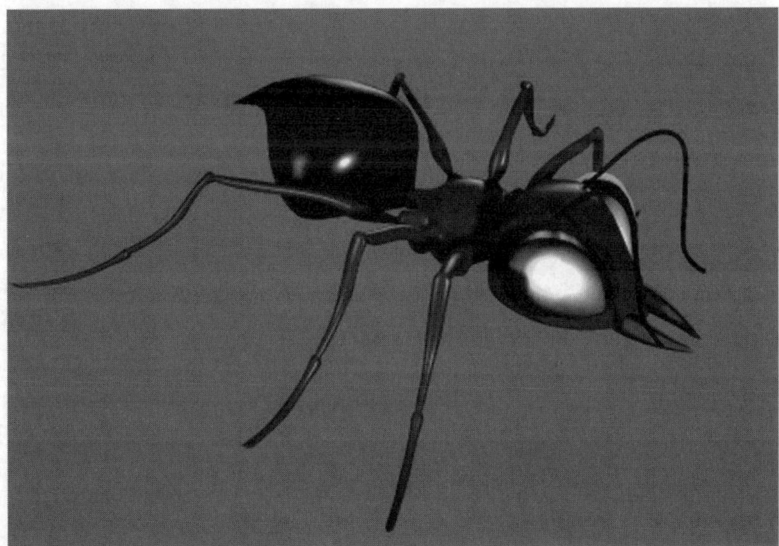

FIGURE 16.2 *After the Red Ant becomes posable, you can animate all of its parts in Poser 3.*

discussion board (http://www.iguanasoft.com/poser/ and http://www.paradise-web.com/plus_le/plus.mirage?who=poser).

You will find the Ant.Phi file and the Red Ant.obj file on this books CD-ROM, in the Extras folder.

A Basic Toy Birdoid[2]

Don't panic. Hierarchies aren't as intimidating as they first seem. The overall view is: Make a model comprised of separate meshes, name the meshes and export the model in .Obj format (the .obj file), list the meshes hierarchically in a text file (the .phi file), put this in your Runtime:Geometries folder, then let Poser 3 convert it all to a model you can position for use in another 3D scene, use as a reference object in painting 2D images, or animate in Poser. The number of things you can do with a Poser model grows with every new version of Poser.

Poser is adamant about a few issues: You must place the folder containing your hierarchy in the Runtime:Geometries folder, and before the files are converted, there must be nothing in your folder but the .obj and .phi files. (After the conversion Windows users will see an additional file, .rsr. This file is hidden on the Macintosh.)

My initial experience with hierarchies consisted of one successfully converted string of spheres, and then nothing. Nothing but crashes, errors, and the dreaded message, "no geometry to match nodes;". I had begun piling new .obj and .phi files into the same folder and leaving it to Poser to sort it out. Poser, in no uncertain terms, declined to do this. After MetaCreations tech support showed me the error of my ways, all went smoothly, and now I'm sure you can make an animatable object out anything.

So, to begin with, you need a model to work on. You can grab something from the Hierarchies folder on the Poser CD, but sooner or later, you'll want to make your own from scratch. The Toy Birdoid is a basic introduction to hierarchy objects for those fairly new to modeling (but who have read the manuals thoroughly), and an exercise small enough to deal with when the inevitable booboo crops up (Poser is worse than your third grade teacher about spelling). Birdoid is also an example of a model made using MetaCreations' Ray Dream Studio 5.02 , a natural modeling companion to Poser. Since the model is all primitives with a minimum of tweaking, it goes fast—the quicker to get it into Poser.

These are the steps to making the model and exporting it from Ray Dream Studio.

---

[2]Written and illustrated by Cecilia Ziemer.

MAKING THE BODY IN RAY DREAM STUDIO

1. Drop the magnet icon into the perspective window to open the mesh modeler.
2. Create a sphere for the body and subdivide it twice (**Menu>Selection>Subdivide**)
3. Set the camera to top view (**Cmd/Ctrl-8**) and select a vertex at the back of the sphere.
4. Use the magnet tool to drag vertices from right to left. This will be the Birdoid's tail end. See Figure 16.3.
5. Switch to the left view (**Cmd/Ctrl-4**) and drag the vertices downward, then a little toward the head end. This is as much shaping of the body as needs to be done right now. See Figure 16.4.
6. Set the camera back to default position (**Cmd/Ctrl-0**). Select the body object (**Menu: Polymesh/Name Polymesh**) and name it "bod" (to prevent confusion with "Body" once it's in Poser).

THE BIRDOID NECK

7. Create a cylinder for the neck, and resize it smaller—exact proportions don't matter here, you know what a toy bird looks like. You can subdivide the neck object if you wish to give it more shape. See Figure 16.5.

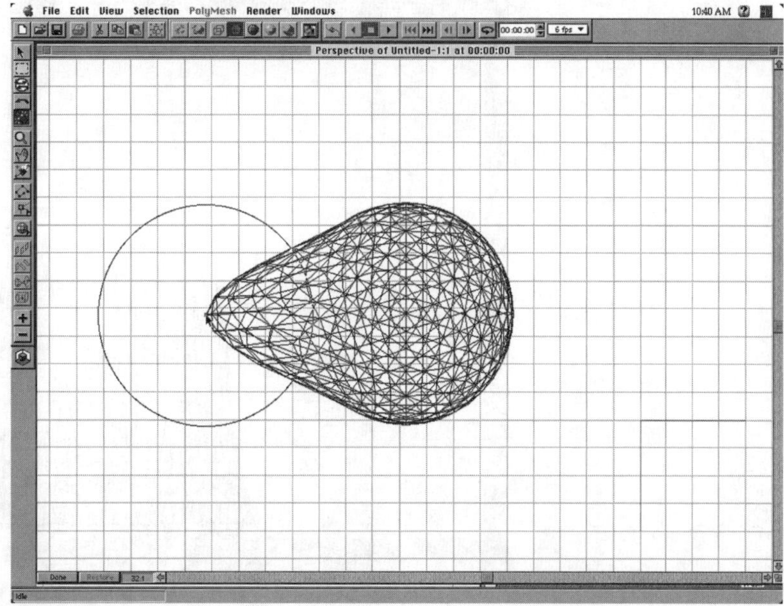

FIGURE 16.3 *The Birdoid's tail end is created.*

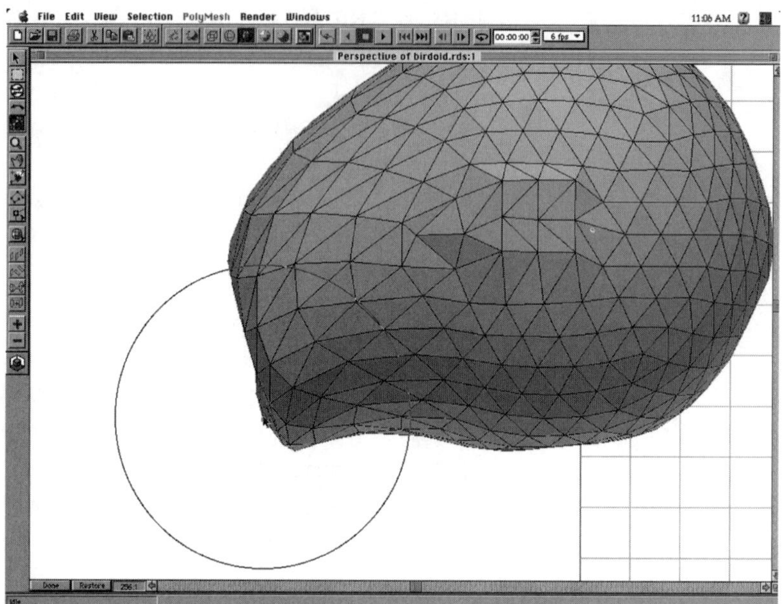

FIGURE 16.4 *The initial body shape is created.*

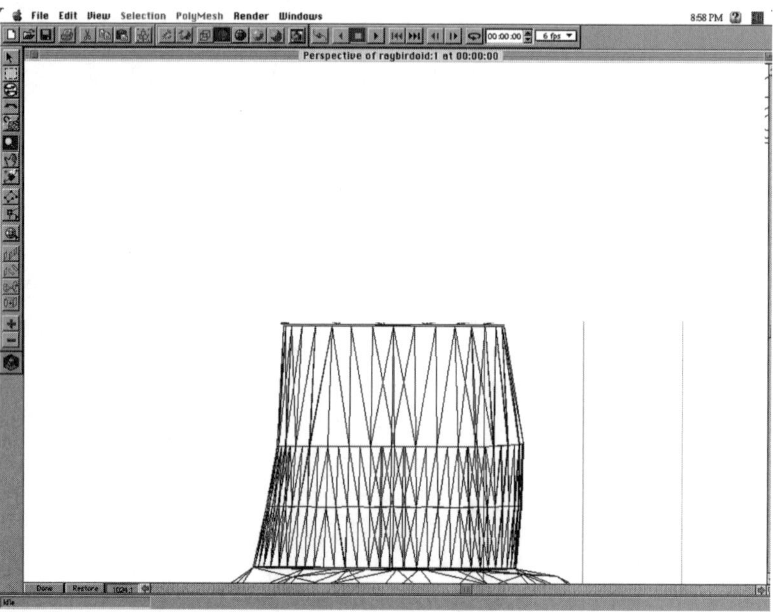

FIGURE 16.5 *The Birdoid's neck is created from a Cylinder.*

8. With the front view camera (**Cmd/Ctrl-1**) select the cylinder (double-click to select one vertex, then hold down the shift key to select entire objects) and drag it up above the top center of the body object
9. Switch to left view and drag the cylinder above the head end of the bird bod, but not yet touching—just move it close for reference.
10. Flatten the area of the sphere on which you wish to place the neck by selecting a thin line of vertices at the top head-end of the body and dragging downward.
11. Use the magnification tool to enlarge the view of this as much as you need. Objects comprising the model should barely touch, but not overlap. Exporting in the .obj format can cause overlapping vertices to weld together, thus creating a new object that, having no name, isn't listed in the .psi file and is thus unrecognizable to Poser.
12. Move the neck down until the it touches the flat space on the body. Select the neck object and name it "neck."

THE BIRDOID HEAD

13. Create and subdivide (**Menu>Selection>Subdivide**) a sphere for the head and, switching among front, top and left camera views position the head very close to the top of the neck.
14. Tweak the top vertices of the neck into position to touch the bottom of the head sphere. Select the head object, and name it "head." See Figure 16.6.
15. Select the head object and the vertices at the extreme head and tail ends of the body object and hide them (menu select hide selection: this makes the next step easier to see).

CREATING THE BIRDOID'S SHOULDERS

16. Using front and top views, select some vertices on each side of the body where you wish the wings go (I put mine bang in the center for this) and drag them one by one to flatten the area as you did for the neck.
17. Create a cylinder, then resize it (**Menu>Selection>Resize>**) in all dimensions for a shoulder object. See Figure 16.7.
18. With the Camera in Front View, rotate the cylinder 90 degrees.
19. Use the Top and Front Views to position the Cylinder to fit against the flattened area on one side of the body.
20. In the Front View, select the vertices on the end of the Cylinder not touching the body and rotate them a little clockwise.

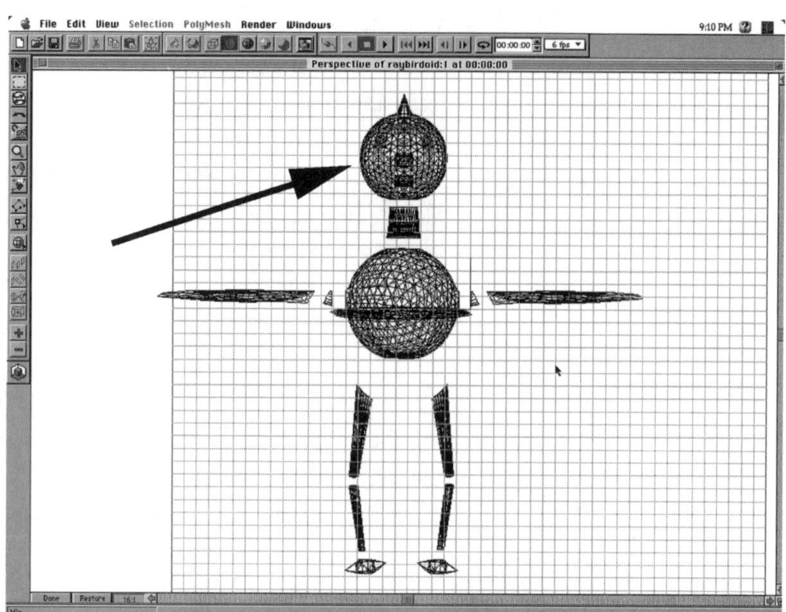

FIGURE 16.6 *The Birdoid's Head is created from a Sphere.*

21. Return the camera to default view (**Cmd/Ctrl-0**) and make the left drawing plane active (**Opt/Alt**-click on the left side of the icon at the bottom of the toolbar). Select the shoulder cylinder and duplicate with symmetry (**Cmd/Ctrl-D**). Decrease magnification to find the duplicate object—it will be on the far side of the active plane.
22. Drag the duplicate to the other side of the body and in top and left views check its Y and Z alignment to the first shoulder object.
23. Select the shoulders and name them respectively "rshld" and "lshld."
24. Make the rest of the model visible (**Menu>View>Reveal Hidden Vertices**).

CREATING THE BIRDOID'S LEGS

25. For the thigh object, create a Cylinder and resize its X and Y dimensions—in the Properties box this should be the default 8 units in the Z field, and around 2 in the X and Y fields.
26. With camera in Left View (**Cmd/Ctrl-4**), select the bottom vertices and drag them to the left.

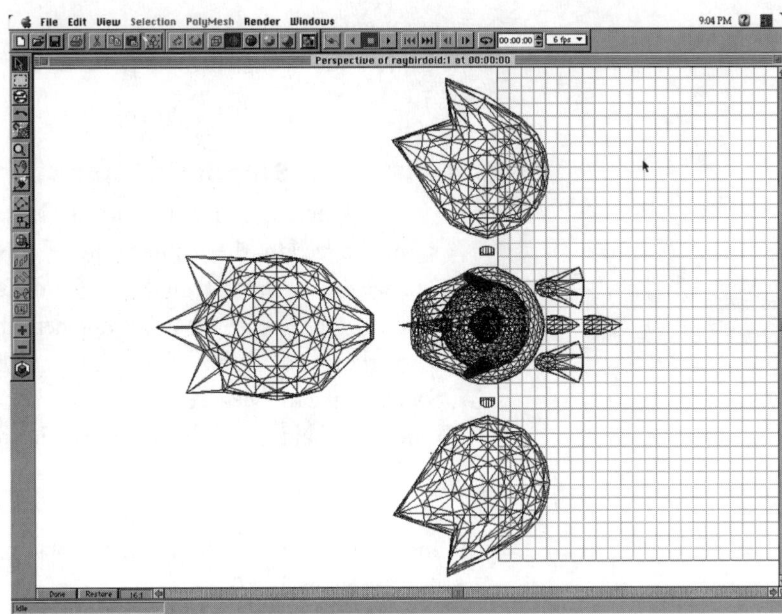

FIGURE 16.7 *An exploded view from the top camera shows some relative proportions.*

27. Then, with the camera in default view and the bottom drawing plane active, select the thigh cylinder and duplicate with symmetry. (Again, you will have to decrease magnification to find the duplicate.) This gives you the start of the shin object (which you can temporarily hide).
28. In Front View select the top vertices of the thigh cylinder and position them against the body, touching, but not overlapping. See Figure 16.8.
29. Next, select the entire thigh, make the left drawing plane active, and duplicate with symmetry. Drag it to the opposite side of the body.
30. Make the shin visible, select it, and drag it underneath the thigh, positioning it to touch but not overlap the thigh. Select the bottom vertices and resize them down just enough to produce a little tapering at the bottom.
31. Select the shin and duplicate with symmetry for the other shin.
32. Create a Cube and resize it for a foot. You can subdivide it and reshape it if you like.
33. Duplicate with symmetry and position each under its respective shin.
34. One by one, select and name the leg objects: "rthigh," "lthigh," "rshin," and "lshin"; name the feet "rfoot" and "lfoot," keeping all consistent with the right and left shoulders.

Now for the wings and tail (Refer back to Figure 16.7, which shows a top view of the entire Birdoid, exploded. You can use this as a guide to wing and tail shapes.)

CREATING THE BIRDOID'S WINGS

35. Create a sphere and squash it (**Menu>Selection>Resize**) to about 30 it in the Z direction (the Z dimension in RDS is the Y in Poser).
36. Change the camera to Front View (**Cmd/Ctrl-1**). Position the squished sphere at the same height as the shoulders, then select and drag it so that it's on the side of the bird closest to the toolbar.
37. Switch to the top view, select a few vertices, and shift-drag them out toward the shoulder. You should be dragging toward the top of the screen. See Figure 16.9.
38. In the front view, tweak the dragged-out vertices into a line, then select and rotate them using the rotation tool to match the angle of the shoulder. See Figure 16.10.
39. Go back to the top view and shape the wing such that it's not a disk—the shape its up to you.

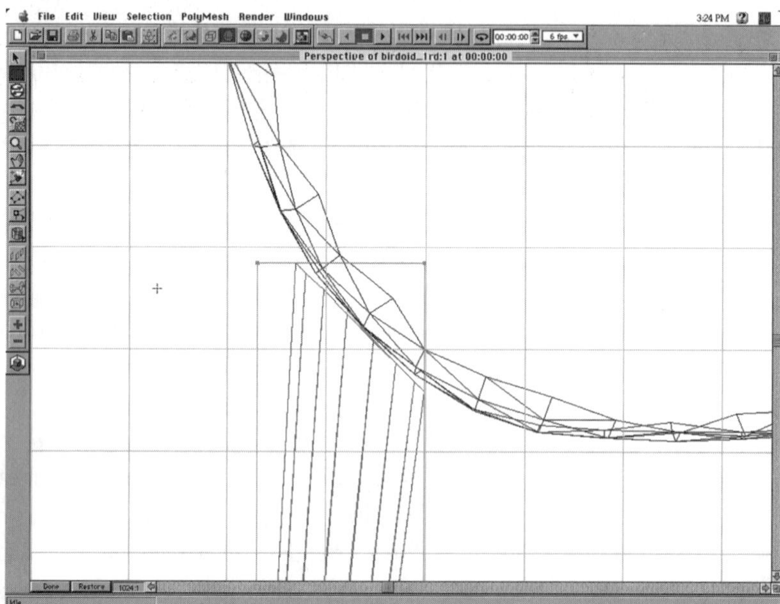

FIGURE 16.8 *The Birdoid's Legs are placed.*

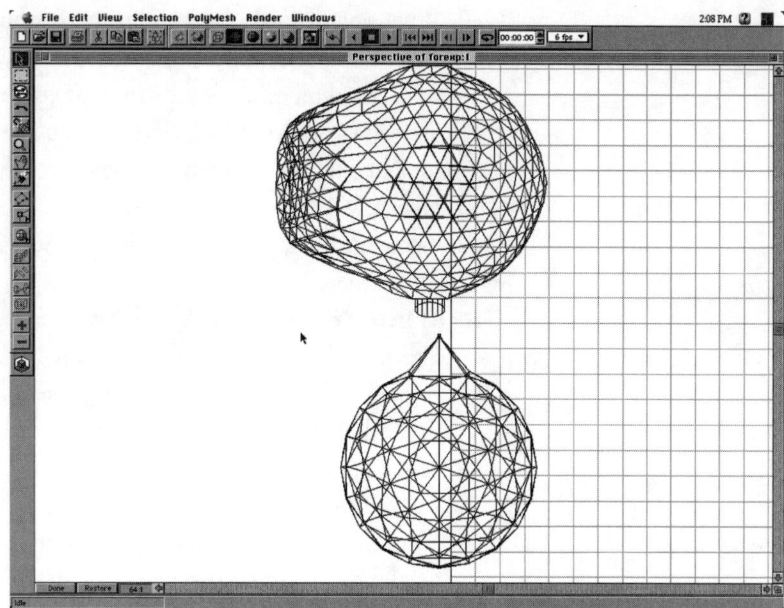

FIGURE 16.9 *The Wings are shaped.*

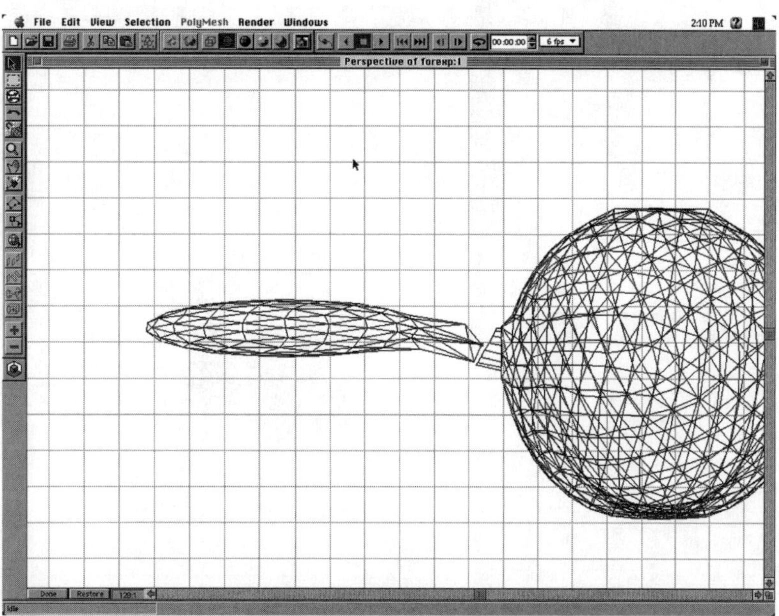

FIGURE 16.10 *The Wings are positioned.*

40. When you've finished this wing, go to default view **Com-0**, make the Y plane active, select the wing, and duplicate with symmetry. Decrease the camera magnification if the wing isn't visible.
41. Shift-drag the wing to the second shoulder. Leave the wings sticking straight out from the body and looking goofy—you'll do the rotations in Poser.
42. Name the wings "rwing" and "lwing." See Figure 16.11.

CREATING THE BIRDOID'S TAIL

43. Create a sphere, subdivide it, and resize its Z dimension to 30.
44. In the Left View, position the tail sphere directly behind the tail-end of the bird, then do the same in the Top View, centering it behind the body.
45. Select and shift drag some vertices toward the body and do any shaping you wish to do from the Top View.
46. From the Left Camera View, position the tail with respect to the body, touching, but not overlapping. As with the wings, leave the tail sticking straight out behind.
47. Name the tail "tail1."

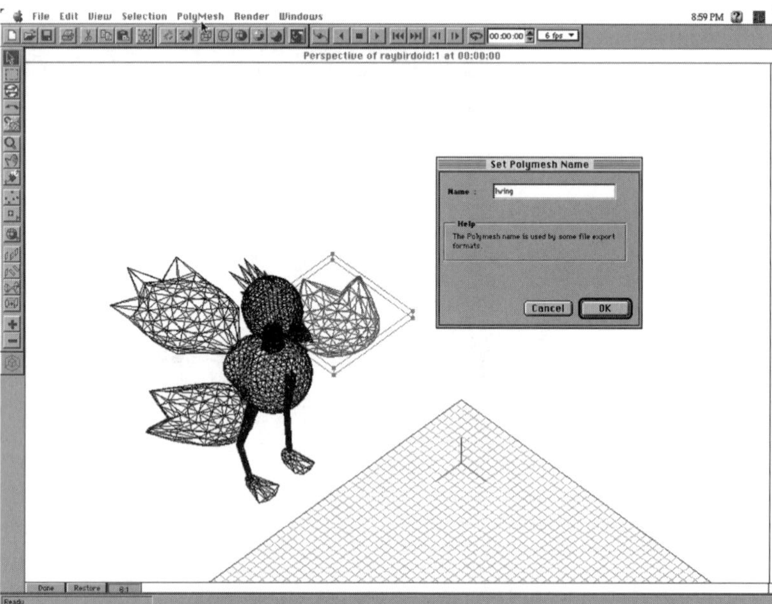

FIGURE 16.11 *The Wings are finished and named.*

SHAPING THE BIRDOID'S BEAK

48. For the top of the beak, create a Cube, resize and subdivide. (The size of the beak isn't critical but it should be longer in the Y dimension than in the Z.)
49. With the camera in left position, select the vertices at the cube edge away from the head and weld them (**Menu>Selection>Weld**). See Figure 16.12.
50. Make the bottom plane active, select the beak, and Duplicate with Symmetry. Resize the duplicate (**Menu>Selection>Resize**) from 100 to around 90 in Y and Z dimensions.
51. Tweak both sections of the beak to fit the head—for speed, I just dragged some of the head's front vertices to make a flat area, then moved the beak parts to barely touch this.

The joints are awkward looking here—but very informative once the model is in Poser and you're setting joint parameters.

52. Name the top beak object "tbeak" and the bottom, "bbeak."

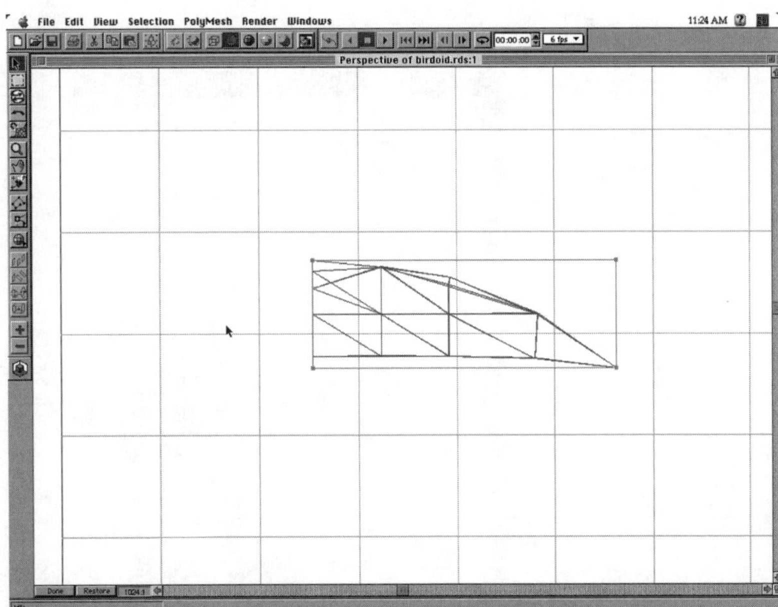

FIGURE 16.12 *The Birdoid's Beak is created.*

RECHECK THE OBJECT NAMES

53. One by one, select the objects one last time to be certain each object has its name and its integrity as a separate object—just a good habit to get into. While this isn't a problem for models with simple joins, polymeshes made from single object models being prepared for a Poser hierarchy by Detaching Polymesh sometimes don't detach completely, or reattach. You know this has happened if you can't select individual objects, or if the objects have lost the names you have given to them. When you're satisfied that all the meshes are indeed separate and named click 'done' to leave the mesh modeler. Save your work. See Figure 16.13.

EXPORTING YOUR MODEL FROM RDS

1. Orient your model as you prefer it if that has not yet been done. **Cmd/Ctrl-t** to open Object Properties, then enter a value of 0 into all translation and rotation fields.

Do not change the model's size at this stage.

2. Select the Birdoid and choose **File:Export** from the Menu bar at the top of the screen.

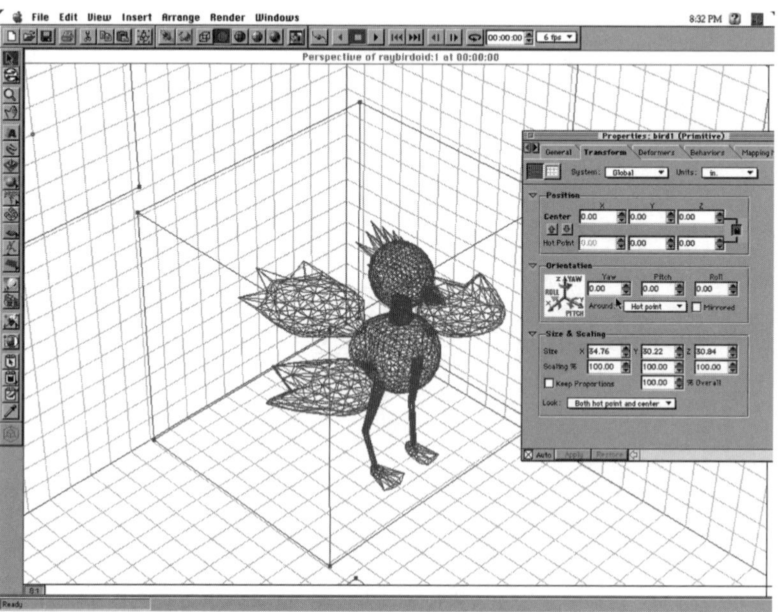

FIGURE 16.13 *Enter values in Object Properties in Ray Dream.*

3. Create a new folder in the Poser Runtime Geometries folder; name it "goonybird."
4. Choose Obj from the Format pulldown and export the Birdoid as "Birdoid.obj" to the goonybird folder.
5. Close RDS. If you've been staring at the screen all this time, go run around the block!

MAKING THE TEXT (.PHI) FILE

1. You can write the hierarchy (.phi) in any plain text editor—Simple Text, Notepad, any plain text editor. Refer to the Poser *Advanced Users' Guide*.
2. This is the .phi file for the Birdoid example:

```
objFile :Runtime:Geometries:goonybird:Birdoid.obj
1 bod yzx
  2 neck yzx
    3 head yzx
        4 tbeak zyx
        4 bbeak zyx
  2 tail1 zyx
  2 rshld yxz
    3 rwing xyz
  2 lshld yxz
    3 lwing xyz
  2 rthigh zxy
    3 rshin zxy
        4 rfoot zxy
  2 lthigh zxy
    3 lshin zxy
        4 lfoot zxy
ikChain rthigh rshin rfoot
ikChain lthigh lshin lfoot
```

The first line tells Poser what its looking for and where to find it; this line must be present at the beginning of the text file. The .obj file must be in the folder and both .obj and folder name must be listed *exactly as they are named.*

The numbered lines are the segments of the model and must be listed exactly as you named them in RDS. The rotation order must be listed for each object. The direction in which the object twists should be listed first.

1 bod is the parent object for the entire model, the objects numbered 2 are the first children, the objects numbered 3 are the children of number 2. Think of it as a tree, where object 1 is the trunk with everything, ultimately, branching from it. The parent object (1) moves everything,

object (2) moves only its dependents, object (3) moves only its dependents and so on to the end of the hierarchy.

If you, say, wanted to attach spurs to the feet later, these would both be numbered 5 and you would enter them as: 5 spur under 4 rfoot, 5 spur under 4 lfoot.

ikChain lines should be present even if you don't plan to use ik.

3. When you've made your text file (or copied and pasted this one) save it in the goonybird folder as : Birdoid.phi—and be sure there's nothing in the goonybird folder but the Birdoid.obj and Birdoid.phi files.
4. Exit your text editor and open Poser 3.

CONVERTING

These are the steps for converting the object and a text file to a bendable model.

1. Delete the current figure (**Menu> Figure> Delete Figure**)
2. Under **Menu: File** select **Convert Hier File**, then select Birdoid.phi from the goonybird folder.
3. If everything is working correctly, a box should appear mid-screen prompting you to name the new object. (You can save something as New Set only once per library so name the object Birdoid).
4. Do not fear! The object doesn't automatically appear on-screen—you'll find it under Figures: New Figures in the Libraries pulldown.
5. Select Birdoid (the name appears in the New Figures library under a Poser Shrug icon), click on the double arrow to add it to the screen, or click the single arrow to replace the default figure if you haven't deleted it—and if you haven't, do it now.
6. You still may not see the new figure—it comes in huge. From the pull-down list at the bottom of the screen select **Body**.
7. Use the scale dial to resize Body to 8 or 9, at which point you should see a naked and eyeless toy bird to which you can apply Joint Parameters, as described in the *Advanced Users' Manual.* Save the Poser scene.
8. In general, Joint Parameters speak for themselves. Green starts, Red stops, and the blend zones are in between. Set the screen display to line, and it may all be easier to see with the background set to white, and the foreground set to black.
9. The first thing to do after opening the Joint Parameter window is to find the center of each object and drag it to the point on the body part you want to pivot from. Usually, the default center settings are correct for ob-

jects but bird toys with knees on backward (unless you're a bird) aren't normal objects. You will need to set the tail center close to the body and readjust the leg centers.

10. When centers are centered, set the rotation parameters. If you tie the model in knots, Zero Figure will untie them, or you can Opt/Alt-click on the dials. See Figures 16.14 to 16.16.
11. Add a couple of spheres for eyes, scaling them down and sticking them onto the head, then making them the child objects of the head.
12. Then you can add textures, by either importing a bitmap or by painting on the creature in a 3D paint program such as MetaCreations Painter 3D. When the Birdoid is finished click the + to add it to the Library.

NEED THE BOMB SQUAD?

Check the following if your hierarchy doesn't come booming into Poser 3 with a New Set Name prompt.

- If you get an error message instead of a New Set Name prompt, first check your folder to be sure everything is where it's supposed to be. If you're using a Mac, also check that the .obj file you exported from RDS

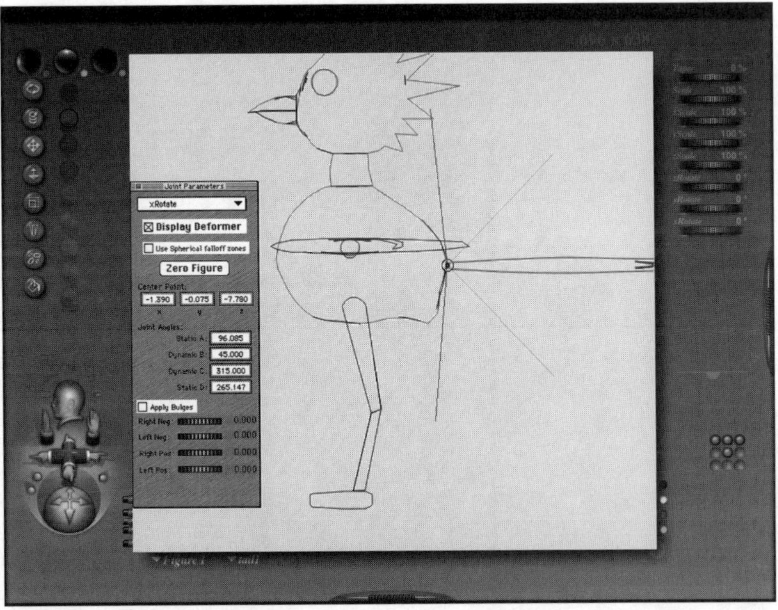

FIGURE 16.14 *The tail's X Rotation.*

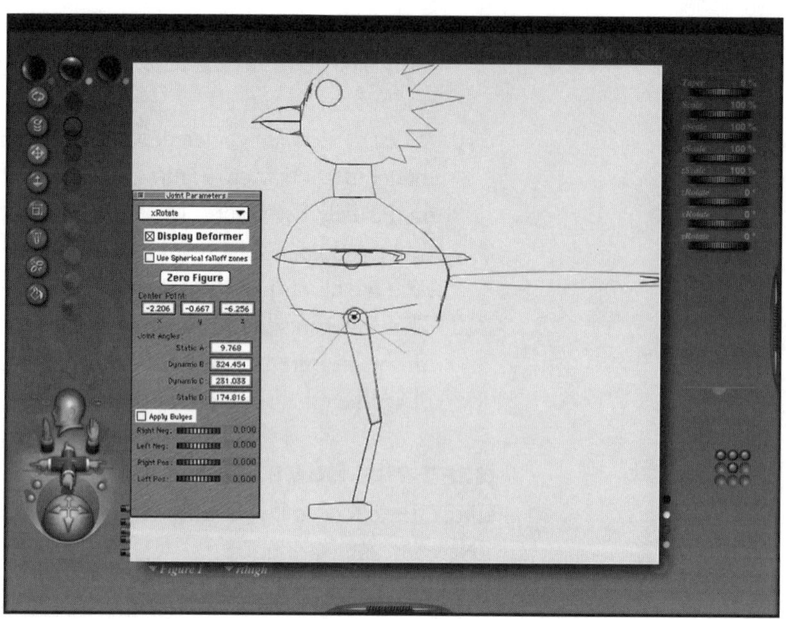

FIGURE 16.15 *The X Rotation of the Thigh.*

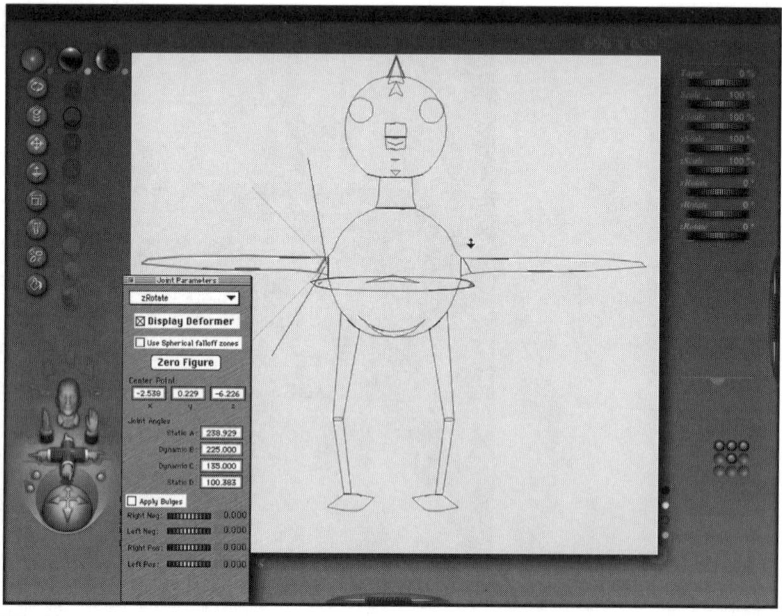

FIGURE 16.16 *The Wing's Z Rotation.*

does indeed have the ".obj" after the model's name—this is automatic in Windows. but on the Mac you need to add it—if it's missing, you will get the "no actr..." message. If it looks right, then open the .phi file and check the spelling—Poser is inflexible about spelling and typos—also see that the names in the top line are the same, letter for letter, as the model's and the folder's names.

- If you've copied and pasted parts of your hierarchy list that duplicate (arms, hands, legs, etc.), make sure that you didn't overlook changing the handedness of the duplicates (although in some instances Poser will convert the hierarchy anyway and what appears on the screen is a partial model).
- Check to see that you have only one parent object (object 1) in the model.
- If none of this works, open your modeling application and import the model. Then open the .psi file and check polymesh names against the list. If you're unable to select a polymesh, one or more vertices may be shared with another mesh—this can happen even with a model as simple as the Birdoid if you deformed or resized the model before exporting it as an .obj. To correct this, select all the vertices of the offending polymesh, then detach them as a new object. Name the new mesh and select and rename the mesh from which it was detached, then make the corrections to the .phi file and save it.

Now try the conversion in Poser 3 again.

If you've converted an object, saved it to a library, and have then removed the hierarchy folder from Runtime:Geometries, Poser will be unable to re-create it from your selection of from the Libraries palette and may even crash. When you remove a converted hierarchy object folder from Runtime:Geometries folder, also delete the Library entry.

Karuna! You will find the Birdoid.Phi file and the Birdoid.obj file on this books CD-ROM, in the Extras folder.

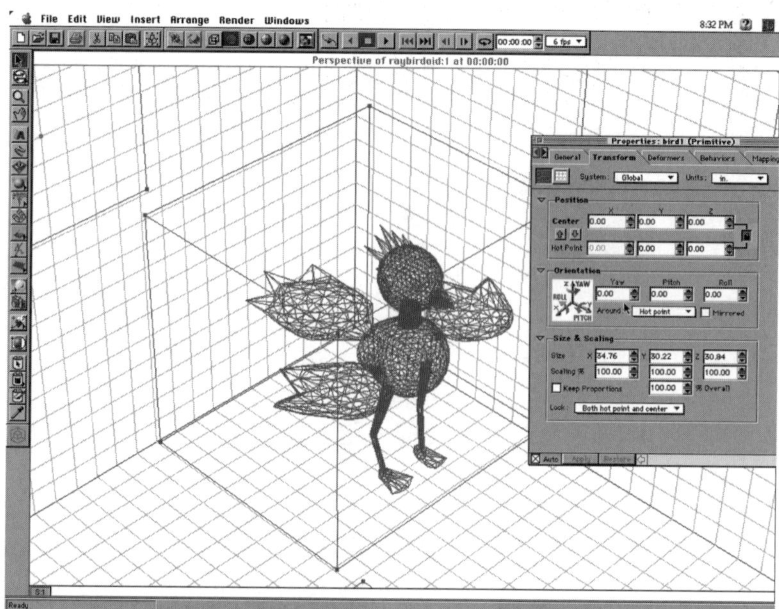

FIGURE 16.17 *The finished Birdoid model can be animated in Poser 3.*

Moving Along

In this chapter, two very detailed tutorials were presented that should help you to create your own models and their associated hierarchy files for import into Poser 3. In the next chapter, we'll explore some important ways that you can enhance your Poser 3 projects by handshaking with other applications.

CHAPTER

17 Handshaking

Poser is capable of communicating with other applications—handshaking—in a number of interesting ways. The closest association it has is with Ray Dream Studio, MetaCreations flagship 3D environment, with which WaveFront OBJ files can be passed back and forth. Since Poser can read in DXF, 3DMF, and 3DS file formats, as well as OBJ files, Poser can also communicate with 3D Studio output, and with any other applications that output 3DMF or DXF files (all used for developing props for Poser). It can also read a number of bitmap file formats, which it uses for texture mapping. This allows it to handshake with Painter, Photoshop, and other bitmap painting and f/x software. Poser outputs QuickTime and AVI animations, in addition to single-frame sequenced animations, so its output can be tweaked and customized in many post-production packages. Poser 3 can utilize audio files, so handshaking with various Audio applications is possible. Some applications allow you to paint on objects in a virtual 3D environment, to create more intuitive texture maps, so suitable 3D Painting applications should be mentioned. Then there are the Motion Capture data files that Poser 3 can utilize, making it open for transferring Motion capture data with other applications. In this chapter, we'll take a brief look at each of these handshaking capabilities.

Ray Dream Studio

If you are doing professional work with Poser 3, or plan to, you must also have Ray Dream Studio. Ray Dream and Poser are part of a suite of animation solutions, and their connectivity will only grow deeper over time. Here are the attributes in Ray Dream that make it such an important part of the overall Poser environment.

Read-Write OBJ Files

On the Poser CD (and also contained on the MetaCreations Web site), there are plugins that allow a direct link between Poser and Ray Dream. One very important part of this link is the Ray Dream Import/Export plugins that allow Ray Dream to read and write WaveFront OBJ file formats, which is the 3D format that Poser loves the most. If you have enough RAM (at least 48 MB or more), you can run Ray Dream and Poser simultaneously, making the transfer and modification of 3D object data all the quicker.

Mesh Form Modeler

The most important modeling environment, when it comes to creating Morph Targets for Poser objects, is Ray Dream's Mesh Form Modeler. See Figure 17.1.

Using the Sphere of Attraction and other processes in the Mesh Form Modeler, you can very quickly create Morph Targets that are then saved out as alternate OBJ files for Poser Parameter Dial deformations. See Chapter 15 for a very detailed look at this process.

FREE FORM MODELER

Ray Dream's Free Form Modeler can be used to create all manner of original props for Poser, once you get the hang of its use. There is no other modeling environment as variable as the Ray Dream Free Form Modeler in any other application, though it is also complex and demands study and exploration time. See Figure 17.2.

Once elements of a new Poser prop are created in the Free Form Modeler, you can use other tools in Ray Dream to clone them, or to glue them together with other prop elements. Then, export them as WaveFront, OBJ files, or as 3DS or DXF objects.

POSER MODELING IN RAY DREAM

On the Poser CD and also on the MetaCreations Web site is a plugin that allows you to place Poser elements in Ray Dream directly, modifying and animating them without opening Poser. This is the new Poser Modeler for Ray Dream. There are advantages and disadvantages to doing this. The advantage is that you have access to all of Ray Dream's tools and Deformers. The disadvan-

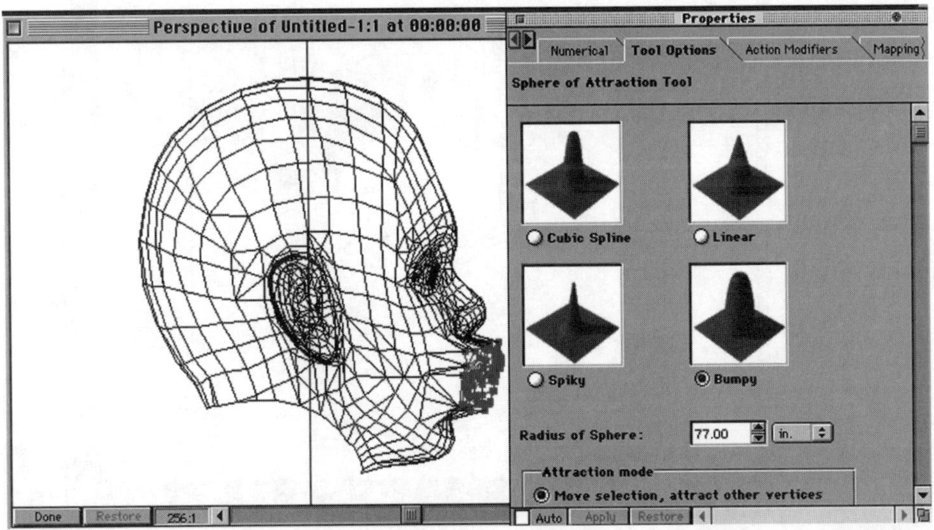

FIGURE 17.1 *Poser OBJ files can be infinitely transformed for use as Morph Targets in Ray Dream's Mesh Form Modeler.*

tage is that Poser itself is faster than Ray Dream when it come to animating these models. To activate the new Ray Dream Poser modeling environment, you simply drag and drop the Poser icon in the Ray Dream toolbar into the Ray Dream scene (see Figure 17.3).

Ray Dream Deformations

Ray Dream Deformations are f/x that alter the geometry of selected objects. Most of these f/x also alter the polygon count of targeted objects, so they are of no value as Morph Target tools. There are a few, however, that do not alter the polygon count, and these are very valuable as Morph Target modifiers.

Morph Target Deformations

The most valuable Morph Target Deformation in Ray Dream is the Spike Deformation. Spike creates extruded polygons from the targeted mesh that end in points, making Spike great for hair creation, and also for bizarre cactus looks. See Figure 17.4.

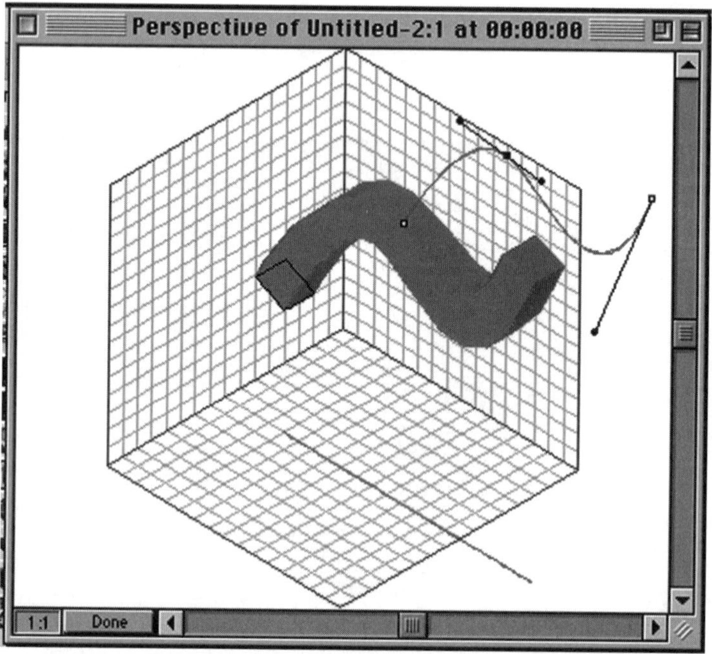

FIGURE 17.2 *Ray Dream's Free Form Modeler can aid you in the creation of any prop you might need for your Poser scenes.*

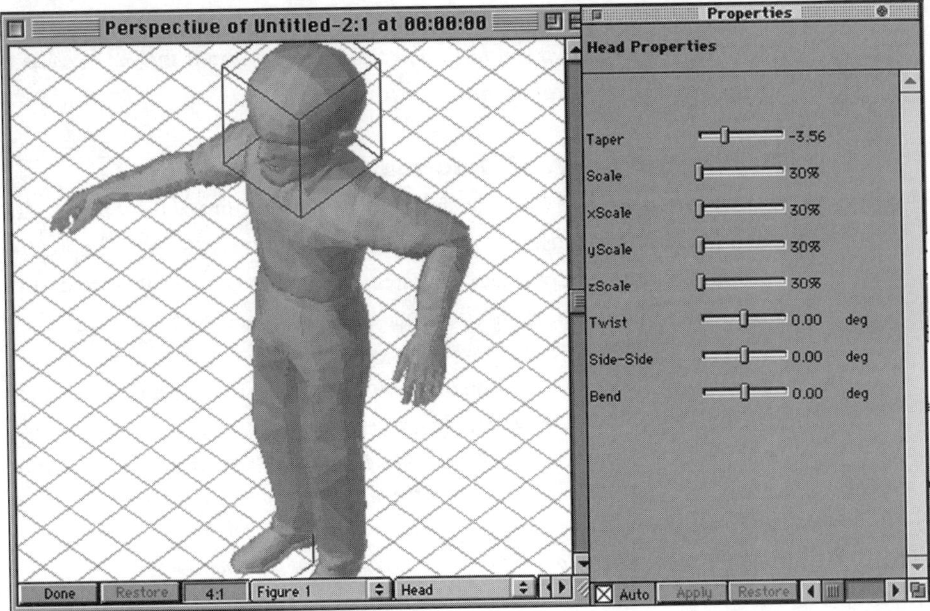

FIGURE 17.3 *Using the new Poser Modeler in Ray Dream allows you to customize the figure's elements with the familiar Poser Parameter Dials.*

FIGURE 17.4 *Using the Spike Deformer in Ray Dream, you can use a Poser Parameter Dial to grow instant spiky hair or other more radical looks on a figure, a Morph Target controlled by a Poser Parameter Dial.*

Other Deformations that can be used to create Morph Targets include Bend and Twist, Non-Uniform Scaling, and Stretch.

Ray Dream Internal Deformations

As long as you use the Poser modeler native to Ray Dream and don't plan to develop Morph targets inside of Poser with Deformations, they are all open for your exploration. Many create animated effects that can't be generated anywhere else without a lot more effort. See Figure 17.5 and 17.6.

When importing a prop, there are times when Poser does not accept it. If that happens, try closing and opening the program again, flushing out any remaining problems. This can happen when the prop is large, like the exploded head displayed in Figures 17.5 and 17.6. Also note that the same prop, when saved as a DXF and a OBJ from Ray Dream, is oriented differently. OBJ props come in at the correct orientation, while DXFs come in with the Z and Y axis transposed.

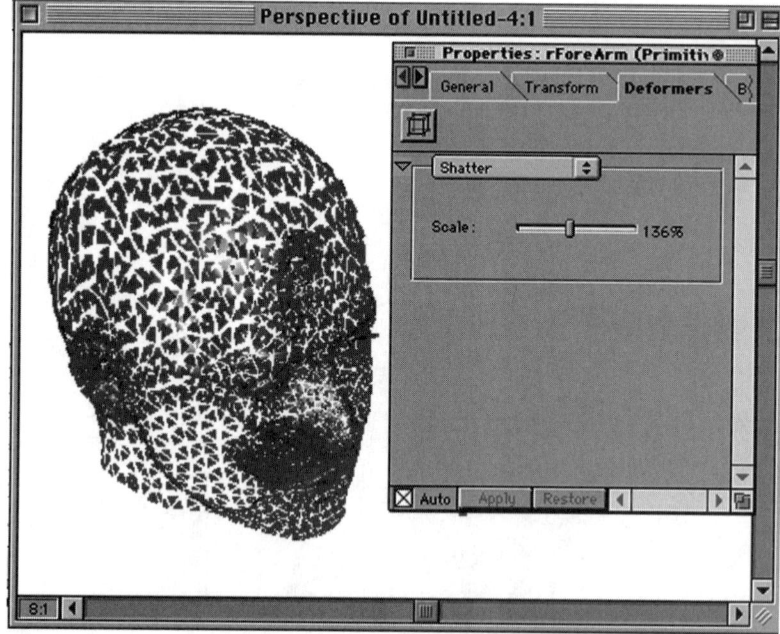

FIGURE 17.5 *The Shatter Deformer applied to a Poser Head in Ray Dream explodes the target into separate polygons. It is not suitable for creating Morph Targets. Any Deformer, however, can create props from figure elements.*

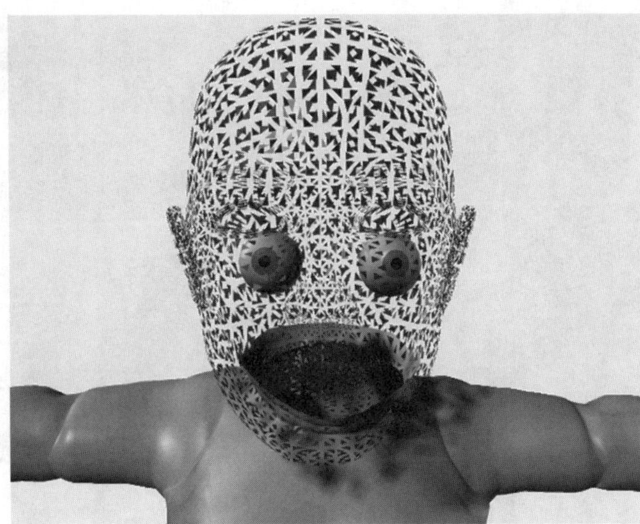

FIGURE 17.6 *The exploded head, saved as a DXF prop, is used here to replace the Sumo baby's head.*

Other 3D Applications

There are more 3D applications whose output Poser can utilize than those we are mentioning here. Those mentioned, however, were selected because they are the author's favorites, and also because each has its own special attributes for doing Poser-associated tasks.

BRYCE 3D

Bryce 3D is another part of the 3D suite of products from MetaCreations, the third member of the triad that includes Poser and Ray Dream Studio. As evidenced by comments from members of the Poser List (a MetaCreations Internet site), Bryce 3D is the application of choice when it comes to placing Poser figures in a rendering and animation environment. As of the 3.1 version of Bryce 3D, Poser figures can only be brought in as models, and not as animated figures. There is a constant clamor, however, rising from the Poser community of users, requesting that this be changed. I would expect that soon, MetaCreations, known for its responsiveness to user requests, will develop the plug-in technology that will allow fully animated Poser figures to be ported to Bryce 3D. Bryce 3D already has the capacity to read in WaveFront OBJ files, as well as to map objects with Parametric (UV) textures, so using the Poser texture maps is no problem.

Bryce 3D renders far slower than Poser, but does include infinite planes, creating a very realistic 3D world in which Poser figures can move. See Figure 17.7.

FIGURE 17.7 *Bryce 3D has the most votes for the final rendering and animation of Poser figures. These Poser Chimps were ported to Bryce 3D as OBJ files, textured, and linked together so they could be animated within Bryce 3D.*

If your rendering camera is not going to move in Bryce 3D, and you need to incorporate animated Poser figures, you might select to animate the figures in Poser. Then, in a post-production application, you could overlay the Poser animations on a Bryce 3D background. The only liability in doing this is that the figures will not cast a shadow in the 3D world.

FORM-Z

Form-Z comes for both Mac and Windows and is one of the most full-featured modeling applications on the market. It is much better suited to object creation than it is to the type of specific deformation needed to create Morph Targets for Poser. Form-Z demands a rather extensive learning curve compared to less full-featured modeling systems, due in large part to its prioritized interface and tools. If you intend using it for Poser projects, use it for the creation of props or figure replacement elements. If you are brave and experienced enough, you can also take a model developed in Form-Z and create a Poser hierarchy for it. As far as file formats that Poser can digest, Form-Z objects can be saved as either DXF, 3DMF, or OBJ. You may also want to explore using Form-Z as a rendering environment. The quality of its textures is superlative, and the RenderZone speeds are almost instantaneous. See Figure 17.8.

Form-Z information at http://www.autodessys.com.

AMAPI

Amapi is available for both the Mac and Windows. It reads and writes a number of 3D object formats, but OBJ is not one of them. It has some unique object modeling tools, but be prepared for a challenging interface experience. It reads. It writes. Amapi is a solid environment for creating and customizing props for Poser. See Figure 17.9.

Contact Amapi at http://www.amapi.com.

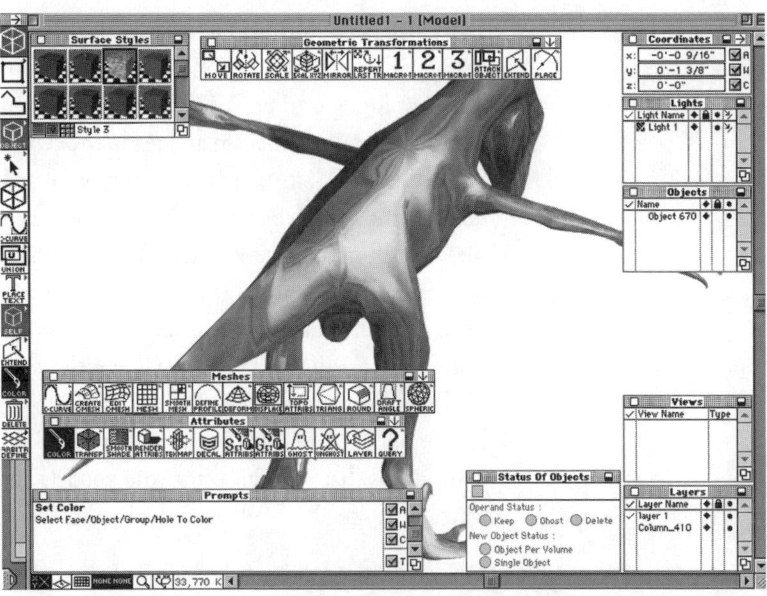

FIGURE 17.8 *Since Form-Z can read and write WaveFront OBJ object formats, you can import the figures in the Geometries library and deform them or create props for Poser.*

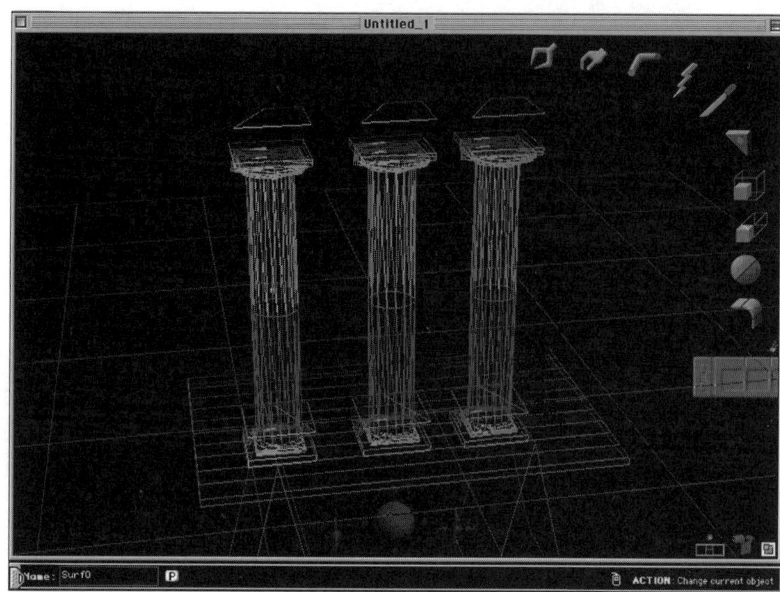

FIGURE 17.9 *Amapi has an interface different from any you will ever experience, and it can be used to create and customize props for Poser.*

INSPIRE 3D (LIGHTWAVE JR.)

Inspire 3D is the light version of NewTek's LightWave and has features that are just right for deforming Poser figures and creating figures and props. It is both Mac and Windows enabled and reads/writes WaveFront OBJ files, in addition to DXF and 3DS. Inspire 3D is your gateway to incorporating hundreds of detailed LightWave Objects (LWO) files into Poser, because it writes out OBJ files. Most times, however, the OBJ files cannot be read directly into Poser. In fact, Poser can't even see them. The answer is that they read easily into Ray Dream and from there can be saved out again as WaveFront OBJ models. Inspire 3D also writes 3DS and DXF models.

The other great feature of Inspire 3D as far as Poser is concerned is that it has a number of deformation tools not found in Ray Dream or anywhere else. This means that you can warp your models and figures in new and exciting ways in Inspire 3D. See Figures 17.10 and 17.11.

CAUTION

Karuna! If you find that Poser looks like it is loading a prop in any format, and then nothing appears, quit and restart the application again. This usually fixes the problem.

Contact NewTek at http.//www.newtek.com.

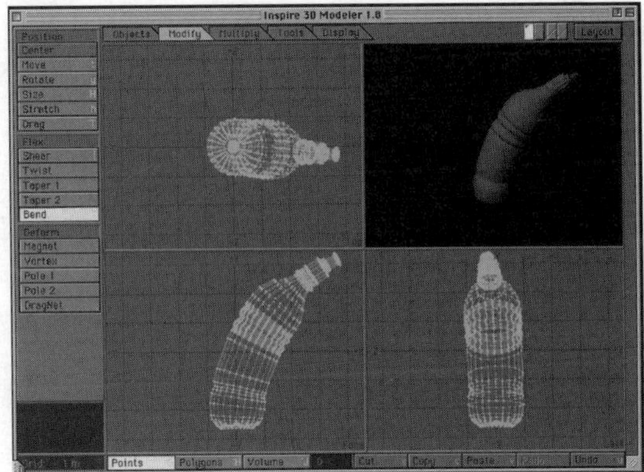

FIGURE 17.10 *On the left is a LightWave object (LWO) bottle, warped in Inspire 3D. On the right is the same object, saved out from Inspire 3D as an OBJ, imported and resaved in Ray Dream, and then read into Poser.*

STRATA STUDIO PRO 2.5

Available for Mac and Windows platforms, Strata Studio has a large collection of modeling and deformation tools and is extremely intuitive to use. It does not address OBJ files, but does read in DXF, 3DS, and 3DMF formats. Strata Studio Pro has excellent modeling features, and they are extremely easy to learn and use. Creating props for Poser with Studio Pro is a simple task. Studio Pro

FIGURE 17.11 *The same warped bottle can be used as a strange helmet for a Poser figure, parented to the Head.*

has one more feature that allows you to animate polygon mesh objects with ease: Bones.

Animating a Boned Poser Figure in Strata Studio Pro

1. Import a Poser figure from the Runtime/Geometries folder into Ray Dream, and save it out as a DXF object file.
2. Open Strata Studio Pro and import the Poser DXF figure.
3. Change the figure to a Polygon Mesh from the Convert dialog.
4. Create a Boned skeleton, and attach it to the Poser polygon mesh.
5. Animate the mesh by rotating the boned skeleton.

Animating facial features using Strata Studios Bones would be far too complex, but you could animate the rest of the figure. You might have to increase the polygons with a smoothing operation so the mesh doesn't fold in the wrong places.

Contact Strata at http://www.strata3d.com.

3D STUDIO MAX 2+

3D Studio Max (Windows only) has a worldwide reputation as a superlative modeling and animation environment. It can handshake with Poser both ways,

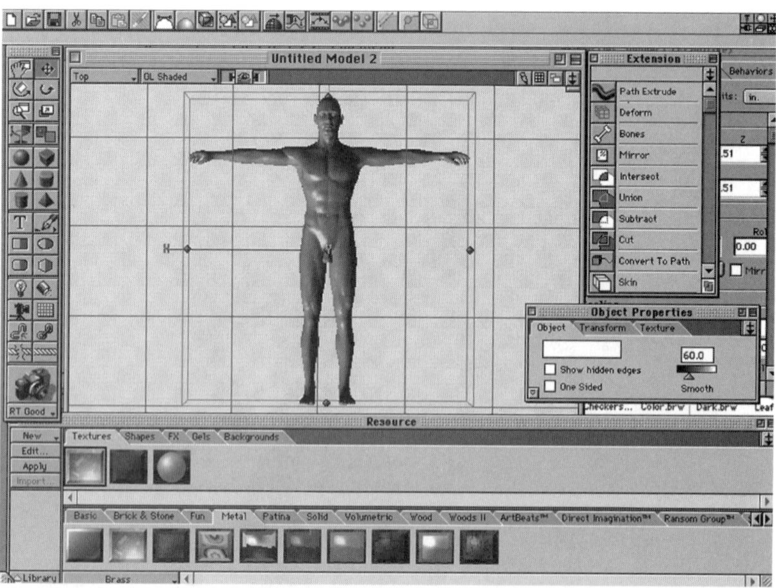

FIGURE 17.12 *You can import Poser figures as DXF models into Strata Studio Pro, transform them into polygon meshes, and animate them with Studio Pro's Bones IK Chains.*

since Poser can read and write 3DS object formats. Working in 3DS Max, there are several ways to create projects that can incorporate or enhance Poser elements:

1. You can import 3DS Poser figures and animate them with the Bones Pro plug-in from Digimation. This is a full-featured Bones utility. It is wiser to use 3DS Max Bones to animate global body movements, but facial boning can be a frustrating experience, so it should be accomplished in Poser itself.
2. You can develop props and body replacement elements in 3DS Max and then export them to Poser for developing your figures. Max plug-ins offer modeling processes found in no other software.
3. Character Studio, a Max accessory, reads and writes BVH Motion Data, and Character Studio also has its own walk generating system. Since both Poser and Character Studio can handshake with Motion data, each one can be a possible help to the other when developing animated movements.

3DS Max information at http://www.kinetics.com.

TRUESPACE 4+

Caligari's trueSpace is a Windows-only application that offers many options useful for Poser figure, animation, and prop development. Poser can write out

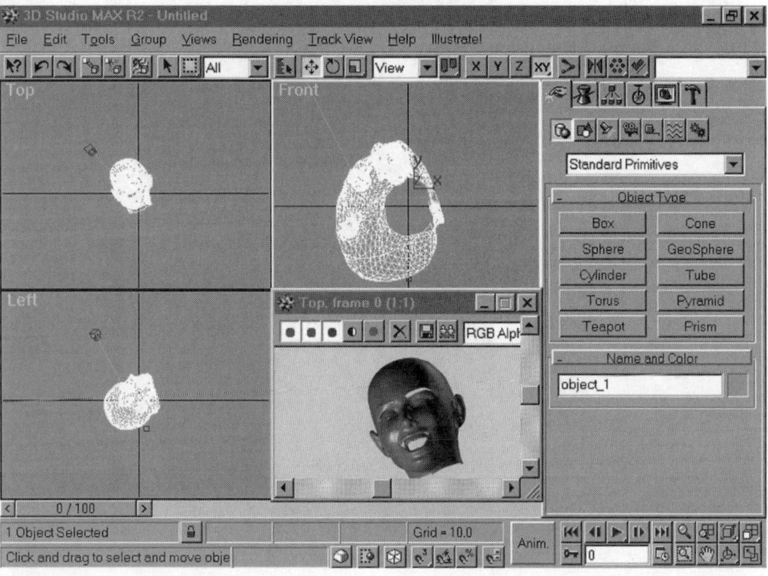

FIGURE 17.13 *3D Studio Max offers an array of possibilities for handshaking with Poser.*

both 3DS and DXF object file formats for use in trueSpace. Although trueSpace can read in OBJ files, it does not write them out. trueSpace has a very intuitive Bone utility, so imported Poser figures can be animated in trueSpace. trueSpace has a number of prioritized object creation and modification tools, so it is a very valuable environment for creating Poser props and replacement elements for Poser figures and scenes. See Figure 17.14.

Contact Caligari at http://www.caligari.com.

ORGANICA

As far as metaball modeling, Impulse's Organica is tastier than sliced bread. Metaballs are modeling elements that stretch out to each other when brought into proximity, so creating very organic-looking components is extremely intuitive. You can use Organica to create entire figures that can then be set up for hierarchies and used as animated figures in Poser. You can also create singular or multiple body elements that can replace any selected Poser body element, or even props to create interest in a Poser scene. In terms of 3D object file formats, Organica (available for both the Mac and Windows) can write out 3DS and DXF files, both of which Poser can read. The main item that differentiates

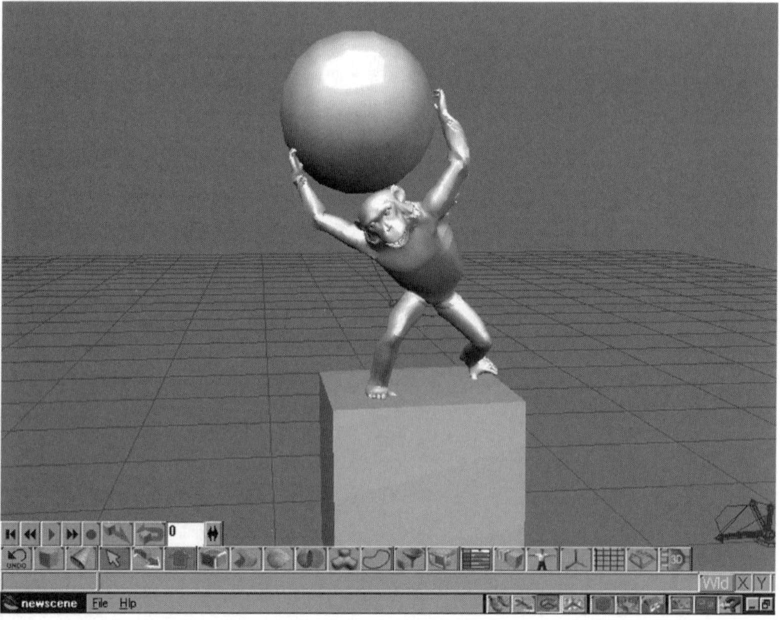

FIGURE 17.14 *trueSpace can read in Poser figures exported as OBJ, 3DS, or DXF formats, but does not write OBJ files.*

Organica from other metaBall modeling utilities is that it includes a large library of primitive shapes, in addition to spheres. Organica is not a good choice for developing Morph Targets, because it adds and subtracts polygons as you work and save. See Figure 17.15.

Contact Impulse at http://www.impulse.com.

NENDO

Nendo is Nichimen Graphics polymesh modeler. It can import both 3DS and OBJ files, and it can output 3DS and OBJ files. Nendo is mainly a polygon mesh modeler, using its own primitives as a start, and is less intended as a 3DS or OBJ customization application. Though you can import OBJ and 3DS models into Nendo, it does this extremely slowly, and it overloads easily. Its best use as a Poser helper is as a prop modeler, a task it performs extremely well. Nendo is one of the easiest polygonal modelers around, and it also features a full 3D painting module. The 3DS models it creates are made to load very quickly into Poser and Bryce 3D. See Figure 17.16.

Contact Nichimen at http://www.nichimen.com.

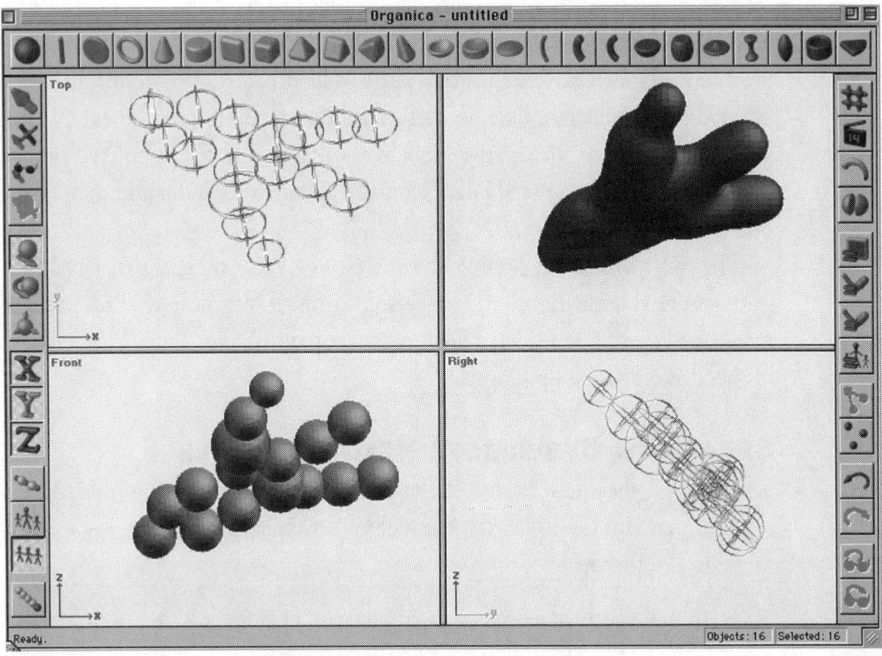

FIGURE 17.15 *Impulse's Organica is a perfect organic modeling system for developing Poser figures or figure parts, like this foot.*

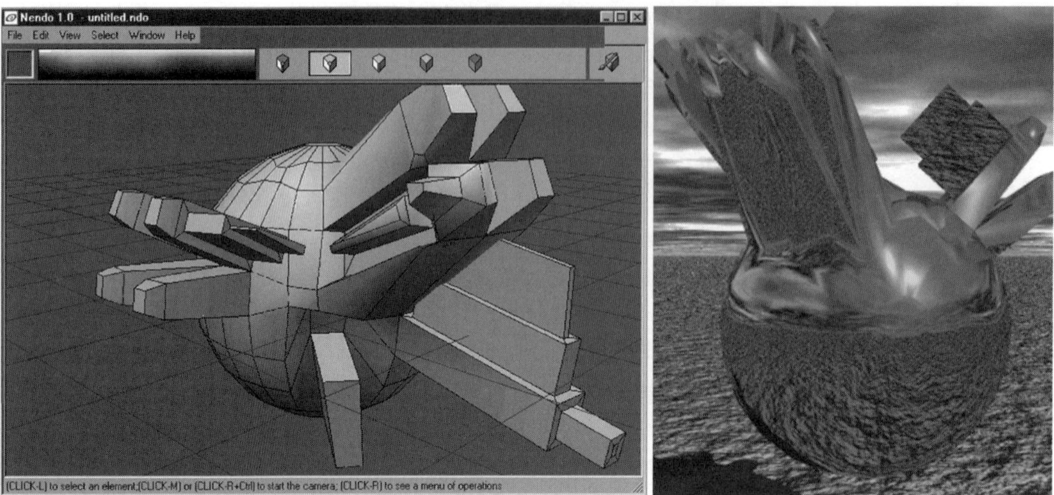

FIGURE 17.16 *Nichimen's Nendo makes prop modeling easy because you can generate very complex volumes from a single primitive. This complex object started as a basic sphere. A Bryce rendering is on the right.*

CyberMesh Is a Must!

Knoll Software's CyberMesh is a 3D application that lives as a plug-in in Adobe Photoshop, a 2D bitmap graphics application (for Mac and Windows users). Though it exists in a 2D world, it creates 3D DXF object formats that can be used in Poser as replacement body parts or as props. CyberMesh transforms grayscale art into height data, so that a flat bitmap painting becomes a 3D object. The lighter the bitmap, the "higher" the object is at that point. You can use CyberMesh to wrap your 3D data around a sphere or cylinder and then save it out as a true 3D object.

The most important use for CyberMesh for Poser users is that facial portraits can be translated into 3D objects, making all sorts of new heads or facial masks for Poser figures. Here's how to do it (obviously, you'll need CyberMesh installed as a Photoshop plug-in).

CREATING A CYBERMESH HEAD FOR POSER

To create a CyberMesh head for a Poser figure, do the following (this tutorial requires that you have placed a copy of CyberMesh into the Plugins/Exports folder in Photoshop):

1. Take a picture of a head with a digital camera, or use a copyright free picture of a head found on a CD-ROM collection.
2. Bring the image into Photoshop. Make the resolution 72 DPI and shrink the image to no more than 256 pixels wide.

3. Translate the image into Grayscale from RGB.
4. CyberMesh creates the best 3D objects when the image it references is vertically symmetrical, so do the following. Select the left or right half of the image, whichever looks better, and copy-paste it, creating a new image layer. Move the half that you pasted over the other half, creating a perfectly symmetrical image left and right. This balances out the lights and darks, which is what CyberMesh uses as a reference to create height data.
5. Blur the image several times. Make the nose slightly lighter than the rest of the head, so that it is a little higher.
6. Go to File/Export/CyberMesh. Play with the controls in CyberMesh until you can see a 3D mapping that you like. In general, start with the Rectangle map, with a height of about 20, and Full Resolution. When you have created a 3D map that looks OK, Save out the DXF.
7. Bring the DXF head into Poser, and use it to replace the head of a Poser figure. See Figures 17.17 and 17.18.

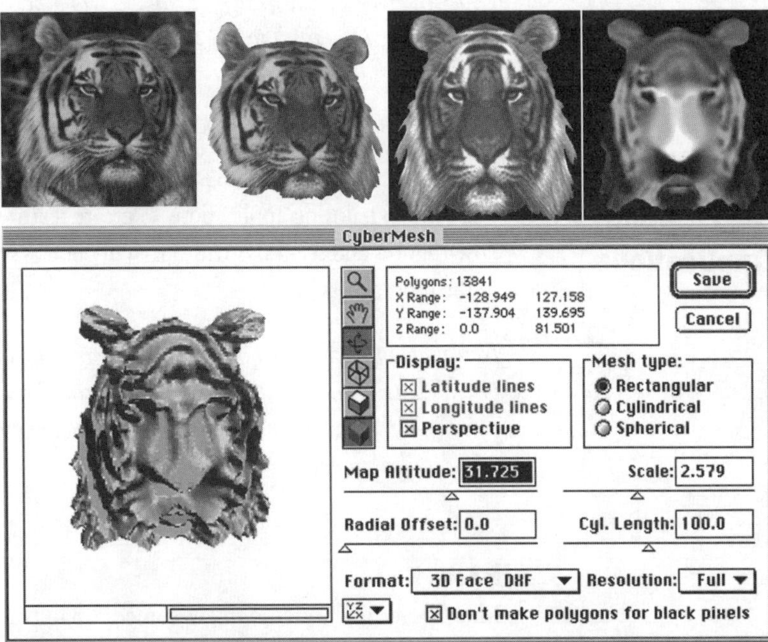

FIGURE 17.17 *A progression of images, showing the transition of a CyberMesh operation from bitmap to Poser 3D Head.*

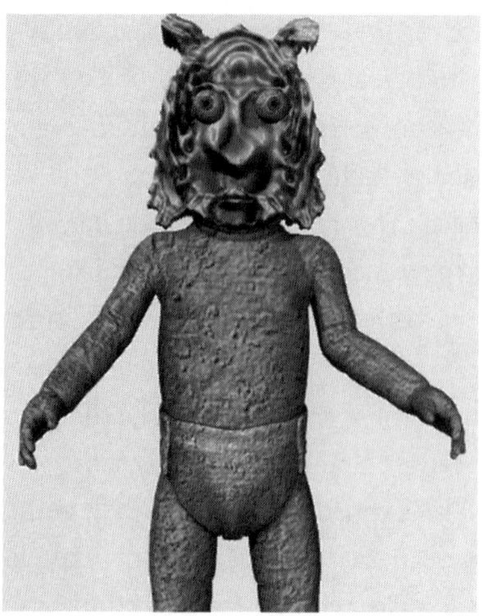

FIGURE 17.18 *The finished CyberMesh Head is used to replace the head of a Zygote baby figure, keeping the eyes intact. The Ground Texture was used as a Bump Map on the baby's body for effect.*

NOTE

CyberMesh heads work best when your Poser animation views the head from a fairly straight-on position. They look less suitable when the head is seen in profile. CyberMesh heads are really 3D masks. The best way to make them serve as 360-degree 3D heads is to place them inside of a hood or another prop that hides their somewhat flat nature.

For more information on CyberMesh, call (415) 453-2471

2D Painting Applications

Use bitmap painting applications to create textures and backgrounds for your Poser figures and scenes. A wide array of choices is available, but here are some of the most accessible.

NOTE

Note that our discussion of 2D Bitmap Painting applications in this chapter is fairly brief. That's because Chapter 18, Customizing Templates, deals with a more important and direct 2D handshaking Poser related option, template painting, in a very detailed manner.

PAINTER

MetaCreations Painter is an awesome bitmap painting application with loads of brushes and other image enhancing options. It is extremely complex to master, but easy to get a basic understanding of. For textures, my favorite tool is its Image Hose, a utility that allows you to spray sizable images. The Image Hose has a large collection of Nozzle libraries to select from. See Chapter 18.

Contact MetaCreations at http://www.metacreations.com.

PHOTOSHOP

Photoshop is the most common and widely used bitmap painting application. besides being the repository for a huge library of plug-in effects, it has an excellent (and industry standard) layering capability. This makes it a gem for creating Poser associated textures and backgrounds. See Chapter 18.

Contact Adobe at http://www.adobe.com.

COREL PHOTOPAINT

Corel's PhotoPaint has effects and tools that Photoshop lacks. It also has the capacity to load animation files, so you can add painted effects to every frame, before saving the animation out again. PhotoPaint is useful for Poser texture and background creation because it contains effects normally sold separately as plug-ins.

Contact Corel at http://www.corel.com.

GREAT 2D F/X PLUG-INS

This single topic could be five books in itself. There are literally hundreds of plug-ins that create a wide variety of effects in Photoshop and Photoshop-compatible applications. So I asked myself, if I was marooned on a desert island with my graphics systems, Poser, and Photoshop, which six 2D plug-in effects would I want along to develop textures for Poser figures? Here are my six top Poser-related choices (though I use a lot more), and why I would choose them:

Kai's PowerTools 3

What computer graphics artist could live without Kai's PowerTools from MetaCreations? It is the most popular effects plug-in collection ever developed, setting a high standard for others to follow. Kai Krauss's interface design rocked the industry and gave ideas to a whole generation of designers on how interfaces could be both effective and interesting. This is a large collection of tools, with my favorites for Poser textures being the Texture Explorer, Vortex Tiling, and the Spheroid Designer.

Contact MetaCreations at http://www.metacreations.com.

Alien Skin's Eye Candy

Eye Candy was developed by Alien Skin Software as a successor to their Black Box collection of plug-ins. It pushes the variety of plug-ins a lot farther, adding such effects as Smoke and Fire. A later collection by Alien Skin is Xenofex, adding even more possibilities for texture creation. I prefer the Eye Candy collection, however, since I must select only one.

Contact Alien Skin at http://www.alienskin.com.

Xaos Tools' Terrazo

Terrazo is the mother of all tiled-texture plug-in applications. If you are looking to create patterned clothes textures for your Poser figures, go no farther. Terrazzo's easy to understand interface and optional patterns make it a great Poser asset.

Contact Xaos at http://www.xaos.com.

Virtus' Alien Skin Textureshop

This is another Alien Skin creation, but since it was created for Virtus Corporation, I thought it righteous to slip in here. It is also a pattern creator, one with blends and organic looking possibilities that make it just right for creating skin and scale textures for Poser figures.

Contact Virtus at http://www.virtus.com.

Andromeda F/X

Andromeda F/X are spread across a number of volumes, each offering unique painting and texturing tools that can help you create texture maps and backgrounds for your Poser work. My favorites are Screens and S-Multi.

Contact Andromeda at http://www.andromeda.com.

Photoshop's Internal Effects

Photoshop comes with its own libraries of plug-in effects already installed internally. They are listed under several headings: Artistic, Brush Strokes, Distort, Noise, and more. For Poser texture development, I like the Distort options best. My favorite Distortion effects for creating Poser textured fabrics are Ripple, Glass, and Wave.

Contact Adobe at http://www.adobe.com.

Post-Production Editing

Painter

The one attribute that Painter has that allows it to be listed as a post-production as well as a painting application is its ability to load and save animations. When you load an animation into Painter, it is separated into frames, so that you can paint on each one before saving the animation out again. This means that all of Painter's brushes and effects are animation-oriented as well as being able to address textures and backgrounds for your Poser work.

Contact MetaCreations at http://www.metacreations.com.

ADOBE PREMIER

Use Adobe Premier to stitch your Poser animations together into longer sequences. The separate segments can be attached start to end, or a transition effect can take you from one segment to another.

Contact Adobe at http://www.adobe.com.

ADOBE AFTER EFFECTS

Adobe After Effects sets the standard for adding effects to animations, and hundreds of different effects plug-ins are available to increase its functionality even further. Many of the animations on this book's CD-ROM were processed through After Effects. If you need to composite your Poser animations to another background, Alpha, and effects layers to create specific effects sequences, you should think seriously about investing in After Effects as part of your professional tools.

Contact Adobe at http://www.adobe.com.

COMMOTION

If After Effects is important to your work, then Puffin Designs Commotion is also a must. Commotion adds much more functionality to your post-production needs, like the ability to playback Poser animations from RAM in real time, and the ability to paint on your sequenced frames. Commotion also allows you to use spline masks to composite elements with other content layers.

Contact Puffin Designs at http://www.puffindesigns.com.

MEDIA STUDIO PRO

Ulead's Media Studio Pro is a Windows-only application that offers a whole collection of post-production editing capabilities. With Media Studio, you can translate your Poser animations from one format to another and take advantage of a number of image effects to alter the look of your animations. Media Studio Pro is really a multimedia component package, consisting of an

Audio Editor, Video Capture module, and the Video Editor. The Audio Editor has a full mixing console on board. Just what you need to craft the perfect audio files for your Poser masterpieces. Using the Video Capture module, you can record sequences from your video camera or player direct to hard drive, using your audio interface or card.

Contact Ulead at http://www.ulead.com.

Animation Painting

This class of post-production applications allows you to add painting effects directly to your Poser animation frames.

SkyPaint

SkyPaint is a special application that allows you to paint on Panorama files. Panoramas are interactive visualizations that allow you to view an image as if it were mapped on a cylinder or sphere, with the viewpoint in the center of the scene. Once a Panorama is stitched together (Bryce has a cylindrical Panorama renderer), it can be posted to the web or used on a CD for viewers to interactively navigate. Until SkyPaint, there has never been a way to paint on a Panorama after it has been created. SkyPaint comes with a Photoshop plug-in that allows you to port the Panorama in sections to Photoshop for painting and effects, and then back to SkyPaint for interactive animated viewing.

SkyPaint information at http://www.wasabisoft.com.

MediaPaint

Strata's MediaPaint is an awesome package for developing animated effects that can be overlaid on your animation frames. MediaPaint offers you painting and a number of environmental effects. Most 3D applications take a long time to render particle and other effects, used to simulate nature (fire, clouds, smoke . . .). With MediaPaint, you can paint these effects on your completed animation. This is a way to allow your Poser figures to breathe fire or release bubbles underwater.

Contact Strata at http://www.strta3d.com.

Paint

Discreet Logic's Paint is an interactive vector and object-oriented painting and animation system. Paint allows you to paint and animate paint strokes, geometry, text, and effects, and it is Photoshop plug-in compatible. One of Paint's biggest assets is its plug-in handshaking with 3D Studio Max. This is important if you plan to use Max as your Poser animator, since you can use Paint to develop textures for Poser objects in the Max environment.

Contact Discreet Logic at http://www.discreet.com.

Aura

Aura (Windows only) was created to add animated 2D painting effects to movies, specifically for LightWave and Inspire 3D frames. It can just as well be used to add all sorts of animated f/x to your Poser movies. Aura is a perfect tool for rotoscoping, and allows you to use "Anim Brushes," which are animated sections of the footage that can then be painted down. Aura addresses a number of animation and graphics formats and can address Poser animations you import. Many of Aura's tool are not duplicated in any other animation paint system, and high-resolution transparency and blending is supported at the pixel level, for very high end output. Aura supports a number of nonlinear editing boards directly. Since it also writes out Toaster Flyer Clips, Aura is useful for animators planning to animate Poser figures in LightWave.

Contact NewTek at http://www.newtek.com

3D Painting Applications

3D Painting applications allow you to apply colors, textures, bump maps, and other channel effects directly to your 3D objects, so no special wrapping conventions are needed. For 3D painting to map correctly, the object has to accept UV (Parametric) mapping.

PAINTER 3D

MetaCreations Painter 3D is a natural choice for most Poser users in terms of 3D painting. It features the painting and texturing options of Painter itself, so you can even use the Image Hose to create textures for your Poser figures. This is very important if you need to develop Poser texture maps that encompass nature looks, such as leaves, clouds, branches, and more. The Celtic mythic figure of the Green Man, for example, can be emulated in Poser by using Painter 3D and the Image Hose. Just load a leaf nozzle into the image hose and create a figure texture of variegated leaves for the figure, head to toe.

Contact MetaCreations at http://www.metacreations.com.

4D PAINT

4D Paint from 4D Vision is best used to paint in 3D on 3D Studio Max objects, though you can also import LightWave and OBJ files as well. 4D Paint contains a plug-in for 3D Studio Max, so that a selected Max object can be transported directly to 4D Paint. Once there, it can be interactively painted on, have channel maps (bump maps, transparencies, secularities, etc.) applied, and be shipped right back to 3D Studio Max for rendering.

Contact 4D Vision at http://www.4dvision.com.

TRU-V

Positron Publishing's trU-V is the result of years of exploration and development centered on the best way to create textures that show no seams or stretches once a 3D object is rendered and animated. As of this writing, it is 3D Studio Max and LightWave enabled, with more 3D object formats soon to be implemented. trU-V creates a polymap, a stretched out gridded map that addresses the selected polygonal object and is then used as a painting reference. After developing a trU-V map, go to 3D Studio Max. Open the Material Editor, select a surface and add a Diffuse bitmap. Find the trU-V PolyMap image that was saved out (probably in the TrU-V folder). Select Show Map In ViewPort and copy the material to the selected object. It should map perfectly, showing the texture map as a series of placed grids. If it looks OK, you can port it to any 2D (Painter, Photoshop, etc.) or 3D painting application (like Positron's MeshPaint 3D) from there, creating whatever texture looks you like.

Contact Positron at http://www.3dgraphics.com.

SURFACE SUITE PRO

This application started out as a 3D Studio Max plug-in and has recently become a stand-alone 3D texture creation utility. Though not exactly a 3D painting application like the others mentioned, it does allow you to create seamless textures that wrap around objects. Unique to SurfaceSuite Pro is its use of Control Points to develop seamless textures for objects that show no stretching across complex surfaces and that can "relax" to mold themselves perfectly to any object that SurfaceSuite addresses. This application also features unlimited layering, so that textures can be developed from a number of sources in a composite. Surface Suite will import 3DS, OBJ, LWO, and DXF models, as well as a number of 2D bitmap formats. It exports 3DS and OBJ files, plus a number of bitmap formats so you can tweak the resulting textures, and is absolutely perfect for Poser uses.

Contact Sven Technologies at http://www.sven-tech.com.

BVH MOTION CAPTURE DATA: CREDO INTERACTIVE'S LIFE FORMS*

Credo Interactive's Life Forms application is an absolute must for Poser users who plan to be doing a lot of work with Motion Data files. Poser, along with many other 3D applications, is able to both read and write Motion Data files. Poser's Walk Designer (see Chapter 14) is an exquisite utility that allows you to create realistic walks and runs that can then be saved as Motion Data files. But

* By Pamela Chow of Credo Interactice, Inc.

Credo Interactive's Life Forms offers far more extensive Motion Data file editing than Poser, or any other application. What's even better is that LifeForm data can be ported directly to Poser. The following information, detailing the Life Forms/Poser connection, was contributed by Credo Interactive.

Poser 3 users can import BioVision motion capture files from motion composition software such as Life Forms because of the complementary nature of Poser 3 and Life Forms 3. The following tutorial shows you how to bring motion from Life Forms into Poser 3. This tutorial is for any Poser 3 user who wants to use Poser's new BVH motion import feature to bring in animation from Life Forms, a high-end motion composition and editing application.

Because Poser models are single-skin meshes, their joints have a more limited range of rotation than models in Life Forms. When the joints of Poser models are over-rotated, the mesh will be distorted. You can still use Life Forms to apply motion data to the Poser Models, and then apply Limits and Inverse Kinematics in Poser to reduce or completely remove the distortion. In Life Forms 3 or Poser 3, you can edit the motion data so that the motion does not tear the mesh in Poser.

What you need for this tutorial:

- Poser 3. (Poser 2 does not have BVH motion import feature required)
- Life Forms Studio 3

For this tutorial we will assume that you are using the Life Forms 3.0 Demo. This demo can be downloaded for free from http://www.credo-interactive.com. Note, however, that the demo version is limited to exporting only five frames of animation.

Animating in Life Forms

Motion editing functions are explained in depth in the *Life Forms User Guide*. We'll describe briefly how Life Forms is used for animation.

- ***As a Motion Editor:*** When you need to make changes to a sequence, you can use Life Forms graphical timeline to quickly navigate through the animation. Then, use the Range Edit function to apply a relative or absolute rotation to one or more joints. For example, let's say you have sequence that is perfect for your needs, except that the head should be looking down instead of forward. In Life Forms, this is simple matter to fix. Simply select all frames and apply an absolute or relative rotation to the head so that it faces the desired position. You can also quickly change the rhythm or timing of a sequence by adding empty frames and by expanding or compressing a range of frames.

- ***As a Keyframer:*** Life Forms is a specialist in Keyframing. When you want to create custom animations from scratch, Life Forms is the tool to use, because it has the following: a Figure Editor for fast and accurate positioning of joints; simple controls for adjusting location and facing angle of the figure in the Stage window; and a graphical Timeline that gives you the ability to navigate through the animation and expand or contract selected frames.
- ***As a Library of Motions:*** Life Forms Studio 3 comes with a library of models and motions called PowerMoves. This library contains 120 motion captured sequences and over 600 other sequences that you can reuse as is, recombine, or modify, and then port to Poser 3.
- ***For Smart Paste Functions:*** With Life Forms you can paste one animation in front of, following, or in the middle of another animation. Life Forms automatically recalculates the location values to produce a continuous path. This means that you can quickly assemble a longer animation from short pre-made sequences. You can also paste motion sequences from one model to another. The Joint Map editor lets you control how motion data is applied from the a source to a destination model.

Setting up Motion Sequences for Poser

There are two ways to create motion for Poser 3: by using motion captured animation and by keyframing your own animation.

Using Motion Captured Animation The PowerMoves 1 & 2 Library that comes with Life Forms has over 120 BioVision motion capture (mocap) sequences that you can use. Mocap sequences are recorded with a live actor using motion-sensitive equipment. When you open a mocap file in Life Forms, you will see a BioVision skeleton figure. Its motion is recorded at a frame rate of 30 FPS. This dense motion data produces very realistic movement.

To bring those sequences into Poser 3 simply export the motion capture animation from Life Forms as a BVH file.

Example:

1. Open the motion-captured animation in Life Forms that is contained on this book's CD-ROM in the Credo folder. Open this file by choosing

File menu > Open. Browse and locate mt5948 Kick Fly Spin.lfa. This animation is in the same directory as this document.

2. Export the motion as a BVH file. Open the Export dialog box by choosing **File menu > Export**. Select BioVision BVH file format from the Export Format list. Make sure that all export option checkboxes are cleared. Click OK. The Demo version of Life Forms only allows you to export five frames, but we've included the full BVH export in mt5948 Kick Fly Spin.bvh as a sample file for this tutorial.
3. Import the BVH motion into Poser 3. Choose **File menu > Import > BVH motion**. Browse and select Kick Fly Spin.bvh.
4. Align Arms along the X axis. A dialog box appears. Click along the X axis. Poser will now import and apply the motion to the model selected in Poser.
5. For this animation, we did not choose Use Limits and no editing was required. See the Poser file Kick and the movie file Kick.mov in the same Credo folder. After the motion has been imported, examine the animation by stepping through the frames. Check to see that the mesh intersects or breaks at various points in the animation. If so you may try applying Use Limits, and try turning on Inverse Kinematics for the arms and leg joints to see if the animation improves. You may also find it necessary to edit several frames in the animation to remove unwanted wrinkles or distortions in the mesh if they occur.

See Poser File: Kick and the Kick.mov in the Credo folder on this book's CD-ROM.

Keyframing Your Own Animation You can keyframe your own animation using one of Life Forms Default human models and then export it to Poser 3. There are four steps in this process:

1. Create the Keyframed animation.
2. Adjust the Frame Rate to 30 f/s.
3. Export the Motion in a BVH file.
4. Port the BVH motion into Poser 3.

To Create a Keyframe

1. Open a new animation. Choose **File menu > New Animation** to open a new animation.
2. Add a new figure to the animation. Choose **Figure menu > New Human Figure** to insert one of Life Forms' Default human models.

3. Position the insertion point in the Timeline. Do this by clicking in any frame in the Timeline.
4. Open the Figure Editor window. Open the Figure Editor window by choosing **Window menu > Figure Editor**. You can also open the Figure Editor window by double-clicking on the figure in the Stage window.
5. Position the joints to create a new shape or pose. In the Figure Editor window, drag the joints to create the desired pose. This pose will appear in the Timeline at the insertion point.
6. Complete the animation and improve the timing. Repeat this to create the animation you want. Insert empty frames between the keyframes to improve the transition between keyframes.
7. Preview the animation. Preview the animation by clicking Play in the Control Panel. You can preview the animation in Rendered mode by opening the Rendered window.

Adjusting Frame Rate before Export

The default frame rate in Life Forms is 3 f/s. Before exporting animations to Poser 3 as BVH file, you'll need to increase the frame rate to 30 f/s. The following steps show you how to increase the frame rate of keyframed animations to 30 f/s without changing the duration of the animation.

To increase the Frame rate to 30 f/s:

1. Note the current frame rate and duration of the animation. For example, let's take a frame rate of 3 f/s and duration of 60 s.
2. Choose **Control menu > Frame rate**. Enter 30 in the Frames/sec field.
3. Notice that the duration of your animation is now 6 s instead of 60 s. You will need to expand the animation to the desired duration. First zoom out of the Timeline as far as possible by using the Zoom bar.
4. Select all the frames by clicking in the gray area to the left of the timeline.
5. Then, position the cursor over the Selection handle until it becomes a double-headed arrow. Now, drag the cursor to the right. Do not release the mouse. While dragging the mouse keep an eye on the Current Frame box in the bottom left corner of the Timeline window. This will give you the percentage by which you have expanded the animation. Drag until the animation has been expanded by 1000% or 10 times.

To Export BVH Files

1. Make the animation you want to export the current animation by clicking in one of its windows.
2. Choose **File menu > Export**.

3. In the Export Format list select BioVision BVH.
4. Make sure that all export options are cleared. Then click OK.

To Import BVH Motion Data into Poser 3

1. Choose **File menu > Import > BVH motion**. Browse and select HipHopC.bvh.
2. Align Arms along the X axis. A dialog box appears. Click along X axis. Poser will now import and apply the motion to the model selected in Poser.
3. Several messages will appear warning you that certain parts are missing. Keep clicking OK until all these messages are closed. After the motion has been imported, examine the animation by stepping through the frames. You may see the mesh intersect or break in certain frames of the animation. If this happens, try applying Use Limits. You may also try turning Inverse Kinematics on for the arms and leg joints to see if this helps.
   Contact Credo Interactive at http://www.credo-interactive.com.

See the Kick.mov in the Credo folder on the CD-ROM.

Fashion Studio

If clothes for your Poser figures are important to you, and you relish the idea of designing Poser wardrobes, then Fashion Studio will be a necessary component of your Poser toolkit. Fashion Studio is a professional clothing designer's application, with loads of functionality for Poser users. With it, you can fit clothing to a model and save the results to a DXF file. The clothing can be animated, using gravity, wind, and other factors in Fashion Studio. To animate it in Poser, however, means computing all of the necessary bend and hierarchy Parameters necessary. Fashion Studio imports DXF files, so you have to make sure to save the Poser figures you want to clothe as DXFs from Poser first, using them as designer models in Fashion Studio. You can download a demo from the Web. See Figure 17.19.

Fashion Studios information at http://www.dynagraphicsinc.com

Media Conversion and Compression

Available now for the Mac, and coming in the first quarter of 1999 for Windows, Terran Interactive's Media Cleaner Pro may be the most valuable utility around when it comes to compressing your Poser animations in a multitude of display formats. A Poser animation that writes out as a 10 MB file can typically

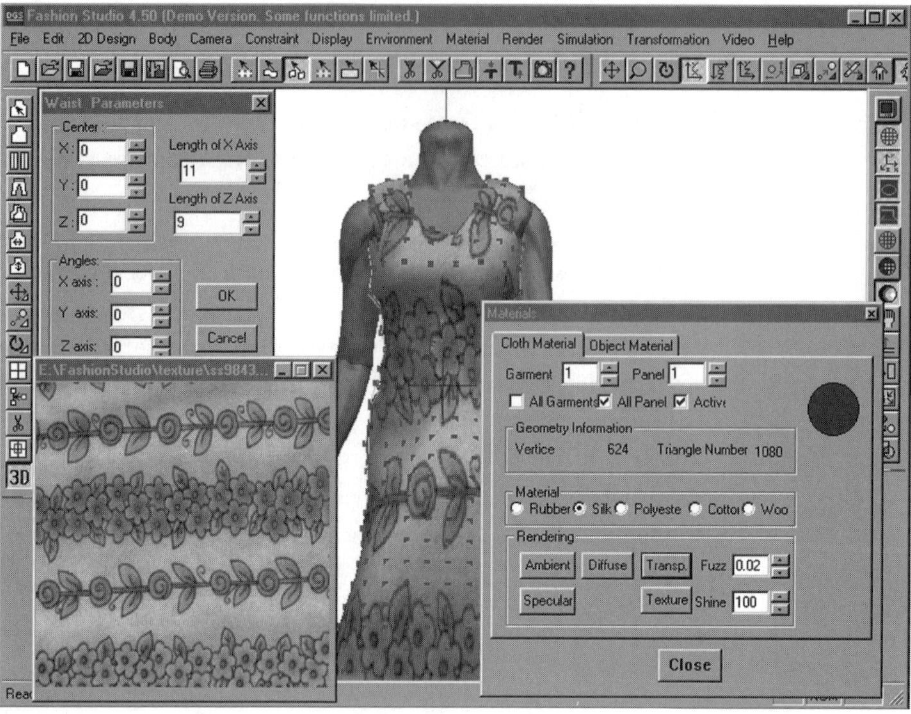

FIGURE 17.19 *In Fashion Studio, you can design garments that can be saved as DXF files and placed on Poser figures.*

be compressed by Media Cleaner down to 4 MB, with no visible image loss. When you consider the amount of space that can be taken up by multiple Poser animations, you can see that being able to reduce them in size by 50% or more is quite a savings of storage space. For Web animations, Media Cleaner includes the Sorrensen Video Codec, so that your Poser animations download to Web viewers systems much faster.

Contact Terran at http://www.terran.com.

Necessary Content

The world is flooded with CD-ROMs that offer 3D objects, texture maps, and other content that you can use to make your Poser productions richer. Here are a few that you definitely should consider.

CHRIS DEROCHIE

In Chapter 20, which is devoted to Master users, you will read a piece by Chris Derochie. Chris is a professional animator with years of experience in the field. One of his present endeavors is the creation of a series of Poser CD-ROMs, loaded with poses, motion files, and other Poser related material, to be produced quarterly. The first CD-ROM contains 90 animation files of men, women, children, and animals divided into three different frame rates—10, 24, and 30 fps. The 10 fps versions are simplified action with low frame counts for game programmers on a tight frame budget. The 30 fps version is much more refined, with more subtlety and higher frame counts for use by everyone, especially animators looking for references and people transferring to NTSC video. The 24 fps version is a retaining of the 30 fps version without extra refinement. The 24 fps version is best for feature animators needing reference and for people transferring animation to PAL video, which runs at 25 fps. The CD also contains dozens of facial expressions for men, women, and children; lighting sets; hand positions; and 75+ poses for men, women, children, and animals. The animation and poses for the first CD concentrate on everyday actions and basic game animation.

Contact Chris Derochie at derochie@tinet.ie.

BAUMGARTEN ENTERPRISES

Ed Baumgarten has devoted a lot of time and effort to developing garments and props for Poser figures and environments. He is in the process of releasing his creations on a CD-ROM. You will find a number of his sample objects on

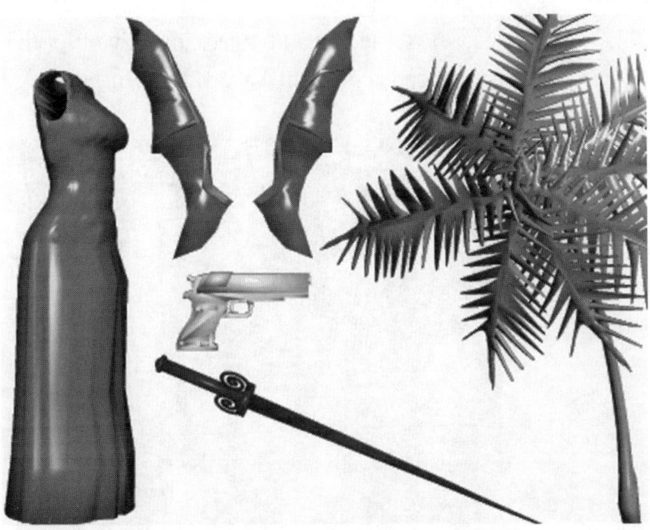

FIGURE **17.20** *A sample of objects from the Baumgarten Enterprises collection, found in the Baum folder on this book's CD-ROM.*

this book's CD-ROM in the Baument folder. A descriptive text of his creation methods is also included in Chapter 20 on Master Users. Visit his Web site (http://www.stewstras.net/baument) for more information. See Figure 17.20.

SB TECHNOLOGIES

On this book's CD-ROM is a folder with object files and Poser files of a jail cell and a bedroom, all from SB Technologies. You can incorporate either environment in your own Poser scenes, simply by loading them from the CD-ROM. If you like what you see, contact SB Technologies for a list of its other available models and props. See Figure 17.21.

Contact SB Technologies at http://www.sbtech.com (or call 412-881-1088 or 412-327-8072).

Karuna! The Jail Cell and bedroom Poser files, and all of the OBJ contents, are in the SBTech folder on the CD-ROM.

REPLICA TECHNOLOGY

Don't miss the Replica Technology Dolphin and Shark collections. The models are exquisite and can be used as animated props in your Poser or Bryce 3D scenes. Of course, if you're brave enough, you can also create hierarchy files that can be animated directly in Poser. A complete installation will require approximately about 65 MB of hard disk space (Objects, Scenes, and Textures). This collection was done using LightWave 3D versions 5.0 and 5.5. You can also load the scene files and objects directly off of the CD-ROM. This collection can be loaded by LightWave 3D and Inspire 3D. To get the objects into Poser,

FIGURE 17.21 *The SB Technologies Jail Cell Poser environment.*

FIGURE 17.22 *These detailed shark models display the high quality of the Replica Technology collections.*

you should have a copy of LightWave, Inspire 3D, or another application that can translate LightWave 3D object formats (LWO) into 3DS, OBJ, or DXF files. Inspire 3D can do any of these translations very quickly from the Modeler's Tools/Custom/3D File Exports dialog.

Replica Tech offers a diverse collection of 3D Objects on CD. Most are LWO files, but there are other formats as well. They include: the Interior Design Collection, the Wright Collection, the Camelot Collection, the Dolphin Collection Vol. 1, the Dolphin Collection Vol. 2, and the Shark Collection Vol. 1. See Figure 17.22.

Contact Replica at http://www.replica3d.com.

ArtBeats REELs

If you are thinking about using After Effects or another post-production editing application to composite your Poser animations with other content layers, then don't make a move without investigating ArtBeats REEL CD-ROM collections. The REEL volumes contain animated sequences of clouds, water, fire, explosions, and other environmental effects that can add just the touch of magic you need to your Poser movies.

Contact ArtBeats at http://www.artbeats.com.

Moving Along

Though we have by no means listed all of the possible applications that can handshake with Poser to enhance your creative endeavors in the chapter, we have presented you with quite a number of hot items to search out. In the next chapter, we'll look at ways you can customize your Poser figure templates to create new texture maps for Poser figures.

CHAPTER 18

Customizing Templates

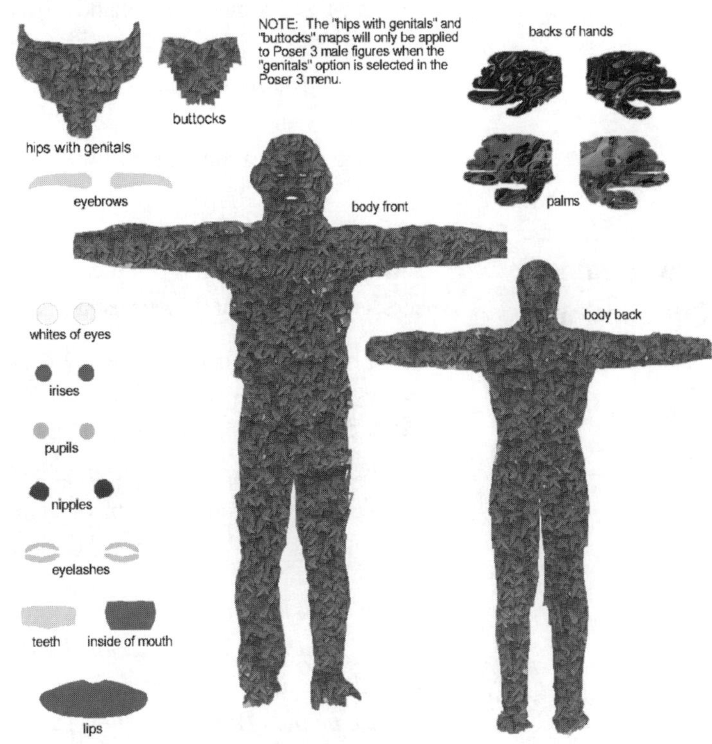

The templates used for demonstration purposes in the chapter were created by Robert Saucier, an active member of the MetaCreations Poser List. Mr. Saucier is a webmaster for a large ERP software company based in Grand Rapids, MI. His high resolution Poser 3 templates are included on this book's CD-ROM in the Templ folder, for your free use, and include new templates for the Zygote models as well. Since they are in high resolution, they allow for much more detail when used to create new textures for Poser figures.

At work, in addition to his webmastering role, he is also responsible for creating and maintaining presentation material for a small but global part of the company. Poser comes in very handy when process flows are needed. A Poser figure pointing out a step gets a little more attention than just an arrow. As a future project, Mr. Saucier plans to recreate the Poser 2 muscle bump maps for Poser 3 use.

See Saucier Creations at http://www.saucier-pages.com.

File Naming Conventions

When you look in the Templ folder on the CD to retrieve the new Poser Templates, you will see that they are named according to the following conventions:

- P1—Poser 1 map templates
- P2—Poser 2 map templates
- P3—Poser 3 map templates
- Px—Map template may be used for one or more of the above
- ZS—Zygote Poser 3 Sampler map templates
- ZA—Zygote Poser 3 Animal Collection map templates

Karuna! In the following exercises, MetaCreations Painter 5 is used as the bitmap painting application. You can use another application if you don't have Painter 5, but you'll have to substitute that application's brush and/or texturing capabilities for those mentioned in Painter.

Creating Textures with Painter

MetaCreations Painter offers you an almost unlimited number and variety of painting effects with which to paint on Poser Templates.

CREATING A NEW HORSE TEXTURE

In this first exercise, we will walk through the creation of an alternate texture map for the Poser 3 Horse. Do the following:

1. Open Painter. Load the P3Horse.Tif file from the Templ folder on this book's CD-ROM. This is the hi-res Horse Template created by Robert Saucier.
2. Click the Magic Wand in a white area of the image. Hold down the Shift Key, and use the lasso to encircle all of the text lines. Under the Selection menu, go to Invert. All that should be selected now are the actual Templates. See Figure 18.1.
3. Select the Bucket icon and make sure a black color is selected. Click once inside any of the outlined areas, and all of the areas will be filled with black. See Figure 18.2.

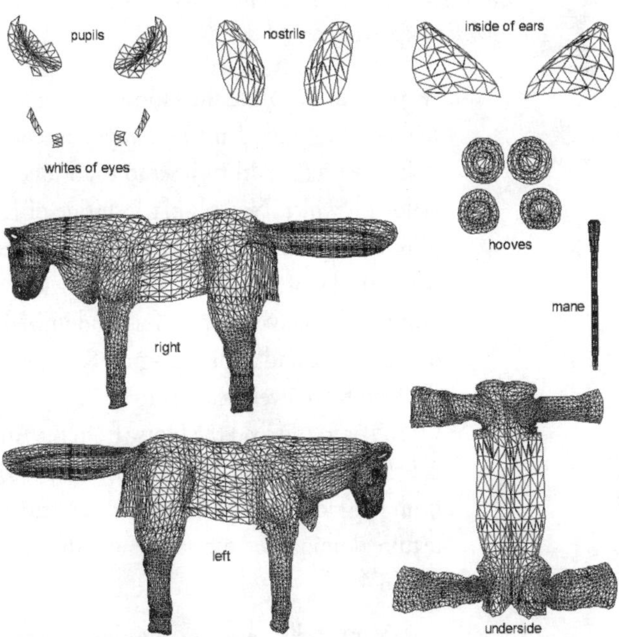

FIGURE 18.1 *Here's what the beginning Template looks like.*

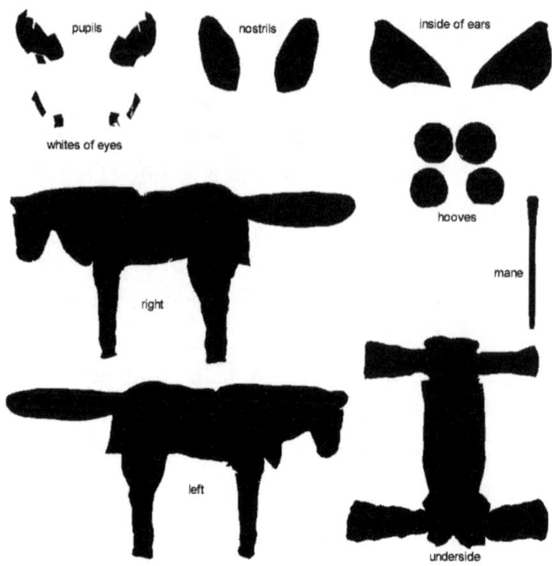

FIGURE 18.2 *All of the areas are filled with black.*

CAUTION

Karuna! It is important that the outlined marquees remain intact and visible for all painting operations.

4. As you can see, all of the Horse's elements are named on the Template, making it easy to identify what you are painting. Paint the elements as follows with the Airbrush set to Fat Stroke: Pupils black; Whites of Eyes yellowish white; Nostrils black; Inside of Ears light pink inside to dark pink outside, with a black outline; Hooves black; Mane bluish white with streaks of gray-blue; Right and left Sides, a yellow-white background with gray-blue patches, randomized; Underside should be a mix of gray-white and light blue-gray. Save the template as a texture map in the textures drawer. See Figure 18.3.
5. Open Poser, and load the Horse from the Animals library. Open the Surface Materials dialog, and load the new Horse texture you just created from the Horse Template. Color all of the Horse elements white so the texture dominates. Pose and render the image and save to disk. See Figure 18.4.

Repeat the preceding exercise, but this time create a new Horse surface texture that would be used for a merry-go-round horse, making the horse and its spots bright primary colors. Use your imagination. See Figure 18.5.

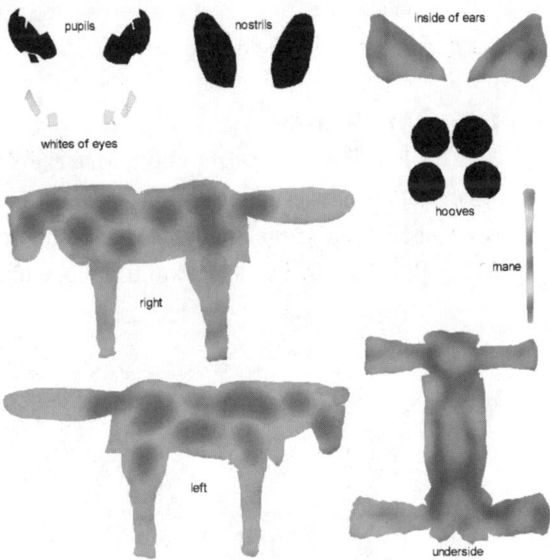

FIGURE 18.3 *The finished Template painting for an alternate Horse texture.*

FIGURE 18.4 *The rendered Horse figure textured with the new dappled map.*

FIGURE 18.5 *The brightly colored renderings of a posed merry-go-round horse.*

You can also use any of Painters Patterns to create a new Horse texture, like this floral design. See Figures 18.6 and 18.7.

THE GREEN MAN

In Celtic lore, it is said that the Green Man exists deep in the woods, granting benefits of the harvest and mysteries of the Earth. The Green Man is the male aspect of Mother Nature, though he has been lost in time. We can bring him back in Poser, at least in a digital world. This exercise especially requires Painter,

FIGURE 18.6 *A Painter Floral Pattern is used to map the Horse.*

FIGURE 18.7 *In this instance, a Green Textured Glass pattern was used as both a Surface and a Bump Map.*

since we are going to use its Image Hose, a tool found nowhere else. Do the following:

1. Open Painter and load the P3ManNude Template from the Templ folder, which will load another of Robert Saucier's detailed maps. See Figure 18.8.
2. Follow the same procedure you used with the Horse to select only the figure's outlined surfaces, and not the background or the callout lettering.
3. Use the Fill Bucket to paint everything a light green at the start, making sure the marquee around all of the mapped content remains active. Open the Painter Image Hose, select the English Ivy Nozzle, and set the Size to 30%. Use the Image Hose to spray this nozzle on the Front, Back, Hips With Genitals, and Buttocks elements.
4. Use the Airbrush to color other elements as follows: Lips and Irises bright red; Teeth yellow; Inside of Mouth dark green; Eyelashes light blue; Nip-

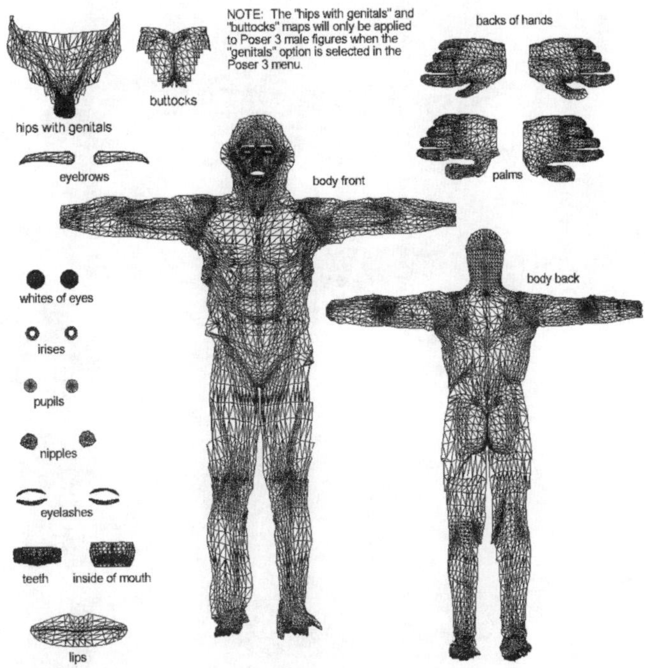

FIGURE 18.8 *The P3ManNude Template.*

ples dark blue; Pupils light green. Use a Turbulence Pattern of 30% to texture the front and back of the Hands. See Figure 18.9.

5. In Poser, load the Nude Man from the People library. Resize the Head with a -14% Taper. Apply the new map you just created to the figure. A close-up of the Head should resemble Figure 18.10.

The Green Man is usually pictured with a wreath around his Head, so let's create one. This will require Ray Dream Studio.

6. Open Ray Dream and place a Sphere in the scene. Squash the Sphere so that it is only about one-fourth as high. See Figure 18.11.
7. With the squashed Sphere selected, go to the Deformers tab in the Properties dialog. Select the Spikes Deformer and set the values as follows: Density 6, Length 100%, Radius .25, Messiness 100%, Flow and Gravity to 0. See Figure 18.12.
8. Export the Spiked Sphere as a OBJ file from Ray Dream and import it into your Green Man scene in Poser 3. Place it on the head of the figure, pose, render, and save. Make the Head the parent of the Wreath. See Figures 18.13 and 18.14.

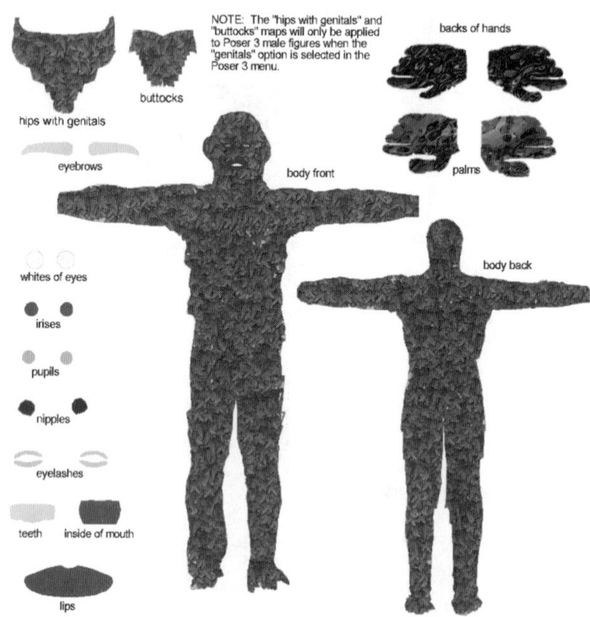

FIGURE 18.9 *The finished Green Man Texture Map created from the P3ManNude Template.*

FIGURE 18.10 *A close-up of the Head of the Green Man.*

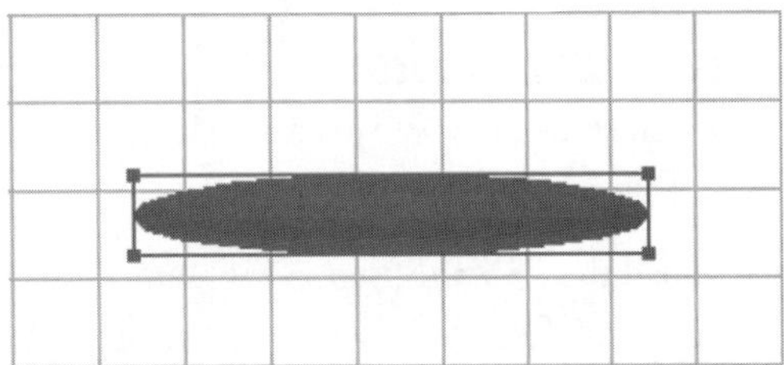

FIGURE 18.11 *Create a squashed Sphere in Ray Dream.*

FIGURE 18.12 *The Spiked Sphere looks like a wreath of grass.*

FIGURE 18.13 *The posed Green Man with a wreath of spiked grass on his head.*

FIGURE 18.14 *A series of Green Man poses, displaying the full texture map.*

LEISURE SUIT LAMBERT

Let's try one more template to create a texture variation for a Poser figure, modified in Painter.

1. Load the P3ManBusiness.TIF Template from this book's Templ folder on the CD-ROM. Color the template whatever colors you like, using the previous examples as a guide.
2. Explore the use of Patterns and Weaves to apply designs to the jacket, pants, and shirt.
3. Use an Airbrush with a light gray color to add beard stubble to the face.
4. After applying this map in Poser, get some Sunglasses and a Hat prop from the Zygote Props library, and parent them to the head. One result of this exploration can be seen in Figure 18.15.

CUSTOMIZING THE RAPTOR TEXTURE

The Raptor Template allows you to explore ways that scales and other texture features can be explored. If you are using Painter, try applying a Paper Texture and also using the Turquoise f/x Brush to simulate scales. Always apply a Bump map of the texture to give scales more depth. For one example of another Raptor look, load the texture Raptor2 from the Templ folder on this books CD-ROM. See Figure 18.16.

CAUTION

Karuna! No matter what you do when painting a Template with anything other than solid colors, your figure will display some seams where the Template views meet. You can minimize this artifact by setting the Camera up so that it doesn't see the offending seams. If this is still troubling to you, then you will have to use a 3D Painting application like Painter 3D, 4D Paint, trU-V, or SurfaceSuite Pro. See Chapter 19.

Creating Textures with Photoshop

Though it is advisable that you purchase Painter for creating new Poser figure textures because of its infinite creative possibilities, it is more than likely that you already own Adobe Photoshop. Photoshop, too, offers you tools and techniques for creating Poser texture maps for figures and props. It features a large number of internal painting f/x, which cannot be operated as plug-ins from other applications. Some of the external plugins you can get for it don't work with anything else.

THE SPOTTED CHIMP OF MARS

In this exercise, we'll use Photoshop to paint on the ZAChimpanzee.Tif template, found in the Templ folder on this book's CD-ROM. Then we'll apply the texture to the Zygote Chimp figure. You will need Poser 3, Photoshop, and the Zygote Animal models to do this tutorial. Do the following:

FIGURE 18.15 *Leisure Suit Lambert wears the highest fashions.*

FIGURE 18.16 *A new Raptor look, achieved with the Raptor2 texture map, a variation of the P3Raptor.Tif Template, included on this book's CD-ROM. Compare this with the default Raptor texture map.*

1. Open Photoshop and load the ZAChimpanzee.tif file from the Templ folder on this book's CD. See Figure 18.17.

NOTE

You'll have to translate the Template from a Bitmap to a Grayscale image to use the Magic Wand in Photoshop.

2. Use the Magic Wand to select just the Chimp's elements on the image, just as you did in the Painter exercises. Then Copy them and paste so that they are placed on a new Layer (automatic when you use Paste). For now, you can keep the original template as the bottom layer, because it contains the call-outs. Before saving your new texture map, however, you can delete the original Template Layer. Use the Airbrush to colorize the elements of the Chimp's body on the Template. See Figure 18.18.
3. Go to the Filter/Texture menu, and apply a Craquelure texture to the Chimp's front and back, with settings of Crack Spacing 14, Crack Depth 8, and Crack Brightness 9. See Figure 18.19.
4. Select the Chimp's face and use a Stained Glass Texture effect with a Cell Size of 7, Border Thickness of 1, and a Light Intensity of 1. This adds a mosaic-tiled appearance to the face.

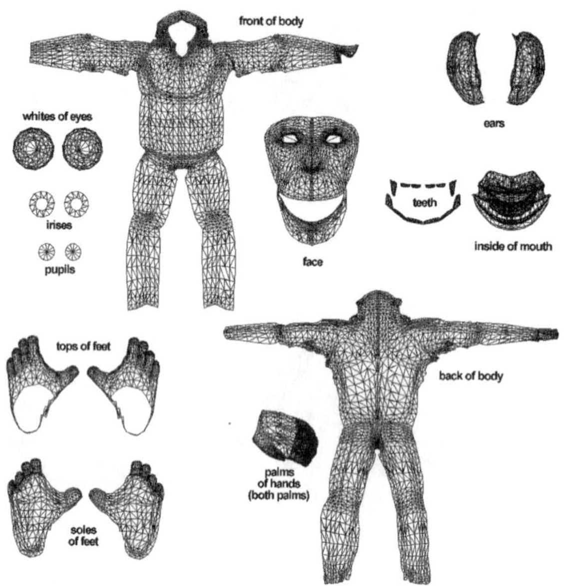

FIGURE 18.17 *The ZAChimpanzee.tif Template loaded into Photoshop.*

5. Now use a solid brush and a yellow color to place yellow dots on the front and back of the image map, trying for a random look. Save the new Chimp texture. See Figure 18.20.
6. Import the new texture into Poser, and apply it to the Chimp figure. See Figure 18.21.

MAPPING A PHOTOGRAPHIC FACE

One of the most frequently asked questions concerning Poser is "How can I map a real face to a figure?" The answer is that it is not worth the try. Why is this so? Real faces are absolutely never perfectly symmetrical. We have a bilateral brain, and each side controls the opposite side of the face. In a sense, each side of the brain is responsible for sensing the world in a different way, which shows in the difference between the halves of our face. The recognizability of a face is based upon its non-symmetry, which makes even identical twins just a bit different when you look closely. Our two eyes are never on the same horizontal plane, for instance. This has a lot of importance when you consider that Poser heads, those that come with the application, are perfectly symmetrical, which is exactly why they always look a little robotic. Perhaps in a future addition, they're be a specific parameter dial for altering symmetry. Until that time,

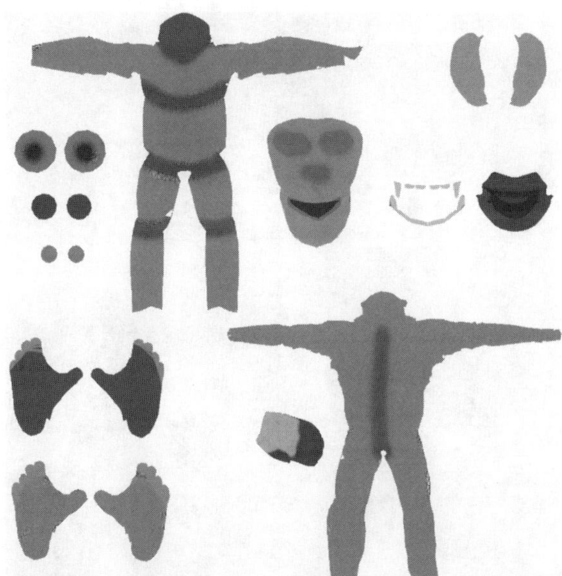

FIGURE 18.18 *The first step in customizing the Chimp texture, using the ZAChimapnzee.tif Template in the Templ folder on this book's CD.*

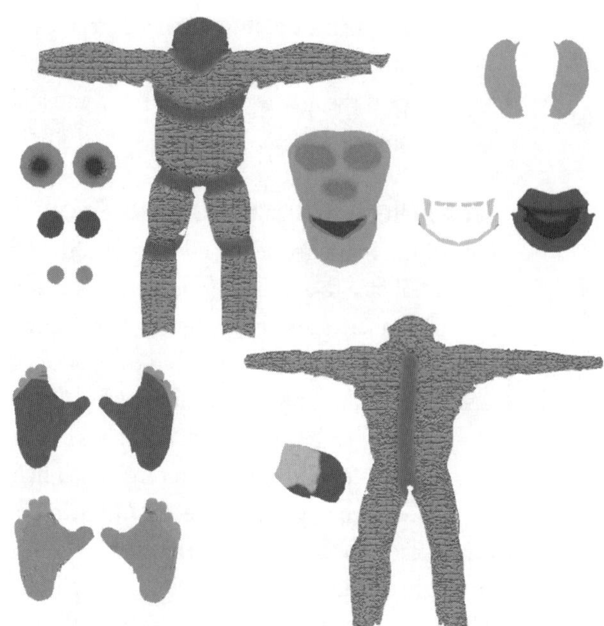

FIGURE 18.19 *The Craquelure textures is applied to the body elements.*

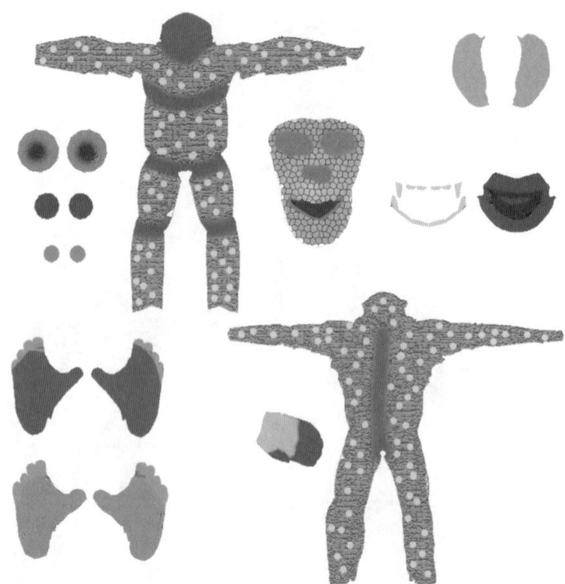

FIGURE 18.20 *The texture map is now complete, with the spots added.*

FIGURE 18.21 *The Chimp is posed and mapped with the new texture.*

however, we have to alter any photos to match the symmetry of the Poser Head object, fitting the image to the 3D structure. This means that the personality of a photographic face—its asymmetry—must be made symmetrical, thus losing the personality of the photo. At the very best, it can add some skin tones to the Poser Head. On top of that, you have to remove the nose from the image map, because the Poser Figure's nose is a real 3D construct that casts its own shadows.

The best way to get a photographic face is to take the image map and translate it into 3D geometry in a suitable 3D application. This is called Displacement Mapping, where the image actually displaces the geometry of a surface. CyberMesh, which we looked at in Chapter 17, does this, but the result is more of a mask than a photo. Many 3D applications, like Ray Dream and LightWave, have a better displacement mapping feature. Then the problem is that unless you spend a huge amount of time developing a hierarchical model of the face that can be controlled with the Parameter Dials in Poser, you won't be able to control the features anyway. For now, it's either develop a complete hierarchical model and associated PHI file on your own, or wait for an advanced version of Poser that offers more of these options.

There is a third option, one that may allow you to get at least a semblance of a Head mapped with a photographic face. Try this:

1. Create an egg-shaped object from a Ball Prop. You will use it to replace the Head of a figure, but don't do that yet.
2. In Photoshop, import a face graphic. Resize its canvas so that the face sits in the middle of a frame 3X the horizontal and 2X the vertical, using the same color as the edge of the face for the canvas backdrop. Blur the edges where the face meets the background. See Figure 18.22.

3. In Poser, Surface Map the face graphic to the Egg. Replace the Head with the Egg. Place Hair on the Egg and render. You may have to adjust the map a bit, but expect that distortion will be a component of this technique. Actually, the distortion creates interesting caricatures. Save to disk. See Figure 18.23.

Note that this technique demands that the face be pretty much front on in the viewplane, since there really is no depth to the nose.

Poser Forum Web Ring

For the newest and best creative Poser techniques, stay in touch with the Poser Web Ring at http://www.iguanasoft.com/poser/ring.html.

FIGURE 18.22 *A photo of a face, with the hair cut away, is the main content of a surface map.*

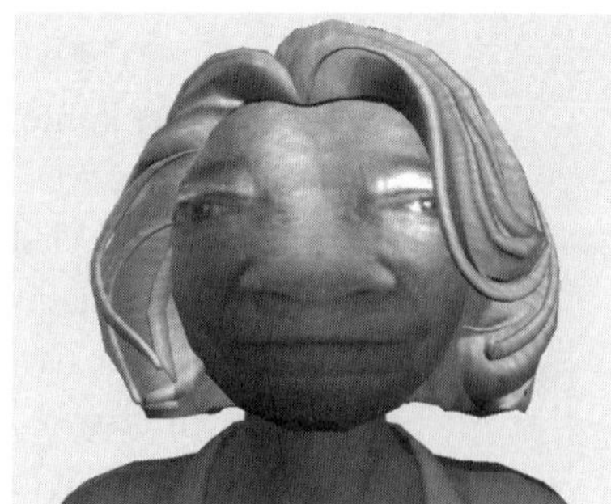

FIGURE 18.23 *The completed mapped figure.*

Moving Along

In this chapter, we've explored a few ways that you can use Painter and Photoshop to create interesting customized textures for your Poser figures. In the next chapter, we'll look at some options for cameras, lights, and rendering.

CHAPTER 19 Cameras, Lights, and Rendering

In this chapter, we'll look at three Poser 3 attributes whose use and modifications can alter your animations in major ways: Cameras, Lights, and Render Styles.

Cameras

Poser 3 features a number of Camera options that add new ways for you to render and record your output, as well as making your compositions easier to navigate. The standard documents cover the general uses of the Cameras, so we'll look at a few ideas about Cameras that are new, ones that you may find useful in your Poser work.

THE ANIMATING CAMERA

Camera movements create automatic keyframes when the Animating Camera is switched on. It is toggled on or off by selecting the Key icon on the lefthand toolbar. Gray is on, orange is off. When it's on, your Camera movements are recorded as keyframes wherever you're at on the timeline. Leave the Animating Camera off when you are posing a figure and turn it on after all figures are posed and separately keyframed. This allows you to worry about one thing at a time and prevents the Camera from animating when all you want to do is to get it to see another view of the scene.

CAMERA LIBRARY ANIMATIONS

Just as you can apply different faces or full poses to alternate keyframes to create an animation, so too can you apply different Camera views from the Camera Library at different points on the timeline. The best advice is to spend a day or two exploring different camera angles and perspectives, saving all of those you like to your Camera Library. When they're needed, for still positions or keyframes, you'll have a good many to select from.

ANIMATED REFLECTIONS

Here's a neat animation that you can create, showing a person moving in front of a mirror. Do the following.

1. Select any one of the Poser figures, or even an animal, as your main character, and place it in the center of your Poser document. Turn the Ground Plane on, and adjust the lighting so the figure is well lit. Make the background a light blue color. See Figure 19.1.

FIGURE 19.1 *This project starts with the placement of a figure of your choice at the center of your Poser document. This is a Business Suited male with a morphed head.*

2. Create a 120 frame animation, set to 30 FPS. Make the figure move however you want it to, but for this project allow its feet to remain in place (you can do this easily by making sure that IK is on for each leg). When you are satisfied with the choreography, render and save the animation.
3. Next, turn IK off for all body parts. Select the figure's Body. Use the Y Axis Parameter Dial to rotate the figure exactly 180 degrees, so its back is facing the camera. Do not alter any other elements of the figure. See Figure 19.2.
4. Now set the Document Size to the same size as the animation you rendered. See Figure 19.3.
5. You can use your favorite 3D application or a post-production application to perform the next step. The object is to reverse (flip) the horizontal for the animation you just rendered. I used After Effects for this task. After reading in the animation, I used the Basic 3D Effect, altering the Swivel Radial Dial to read 180 degrees. Then I re-recorded the animation again, so that it would play with everything horizontally flipped. See Figure 19.4.

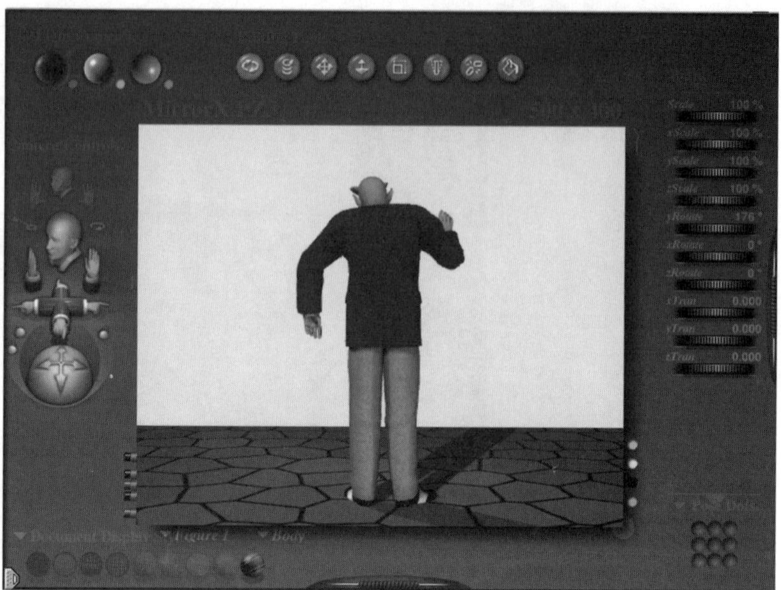

FIGURE 19.2 *The figure is facing away from the camera.*

Set Window Size:

Width: 320

Height: 256

Match background

Constrain aspect ratio

Lock window

Cancel OK

FIGURE 19.3 *Set the size of the Document window to the same size as the animation rendered.*

Why are we flipping the animation horizontally? Because a common mirror flips what is reflected horizontally. Otherwise, the reflection will not match the movements of the figure standing in front of the mirror.

6. After the flipped animation has been rendered, import it into your Poser scene, and use it as a background. Your scene should now look like Figure 19.5.

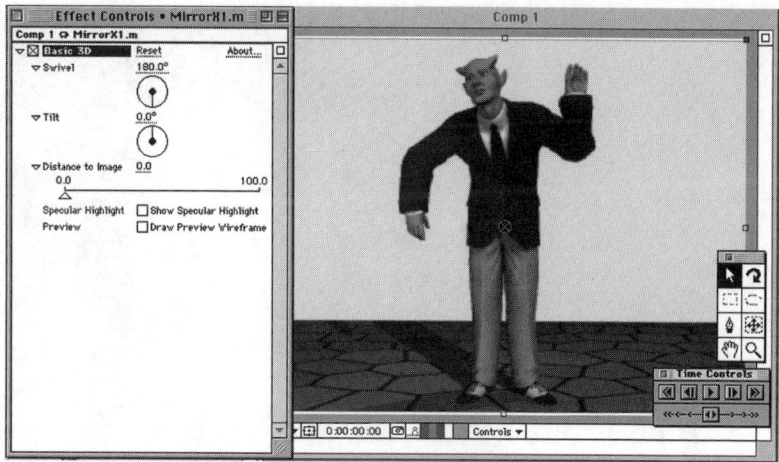

FIGURE 19.4 *If you use After Effects to flip the animation horizontally, access the Basic 3D Effect, and change the Swivel Radial Dial to read 180 degrees. Then record the animation again.*

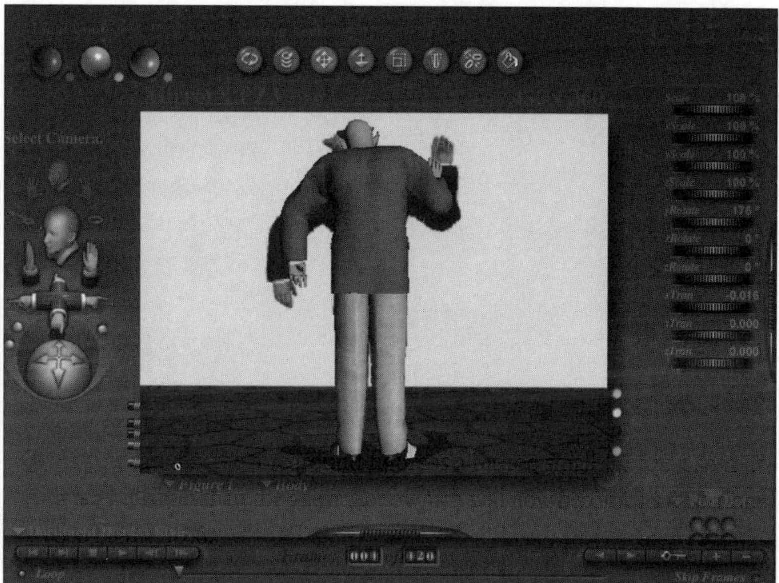

FIGURE 19.5 *The scene will now look like this, with the flipped animation in back of the Poser figure.*

7. As you can see, the foreground figure is a bit too small. Resize it so that it is a bit larger than the animation, which will now become its reflection. See Figure 19.6.

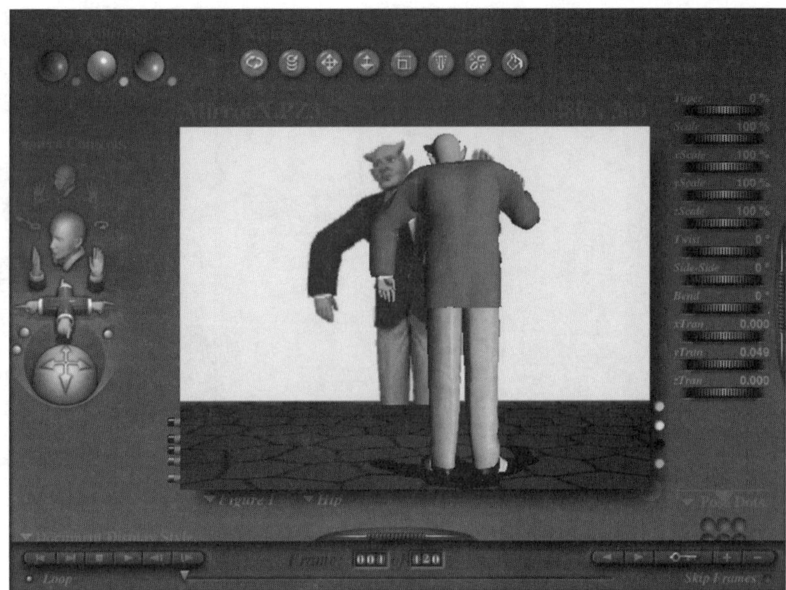

FIGURE 19.6 *The foreground figured is enlarged and moved a bit to the left, so that both figure and reflection can be seen clearly. I have also changed the color of the jacket, making it lighter, so it doesn't conflict with the reflection of the jacket.*

8. Next we have to build a wall, so that it looks like a mirror is inset within it. You can either do that in an external 3D application and import it, or construct it out of blocks, as I have done in Figure 19.7.

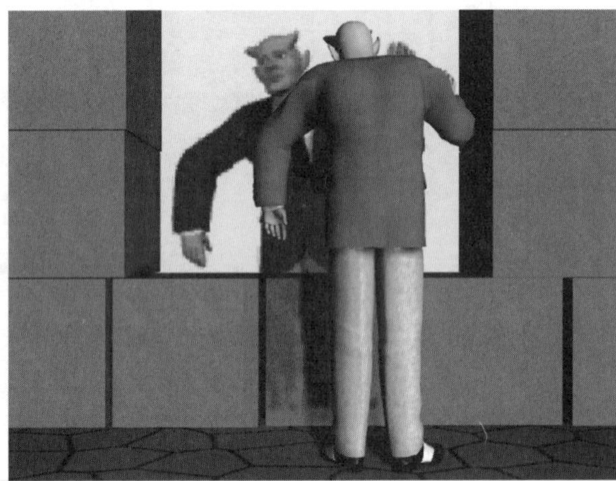

FIGURE 19.7 *The block wall is created, leaving a hole so that the animated figure shows through.*

9. Now animate the whole scene, and you will see the mirrored result. The Camera in this project demonstrates how important it is to keep it the same throughout. Otherwise, the reflected animation will look very strange.

CAMERA CLOSE-UPS AND TEXTURES

One rule to consider whenever you do extreme close-ups (zooms) with any Camera is to use just colors for items that are not involved in zoomed views. For items that are involved in zoomed close-ups, use high-resolution textures. This simulates something computer artists call LOD, or Level Of Detail. Save detailed textures for items closer to the cameras. The same holds for shots that picture an action figure with a crowd of onlookers in the background. If you utilize textures for important figures alone, the viewer will see the background figures as hazed out, and without adjusting the camera itself, you will intimate more depth in the scene.

ON THE INSIDE

There is a strange camera associated operation you can perform that is not documented in the Poser 3 manual, perhaps because it is a bit too esoteric for the average Poser user. All of the objects you place in a document have both an inside and an outside. If you keep zooming in on a selected object or figure, there will come a point at which the Camera is literally "inside" of the construct. In most cases, you will not know it, because it will seem as if you have just passed through the targeted element. This is because most objects in Poser are one-sided polygons, so that the computer does not spend any time rendering their inside faces.

This is not true for the mouth, however, and it's easy to understand why. If the inside of the mouth was constricted from one-sided polygons, then every time the mouth opened, you would see right through the head. Since this is not exactly the way the real world presents itself to us, the Mouth and Teeth are made from double-sided polygons for a realistic view.

What does this have to do with the Camera? Simple, it allows us to fly the Camera inside of the mouth of a figure, so that we can view the world as if we were sitting at the back of a figure's throat. Admittedly, this has limited use, but it may be an effect that you could use when conditions are right. When you place the Camera in the mouth, you can still manipulate the mouth openness and other parameters. This makes the mouth like a window that can be animated, so you can see whatever is beyond the mouth in the direction the figure is facing. See Figure 19.8.

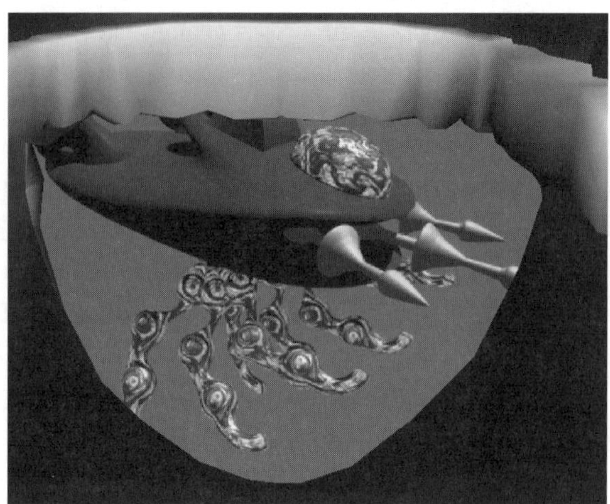

FIGURE 19.8 *A view from inside the mouth of a figure shows the back of the teeth and displays the background layer through the mouth opening.*

NOTE *To animate a sequence using the "Inside the Mouth" camera, make sure Display Settings are used. To create a single image, make a one frame animation using Display Settings.*

"MILKING" YOUR FOOTAGE

The next time you go to the movies, see how many times the same footage, from different vantage points, is repeated. You can especially watch for this on expensive takes, like explosions, though you may also catch it being used when a character is running, walking, or driving. This is a way that directors often "milk" the footage, and you can take advantage of this same option with your Poser animations.

After all, it may have taken you hours or even days to get everything in your scene set up just as it should be, with all of the tweaked nuances timed correctly. Why should you settle for just one run-through of the choreography? Poser's variable Camera options are just what you need to repeat the animation without the kind of repetitive loops that do nothing but bore your audience. Explore these possibilities:

- Render your animation with different Camera types, stitching them together in the post-production process with Adobe Premier, After Effects, or similar applications. When you stitch them together, use smaller snips from each animation, so that the viewer is always presented with different perspectives for shorter (three seconds per snip) amounts of time.
- Try rendering the same animation from the same Camera using different rendering styles, and then stitch these together. This can lend a very subliminal look to an animation.
- Use different zooms, pans, and rotations to add excitement to an animation. You can do this from one Camera type by just changing these options with each animation save.
- Cut in views of the face (Face Camera) of your character during an animated sequence that shows the figure in action. This allows the viewer to intuit how that character is feeling about what it is doing.
- Show the same animation from the perspective of each actor involved. If a flower pot is going to fall on an actor's head, show the view from both the actor and the flower pot. Show the actor looking up and then become the flower pot looking down. Intersperse these views frequently, until the ultimate conclusion. This heightens the tension in a scene. If you have two Poser figures engaged in a karate match, show the view from each of the figures, and then perhaps from someone on the sidelines. You'll only have to choreograph the scene once, but you'll be able to get ten times the footage out of it.
- Allow your camera to fly around the action like an insect, weaving in and out. Do this several different ways on a single animated choreography and stitch them together.
- Use distorted Camera angles to add to user interest, like a view from the ground up that distorts the perspective. Do this in different ways to any single animation.

Karuna! For the quickest way to achieve interesting perspective views, use the Trackball.

- Most importantly, use any or all of these techniques together, adding even more variety (and viewer time) to any animation.

Lights and Lighting

Here's a collection of hints and tips concerning how lights can be used to enhance and modify your animations:

- If you want your character to be influenced by an explosion in its proximity, use a few keyframes to turn a light's intensity to 1000 or more. This will wash out the details of the figure, so that it will seem like a fiery event has occurred nearby. Use a white light for an atomic flash, a red light for a fiery burst, or a blue-green light when the event is being caused by an extraterrestrial source.
- Do you need a night scene, an environment with no moon or stars, but just your actor(s) moving in the dark? Make sure all three lights are set to pure black or a very deep purple. Then take one light and aim it at the actor(s). Set the other two lights so they shine from above. Set the intensity to 1000. You scene will show up clearly, but will be cast in deep darkness. To make your character's eyes glow in the dark when using this lighting method, do the following. Turn off all texture for the eyeballs. Set Highlight to full intensity and select a yellow or yellow-green color. Use a dark blue Ambient color to give the eyeballs a 3D look. This effect is very eerie. You could also use a blood red, giving the eyes a nightmarish glow.

Karuna! If you are going to use a background image or movie, make sure it is appropriately dark as well, since Poser's lights have no effect on background footage.

- For a very dramatic lighting effect, use just one light, switching the other two off. You'll be able to control shadows much more effectively by using this method. Turn the light that is activated so that it casts part of the object in shadow. This effect also creates a better 3D depth than multiple lights. Use this method in conjunction with extreme camera close-ups. See Figure 19.9.

Light Library Animations

Just as you can apply different faces, full poses, or Camera positions to alternate keyframes to create an animation, so too can you apply different light colors and positions from the Lights Library at different points on the timeline. The best advice is to spend a day or two exploring different light configurations, saving all of those you like to your Lights Library. When they're needed, for still positions or keyframes, you'll have a good many to select from.

FIGURE 19.9 *This Ray Dream flower was created in Ray Dream and imported into Poser in OBJ format. Note the detail emphasized by using an extreme zoom camera with only one light. A Poser head was dropped into the flower center for effect.*

Render Options

By Render Options, we mean the rendering styles found at the bottom of the Poser 3 interface, or various rendering options found in the Render dialogue and other menus. You should be aware of all of these.

ANIMATED SHADOW MAPS

You can use Poser to create content for an Alpha Channel in your favorite post-editing application (like Adobe's After Effects). An Alpha Channel contains only grayscale data, and can be either in black and white or in 256 shades that range from black to white. Pure white prints itself on the channel that the Alpha is placed above, while pure black acts a drop-out mask. The grays in between act as different levels of transparency, so that the blacker the gray is, the more opaque it is.

Rendering an image or animation using the Silhouette renderer is perfect for creating Alpha Channel information, since it creates a two-color render. If the background is black, and the figure white, only the inside of the figure will allow data to be written over the next layer down in your post-editing composition.

If all of these terms seem strange to you, you probably have no experience using a post-editing application. In that case, you can either skip this section and move on, or you can avail yourself of a post-editing application to explore what it can do and reach a general understanding of these terms.

Essentially, you would use an Alpha Map to make sure that any effect applied in your post-production software addressed only the Poser figure(s), still or animated. But I have another suggestion for you to explore. Let's say all that you wanted to include on a layer in your composition was a shadow of a figure, perhaps a human, animal, or even a prop. Poser 3 can help you do this, and here's how:

1. Create a Poser animation as you normally would, using any of the tools and techniques required to do the job.
2. Make sure that Ground Shadows are on. Make the Shadow Color White, and the background black. Use the Silhouette renderer. All that you should see in the Document is the White Shadow, with everything else being Black.
3. Move the Object or Figure upward along the Y axis. Notice that Shadow Size does not change. Render the animation.
4. Use this animation as an Alpha Shadow mask in your post-production application. Whatever effects are applied to it will only affect the white areas of this Alpha layer, so creating things like shimmering shadows is a snap.

SURFACE ATTRIBUTE COLORS

In the Surface Material dialog, under the Render menu options, there are three Color selectors: Object Color, Highlight Color, and Ambient Color. There is also a slider that controls Highlight Size. Using different combinations of colors in these three selectors, and adjusting the Highlight Size slider produces different rendering looks based completely upon these Color qualities. Just as the three global Light Parameters on the main screen alter the overall lighting in a Poser document, so these three Color selectors alter the Light Color components for each targeted element in your scene, by acting as additive colors, almost like color gels for the lights. Table 19.1 shows some suggested combinations and what they generate. All of these results are achieved by using just one global light set to white, and with Textures set to None.

Once you have explored these color settings with textures off, try applying a texture over them. You will see that different textures respond in different ways to the same color settings.

Table 19.1 Results of Different Surface Material Light Combinations

Object Color	Highlight Color	Ambient Color	Highlight Slider	Result
Bright Yellow	Black	Black	0%	Yellow object with black shadows Plastic
Bright Yellow	White	Black	100%	Yellow object with brightwhite highlight over yellow area and black shadows Plastic
Bright Yellow	Dark Blue	Black	100%	Yellow object with just a touch of blue around the perimeter of the highlight and black shadow Plastic
Dark Blue	Bright Yellow	Black	100%	Blue object with yellow highlight and black shadows Metallic
Dark Red	Black	Medium Blue	NA	Pink object to purple shadow tones, resembling sunset reflective surface
Any Color	Any Color	100% White	NA	Completely washes out the object in a flat white Bright Ambience outweighs everything else
White	White	Black	0%	Allows light source(s) maximum control over object color
1. Dark Red 2. Dark Blue 3. Dark Violet	1. Light Green 2. Light Orange 3. Light Yellow	Black	100%	Using complimentary object and highlight colors with maximum highlight size creates metallic chromes
Dark Blue	Medium Blue	Light Blue or Light Blue-Green	50–100%	Creates a great water surface color
Black	Bright Red	Black	90–100%	Creates a dark red object with a medium-sized highlight only where the light is shining, making a great ruby
Dark Green	Light Green	Black	90–100%	This creates an emerald-like object

RENDER STYLES

More than any other 3D application, Poser 3 makes it extremely easy to alter the rendering styles on your display screen. Pushing the envelope even further, Poser allows you to select any and all of the elements on screen for different rendering styles (Display/Element Style). This makes it easy to render one part of the document as a silhouette, another as a wireframe, and yet another as a shaded render, leading to all sorts of creative possibilities. Here are a few suggested uses that you may want to explore:

- Create a group animation, using several Poser figures. Use the Render Styles to display your primary figure as a shaded model and all the rest as wireframes. Render and save to disk. You will notice that the non-shaded figures appear very ghost-like in the animation.
- Create a Poser animation that incorporates just one figure. Use the Shaded Render Style to render the head, and render the rest of the body parts as Silhouettes. Render and save the animation. Import the animation into Painter, which will bring it in as single frames in a stack. Go through the stack and apply a texture or effect to the inside of all of the silhouetted body parts, which is easy since they will all be a single color block. Save out the stack as a new animation, and play it. All manner of magical effects can be applied to Poser figures using this technique.
- Create a Poser Head that uses a Hidden Line Render Style, except for the eyes. Render the eyes as a Textured Render Style. This looks very bizarre, and when animated, calls extreme attention to the eyes.
- Create an animation that shows a figure interacting with and among several props. Use the full Textured Render Style on the figure, and the Sketch Render Style on the props. This method creates a lifelike figure moving in a cartoon world.

There are dozens of other mix and match explorations you can make using Render Styles. Take some time to explore as many as possible. See Figure 19.10.

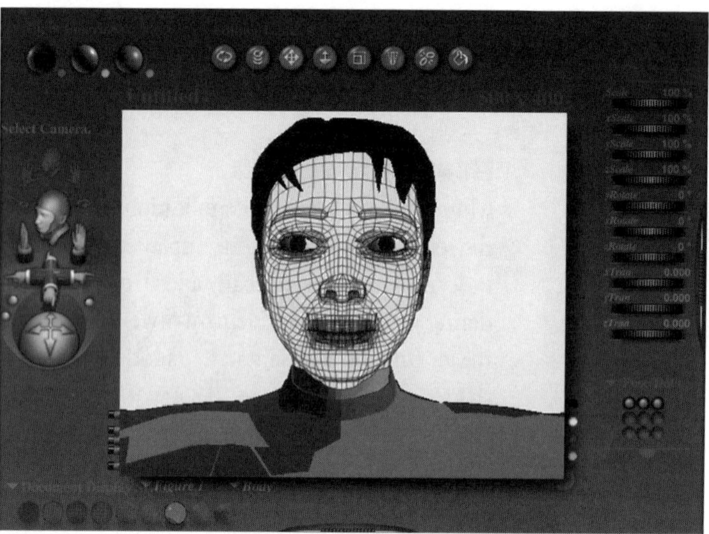

FIGURE 19.10 *In this Render Style example, the Hair is rendered in Silhouette, the eyes as Textured renders, the Head as a Hidden Line, and the lower body as a Sketch.*

Karuna! Rendering Hair using the Silhouette Style can be much more realistic than using a textured Render. This is because we generally see hair as a single color object, except when we zoom in close.

If you want to use the Render Styles in an animation, just make sure that you reference the Display Settings instead of the Render Settings in the animation dialog.

Moving Along

In this chapter, we have explored ways that you can use to make your animations more interesting, using the capabilities of the Camera, Lights, and the Render Styles. In the next chapter, we'll learn more about Poser from some Master Users.

CHAPTER

20 Hints and Tips from Master Users

What defines a Poser Master User? First, a Poser Master User must know Poser from the inside out, having explored not only its tools, but also how to push the tools to the limits. A Master User should also have found ways to bend Poser to his or her personal creative uses, so that the artist's and animator's style shines through. Last, I would say that Master Users are also open to sharing their discoveries with the wider Poser community, since the master of any tool always takes great pleasure in dispersing that knowledge to others, realizing that knowledge passed on is potentially knowledge deepened. Here then, in every sense of the word, are a few examples of masterful Poser user's words and works.

Chris Derochie

Chris Derochie has been animating since 1984. He has worked on eleven animated feature films, twelve Disney CD-ROMs, and dozens of television series, specials, and advertisements. He was born in Canada and worked in Vancouver as a freelance character animator until 1989. He then moved to Ireland to work at Don Bluth Entertainment for four years. He moved to Australia in 1992, where he worked at Walt Disney Television Australia for two years. He returned to Canada for another two years in which he tried his hand at storyboarding and directing as well as animation. He continued his hobby of encircling the Earth by returning to Ireland in 1996. He works from his home, freelancing for major animation studios and sending his animation to them over the Internet. He uses Poser to plan out difficult scenes and is presently producing a series of CD-ROMs containing animation, poses, and models for use with Poser.

APPROACHING A SCENE[1]

Every animator has his or her own ideas on how to approach or plan out scenes. There is no right or wrong way, but some methods are definitely more effective than others. All of the best approaches share one thing in common—the dominant amount of energy is spent on visualizing and planning rather than animating.

Before you begin any animation or even a single pose, you should take the time to ask yourself these questions: "What is this scene *really* about?" "What are my characters thinking and feeling?" "What do I want the audience to look at in this scene?" "Which part of this scene/pose expresses the meaning of the scene the clearest?" Before you are able to communicate an idea through a scene or pose, you will have to be *very* clear on exactly what your idea is!

If you begin posing or animating before you have a solid idea, the scene will

[1]Text and images by Chris Derochie

be lifeless and boring. For example, if you were creating a pose of a woman picking up a jug of water without first thinking of what her intentions were for the jug or what she was thinking while picking it up, she will look like a mindless puppet, picking up a jug simply because someone else pulled her strings. See Figure 20.1.

If you posed the scene with the idea that the woman was angry that her husband wouldn't get out of bed and she intended to dump the water from the jug over her lazy spouse's head, you would find that that thinking changes the way that you would pose every single element of the body, from her face to her fingertips. See Figure 20.2.

FIGURE 20.1 *The woman picks up the jug like a mindless puppet, conveying no human depth.*

FIGURE 20.2 *The woman picks up the jug, with an intention to dump the contents on her husband's head.*

Let's say that her mind is elsewhere—she has lost a child recently and her attention is focused on her grief. Everything she does is lacking in energy as she goes through the motions of her daily routine—if she can even accomplish them at all. You might pose the scene showing her pausing just after she has begun lifting the jug because she hasn't even thought of what she is supposed to be doing with it. She may stay motionless for several seconds before she "wakes up" and continues the action. See Figure 20.3.

As a final example, we'll say that she has just woken up from a very intense nightmare in which her body was on fire. She rushed over to the water jug, still half dreaming, and dumps the water over her head to extinguish the imagined flames. The extreme tension has to be felt in every part of her pose! See Figure 20.4.

As you can see from these examples, it's what you make the character think and feel that is of prime importance, not its positioning. This principle is just as important for animation. Anyone can make a character move around on screen, but your character will only have life if it is seen as a thinking, feeling being. Only then can your audience have any empathy for the character. Have you ever watched a film in which the main character was so poorly written that you didn't care if he lived or died? This is because the writer or film-makers didn't allow you to see into the character's personality. You might even see it as an actor walking around a set, saying his or her lines. How believable would the

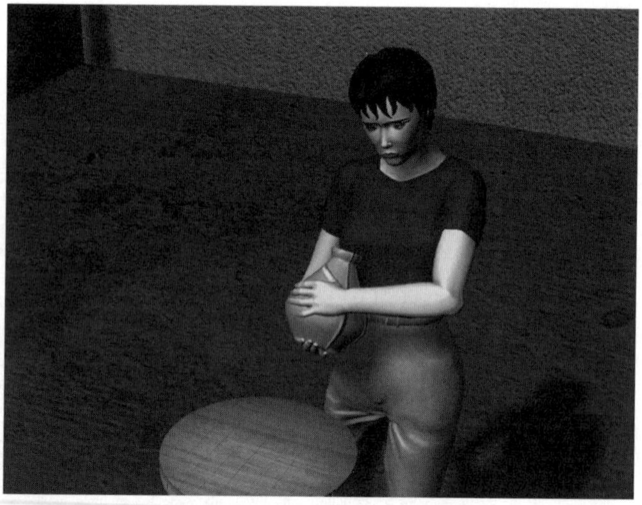

FIGURE 20.3 *The woman cradles the jug while picking it up, lost in grief.*

film be then? It all boils down to this: The action will be determined by what the character is thinking and feeling.

OK, so you've thought the whole thing out, you know exactly what the character is thinking and feeling (its motivation). Now how do you get that Poser figure to look right? This is where talent and experience come in handy! If you haven't spent most of your life as an artist, you'll have to get into a few new habits. You will have to pay close attention to everyone and everything around you. Study the world, go people watching. When you are walking down the street, look at people that you pass by and try to figure out what they might be thinking. Then try to observe what it is about how they are moving and holding themselves that made you come to perceive that they were feeling that way. Don't generalize, "He's sad because he's walking slow" or "She's in a hurry because she's walking fast." Try to look at the details that you normally miss or take for granted. For example, you may see a woman talking to a man and get the impression that she is nervous for some reason.

Get into the details: She's unconsciously fiddling with the zipper on her coat; her gestures are very tense and choppy, yet she keeps smiling at the man that she's talking to; she only gestures when she has to, then she's straight back to her zipper again; she keeps looking around with stiff-necked, darting glances. There may be hundreds of details to see. At this point you could come up with some possible scenarios to explain her behavior. Perhaps she is attracted to this man and she has finally built up the nerve to speak to him, but she's afraid that she'll run out of things to say or that she will say something stupid.

FIGURE 20.4 *The woman is still dreaming of fire as she picks up the jug.*

It could be that she is chatting with this guy, but her boyfriend could be arriving at any moment. The man may be someone whom she hasn't seen in a while and she just gets very excited and hyper talking to people. It doesn't matter if you are correct in any way, but you've just built up your own mental library of real-life situations that you can emulate. Next time that you need to animate or pose a character in a similar situation, you know the types of actions, gestures, and facial expressions that will get that feeling across.

Another good source is live action films. Look carefully at your favorite actors in films that you really enjoyed and follow the same analytical procedure. What is it about their performance that gets their thoughts and feelings across so clearly? If you have a video machine with a good freeze frame, you can make your poses match the character on screen. If you have a video camera, you can film yourself, a friend, family member, or even a model. If you have a capture board in your computer, you can then import the video into poser and use it in the background as reference.

There is one *very* important concept that needs to be understood clearly! Live action and animation are like two very different languages that do *not* translate literally. Think of them as English and Japanese; you know what happens when you try to literally translate them!

The process of taking live action film and directly tracing it for animation is called "rotoscoping." If you have ever seen a film that was rotoscoped or that had rotoscoping in it, you would notice that it looks sluggish and lifeless. Conversely, if you've seen any of those old live action TV series about comic book superheroes, you'll notice that they looked like fools in tights moving around in exaggerated ways. They simply can't be transplanted without being converted. For example, if you had a live action scene of a boxer hitting a punching bag with all of his strength, it would look very powerful in live action. In order to keep that feeling of strength when you translate it to animation, all of the poses must be exaggerated and the timing must be altered. When the boxer twists his torso and pulls back his fist, you need to go even farther and hold that "anticipation" pose a little bit longer. When he swings through, you need to make the swing faster and lean his body farther forward. As his arm and torso follow through, you need to swing the arm farther from the body, end in a more extreme pose, and hold in it a little longer than in the live action. When you view the animation, it will *feel* the same as the live action, but the actual poses and timing have now been converted.

This strange limitation is the reason that motion capture files never feel right because they are the 3D equivalent of rotoscoping. Although motion capture is used extensively in films and games, it is rarely left in its raw form. Animators usually use the motion capture files as a stepping stone and refine the scenes by hand.

If you spend more time observing people and building up a mental library of characteristic movements and expressions, you will find it easier to visualize your scenes. By having a clear idea of what you want the character to be thinking and feeling before you pose or animate your scenes, you will find that your work has more life and appeal than ever before.

Fast and Dirty, Quick and Easy, Slow and Painful: Three Levels of Lip-Synching and Phonemes[2]

Martin Turner is a regular on the MetaCreations Poser List and has expertise in both the shaping of phonemes and in creating clothing for Poser 3 models. Poser 3 leaped through the light barrier by offering animatable faces and the ability to import and graph sounds. This tutorial gives you a fast and dirty way of lip-synching, and then works through some of the more technical aspects of making speech look good.

PHONEMES, A QUICK BUT IMPORTANT NOTE

Phonemes are the smallest speech sounds that make a difference to what word is being said. The difference between *tooth* and *truth* is one phoneme—the "r" sound—even though the spelling is quite different. If you are an English speaker, you probably spent considerable time as a child learning how to read and spell English and discovered that things didn't look the way they sounded. When working with phonemes, you have to forget all that. It is terribly, terribly tempting to look at the way words are written, and try to do your lip-synching on that basis. The result will simply be wrong. The only way (and even trained phonologists do this) to work out which phoneme you should be using is to mouth it to yourself. So bear that in mind as you work through this tutorial.

HOW FAR TO GO

This tutorial is in three parts: Fast and Dirty, Quick and Easy, and Painful and Slow. How far you go depends on how much realism you need. If your character is being animated from a distance, head half turned, using sketch shading to give everything a cartoon feeling, then Fast and Dirty is about all you need. It works from the library palette. If you need more realism, then you still need to work through the Fast and Dirty stuff, but the Quick and Easy, which is about consonants, will give you enough detail to help your character talk sense. If you are looking for the max, then you also need to take into account the Painful and Slow stuff, which is mostly about vowels. There is one step beyond that—useful if you are doing broadcast-quality rendering. That is when you put every-

[2] Text and images by Martin Turner

thing you learned in this tutorial together with careful study of real people speaking and meticulous use of the Poser tools to get everything just right. For that, you are on your own—in art, as in life, only you can take things to the ultimate. No tutorial can do it for you.

FAST AND DIRTY LIP SYNCHING

First, record some speech in your favorite recording application and save it in a format that Poser understands. For Mac, the format is QuickTime, for Windows the format is AVI.

In Poser, choose **File>Import>Sound**, locate your sound, and import it.

Then open the Graph palette. When you import a sound, you can view it in the graph window. The green line is marks the frame you are on, and the red line marks the changes you have set in the selected value. Poser will also play the sound as you move from frame to frame. This graph shows the word "Excellent," with a little background music before and after. The word begins just before the green line, but notice that the mouth opens first—people usually breathe before they start to speak. See Figure 20.5.

Play the sound through several times, so that you get the hang of which sounds go with the peaks on the graph. Essentially, the short changes in level are consonants, and the long ones are vowels. M and n sounds can be very loud, though, and are longer than most consonants, so watching carefully is the best advice.

Now, keeping the graph palette open, go to the libraries palette, take Faces, and select the Phonemes library. The Phonemes in the Faces section of the library is fine for fast and dirty lip-synching, but the results you will get will be very stylized and exaggerated. Unless you are enunciating very carefully, you would never open your mouth like this for "oh." See Figure 20.6.

In the graphing palette, move the cursor onto the first sound, and then select the face in the phoneme's library that goes most with that sound. Load it,

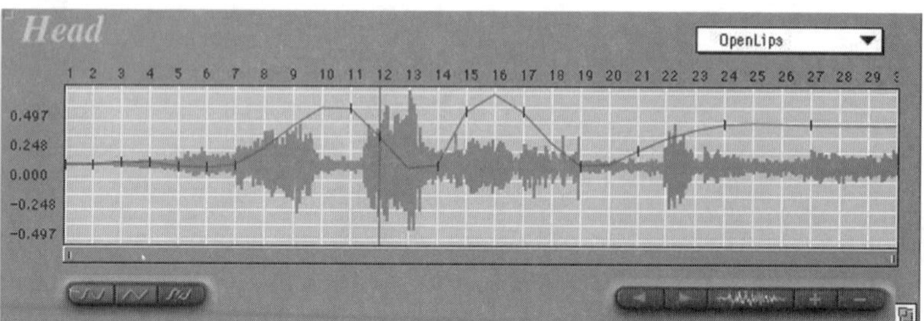

FIGURE 20.5 *The Poser Graph palette.*

and then move the cursor on to the next abrupt change in the sound level. As you move the cursor, Poser will "pronounce" the sound to help you. Repeat the process, using the nearest-looking phoneme in the library until you have finished. Tweak the phoneme shapes by using the Parameter Dials for the mouth. People move their faces differently as they speak. The man in Figure 20.6 is nodding. Some people tilt their heads, wince, or lick their lips. Remember that anyone speaking for more than a few seconds will also blink at least once.

Making realistic phonemes will almost always involve setting a number of the dials. Sounds are influenced by what comes before and what comes after. Expression is very much influenced by how the person is speaking and smiling, frowning, or shouting as he or she talk. Work at it until it looks natural. See Figures 20.7 and 20.8.

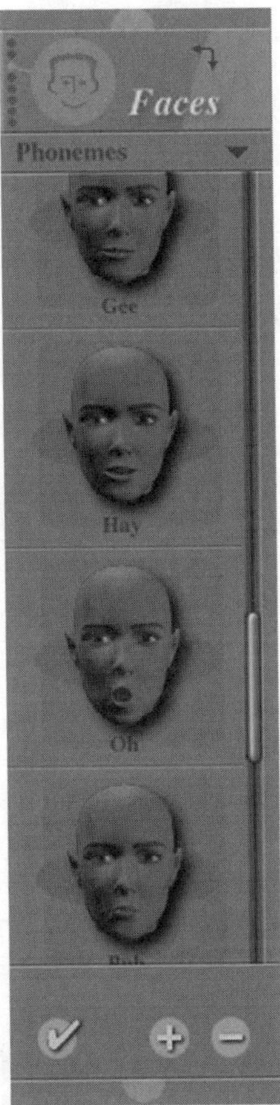

FIGURE 20.6 *The Phonemes Library.*

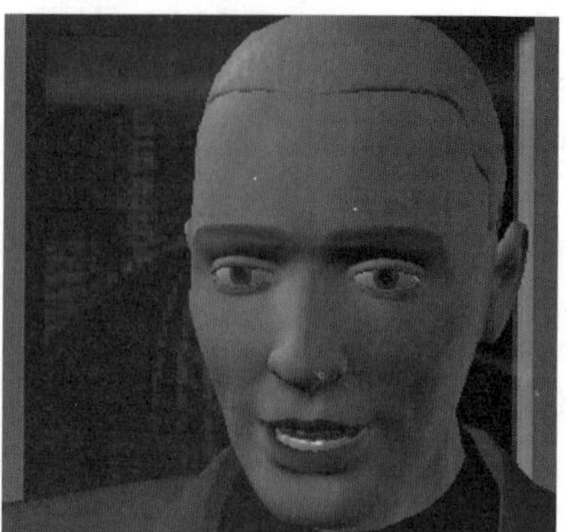

FIGURE 20.7 *Apply the correct phoneme to the selected figure.*

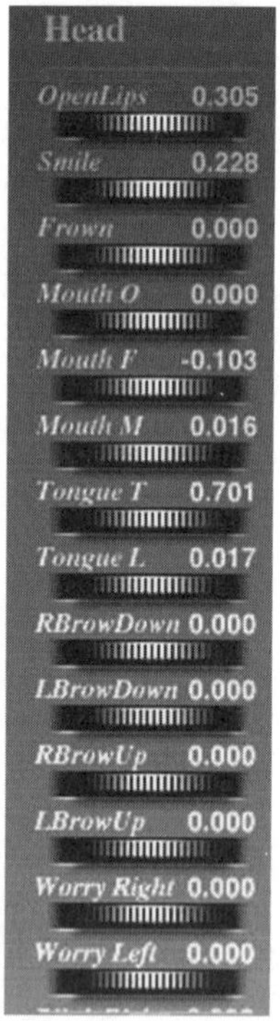

FIGURE 20.8 *Tweak the Parameter Dials for the mouth as needed.*

Problems with Fast and Dirty Lip-Synching

What you just achieved—assuming you tried it—should have taught you all you need to know about the Poser technicalities of lip synching. It's easy and fun. But the result you got will look exaggerated and unnatural. To get a smooth, natural look, you need to know some of the basics of phonology, and you need to use the Parameter Dials that go with the face element, rather than the library phonemes.

QUICK AND EASY CONSONANTS

Consonants can be grouped by where they happen in the mouth, whether they are voiced or unvoiced, and whether they are fricatives, plosives, nasals, and so on. It doesn't matter if this means nothing to you yet—things will become clear when you start mouthing the sounds in Table 20.1. As practice, mouth the sounds in Table 20.1 with your fingers on your mouth to see how it moves.

Table 20.1 The English Consonants, Their Phonological Descriptions, and How to Achieve Them in Poser 3

Voiced	Unvoiced	Type	Poser Notes: Use These Controls
*Bilabials (with both lips)		Mouth M	
b	p	Plosive	Lips coming together sharply
m		Nasal	Lips remain together longer
w			Lips don't quite meet
*Labiodentals (lips and teeth)		Mouth F	
v	f	Fricative	
*Dentals (tongue on teeth)		Mouth t (Higher values of T)	
th (as in the)	th (as in thick)	Fricative	
*Alveolar (tongue on ridge behind teeth)		Mouth t (lower values of t)	
d	t	Plosive	
z	s	Fricative	
l		Lateral	Mouth 1
n		Nasal	
Palato-alvelar (blade of the tongue near the ridge behind the teeth			Just open the mouth a little, plus mabye some Mouth 1
	sh		
j (edge)	ch	Affricate	
Palatal			
	y		Maybe a little Mouth 1
Velar (back of the tongue on roof of mouth)			
g	k		
Glottal (mouth open, vocal chords narrow)			
	h		

i) To construct them, you need to forget the library palette and go straight to the Parameter Dial controls that come up by clicking on the figure's head. Apart from that, the process is the same, just using the Parameter Dials instead of the prebuilt phonemes.

ii) Generally, only those at the front of the mouth will show up. I have starred these in the consonant table. The rest will take the sound of the vowel they *precede*. For these consonants, just close the mouth a little and open it wider for the vowel.

iii) Voiced and unvoiced look exactly the same as far as the tongue and lips are concerned. However, the sound graph will show voiced as about half as loud as vowels, while unvoiced will be much quieter.

iv) The range that Poser offers for "tongue T" and the other controls is much more than the ordinary range of speech. You should experiment with different levels. The louder someone is speaking, the more movement. Women move their lips more than men do (in general). Watch out particularly for Mouth M and Mouth F, where too high values look ridiculous. You will very rarely need to move the dial as high as 1, even for someone shouting.

v) For quick and easy vowel sounds, use a combination of Smile and Open-Lips, except for the O sound, for which you use Mouth O. You should note, however, that in British English the O sound is *not* always made with mouth O, so watch out for this. Vowel sounds are less determined than front of the mouth consonants, so it's less critical to get it right.

vi) The only way to be sure a phoneme is correct is to check what it actually looks like when animated—you may need several tries at first. In general, it is better to underanimate than overanimate. If you are doing a particular accent that isn't yours, watch someone with that accent speaking and remember any particular features.

vii) Each person has a different way of moving his or her lips to talk—the most important difference is the amount of lip movement, but people also vary the way in which they open their mouths wider *during* a vowel. It's important to remake your lip movements for every actor/character, rather than using a standard set, because the way people talk is one of the most important aspects of characterization.

PAINFUL AND SLOW VOWELS

The Painful and Slow section concentrates on vowels. Everybody's vowels are slightly different, and they vary greatly from accent to accent. So this is just a guide. However, it is much more difficult to spot inappropriate vowels than it is bad consonants.

There are six criteria that more or less pin down vowels:

- The part of the tongue that is raised (front, center, or back)—ignore everything but the front.
- How high the tongue rises toward the palate (high, mid-high, mid-low, low).
- The position of the soft palate (ignore this one—you can't see it).
- The kind of opening made at the lips—various degrees of rounding or spreading.
- Length of the vowel—in phonetic script this is marked as ":" for long, hence —i: e:.
- Diphthongization—one vowel after the other. A lot of sounds you think are one vowel are actually two. For instance, in UK southern English (think, how Lara Croft talks), *go* is actually "g-uh-oo," but the "uh-oo" comes so close together you imagine it is one sound. Fifty years ago, and still in other parts of the country, the sound is a straight long o. Incidentally, word on the street is that no language has both long and short diphthongs, although Anglo-Saxon (think J.R.R. Tolkien and C S Lewis) is written as though it did.

Difference in dialect is most likely to be shown in the diphthongs—one dialect might make the *ay* sound as "ah-ee" (which means a mouth movement from smile to no smile in Poser 3), while another might make it as a single sound in the middle of the mouth (just open lips).

What Poser Offers You:

- Mouth O = rounding
- Smile = spreading
- Open lips = non-spread, non-rounded
- Tongue L = various degrees of tongue rising at the front and glides

Glides (the "yuh" sound in *royal*) are very important for speech, but, given that you'll just want a touch of Tongue L for them, you can probably ignore them.

Do diphthongs as one vowel after the other, if there's a visible difference on your sound graph.

Vowels

The vowels in Table 20.2 are UK English (but will be similar for all Englishes). The script is not the conventional IPA alphabet but should be easier to follow for non-linguistics people. I am only listing the vowels you can see, for all others, Open lips, in an amount proportional to the volume of the vowel (but

Table 20.2 Achieving Specific Vowel Sounds

Sound	Poser Parameter Dial
"i" in *cheese*	*Smile*
"a" as in *car*	Some Smile (maybe)
"a" as in *bad*	More Smile
"u" as in *put*	Some Mouth O
"oo" as in *shoot*	A lot of Mouth O
"o" as in *got*	A touch of Mouth O
"aw"	Some Mouth O
"e" as in *bay*	Open Lips
"e" as in *get*	Less Open Lips
"uh"*	Only a very little Open Lips (depending on volume)

*"uh" is one of the most commonly occurring sounds in English—almost any vowel that isn't stressed tends to become an "uh" sound. If your lip-synch looks overanimated, it may be because you are using front vowels rather than "uh."

don't be taken in by m and n sounds, which can be very loud, even though the mouth is closed) will be fine. Remember as you do this that vowels are very idiosyncratic. Experimenting is the key.

Adding Clothing in Poser 3[3]

Following the release of Poser 3, one of the commonest requests on the Poser discussion list was "How do I add different clothing?" The question behind the question is, of course, how do I add clothing that I can animate and that will correctly move with the body? Well, here's how.

First, you need another 3D program in which to create clothing objects. The only real criterion is that it must be one that can import one of Poser's export formats and export a format that Poser can read. For this tutorial, I am using StrataVision on a Mac, which was the package in which Myst was originally created. If you don't have a package, this might be a good place to start, because Strata is currently willing to let you have a copy for the cost of the mailing, from www.strata3d.com. However, whatever package, Mac or PC, the principles are the same, as are most of the steps.

Exporting from Poser

First, open Poser 3 and go to the nude male or nude female figure, using the default size and the default position. Somewhere between Poser and StrataVision

[3] Text and images by Martin Turner

there is a problem. Poser struggles to export 3dMetaFiles, and StrataVision imports Poser's DXF files as individual triangles. If you don't have this problem, then go ahead and export the entire figure in your preferred format, ticking the box to export body parts as individual groups when you are offered the option.

The Strata Maneuver

If you have the Strata problem, the work around is to make every other body part invisible. Do this by double-clicking on, say, the left hand and choosing "Make body part invisible," then leaving the forearm, but making the upper arm invisible, and so on. Once you have done this (it's tedious, but it only takes ten minutes), export the figure as a DXF file. Then do the same thing again, except making all the visible parts invisible and the invisible parts visible. Yes, it's tedious, but you will only have to do this once for the female and once for the male figures, and then never again.

IN YOUR MODELER

In your favorite modeling package, import your Poser figure. It doesn't matter if the import isn't perfect—for example, if there are holes in the meshes—because you are using the figure as a sort of dressmaker's dummy. See Figure 20.9.

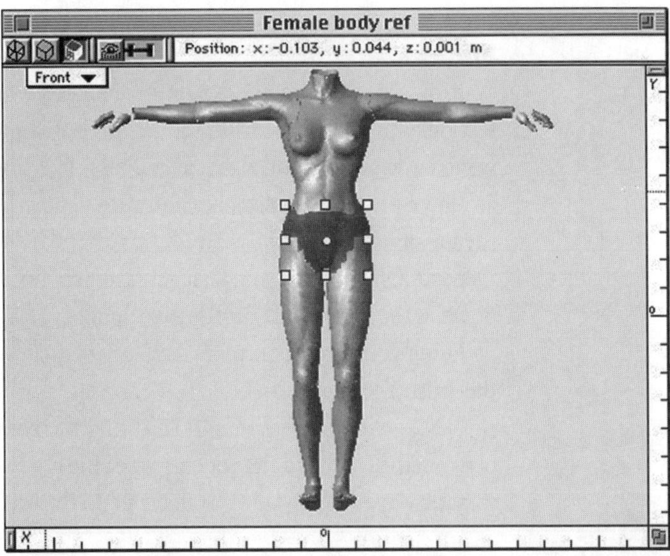

FIGURE 20.9 *Make a dressmaker's dummy figure in your favorite modeling program. This is StrataVision. It may help to give the particular section you are working on its own color. You must cover it completely.*

Lock your figure, so that it can't accidentally be moved or altered. If you are using the Strata Maneuver, make each of your two imported figures a group, give them a different color, and then align them so that you have a sort of composite, harlequin figure. Save this file! Then save again with a new file name so that you don't overwrite it.

MAKING AN ITEM OF CLOTHING

By now, you should have a model where you can clearly see which body part is which. To make a piece of clothing that you can use in Poser, you need to completely cover at least one body part. However—and this is a real saving grace—you don't have to make a piece of clothing for each body part to cover the whole body. Later on, we will see how Poser bends your clothing to suit body parts that it covers.

For this tutorial, we are going to make a mini-skirt. But the principle is the same for almost any garment. One word of warning, though. Poser imposes a split between the hip and the abdomen. While you can cover the legs with a skirt attached to the hip, and the skirt will move with the legs, you can't do this with a dress that is attached to the abdomen, nor can you get the abdomen to follow garments attached to the hip. This is the only body part where the "chain" is broken by default. And, no, there is no way of altering this, so make your jumpsuits and dresses in two pieces.

Mini-skirt

Start by using your cylinder primitive tool to wrap a cylinder around the hip section. Squash it at the front so that it is just larger than the figure mesh at the front, back, and left and right sides. This is like wrapping a square piece of cloth around a physical dress-maker's dummy. The cylinder must extend as high as the top of the hip section, and it must extend below the bottom of the section. Depending on clothing style, it can extend a little higher at the top, and as far down as the feet at the bottom. See Figure 20.10.

Using your node edit tool, "gather" the nodes at the top of the cylinder to the waist. See Figure 20.11.

Next, go all the way round, adjusting the bezier curves so that the "cloth" between the waist and the widest part of the hip hugs the figure. There is no automatic way of doing this. You have to do the beziers one by one.

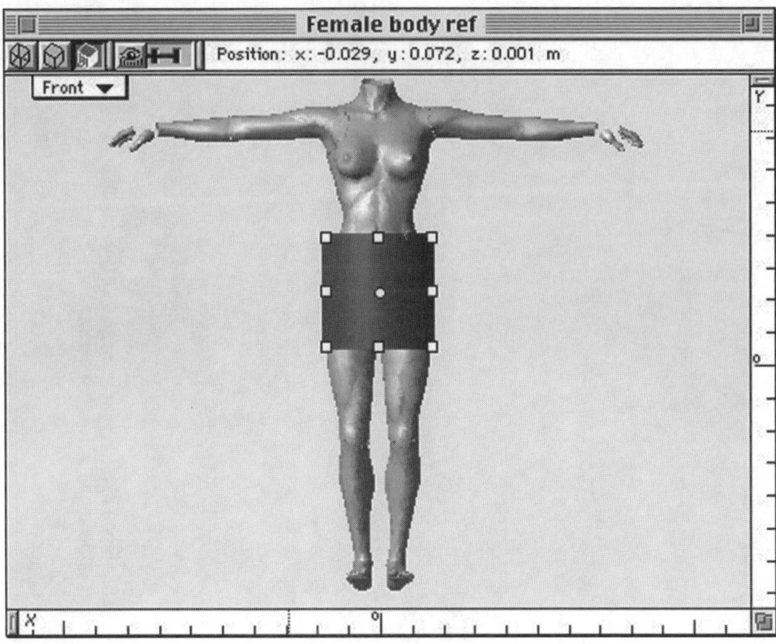

FIGURE 20.10 *Wrap a cylinder around the body, so that it just covers the widest extent of skin at the sides and at the front and back.*

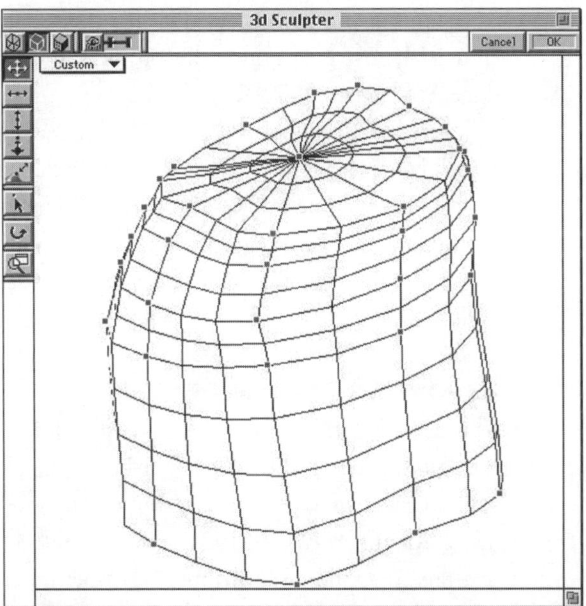

FIGURE 20.11 *Use your node editing tool to shape the cylinder. Keep checking that you are completely covering the body part and not allowing any "flesh" to peep through.*

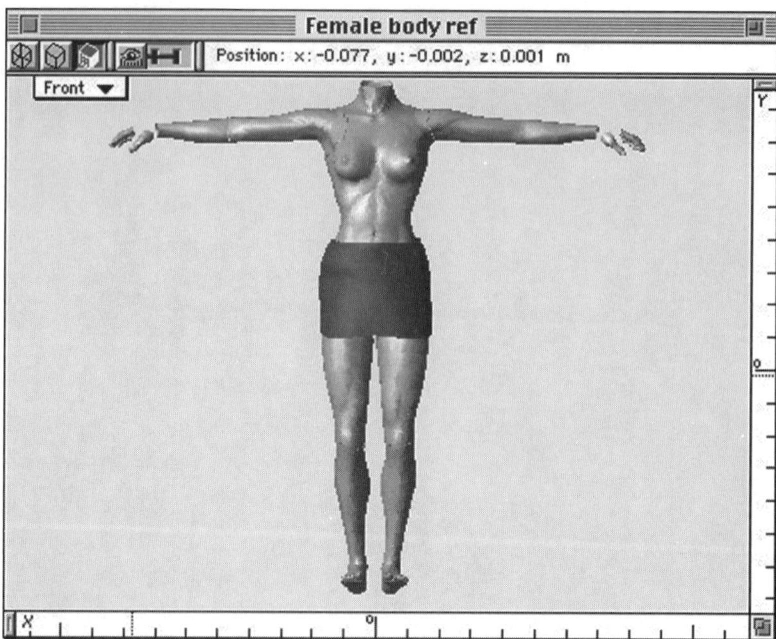

FIGURE 20.12 *Check your garment carefully all around before leaving your modeler—you cannot correct modeling mistakes in Poser.*

Assuming you have covered all the figure's skin, and assuming you have completely covered the hip at the top and at the bottom, your mini-skirt is now done. See Figure 20.12.

There are a number of variations. For example, if you are thinking of a stretch fabric such as Lycra, you can gather the nodes in at the bottom of the skirt as well as at the top. Or if you are thinking of something less severe, you can pull out the nodes underneath to create something of a bell or layering. However, this is for later. You will have a better idea of the possibilities and limitations if we stick with the simple mini-skirt for now.

EXPORTING AND IMPORTING

Choose a file format that you know works for Poser to export just the mini-skirt (not the rest of the figure). The best format is .obj, because it means that you can later export a texture or bump map as well. After that .3DS, followed by .3DMF, followed (as a last resort) by .DXF. DXF was an early 3D format that doesn't support UV mapping. Furthermore, Poser can be choosy about what kind of DXFs it will import. If you are working with .3DMF, you should know that Poser only supports version 1, but shouldn't give any trouble importing meshes (which is what you've got after deforming your cylinder) made with later versions, so just click "Yes" if it asks you if you want to continue.

BACK IN POSER

So, back in Poser, load up the male or female nude figure in the default pose and, from the file menu, import your object. Poser offers you a number of options, all of which are irrelevant. If you need to pick a size, you could start with 100%. If you are lucky, Poser will import your file at exactly the right size. If you are unlucky, it will import it at the same height as the figure. In that case, you will be using the scaling feature to get it right. See Figure 20.13.

With the mini-skirt in Poser, move it to the right place on the body, and scale it so that it looks just like it did in your modeling program. Again, go all the way around to make sure there is no flesh peeping through the cloth. This doesn't matter for the hip section so much, but if there is any thigh or abdomen showing, you need to increase the scale or adjust the position. See Figure 20.14.

Once you are completely satisfied with the positioning, click on the hip and go to Edit: Replace Body Part with Prop. Select the mini-skirt. Poser will now recommend that you turn bending off. In fact, for items of clothing you should leave it on. You should only turn it off for "hard" objects, such as helmets, armor, and some shoes.

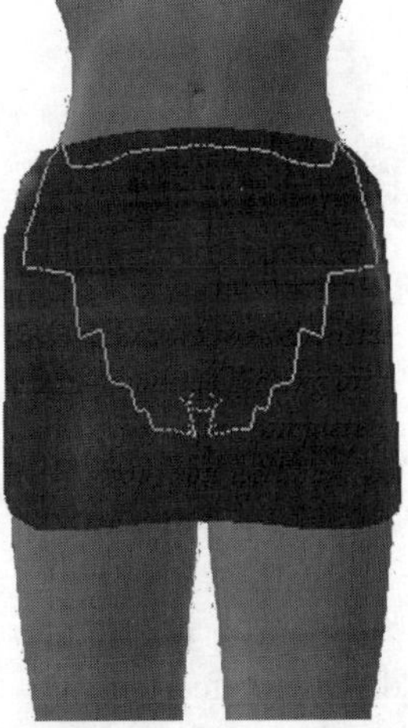

FIGURE 20.13 *Import the skirt, size it, and place it correctly the way it was on your reference model. Clicking on the body part underneath will give you a useful guide to see if you are completely covering it. If there is any body part peeping out over the top, you will have holes in your model when you come to make the replacement.*

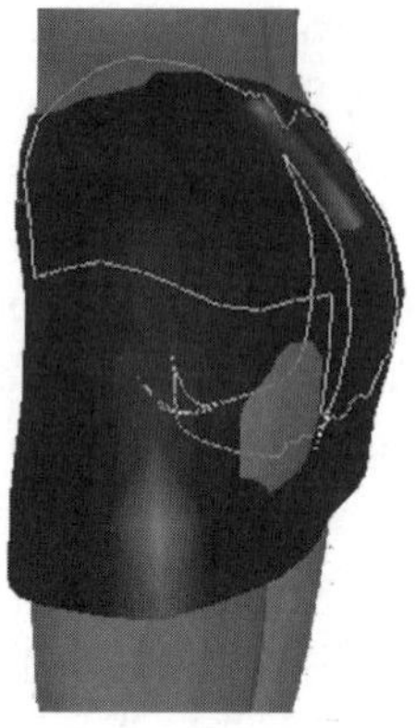

FIGURE 20.14 *This skirt has been scaled too small. If you made your model correctly, it will just be a case of scaling and placement. If you didn't check your garment carefully before exporting it, and it genuinely doesn't fit, you will have to go back and remodel it. When you are completely satisfied, use the* ***Figure: Replace Body Part with Prop*** *to replace the hip with the skirt.*

FIGURE 20.15 *This figure was rounded off with a grunge-look top, hair, and shoes.*

Try a few poses to see what happens. If you have followed the instructions correctly, the skirt should move correctly as you move the legs. Poser will recommend that you turn bending off. In fact, you need to keep it on. That way, the skirt will animate like cloth with the body to almost any position. Shoes can be set to bend (with limits), but "hard" items like armor should be left with bends off. You can apply textures to the garments as required. Note, however, the flesh peeping out through the bottom of the shoe in Figure 20.15. You could fix this in Photoshop, but this would be a real hassle for animation. Better to take the time first to get it just right.

TWEAKING

Unless your mini-skirt is made of some super-Lycra that can take on any form, you need to set limits to how far the legs can move. The longer, narrower, and stiffer the skirt, the less movement is possible. Use the Limits feature to do this.

If you want your skirt to obey the laws of gravity, you will have to introduce some kind of morph-targeting. Poser 3.0 has no "gravity feature."

You can set the color and import a texture map by choosing Surface Materials on the Render menu. Cloth has little sheen, so you should set the highlight to be very broad and with a low value, unless you are thinking of leather or synthetic materials.

If you find that there are gaps at the seams between the garment and the rest of the figure when you render, then you have not completely covered the body part, or you have not hugged the skin sufficiently at the seams.

VARIATIONS AND OTHER KINDS OF CLOTHING

Now that you have the idea, you can see that Poser 3.0 has enormous potential for different kinds of clothing. One of the easiest changes you can make is to create left and right arm pieces to go with the male and female casual figures, which leaves them with a sweatshirt rather than a T-shirt. Full-length dresses are rather more difficult, although they can be very effective. To do a full-length dress, you need to replace the chest body part with the dress. However, because the body chain breaks at the waist, the dress will not follow the movement of the legs. If you have an athletic character you want to animate, the best solution would be to create separate skirt and top pieces, anchoring them respectively to the chest and to the hip. But, for a ball-gown style, simply setting limits on the leg movements will be enough to prevent the legs appearing suddenly through the fabric: People do not tend to run around at social functions.

Going in the other direction, you don't need (and can't use) this technique for underwear or anything that does not completely cover a body part. For that, simply attaching the prop to the figure should be sufficient.

Adding props and replacing body parts uses more memory. The more complex your props, and the more of them, the more memory you will need. Just be aware of this. And remember, more is sometimes less.

Electric Art[4]

POTTED

The apprehensive Plantman is the Poser 3 male nude, slightly distorted on his Y axis and opened for a fast transplant to a pot in Ray Dream Studio 5.02. This is almost misusing the Poser plug-in, which shines its best adding scenery to and editing Poser animations.

In a separate file in RDS, I made aerial roots, the fire-can, the pot, and its potting soil in the vertex modeler (the potting soil is the inside shell of a duplicated pot, resized, with the last cross section filled). Leaves and petals are duplicates of a single mesh modeler leaf, resized, rotated, and perturbed with the magnet tool.

I opened the Poser scene in RDS and pasted pot, fire-can, petals, and leaves into it, then opened the figure in RDS's poser modeler to tweak the Plantman (using Poser's regular tools) into a more vegetative attitude (i.e., translating the feet closer together so they'd fit into the pot) and adjusting angles of head and hands to prevent foliage interpenetration. See Figure 20.16.

When the Plantman was potted, rooted, and blooming, I put cellular shaders on everything but the firing-can, the pot, and the board holding the pot. The atmosphere is 4 Elements Wind; the fire is RadFX fire with a red bulb light hidden in the pot. See Figure 20.17.

FIGURE 20.16 *The poser scene is composed in Ray Dream Studio.*

[4] Text and images by Cecilia Ziemer

FIGURE 20.17 *The finished artwork.*

JUNKYARD FAIRIES

Just so. In fine gardens, fairies are made of gossamer and moonlight, wear silken robes, and dine delicately on dew. These two guys are the other kind, raucous, muddy, deranged, and devolved, wearing shreds of moss and the grime of ages; it's best not to speculate on their diet or pastimes. Only the wings allude to their species.

To make an ugly creature from a handsome Poser model, I started with the Poser 3 male nude, gave him Toddler's height, and rescaled him in all directions. The potbelly, combined with the sway-backed flatfooted stance, required a little tapering on most of the torso parts, and some major adjustments of scale and joint parameters for both hip and abdomen to prevent tearing and separating. See Figure 20.18.

By the time the figure was mauled into proper uglification, no body part remained undistorted or with its normal scale. The eyeballs were scooted forward on the Z axis, until they barely cleared the eyelids; a value of -1 on the Worry dial brought the eyebrows down at the right angle to give the eyes a little shadowing from the top.

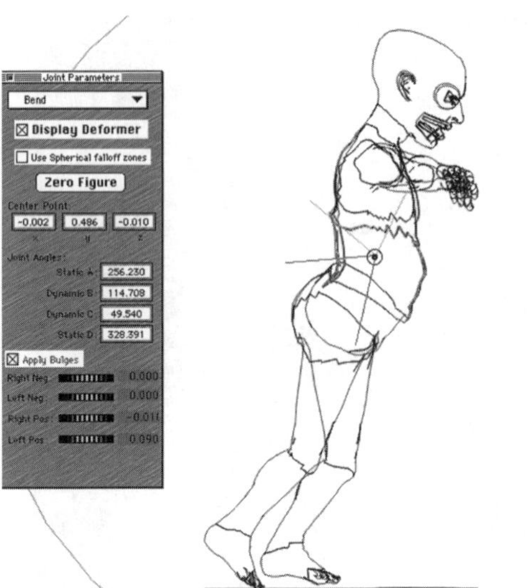

FIGURE 20.18 *The model is first composed in Poser.*

The head extension is a Woman's Hair, cropped and remodeled in Ray Dream Studio 5.02; the wings are three objects, also made in RDS. The outline for the membrane and the cross-section shape extruded for the veins were drawn in Adobe Illustrator and imported; these had to be separate meshes for later texturing in Bryce. Lunch is a piece of Skeleton exported from Poser and dismantled in RDS. I exported hair and wing parts from RDS as individual .Obj. See Figure 20.19.

In Poser, the hair is attached to the head as a prop, and wing-groups are attached as children of the collar sections. Then I imported the bone and curled the hands around it, and bent hands and bone close to the mouth to afford him a good gnaw. I exported it all to Bryce 3D as separate groups for body parts. The second fairy, seated and pondering a large and unshared bone, is the same model, repositioned in Poser and exported. See Figure 20.20.

The hairy-pod-thing is a Ray Dream cylinder mesh, subdivided, spiked, twisted, and spherized; the branches are Ray Dream vertex modeler branches. The materials are all Bryce procedurals: I made a custom material based on Stucco Noise and applied it to the bodies and hair after ungrouping, then regrouping without eyes or wings. The eyes are the default "What are You Looking At" recolored and with a 50% Ambient setting. See Figure 20.21.

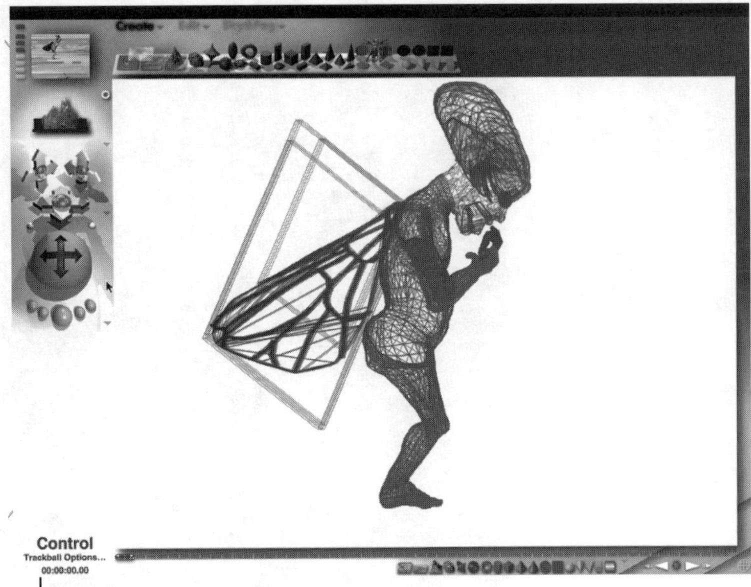

FIGURE 20.19 *Parts modified in RDS are imported into Bryce 3D.*

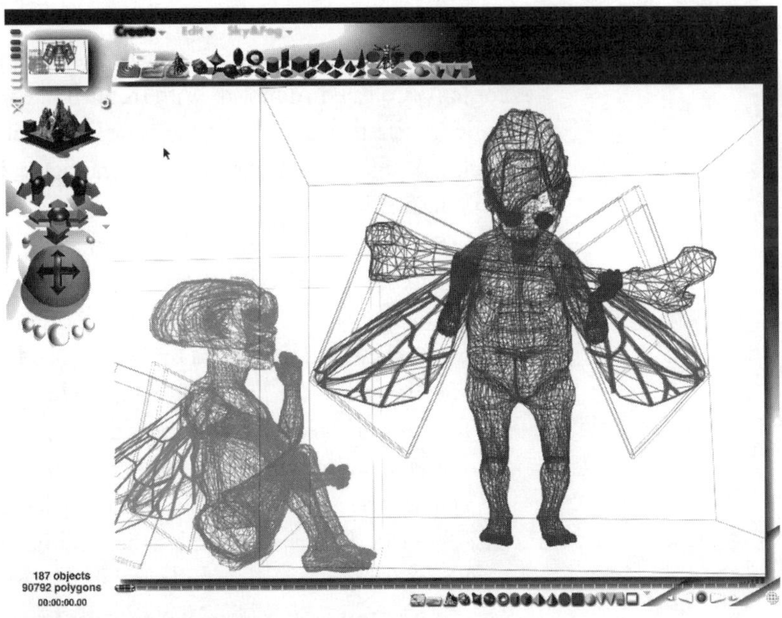

FIGURE 20.20 *The final scene is composed in Bryce 3D.*

FIGURE 20.21 *The final rendering in Bryce 3D.*

RAGDOLL

The four-armed mud-creature crouched on the pier is the same figure I used for Junkyard Fairies, doubled. With IK unchecked, I positioned the figure in its basic crouch, then added it to the New Figures library. Viewing with the side camera, I added the new figure as a second figure; it opened accurately aligned with the first figure.

I moved the second figure downward along the angle of the first figure's spine until the shoulders were clear of the first figure's shoulders. I bent all the arms into position, and made invisible on the first figure (the upper) everything below the chest, and the second figure's head and neck. See Figure 20.22.

Then I attached the "hair" and exported it.

The winged object of contention is the same figure (again)—squashed a little shorter, repositioned, and rescaled down to about 50%.

The tentacle is a RDS spiral with a few spikes here and there. This was the first object in the scene, since placement of the other two figures and all the objects floating in water and sagging in air (except the pier) depended on tentacle placement—it had one angle suitable for an ankle grab. Other objects in the image are Bryce primitives, including the kitchen match (these are little guys) for light. The wings were added and scaled down at the last. See Figure 20.23.

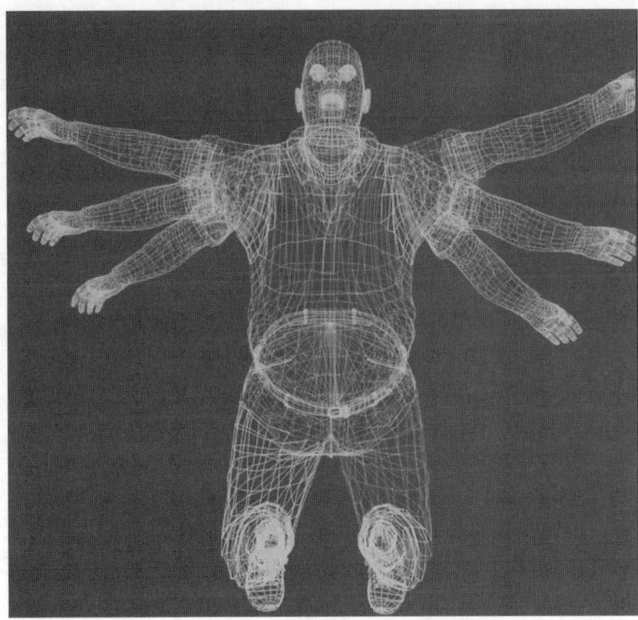

FIGURE 20.22 *Here is the process using three figures with only arms and collars visible.*

FIGURE 20.23 *The finished Ragdoll composition.*

BONES

Karuna! See the Bones animation in the Quicktime folder on this book's CD-ROM.

Who knows what's on parade in the depths of the galaxy? Or as what strange apparitions and devices Poser's four-handed camera translation tool will appear to us in dream? Or what good are a baby and a dismantled skeleton? See Figure 20.24.

The bones for the wheel (originally the Poser skeleton) and the mesh forms of the tail are hierarchy conversions; the baby is a distorted Zygote infant from the Zygote People disk, with its head replaced.

The "wheel" is one shin with foot attached, adjusted in Ray Dream Studio's Mesh Form Modeler. I detached the polymeshes on the foot (for a little toe-bending later), naming arches, heels, and toes as they came apart, and elongated the shin-bones. This I duplicated in the perspective window and one by one, named all the parts of each duplicate and centered the duplicates around a cylinder. The bones group and the cylinder I exported as separate .obj files.

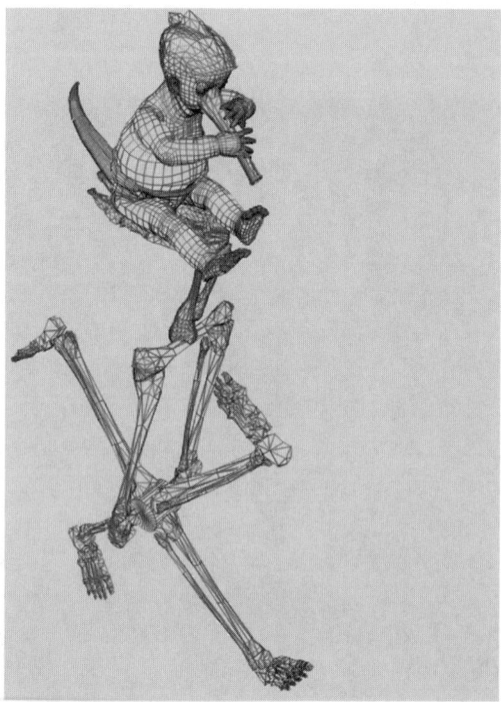

FIGURE 20.24 *A Poser composition created from a Baby figure and a dismantled skeleton.*

Then I wrote the .phi file in SimpleText, before mesh names flew out of my mind.

Using the left-over cylinder in RDS as a spacing guide, I resized one unemployed shinbone and poked it longways through the cylinder's center, attached two more bones at the ends of the resized bone, then attached a duplicate of the resized bone at the top. Yet another resized duplicate and an enlarged hand makes the seating arrangement; with the center cylinder removed, this bony frame/seat was exported as a solid group. See Figure 20.25.

Now for the snoot-flute player (in space, no one can hear you practice . . .) after enlarging his belly and feet, narrowing his shoulders, and generally distorting the whole body in Poser, I duplicated him and exported the duplicate to RDS for dismantling in the mesh modeler—all I needed was the head.

With the magnet tool I distorted the head a little to the back and pulled some vertices on the top for the head fins. The nose and mouth area I selected and decimated, flattening it further, vertex by vertex. The snoot-flute itself is just a lathed object, fit to the face at one end and reshaped a little on the other. Head-with-snoot went back to Poser as a prop for head replacement on the original figure.

The tail was modeled in the RDS Vertex Modeler and broken apart in the

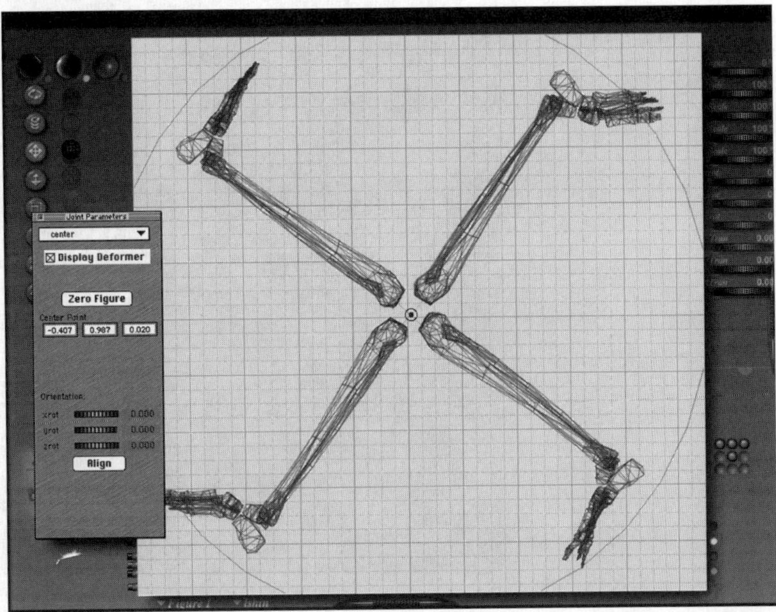

FIGURE 20.25 *The Wheel object.*

Mesh Form Modeler. After replacing the head and positioning the hands for snoot-playing, I converted the wheel and tail to Poser models. Snoot-player was positioned in the bony hand and attached as a child object to the frame, as were the cylinder and the wheel. The wheel's center aligned to the cylinder and the whole works is moved by dragging the frame, the easiest part to grab.

For animation, the wheel was rotated in 90-degree increments with the toes flexing slightly; the tail swayed, the baby boogied. I set depth cueing on, shadows off, made the background color blue, the foreground gold, and the lights blue and orange; the sky is a Bryce PICT—it has several comets, but they're very hard to see. There's no texture map; only a high ambient setting and reddening for the eyes. See Figure 20.26.

Karuna! Load PHI Builder from the PHI folder on this book's CD-ROM.

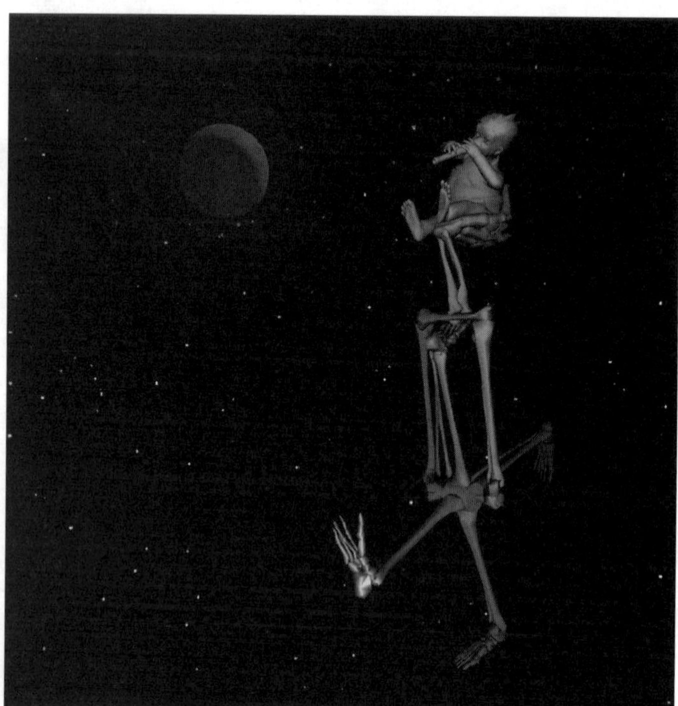

FIGURE 20.26 *A rendered frame from the Bones project.*

PHI Builder[5]

PHI Builder V2.1 is a 32-bit Windows application for aiding in the creation of PHI files. PHI files are the means by which you can import your own models into Poser and set them up so you can actually pose them. This is one of the most exciting new features found in Poser V3.0; unfortunately it's also one of the hardest things to do. PHI Builder's purpose is to make the creation of your PHI file as easy as possible and point out any possible problems, so Poser won't encounter any errors when you load it in. If you don't already have PHI Builder installed, all you have to do is unzip it into your Poser directory. You can check for the latest update at http://edge.net/~fur/index.html.

The first step when making a model for use within Poser is to create your model, or convert your model, into Wavefront's OBJ file format. You should also save your OBJ in its own subdirectory under Runtime\Geometries, because that's what Poser wants. Each piece should be separate from the others—use the existing Poser figures as your guide when splitting them up. This is done in your favorite modeling package of your choice. In my example, I'm using MAX V1.1 with a model of a dancer, provided by CacheForce (www.cacheforce.com). See Figure 20.27.

The second step is to create a PHI file, or a Poser Hierarchy file, to tell Poser how to build the joints between each part. Load up PHI Builder and pick Add

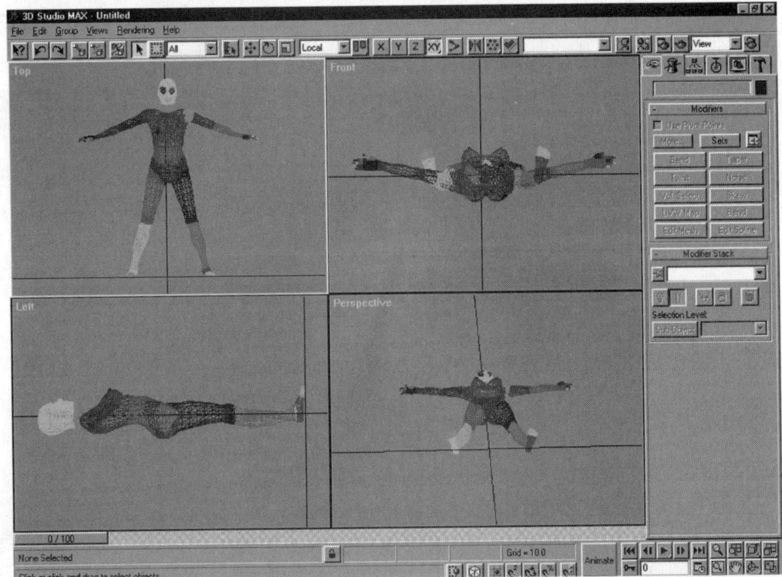

FIGURE 20.27 *I've split this figure up in the exact same manner as the models provided with Poser. It always a good idea to first import your OBJ into Poser just as a test. If that succeeds, you may continue on.*

[5] Text and images by Roy Riggs

OBJ. This will create a default hierarchy, which you will have to rearrange to match your model. See Figure 20.28.

If you have the maintenance patch, this problem should be fixed, otherwise you'll have to find a way to convert the OBJ file. Now, you might have to manually fix some of the level numbering, PHI Builder's artificial intelligence needs some work, but it's only making guesses based on the name of each part, it's not actually looking at the geometry. You cannot switch into the tree editor mode of PHI Builder until you have a syntactically correct PHI file. If you try to switch into the tree mode, it will automatically verify the PHI file before switching over. Once switched over, you can drag and drop the nodes, and double-click on them to edit them. Figure 20.29 shows the PHI after it has been rearranged.

Now you'll need to add the IK Chains for your model. If you select the parent part of your chain and select the Tree/Add IKChain menu item, PHI Builder will bring up a dialog with the remainder of the tree under the parent item, and it will have already selected the most likely child part. All you need to do is supply the name of the IK Chain. See Figure 20.30.

At any time, you can press the Test button and PHI Builder will test the PHI and OBJ files for problems. Naturally, the File/Open and Save features work as expected. PHI Builder will register itself as the owner of PHI files, so your PHI files will get a little icon in the Explorer window. You can double-

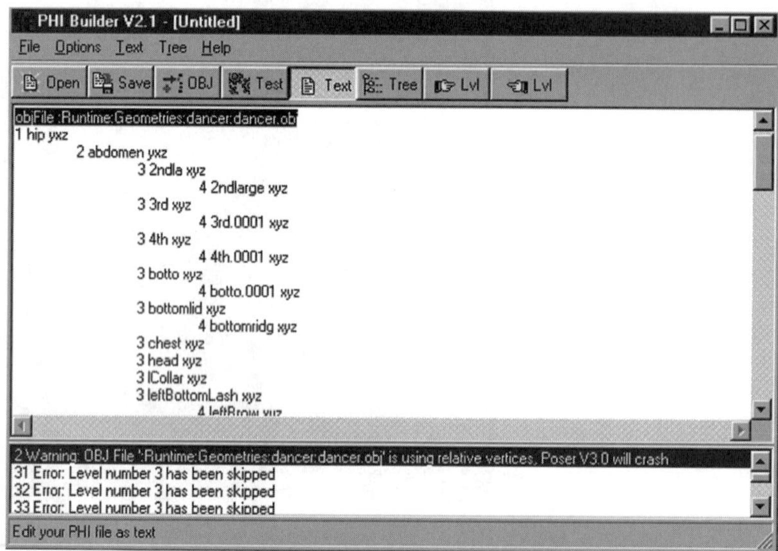

FIGURE 20.28 *This shows that PHI Builder has already noticed a common problem—the OBJ file format exported by MAX is incompatible with Poser V3.0.*

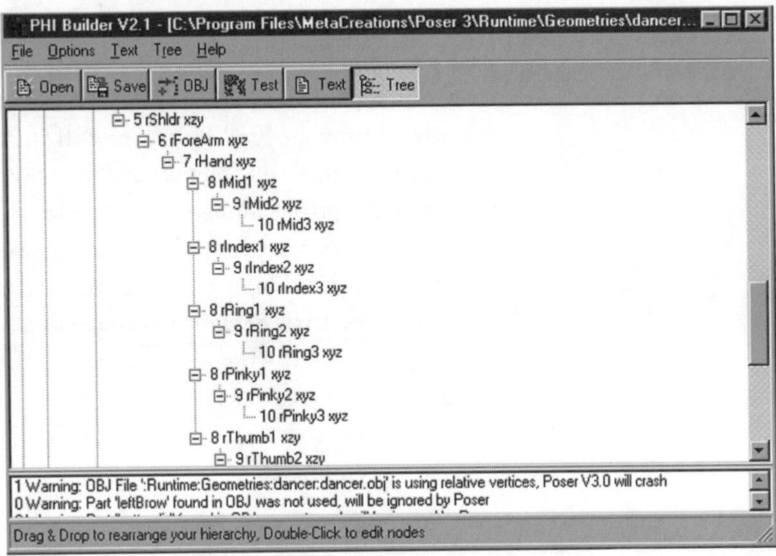

FIGURE 20.29 *Here's how PHI Builder looks after the rearrangement is completed.*

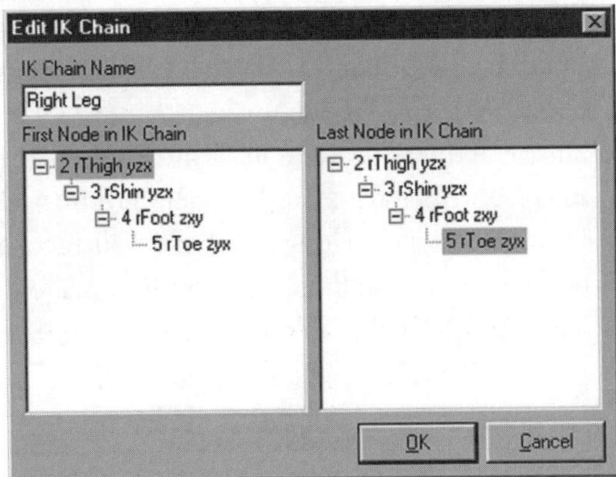

FIGURE 20.30 *The IK Chain is supplied.*

click them to launch PHI Builder, or drag and drop them to the PHI Builder window. Additionally, PHI Builder keeps track of the most recently used PHI files to make switching between them easier. PHI Builder does come with context-sensitive help, but it will not replace MetaCreation's advanced manual.

The third step is to use the File/Convert Hierarchy File menu inside Poser. Poser will read the PHI file, and any OBJ files it includes, to create a .CR2 and an .RSR file to go along with your OBJ. This RSR file basically serves as a compiled version of your OBJ, which Poser can load in faster. If you ever make any changes to your OBJ or PHI file, you MUST delete any previous .RSR files before reconverting the PHI! Hopefully, PHI Builder will have already caught anything that might trip Poser up, and this step should go without a hitch. If you are having problems, make sure the original Poser 2 man is loaded as default, as this was reported to fix a problem some users were having.

The final step is editing all of the joint parameters for your model inside Poser. For more detailed information on this process, read MetaCreation's *Advanced Poser Manual* (ftp://ftp.metacreations.com/pub/Applications/Poser/goodies/advanced_techniques.pdf).

If you want some more PHI tutorials, try Bushi's Graphics Page at http://www.spiritone.com/~bushi/.

Baumgarten Enterprises

On the CD-ROM that accompanies this book is a folder called Baum. In it, you will find a number of object accessories for your Poser scenes, all provided by Baumgarten Enterprises, free for your use. Baumgarten Enterprises (established in 1988) has been modeling in 3D for many years, offering custom model building for hire to hobbyists and professionals alike. With the release of Poser 2, requests for additional parts for the Poser people began flooding in. Since that time, they've created a multitude of object accessories and parts to be used with Poser, Bryce, and virtually any other 3D application that allows the importing models. Using a prebuilt model in a scene or animation is a wonderful way to expand your creative horizons. Adding a prebuilt model into a scene can inspire you to try a whole new choreography. With the release of its first CD (1st quarter 99), Baumgarten Enterprises ventures into the commercial model collections market. Visit Baumgarten's web site at www.stewstras.net/baument/downloads.htm

Moving Along

In this chapter, we have benefited from the viewpoints and work of three Poser masters. In the next chapter, the Zygote Media Group gives us a tour of its facility and lets us in on the creation of the Poser figures.

CHAPTER 21

The Zygote Media Group

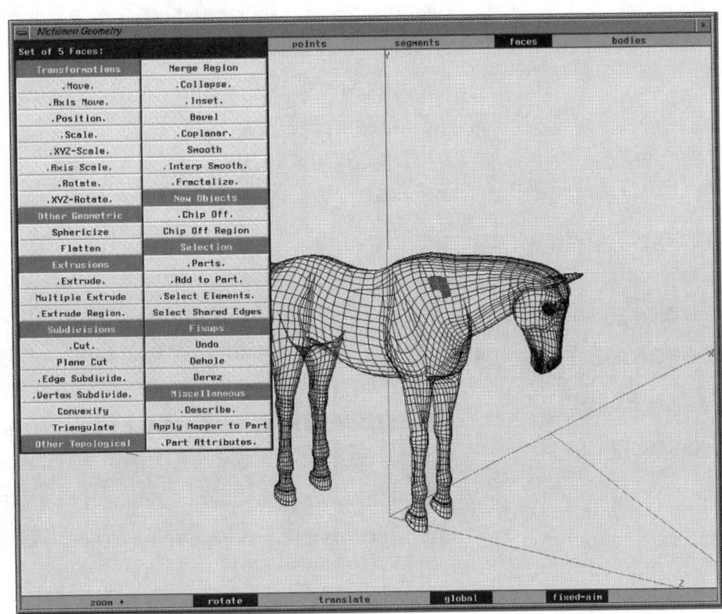

The Zygote Media Group has a reputation for creating the highest quality custom models for clients such as Digital Domain, Pixar, and DreamWorks. Zygote brings that same expertise and quality to MetaCreations Poser 3, one of the most anticipated software releases of 1998. The new human and animal models in Poser 3 owe their existence to Zygote, a fact that should make Poser 3 users shout with joy. At last . . . Poser models that look detailed and natural at any zoom level and that maintain their believability even when animated. Instead of writing this chapter by interviewing the team at Zygote, it was decided that the best way to give you this information would be to let a representative of Zygote do the talking. The following text was written and illustrated by Tom Wheeler, who wears many hats at the Zygote Media Group.

http://www.zygote.com
tom@zygote.com
1-(800)267-5170
1-(801)375-7220

How Zygote Developed the Models for Poser 3

Reading the following ways that Zygote used to develop the models for Poser 3 may help you to create your own Poser 3 models.

HISTORY OF THE PROCESS

At the start of the project, Larry Weinberg (Poser 3's main programmer at MetaCreations) and Steve Cooper (Poser 3 Production Manager at MetaCreations) came and visited Zygote to get to know us and train us on the process

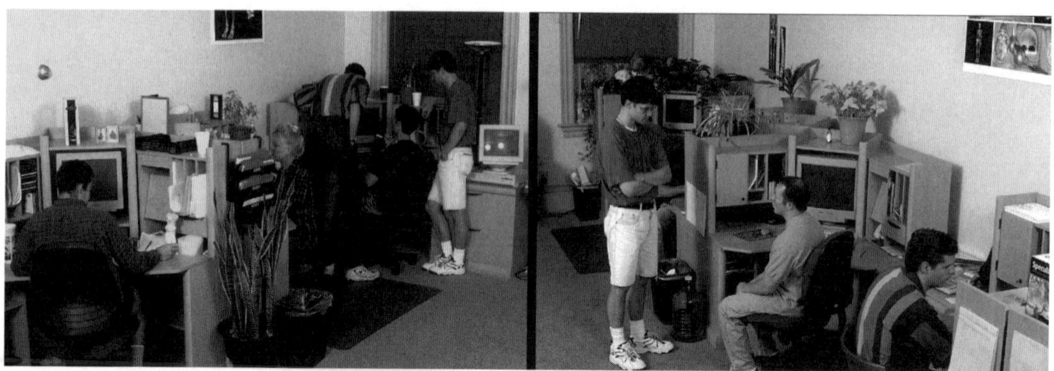

FIGURE 21.1 *The Zygote team at work.*

of optimizing models for Poser 3. At the very beginning, Larry's idea was for Zygote to provide animals for Poser 3. At some point it was suggested that Zygote model a new head for the Poser human male. Zygote had an existing "ideal male," which Larry pulled into what was then Poser 3 at its young stage and placed it side by side with the Poser 2 nude male. Soon a careful scrutiny began to take place. Chris Creek was called over to look carefully at the anatomy with Steve and Larry. The realization was made that things could be improved on both nude male models.

Needless to say, Zygote soon had created not only a new male model that was more anatomically correct, but also had a contract to model all the new humans and the animals. Figuring out the process of preparing a model and getting it into Poser was a long and difficult challenge. Many issues had to be addressed, at times requiring that new tools be created, and ongoing communication about problems and solutions was mandatory. Justin Wilson and I (Tom Wheeler) were leading the Zygote work. Justin was modeling, while I was trying to figure out all the technical ends of setting up models and dealing with blend zones, though there was some crossover on both our parts. Larry Weinberg was our savior on the programming end, answering questions, teaching, and occasionally working those programming miracles he has become known for. Initially, the work was going slowly, much slower than anticipated. It was difficult due to the newness of the tasks. Mistakes were made that cost days, and much of the setup work was fine-tuned by Larry. After about two months of real difficulty, it became apparent that we needed more help and that setting up models was more than a one-person job. Once Tony and Chad were brought on to the job, a sort of assembly line production method began with each person handling one or two sections of the setup job. This has worked well for us.

What's Involved in Setup: A Basic Outline

A. Build the model: Of course, there's a whole science and art to this, but I completely understand artists who want to create their own content—if you want to try it make sure it's completely clean with no holes or reversed normals. There is one other note: 5-sided polygons in Poser drop out, so the mesh needs to be 4-sided polygons or less.

B. Group it for Poser, again for materials, and again for texture mapping: When you look at a model in Poser, you can see that it is grouped out where it will bend, at the joints. These are the only groups in the .obj file that Poser will handle, and they must be named specifically. The naming of the groups is case sensitive and a critical element of success in even reading in a model to Poser. A text .cr2 file is created with every .obj file, and the names of groups must exactly match. Naming is also important for the Poser's walk designer to function properly.

You will also notice when you start working with a model in Poser that different parts of the model can have separate changeable colors. These are the materials of the various parts. Before it was read into Poser, the model was grouped out for those materials in WaveFront. The materials were applied to the .obj file, and then that material grouping information was removed. As you get ready to paint a texture map for a model, you might take the opportunity to view the default texture map or texture template in a 2D paint package. If you do, you'll see separate sections of the model laid out like an unfolded world map (I'll explain why and how later). This means that at some point the model was grouped out again for these sections of UV coordinate mapping, the coordinates were projected onto the model, and these groups were removed.

C. Assign materials: The materials initially applied are just white—color is irrelevant because it will be changed within Poser. The only thing to be concerned with is that each appropriate group has a separate material assigned. Then, even though the groups will be removed, the .obj file still retains the materials information that Poser is able to access.

D. Project the UV texture coordinates for mapping: We use WaveFront to project the planar coordinates through each particular part. This is done in a unique manner, however, because all the parts of the model are included within the same map. We actually scale the planar projection to be huge in comparison to the model, activate a group, and project. Then we move the plane a little, activate another group and project for that group. We do this for each group, each time moving the plane slightly so there's no overlap in projections. This procedure will allow for one map of the entire model, with each part represented. When the 2D representation of this projection is opened inside Digits N' Art's "Flesh," all the parts will need to be scaled up and positioned in an orderly fashion.

E. Layout and unfold the UV coordinates for mapping and save out a texture template: Within Flesh, the UV coordinates can be unfolded. The reason this is done is to minimize the problem of stretching when maps are applied later. A texture map is a 2D image anchored to the mesh by the UV coordinates. With Flesh, UV coordinates can be manipulated apart from the mesh and affect the placement of the texture. The projections made were simple planar projections, so as you look at the UV coordinates, you see a clear image of the head in the middle, but around the edges they overlap each other (because the geometry was going back into space). These edges need to be pulled out to allow paint to be applied separately to all these polygons along the edges. The coordinates, once they are pulled out and unfolded, are then scaled and placed to maximize the use of space in the map, in as orderly a fashion as possible. A gray wash is applied and this texture is saved out to serve as a template so that users can paint maps. There are some real benefits to this procedure, but also some drawbacks. Because models are unfolded by hand so to speak, rather than in some automated controlled way, it has been difficult for users to match up seams when they want to paint stripes on clothing. The texture map templates are designed to be painted on within either a 3D or 2D paint package. They can be scaled up to any resolution, then painted on, and applied as maps to the geometry.

F. Delete all grouping but the Poser grouping: At this point, the model's grouping information will be removed. The model can't have overlapping groups in Poser, so material groups and UV groups will be removed. We found that we needed to save backups at every step of this process, and also set up a naming convention so that we would know internally what obj file had been through which steps. This isn't so important if you're only working with one obj file, but when we were setting up multiple models, organization was a lifesaver. Of course, we learned that lesson the hard way.

G. Create morph targets: Now that the model has been through the UV stage, it's a good time to create the morph targets you need. You don't want to do it before the UV stage, because then the targets will still need to go through these steps. Justin Wilson created all the morph targets for all the models in Wavefront. When creating morph targets, you must work from the exact data you want to morph. In other words, to create a smile for the nude man, the head was taken from the nude man, the vertices are pulled to create the smile, and this new head is saved out. Make sure the software is retaining the exact order of the vertices in the obj file, or the morph won't work. Only Wavefront was used in creating morphs because we found that Nichimen would reorder the vertices.

H. Either create a hierarchy file to start from scratch, or modify an existing .cr2 file to read in the model to Poser: Once extra grouping has been removed, the model is ready to be brought into Poser. This can be done several ways: An existing .cr2 file could be used, or a .hier file could be created. Both of these options require the use of a text editor—we used BBEdit on the Macintosh. All the .cr2 files for all the figures in Poser are contained in Runtime: libraries: character. You can open these in text editors to see what they look like. In the .cr2 file option, the names of all the groups in the .obj file obviously have to match those listed in the .cr2 file. Then there are two locations near the top of the .cr2 file where the reference to the obj file would need to be changed. Using an existing .cr2 file can be a great time saver: If the geometry is similar, the blend zones may not need to be adjusted too much. Its also helpful for matching up blend zones if the models are the same scale. Of course, sometimes you don't want models to be the same scale, depending on what type of figure you're working on. If, however, you're determined to bring a frog model into Poser, you would need to start from the .hier file stage. This is a simple file that describes the hierarchy of the groups in the model that Poser will use to generate a .cr2 file when you choose **convert .hier file** under the file menu. This command brings up a dialog box allowing you to locate the .hier file you've created. I believe that the process of creating .hier files and adjusting blend zones is spelled out in the *Advanced Poser Techniques* manual on MetaCreation's web site. The .obj files that are referenced by either of these methods should be placed in Runtime: Geometries.

When the model doesn't come in the first time, comes in partway, or causes a crash, you get the happy task of hunting down whatever step it was you overlooked. One important step that often causes problems is naming for the groups. If groups are dropping out once the model is in Poser, it's because the group names don't match exactly from .obj files to .cr2 files.

I. Adjust blend zones until the sun goes down: No matter which course you used to bring the model into Poser, you will need to adjust the blend zones. If you start from a .hier file, blend zones will need to be set up from scratch. I usually work from the inside out on a model and just methodically set up each zone and test it as much as I can. I might start on the chest region and set up blend zones for each channel (center, x,y,z, and scale zones). By "set up blend zones," I mean adjust the zones that Poser created at the joint, so that it works well when the joint bends in its various positions. By looking at the movement in wireframe mode, you can see exactly how the geometry is getting deformed, which sometimes helps. When you think about how many joints there are on a human and how many rotation channels there are on each joint, you can begin to see the task ahead of you if it's human characters you want.

The first step to setting a blend zone is to see that the center point is where you want it. This is typically at the pivot position of a joint, but collars and thumbs can be tricky. The "twist" is usually what I set next. This is a simple gradient bar indicating how the body is going to twist along the axis. Then the remaining two rotation channels are controlled with the "handlebars." These are also straightforward: Two handles are green and two are red; the space between the greens and reds is affected by the deformation. So you can move these handlebars around and see how the mesh is affected. There are several general guidelines to bear in mind as you try to set up blend zones. First, set up the zones initially with the model at its zero position, because the zones move in space with the body part. And remember that the child body part is blending up into the parent. Sometimes it gets confusing—the blend zones for the thigh should be located up near the hip, not down at the knee (even though it's all the thigh group). This might seem obvious, but you would be surprised how your mind can get turned around. Nothing is more frustrating than working for an hour or two to get a body part working right, move to the next joint and realize it belongs at the position you thought you just finished. The collars blend into the chest, not the shoulders. The shoulders blend into the collars, and so on. It just helps to keep that hierarchy in mind. An optional but often necessary tool is to set up the spherical fall-off zones. These spheres can be moved and scaled into the desired position (it's often quicker to switch to "bounding box mode" when trying to manipulate the spheres) to affect the bend of the particular channel. Basically, everything inside the green sphere is affected by the rotation, everything to the outside of the red sphere is unaffected, and everything in between the spheres gradually tapers from the green to the red. It's important to remember that these spheres work in conjunction with the handlebars—they do not take the place of the handlebars. Often, I'll spent a lot of time manipulating the spheres into all sorts of sophisticated positions with no real improvement at the joint, and then I move the handlebar slightly and the problem gets fixed.

But the spheres do have real purposes and real effects. They are primarily used for joints where you only want a portion of the geometry to be affected, like a thigh coming into a hip. The hip, in this case, is the parent of the thigh, but it's actually the parent of both the right and left thighs. So you would set up spheres such that when the right thigh bends the hip is only affected in the area over the right thigh, not the area over the left thigh. You can toggle the display mode of the spheres, change them to "lit wireframe" mode, for example, to get a better 3D feel for what they are doing and where they are placed. Setting up blend zones for a figure can be very time intensive, and there is a subjective nature to it. Its important to test the zones by bending the parts all around. You might adjust the zones to a certain position, which causes the thigh to look good as it bends forward, but this may screw up the bend backwards. It gets particularly difficult when you see how one channel affects another. For instance, a thigh bend might look right when it's bent to a certain degree in X, but combine that with a Y rotation and see what happens.

I should mention one improvement that was made to the process that is a huge time saver. Notice within Poser under **Figure/Symmetry** there are mirror commands. This simply allows you to pose a portion of the figure, and then mirror that position to the other side. Big deal, right? Well . . . if you hold down the "option" key on Mac (probably "alt" on the PC?) as you drag over these commands, when you mirror one side over, the blend zones also get mirrored! Spherical zones, handlebars, center points, the works except limits, these will still need to be set. It cuts your work in half, though. Larry Weinberg worked that out in a weekend after he got tired of my complaining to him. Thank you Larry!

During this blend zone process, because you're moving the body parts all around, it's also a good time to set the limits for each body part. Obviously, try to set the limits at the farthest range the motion can take. I haven't mentioned setting up the scale zones. These can get a bit tricky, and MetaCreations needs to still refine the tools there. They basically work as ramps, rather like the twist. The weird part is that there's a zone going from parent to child, and a zone going from child to parent, but they are really the same zone. Whichever one you set is the one that is activated and takes effect. I don't really know of any secrets as to how these work—I just set them and start scaling to see if I like what it's doing. The spherical zones can also be helpful on these. The most difficult place for scale zones is going from a parent that has multiple children, such as a chest. I usually start at these types of parents and work outward it seems to do work all right.

J. Test texture mapping and fine-tune all materials: At this point I scribbled different colors on the texture template to make sure the coordinates are functioning properly and to make sure nothing was left out. You could take the time to paint texture maps now as well. If the model's UV coordinates are messed up, you can just go back to that step, fix the problem, and plug that .obj file back into the Geometries folder in Runtime. You can use the blend zones you've done on the fixed .obj file. As long as all the groups still match, there's no problem. Default materials can be set now as well. Use the paint bucket to set material color, then, by holding down the command key on the Mac, you can set the highlights. You can also position the model to work properly with the IK chain, by giving the parts a slight bend in the direction they would need to go. We chose not to do this on our animal's CD, just because it leaves the animals looking so strange. We felt the animals should come up in the zero position, and the users could set the IK pose.

K. Save out the model (actually do this along the way, but at the end create a nice icon): The final step would be to capture a nice icon for the model. You should save your work periodically throughout this process. The little plus sign at the bottom of the library drawer saves the file into the library. Sometimes you need to do it twice for the icon to actually show up.

And there you have it. Those are the basics, along with some helpful tips from the frazzled guy who spent months working with the process while the process itself was evolving.

What's Coming Next for Poser 3 from Zygote

We have been bombarded with requests, ideas, and suggestions from Poser users for new models. It has actually been extremely difficult to determine what sort of content to begin developing, because of the wide variety of responses out there. Many people would love to see more costumes and clothing for the figures. But, on the other hand, many people use the nude figures more than they use the clothed, because they actually paint clothes on the figures for 2D images. So some users actually want nude versions of the clothed people we have available. Also, animals are a big hit, and many people have asked us for more. People have specifically sought for birds and reptiles. We have considered doing a fantasy/sci-fi character collection, and there has been an excited response for this also.

There are many collections and models we would like to build for Poser. We recently received an entertaining letter from a user in England, with several model suggestions. He is apparently a comic artist, and would like to see a collection of stereotyped characters. Some he mentions are: teacher, police officer, soldier, diver, secretary, nutty professor, thug or gang member, crime lord, mad genius, military general, newspaper publisher, glamour model, college student, martial artist, low-down bum, bag lady, super hero, actor, and fast food worker. We've also received requests for more hairstyles, shoes, accessories, and many other items.

We would love to build all of these models and would have a great deal of fun doing it. We are currently training and adding to our Poser production team, and this process takes a little time. We must also be careful to maintain profitability. It is important for us to build models that will have the widest market appeal. Zygote has been involved in a number of custom jobs for Poser users lately, and many of these models will be released to the public for resale as well.

Aside from collections of models, there are also several ways we would like to take advantage of Poser's ability to use morph targets. This really opens up Poser in whole new ways. We could create multiple morph targets for heads and figures (although morph targets for bodies at this point isn't quite possible) and essentially turn Poser into a modeling application using only morph targets. Imagine a head with 60 or 70 dial parameters along the side; ear dials, nose dials, eye dials, lip dials, head shape dials, jaw shape dials, and on. This may be a direction we can pursue with MetaCreations in upcoming versions of Poser. The file sizes needed to really do this well would be large, however.

Custom Modeling Assignments at Zygote

Because so many Poser users are also involved in modeling their own objects and figures, and because there remains a high interest in the ways that modeling work is done for clients, here is a basic outline of how Zygote goes about the process of creating custom models for clients.

Typically, a custom modeling assignment starts when a client or potential client contacts us. The client describes the kind of model he or she is looking for, and tries to find out how much this would cost. If we do not already have a model that fits the bill in our standard model library, we begin the process of generating a bid. To generate an accurate bid we need to know as many specifics of the job as possible. Can the client provide us with drawings or other reference for the model? If it's a character, we would like to see drawings or pictures from the front, back, and side views. Perhaps there is even a sculpture or physical 3D model of the object that we can mark up and digitize. Also, we need to know what type of software the client is using. There may be additional setup time involved to get a model ready for various software packages. Once we have this information, we can give an accurate bid.

Often during this bidding process, we find that we need to have a clear communication path. It doesn't help when there are two or three people trying to communicate for the client, each telling us different things to do (which actually happens more than you might think). Because modeling, like any commercial art form, is subjective, it's important to know who needs to be satisfied with your work, and exactly what will satisfy them.

BUSINESS CONCERNS WE ALL DEAL WITH

What happens if we build a model, send it off to a client, and the client doesn't like it? In this case, we have to determine exactly what has happened. Did we accurately represent the resource material, but the client has changed his or her mind about what he or she wants? Or did we really screw up? Both of these events occur every so often. I should say, models that Zygote sends out have what we refer to as "clean geometry," meaning there are no holes, reversed normals, or other common problems. And the mesh is laid out in a smart manner, so that it follows the form and will animate as easily as possible. We also have some very advanced tangency techniques in NURBS modeling that were developed at Zygote and that to our knowledge are only used by us. However, even though the model is clean, clients often come back with concerns. Actually, it's rare that a model goes out the door to a client and the client doesn't request some tweaking in one area or another. That's just the nature of the business, and no one is offended by that sort of thing. This is why it's important to get as much information up front before the job has begun.

BUILDING THE CUSTOMIZED MODELS

If the client approves the bid, we get the resource material and begin working. We don't use any digital scanners at Zygote, for several reasons. Generally, the mesh that is created by these scanners is extremely heavy (many polygons) to get good realism. We can build a much lighter model (light in polygons) and get the same realism in a model that's not impossible to work with because of its file size. Also, with scanner technology, the mesh is generated not from the human's point of view, but from the machine's point of view. This results in a mesh that is not clean or well laid out. Yes, it captures the detail, but will it animate without breaking or tearing? The modeling process usually doesn't even involve hand-digitizing anything, most often we work straight from drawings. But if we can digitize an object to get a start, we will. Zygote has a Microscribe digitizing arm from Immersion, which we use in connection with a program called Hyperspace. We run the digitizing program on a Macintosh. This gets us the form in its roughest shape, and hours will still be spent in cleaning up the model, welding vertices, and fine-tuning.

When we start from drawings or other resources, depending on the object, we can often start from a preexisting model. Say, for instance, we needed to build an overweight old woman. We might start from a young woman we already have; a process we refer to as "frankensteining." With the extensive model library we've developed, it's rare that we ever need to start a complex model from scratch. We use Silicon Graphics (SGI) workstations to do the modeling work, though at present there is some simple modeling going on at the PC level. Zygote currently has seven SGI stations, each with various programs loaded (Zygote is a small company, currently with fourteen employees). We also have four IBM compatible PCs and three Macintosh computers. The non-SGI machines are involved in a wide variety of tasks, some of which would include file translation, texture mapping, work in Poser and various other PC level 3D applications, and of course office management tasks.

We use primarily two software packages in combination to create all polygon models. These are WaveFront from Alias/WaveFront, and Nichimen Geometry from Nichimen Graphics. See Figures 21.2 and 21.3.

These both run on SGI workstations. We like WaveFront for its ability to visualize the model, to see how the various parts will smooth shade in total detail. Wavefront has been around for over a decade, with virtually no changes over that time period. But in our view there hasn't been a huge need for upgrades, because WaveFront does what it does so well. The interface is clean and organized, and the tools are extremely valuable for polygon work. There are also some important tools for cleaning the geometry: checking for seams, booleans checks, and database checks. Also, WaveFront has great tools for grouping the models. It also allows you very quickly to focus in on a certain area of interest even within a complex model. For instance, if a seam is found in

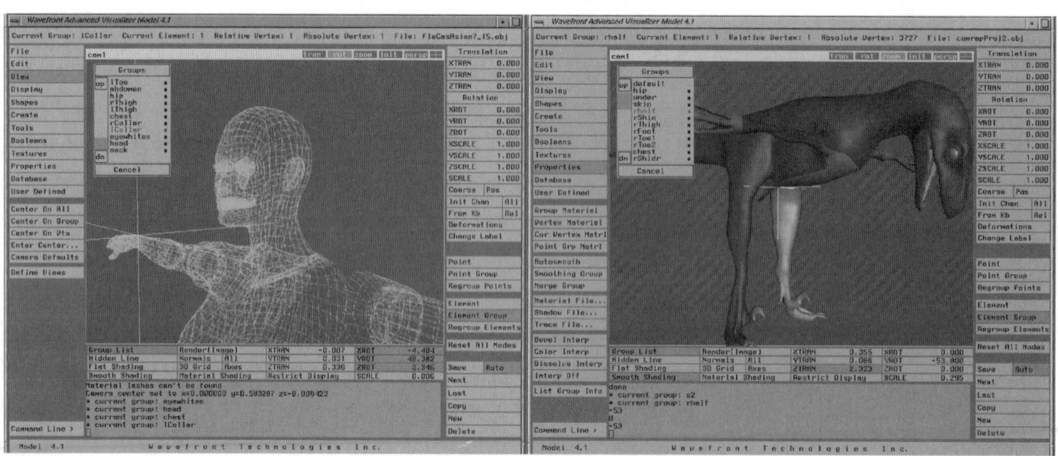

FIGURE 21.2 *This shot of the Alias/WaveFront interface shows two Poser models in development.*

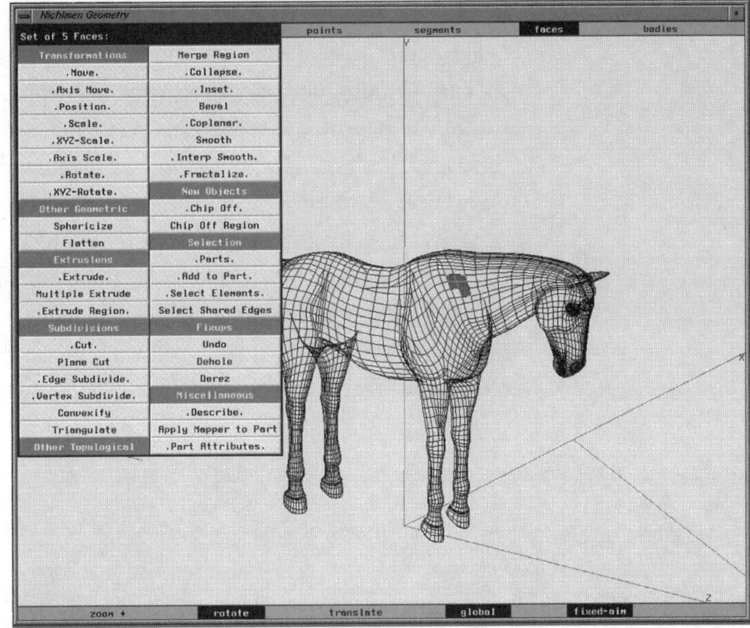

FIGURE 21.3 *Poser 3 models were also developed with the help of Nichimen Geometry from Nichimen Graphics.*

the underarm area of a human model, the entire model can be hidden except for the specific area you're concerned about, so there's no lag time trying to rotate around with a huge amount of data. It handles large files well, and often when we've created pieces of complex models in Nichimen, we will assemble and position the pieces in WaveFront. When you save out a model from WaveFront after doing all the checks and fixes, you know it's clean and will import or translate into any polygon software package.

Nichimen Geometry is also an extremely valuable tool for its modeling abilities at the vertex level. We really feel there is no better application for manipulating points in 3D space. Nichimen's pop-up menu style allows for the ability to conceal a multitude of sophisticated commands without cramping work space. The tools also go way beyond the typical XZY translation. You have the ability in Nichimen to select by points, segments, faces, or bodies and then to manipulate these elements with reference to other points, segments, or faces. In other words, you can move a point along a specific segment toward another point. Or you could move a face toward a point or a segment. You could also move a face or segment out along its normal. Or scale a face in towards a segment or point, or away from it. Or you could collect these elements and perform the same types of functions on groups of elements. There are beveling tools, tightening commands, cutting, extruding, any number of scaling options, splicing, dicing, cooking, cleaning, and so on. You name it, Nichimen's got it.

Both of these programs also can do a lot more than just the functions we use them for. They both have animation and rendering sides to them that we have really not even explored much. For modeling in NURBS we currently are using Alias' Power Animator, though we also have MAYA and Soft Image. Though there are some very powerful tools in these programs, the general consensus here and from others we've talked to is that Power Animator still has the best tools for modeling. Digits N' Arts Flesh is used a lot for working with UV coordinates and texture mapping. This program was used extensively during pro-

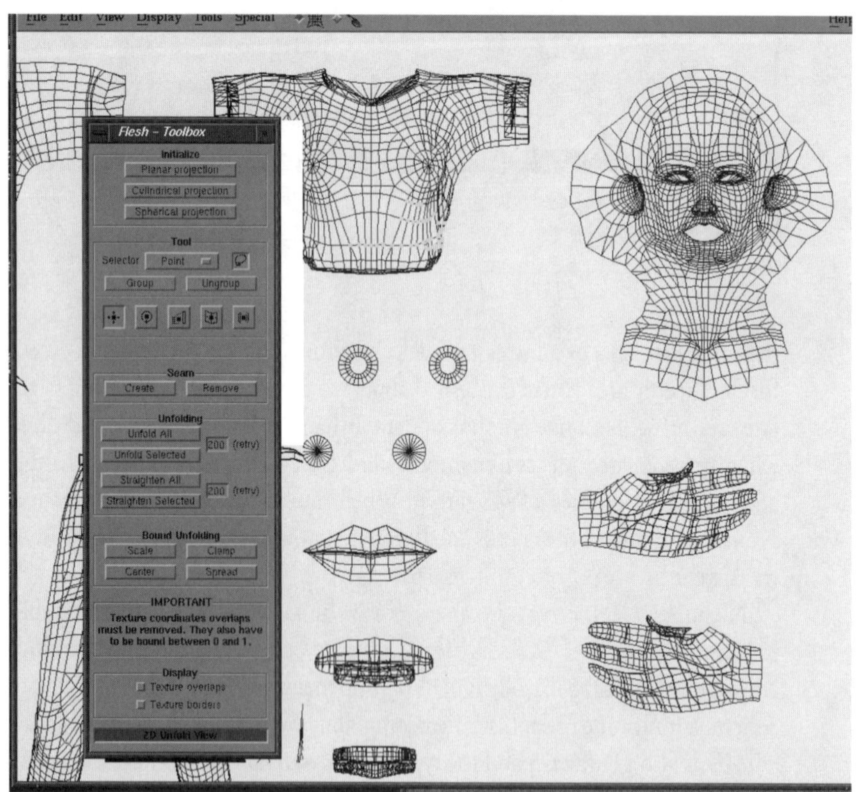

FIGURE 21.4 *Digits N' Arts Flesh was also used to develop the texture maps for the Poser 3 models.*

duction for Poser. Flesh also runs on the SGI platform, and is a unique and powerful tool. See Figure 21.4.

Working for Zygote

Zygote has been fairly restrained in its hiring policy. The nature of this business has been such that work comes in waves. We are attracted to real talent, and when someone presents a very strong portfolio, we will usually find a way to bring that person in. We also subcontract on a very limited basis, typically to past employees who have left the area, or to others we know of by reputation. Up to now we haven't licensed models from freelance artists, but we are interested in looking into it.

How do we keep up with industry developments? Each year Zygote has a booth at SIGGRAPH, and this is typically the event we gear up for the most. We have been able to send nearly all our employees to SIGGRAPH each year. We also usually have a booth at CGDC (Computer Game Developers Conference), and we have representatives at a few other major tradeshows. We advertise in several trade publications, *Computer Graphics World, 3D Artist, Game Developer, Serious 3D, Digital Magic,* and others.

Zygote's New Stuff for Poser 3

On this book's CD-ROM, you will find a "click-me" file for Zygote's Stuff for Poser 3 Sampler CD. The presentation will give you an overview of what extras for Poser 3 Zygote offers. These collections are available for purchase by phone directly to Zygote Media Group, (800)267-5170, (801) 375-7220, or via the secure online order form.

SAMPLER FOR POSER $19.95

This collection contains a sampling of fun 3D data that will give you a good feel for our high-quality products. This CD includes 15 accessories, 2 figures (the wrestling baby and the alien), 1 animal (a doe), and the following motion capture files: (1) Pulling Rope, (2) Multi Punch, (3) Walk and Shake Hands, (4) Do a Little Dance, (5) Round House Kick.

PEOPLE $149.95

This collection contains 14 high quality human figures ready for posing and animating within Poser 3. Each figure comes with the complete speech postures, facial expressions, and texture maps. The figures can be easily animated with real human motions by importing specially prepared motion capture files. People Collection includes:

African American man—Business
African American man—Casual
African American woman—Business
African American woman—Casual
Asian man—Business
Asian man—Casual
Asian woman—Business
Asian woman—Casual
Heavy Man
Heavy Woman
Senior male
Senior female
10-year-old female
Infant in diaper

ANIMALS $149.95

A sweet new addition to Poser 3, Zygote introduces a collection of animals! All 12 animal models come completely texture-mapped and ready to animate. We've also included templates so you can customize the texture maps to your heart's content. Animal Collection includes:

Chimpanzee
Lion
Frog
Cow
Zebra
Penguin
Grizzly Bear
Buck Deer
Gray Wolf
Killer Whale
Shark
Largemouth Bass

MOTION $99.95

Add motion captured from real people to create lifelike poses and animation! Motion capture is the process of digitizing fluid human motions from live actors. These 52 specially prepared motion files from "House of Moves" can easily be applied to Poser 3 figures. Use the motions to move your models to the perfect pose or for realistic animations. Amazing results have been made unbelievably simple. You won't find a motion capture collection like this anywhere else in the world. High-end special effects studios pay thousands of dollars for motion capture, but this collection is a steal!

ACCESSORIES $34.95

100 various models designed to complement Poser 3 figures. Decorate your 3D environment with these high-quality objects optimized for use within Poser 3. Those who have Poser 2 may already be familiar with these objects; however, there are important improvements we have been able to make because of Poser 3. The objects now have separate materials assigned to groups (allowing the user to change colors on the various parts of a prop), sharper edges, and texture templates for painting maps.

Zygote History

Zygote's mission is to establish its reputation as the premier provider of high quality 3D models and related computer graphic products. We maintain a working environment that enhances productivity, creativity, and job satisfaction, and increases company value and profitability each year.

In September 1994, Zygote Media Group began operation. Three leading modelers in the industry—Chris Creek, Roger Clarke, and Eric Merritt—saw an excellent opportunity to capitalize on their skills in the fast growing 3D modeling market. Zygote Media Group, Inc. is a Utah-based company providing 3D computer models and texture maps for clients mainly in the entertainment industry. The name "Zygote" signifies the first stage of life, just as computer modeling is the first stage of a 3D computer animation. The name also conveys Zygote's main expertise and targeted market niche: building organic-shaped models such as humans and animals.

In 1994, Zygote built models for a computer game called "Titanic: Adventure through Time" by Cyberflix, Inc. Since that first custom job, Zygote has produced models for several high-profile clients including DreamWorks, Digital Domain, and Hanna-Barbera. Zygote's artists have built models for such feature films as "The Fifth Element," "Godzilla," and "Dennis the Menace 2," as well as a number of Coca Cola, Southwest Airlines, and other television commercials and TV shows. Zygote's modeling talents have also been seen in numerous computer games such as those by Dynamix, Inc., and Sierra on-line,

Inc. In addition to custom work, Zygote is also involved in creating products for resale, such as our "Stuff for Poser 3." We have several other products and more in development. Our "Mix N' Match" collection has been a very popular CD. It contains a high-resolution nude man and woman, with various articles of interchangeable clothing and hairstyles. We have also created "24 Zygote People," which includes several new figures. This product is a major follow-up to our previous "18 Perfect People." The "Mix N' Match" and "24 Zygote People" collections are not optimized for Poser 3, but are designed for the various other 3D software applications on the market.

THE ZYGOTE DEVELOPMENT TEAM

Christopher H. Creek: President

Prior to co-founding Zygote Media Group in September 1994, Chris was employed by Viewpoint Datalabs as the anatomy team leader, where he played a major role in developing top-selling anatomical models. Publishing companies he has worked with include William C. Brown, McGraw-Hill, and Morton Publishing. He recently co-authored a photographic atlas of human anatomy. Chris' professional experience includes managing the anatomy team at Viewpoint Datalabs and working as a successful freelance medical illustrator for over a decade. Chris has also been an instructor at Brigham Young University.

FIGURE 21.5 *Though everyone at Zygote had a hand in developing the models for Poser 3 at some point, these five members of the Zygote team played the most significant and constant roles. From left to right: Chris Creek, Tom Wheeler, Justin Wilson, Chad Smith, and Tony Avila.*

Roger D. Clarke: Corporate Secretary, VP of Production

Prior to co-founding Zygote Media Group in September of 1994, Roger was employed at Viewpoint Datalabs as 3D modeler, where he worked closely with Chris Creek in the development of Viewpoint's figure collection and anatomical models. He has done medical illustration for McGraw-Hill and Morton Publishing. Along with modeling anatomical objects and characters, Roger's responsibilities include production management.

Eric P. Merritt: Vice President

Prior to co-founding Zygote Media Group in September of 1994, Eric worked as the Organic team leader at Viewpoint Datalabs. Eric was the fourth modeler hired at Viewpoint Datalabs and has the most 3D modeling experience at Zygote. His modeling expertise lies in the complex mechanical models, which he produces from technical drawings or actual physical objects. At Zygote, he has been instrumental in product conceptualization and development.

David Dunston: VP of New Technological Development, Art Director

Prior to joining Zygote Media Group, Dave Dunston worked at Viewpoint Datalabs where his responsibilities included art direction, employee training, and research of new technological tools. Dave was also responsible for complex polygonal and surface remodeling. Some of Dave's better known achievements include the spacecraft in "Independence Day," and the model used in the opening scene of "Star Trek Generations." Dave has a strong art background in painting and sculpting. His professional experience includes artistically reconstructing dinosaur fossils for a paleontology company. Dave researches new modeling, texturing, and animation tools.

Daniel B. Farr: VP of Sales and Marketing, Treasurer

Prior to joining Zygote Media Group, Dan Farr was employed at Viewpoint Datalabs as the Custom Sales Manager. Dan brings to Zygote numerous industry contacts and a tremendous ability to generate new contacts. Dan has owned and founded other successful companies, including a successful audio/video company, a photography business, and a recreational vehicle rental company.

Thomas Wheeler: 3D Digital Artist, Sales Director

Tom has a background in both digital graphics and traditional media. He recently completed animation used in movie trailers for the feature film "Soldier," starring Kurt Russell. Tom has rather eclectic responsibilities at Zygote: He has done 3D modeling, graphic design, created and maintained the web site, and for the past several months has led the Poser production team.

Justin Wilson: 3D Modeler

During his time at Zygote, Justin has worked on a wide variety of projects. His models can be found in various video games, software, TV commercials, and TV programs. Some of his animals were recently used on a Discovery Channel special. He modeled all the new humans and animals that come with Poser 3, as well as many of the models in Zygote's new "Stuff for Poser 3" collections.

Chad Smith: 3D Digital Artist

Chad enjoys working in both digital and traditional media. His background includes freelance illustration, figure drawing, storyboarding, and character/concept development. He worked on the Poser 3 team setting up blend zones and UV coordinates for the figures.

Tony Avila: 3D Modeler

Tony's favorite subject matter for drawing, painting and modeling is human anatomy. He worked on the Poser 3 team setting up blend zones and UV coordinates for the figures.

CHAPTER

22

Poser Projects

The following three projects represent a recap of the things you have learned while working through the tutorials in this book. You will find that they are useful on their own and also act to reinforce your creative Poser skills.

The Carousel

The following exercise can be completed without your having to own the Zygote Poser collection. It will require Poser 3, Photoshop (version 5 is best, or another suitable bitmap painting application like Painter will also work), the Kai's PowerTools version 3 plug-in installed, and Ray Dream Studio (version 5 is best, or another 3D application can be substituted, as long as it writes out formats that Poser can read in). If you have worked through the tutorials in this book and have also explored all of the Poser 3 documentation, this project should take you a maximum of about six hours to complete.

HOW TO PROCEED

Horses

1. Open Photoshop, and load in the Horse texture.pict from the Poser 3.Runtime/Textures/Poser3 Textures folder. This is the default texture map for the Poser Horse. Using this as our base, we can see how it is treated to texture the default Horse. See Figure 22.1.
2. Use the Magic Wand and click on the Horse's light brown skin. Go to the Select menu and select Similar. This places a marquee around all of the light brows in the texture map.
3. Go to the KPT 3.0 filters and to Texture Explorer, which will open its interface. See Figure 22.2.
4. Assign a KPT Texture to the selected brown skin areas of the Horse.

The preceding step assumes you know how to navigate in the KPT Texture Explorer interface.

5. Repeat this procedure for the gray areas of the Horse texture. Save the result as HorseText2.pict to the same folder. Repeat this entire process until you have created four separate and colorful textures for the carousel. Do not use Bump maps and push the Highlight to the max, since we are looking for enamel painted ponies. See Figure 22.3.
6. From the Top Camera View, rotate and move the horses so that they are in a circular arrangement. See Figure 22.4.

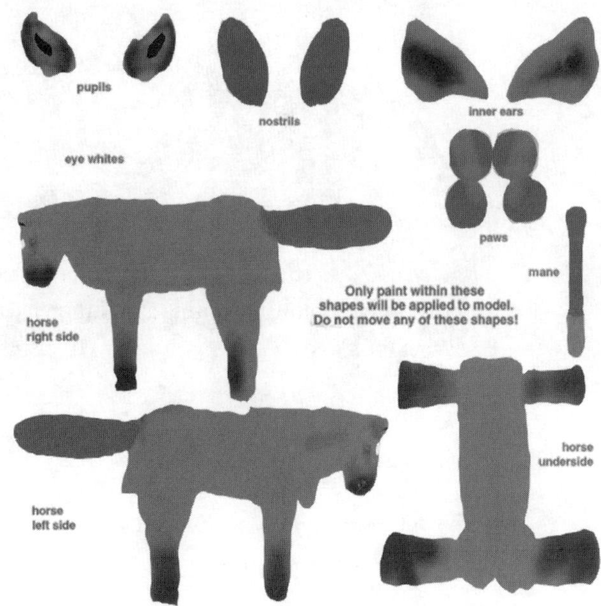

FIGURE 22.1 *The default texture map for the Poser Horse.*

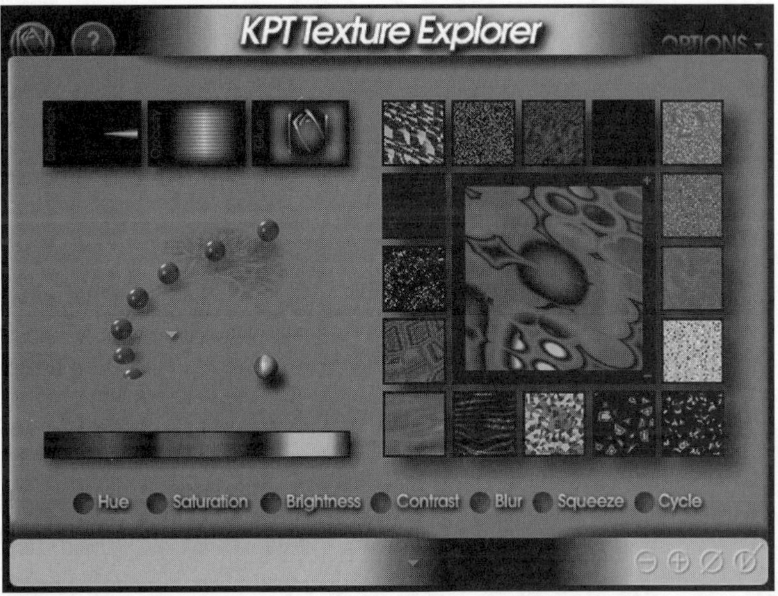

FIGURE 22.2 *The KPT 3 interface.*

FIGURE 22.3 *Four colorful ponies for our Carousel.*

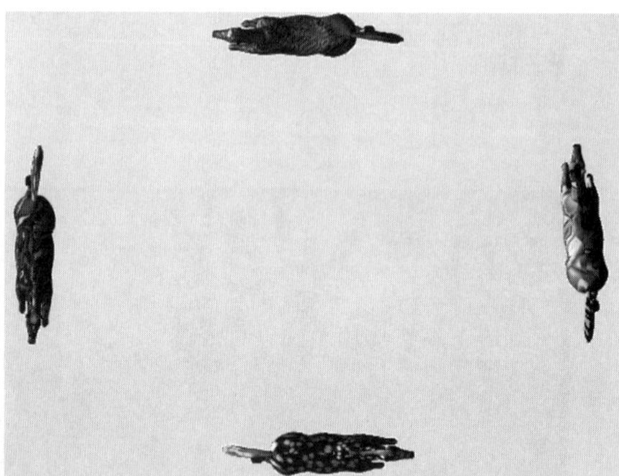

FIGURE 22.4 *The Horses are moved into a circular arrangement, as seen from the top.*

The Main Carousel Structure

We'll create the main structure out of two Poser Cylinders, a Cone, and four Balls. Do the following (see Figure 22.5 as a visual reference to these steps):

1. Create Cylinder 1 as the base. Leave some room between the top of the base and the Horses' feet. Size the base so that it covers the area that the four Horses cover (top view Camera). Reduce the Y dimension of the base to about one-fourth of the Horse height.

2. Cylinder number two acts as the spindle for the Carousel. Size it so that it pokes through the base and extends about twice as high as the Horses. Place it in the center of the base, as seen from the top Camera view.
3. Make the cone the same diameter as the base as seen from the top. Place it on the spindle, and flatten its Y dimension so it looks more like a canopy.
4. Create four spheres, using Figure 22.5 to reference their size. They should all exist on the same horizontal plane and be placed over each Horse to the top of the bar we will soon put through the Horse, so it can move up and down.
5. Parent everything as follows: All four Horse Body elements should have the Base as their Parent. The Base references the Spindle as its Parent, as does the Cone. The Balls have the Cone as their Parent.

Designing and Placing the Poles

You can use simple cylinders for the poles, but I decided to make them a little more complex, using Ray Dream Studio 5. Do the following:

1. In Ray Dream 5, place a Modeling Wizard icon (the Top Hat) in your scene, which opens the Modeling Wizard dialog. Select the Twisted Object/Twisted Column. When it is written to the screen, increase its Y dimension to 44. Save it as a OBJ file, and quit Ray Dream Studio. See Figure 22.6.

FIGURE 22.5 *The basic structure is finished and parented. You may want to add a texture to the Cone-canopy as was done here.*

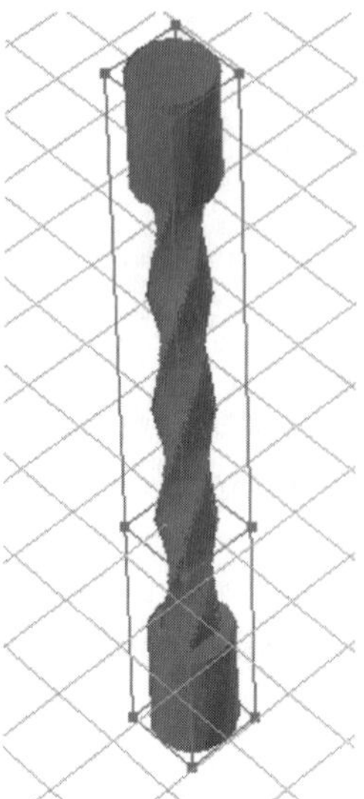

FIGURE 22.6 *The Twisted Column is designed in Ray Dream, for use in the Poser scene*

2. Import the Twisted Column into your Poser carousel scene. Make it tall enough (Y axis) so that it can embed itself in the base a little, go through a Horse, and then embed itself at the top in one of the balls. When you have accomplished this, save the Twisted Column to the Poser Props library. Now you can add its clones to any scene.
3. Place four Twisted Columns through the four Horses as indicated in Figure 22.7, and make the ball at their tops the Parent objects.

FIGURE 22.7 *The Twisted Columns are now the poles that allow the Horses to move up and down.*

Riders

Of course, you'll want riders on the Horses. You can select any of the Figures on the Poser libraries for this. Make sure you seat them the way they should be posed, and then make the Horse they're sitting on their parent object. See Figure 22.8.

Animating the Carousel

Here are some ideas to explore when you want to animate the Carousel:

- Give all of the riders some movement. It doesn't have to be extensive, but even a waving arm will add viewer interest.
- Make the opposite pair of Horses move up and down in unison. The other two should be down when the selected two are up, and vice versa.
- Adjust the lighting so that you are using different angles. Shadows will mingle and look more interesting. Also turn two of the lights down, with an intensity of 60%.
- Select a Camera angle that gives you an interesting perspective. For more interest, shoot the animation two or three times with different angles and close-ups, and then stitch the animations together in an appropriate post-production application.

FIGURE 22.8 *Now the Carousel looks interesting, with some different figures riding the Horses.*

Dragoid, Son of Birdoid

This next project is based upon Cecilia Ziemer's little Birdoid character, found in the Celia folder on this book's CD-ROM. The project makes use of the completed Parameter Dials for the figure, but replaces all of the body parts with new elements. You may use any 3D application you wish to accomplish what this tutorial teaches, and you may design any objects that you find suitable. We are going to use the Birdoid Parameters to create a dragon figure.

HOW TO PROCEED

Do the following:

1. Import the Birdoid Project file, Birdoid.Pz3, located in the Celia folder on this book's CD-ROM. Explore adjusting the Parameter Dials to get a feel for how they control the figure. See Figure 22.9.

For the modeling part of this project, we are going to use Impulse's Organica, a MetaBlock Modeler. You may use any 3D application you wish and shape the parts any way you like. What is important here is the replacement of the Birdoid body parts, and not how they are modeled. For that reason, the modeling processes will not be detailed, since your experience with whatever modeling application you use, and what your object design is, will determine the look of the final figure.

FIGURE 22.9 *Ziemer's Birdoid provides all of the parameters for control.*

FIGURE 22.10 *The finished replacement elements as modeled in Organica. You can model replacement elements in any 3D application you are familiar with.*

Essentially, you will need to create model elements for the following: Head, Upper and Lower Jaw, Neck, Left and Right Thigh, Left and Right Shins, Left and Right Foot, Tail, Left and Right Wings. All Left/Right combinations can be mirrored versions of the same construct. See Figure 22.10.

NOTE

To get the hang of this process without going through extensive 3D modeling, just replace the Birdoid's body parts with any selected props in the Poser library. (See Figures 22.10 and 22.11.

The Centaur

The mythic centaur has always intrigued artists and animators. Walt Disney's "Fantasia" features a scenario that starred the Centaur as a romantic hero, though many times the Centaur is not depicted so positively. Piccasso uses the Centaur as a stand-in for his own instinctual self. In this exercise, we'll combine two Poser figures to create an animated centaur.

FIGURE 22.11 *Renderings of the Dragoid, displayed from different angles to show the effectiveness of replacement figure modeling.*

How to Proceed

No other applications except Poser is needed to complete this project. Do the following:

1. Load the Horse and the Nude Male to the screen. Resize the Nude Male to Heroic proportions, and then resize him to 135%. See Figure 22.12.
2. Make the following elements invisible: Horse Upper Neck and Head; Man's Hips, Thighs, Shins, Feet, and Toes. See Figure 22.13.
3. Select the Horse's Lower Neck and rotate it to -60. Rotate the Man so he is facing in the same direction as the Horse. Select the Man's Body and

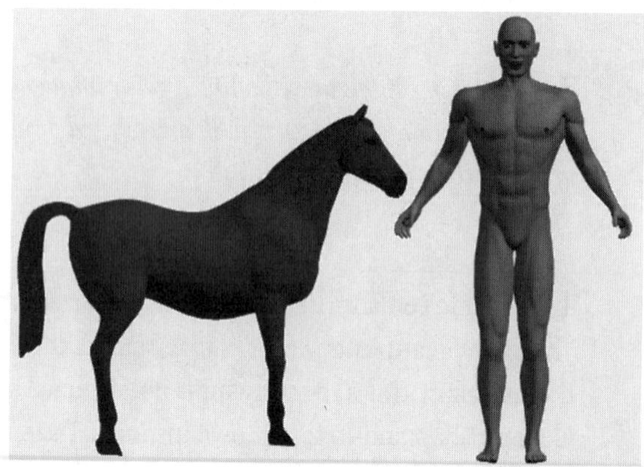

FIGURE 22.12 *The size of the Horse as compared to the Nude Male should look like this.*

move him into position over the open Neck of the Horse. Make the Horse's Lower Neck the Parent of the Man's Abdomen. See Figure 22.14.

When you create a composite figure, color both components the same and leave the texture map off. That way, it'll look like one figure and not two. You can also explore using the same texture on both figures, like the default ground texture.

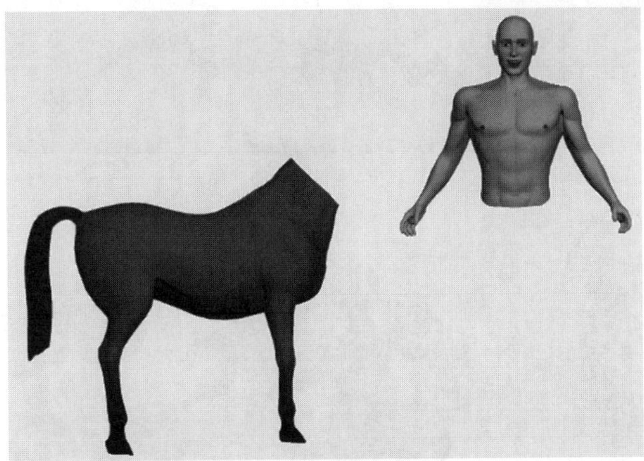

FIGURE 22.13 *Parts of each figure are made invisible.*

FIGURE 22.14 *The Man is placed in position over the Horse's rotated Lower Neck. The Man's Abdomen is Parented by the Horse's Lower Neck. Both are colored the same, and mapped with the Default Ground texture.*

FIGURE 22.15 *The Head is enlarged and Hair and beard are added.*

FIGURE 22.16 *The Centaur figure brandishes a shield and a spear and is ready for any challenge.*

4. Resize the Man's Head to 130% to make it appear more mythic. Place long black Hair on his head. Use another Prop Hair to give him a black beard. See Figure 22.15.
5. The Zygote Props/Weapons has a nice Shield and a Spear. If you have purchased the Zygote collection, you may want to add these elements. Remember to use the Grasp Parameter Dial on the Hand that holds the Spear and to Parent all props to the appendage they belong with. See Figure 22.16.

In Closing

We hope you have enjoyed this journey through the intricacies and pathways of Poser 3, one of the most startling and versatile applications ever written for digital art and animation. The only way to master Poser is to keep on exploring and pushing your creative efforts as far as possible. Enjoy!

Appendix

About the CD-ROM

The purpose of this CD is to provide extra content to The Poser 3 Handbook projects. There is a variety of content on the CD from a number of different sources and contributors, as detailed below. All of the material on the CD can be used in your own projects, except for the animations in the ANIM folder, which are included so that you can see some examples of finished Poser 3 movies.

Contents of the CD

- ANIMS Folder. There are over sixty Poser 3 QuickTime animations in this folder. You must have QuickTime installed and at least 32 MB of RAM to see them. QuickTime is available for both Mac and Windows platforms from Apple's Web site (http://www.apple.com). If you have QuickTime installed, do the following:

  Mac: With this book's CD inserted, and the ANIMS folder open, simply double-click on any animation, and it will load. Click on the start button to run the animation.

  Windows: Open the QuickTime for Windows MoviePlayer. Go to the file menu, and Open any of the QuickTime animations in the ANIMS folder on this book's CD-ROM.

- ANT Folder. This content is from Jeffrey Howarth. In the ANT folder, you will find the Red Ant PHI file here. You can utilize this material after you have read the Poser 3 advanced documentation (available for downloading at http://www.metacreations.com) on PHI files and chapter 16 of this book on the Red Ant.
- AVIz. A selection of animations in the Windows AVI format. Double-click to view. Note that AVI animations will also run under QuickTime 3 or above if you have that installed (Mac or Windows).

- BAUM Folder. This content is from Baumgarten Enterprises. It consists of a variety of Poser 3 Props that can be used to enrich your Poser 3 documents. Most of these objects are in the 3DS format. They can be used for both Mac and Windows Poser 3 documents. Simply load the prop you want to use by selecting the Import/3D Studio option from the file menu. Find the BAUM Folder, and select the prop you want to load. If the prop is a DXF file, then select Import/DXF from the file menu, and load that prop.
- Brycez Folder. For Bryce 3D users, there are two Bryce 3D projects in this folder. 2Apez.br4 is for Mac users, and NENDOX1.BR3 is for Windows users. Open Bryce 3D, and load the appropriate project. For more Bryce 3D projects, see the Bryce 3D Handbook (Charles River Media, 1998).
- CELIA Folder. This content is from Cecilia Ziemer, referencing her text in chapters 16 and 20 of the book. It contains the Mac and Windows Birdoid PHI and Object files, sample movies, and the Birdoid PZ3 file. Read the Celia Ziemer sections of these chapters to explore the use of these files for your Poser 3 projects. As detailed in chapter 22 of this book in the section labeled "Dragoid", you can use the basic Celia Birdoid replacement structure for your own unique figure elements.
- CREDO Folder. This content is from Credo Interactive. Before using the BVH files presented here, you should download the Credo Interactive LifeForms demo software from their Web site (www.credo-interactive.com). Follow the Credo text in chapter 17 of the book to see what is involved.
- MBScanz Folder. This folder contains scanned pages from the copyright free Muybridge images, detailed in chapter 12 of the book. Load any of these images into a bitmap application (Photoshop, Painter, etc.) to view them. Study the frames in order to get a better idea of how to animate animal motion in Poser.
- PHI Folder. This content is from Roy Riggs, and is for Windows only Poser 3 users. Read chapter 20 very carefully to see how PHI Builder, contained in this folder, can help you in the creation of PHI files for Poser 3. Do not attempt to use PHI Builder until you have successfully explored the creation of your own Poser Figure Hierarchies once or twice, as detailed in both the Poser 3 documentation and in chapter 20 of this book.
- PROPS Folder. Here's another twenty-three 3DS and DXF props you can use in your Poser 3 scenes. Use Import/3DS or Import/DXF to load them.
- PROJECTS Folder. Twenty-four Poser projects can be found there. They range from about 1 MB to 15 MB, so you must have enough

RAM to load the larger ones. At least 32 MB of RAM, above that needed for Poser 3 itself, is recommended.

- SB_TECH Folder. This content is from SB Technologies. It consists of Poser 3 project files (.PZ3) for Windows Poser 3 users. The complete Jail Cell and Bedroom environments are included, along with all of their separate props. Load either the Jail Cell or Bedroom project file by selecting File/Open. Populate either scene by placing and posing your Poser 3 figures.
- TEMPL Folder. This content is from Robert Saucier. It consists of high resolution templates for all of the Poser 3 and Zygote extras models, so you can create high resolution texture maps for them. The texture maps that come with Poser 3 are not in high resolution, so details of the texture are not as sharp as they otherwise would be when using high resolution texture maps like these. Read the Poser 3 documentation to gain the necessary knowledge about modifying and customizing texture maps, and also read chapter 18 ("Customizing templates") in this book.
- TXTRS Folder. The carousel project (chapter 22) and the Green Man textures (chapter 22) are included here for your use with the proper project files (located in the Projects Folder on this book's CD-ROM).
- ZYGOTE Folder. This click-me presentation is from the Zygote Media Group, and gives you an overview of the extra content they have developed for Poser 3, as referenced throughout the Poser 3 Handbook. Just double-click on the "Click-Me" icon.

System Requirements and Installation Instructions

To make use of this book's CD-ROM, you must have Poser 3 and a CD-ROM installed on your Mac or Windows system. Recommended RAM is 32 MB in addition to that required by Poser 3, so that you can load in extra props or other selected items on the CD as needed. More RAM is always better. There is nothing to install on the CD-ROM. You should have QuickTime installed in order to run the animations, though you can also see many of the animations by double-clicking on one of the movies in the AVIz folder on the book's CD-ROM. The latest edition of QuickTime will also run AVI movies. As detailed above, the various contents inside of the CD-ROMs folders are accessed in Poser 3 according to what they are. It is vital that you read the Poser 3 documentation and the book, so that you know how and when to access this content. You can copy any of these files to your own hard drive, or to save space, access them on the book's CD-ROM.

Index

A

B

H

N

O

P

S

T

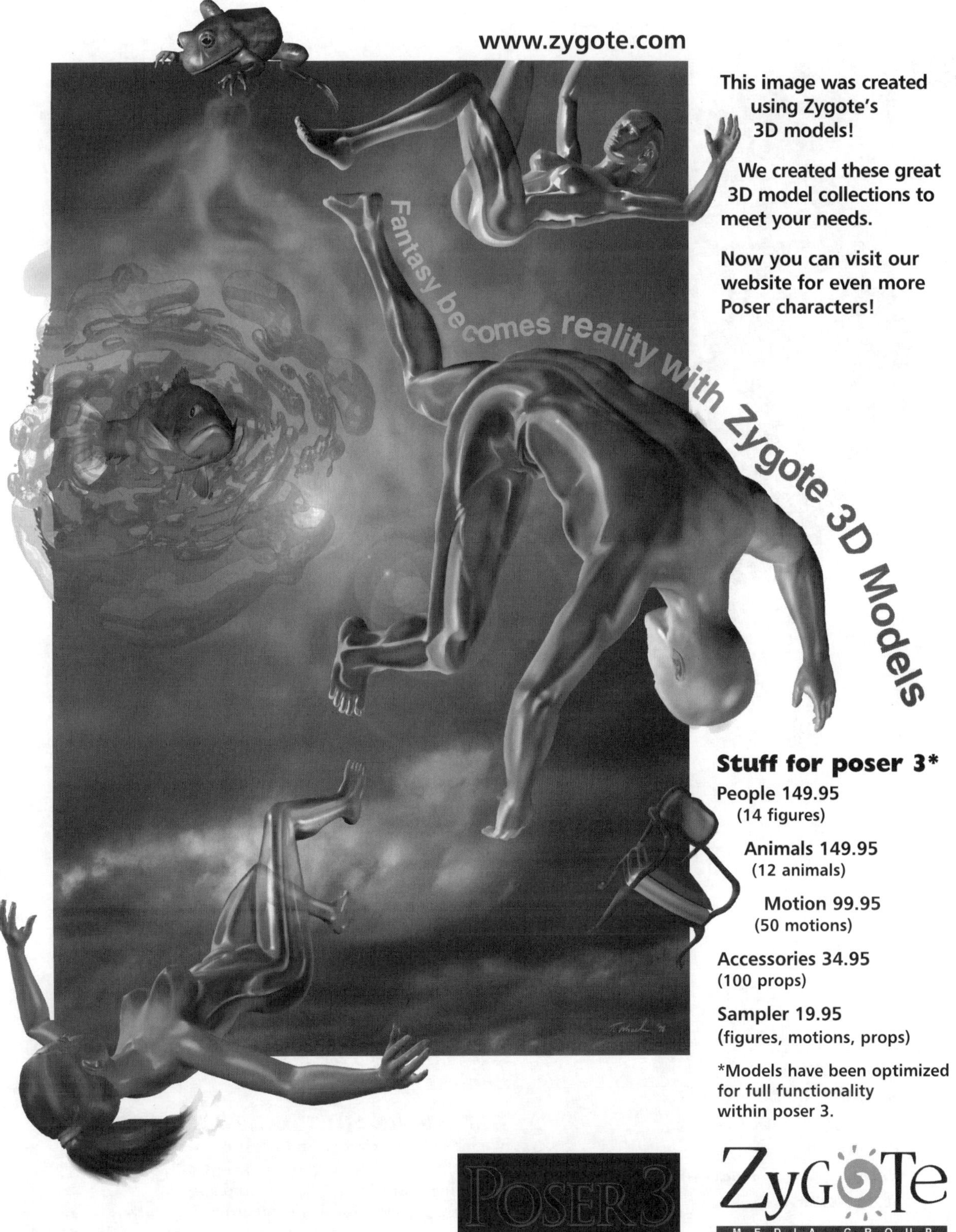
www.zygote.com
This image was created using Zygote's 3D models!
We created these great 3D model collections to meet your needs.
Now you can visit our website for even more Poser characters!
Fantasy becomes reality with Zygote 3D Models
Stuff for poser 3*
People 149.95 (14 figures)
Animals 149.95 (12 animals)
Motion 99.95 (50 motions)
Accessories 34.95 (100 props)
Sampler 19.95 (figures, motions, props)
*Models have been optimized for full functionality within poser 3.
POSER 3
ZyGoTe
MEDIA GROUP
1-888-3dmodel or 1-801-375-0553•Fax 1-801-375-7389•One East Center St.#215 Provo, UT 84606